An Uncertain Tradition

An Uncertain Tradition

*Constitutionalism and
the History of the South*

EDITED BY

Kermit L. Hall
James W. Ely, Jr.

The University of Georgia Press

ATHENS AND LONDON

© 1989 by the University of Georgia Press
Athens, Georgia 30602
All rights reserved

Designed by Nighthawk Design
Set in 10 on 13 Linotron 202 Meridien

The paper in this book meets the guidelines for
permanence and durability of the Committee on
Production Guidelines for Book Longevity of the
Council on Library Resources.

Printed in the United States of America

93   92   91   90   89   5   4   3   2   1

Library of Congress Cataloging in Publication Data

An Uncertain tradition.
  Bibliography: p.
  Includes index.
    1. Southern States—Constitutional history—
Congresses.   I. Hall, Kermit.   II. Ely, James W.,
1938–
KF4541.A2U53   1989   342.75′029   88-5579
ISBN 0-8203-1055-7 (alk. paper)   347.50229
ISBN 0-8203-1075-1 (alk. paper): pbk.

British Library Cataloging in Publication Data available

To the memory of Stephen Botein,

who was to have participated in the symposium from
which the essays in this volume are taken.

All earnings derived from the sale of this book will be
contributed to a special research fund at the American
Antiquarian Society in memory of this gifted historian,
erudite scholar, and compassionate human being.

Contents

Contents

Acknowledgments

This book began as a symposium, "The South and the American Constitutional Tradition," held at the University of Florida in early March 1987. All of the papers presented at that conference are contained in this volume, and they are much the better for the insightful, humorous, and sometimes pungent commentaries given by Don E. Fehrenbacher, Jack P. Greene, Paul L. Murphy, J. Woodford Howard, Jr., and Bertram Wyatt-Brown. These distinguished scholars are due special thanks for their contributions to the symposium and their shaping influence on these essays.

Scholarly enterprises such as this one require considerable institutional support. As the organizers of the symposium, we extend thanks to Dean Charles Sidman, College of Liberal Arts and Sciences, University of Florida; Dean Frank T. Read, University of Florida College of Law; Associate Dean Jeffrey Lewis, also of the University of Florida College of Law; Dean John J. Costonis, Vanderbilt University School of Law; Ann Henderson, Director, Florida Endowment for the Humanities; The University of Florida Humanities Council; the Eighth Circuit Bar Association of Florida; and the Florida Bar. Elizabeth B. Monroe oversaw much of the conference planning; David Bodenhamer, of the University of Southern Mississippi, provided valuable guidance; William T. Coram ably handled local arrangements; and Rachel Engelhardt managed to keep the books balanced.

Malcolm Call, the Director of the University of Georgia Press, was an early, enthusiastic, and patient supporter of the editors' efforts to bring these essays to press. We and the authors trust that the results warrant his confidence.

Kermit L. Hall
Gainesville, Florida

James W. Ely, Jr.
Nashville, Tennessee

December 1987

Part One

Introduction

The South and the American Constitution

Kermit L. Hall and James W. Ely, Jr.

The bicentennial of the federal Constitution has come and gone, and its occasion provided an opportunity to take historical stock of our constitutional traditions. The essays in this volume inquire into those traditions and the special poignancy they have had for the inhabitants of the eleven states of the former Confederacy. Slavery, secession, Confederate nationhood (which included its own national constitution), Reconstruction, and legally mandated racial segregation shaped not just the section's attitudes toward the federal Constitution but the course of the nation's constitutional history. To inquire about the place of the South in the American constitutional tradition, therefore, is to probe more generally for the sinews of authority in the federal system.

Since the late nineteenth century, the search for the roots of southern distinctiveness has been part of a larger effort to explain the impact of section on the American nation. The importance of section as an organizing principle of historical analysis has ebbed and flowed during these decades. The sectional school of Frederick Jackson Turner, with its underlying assumptions about the powerful relationship between geography and history, was modified and recast in later years by C. Vann Woodward and David M. Potter, in history, and Julius Turner and V. O. Key, Jr., in political science.[1] Woodward and Potter, while interested in the sectional phenomenon, also questioned Turner's assertions about the geographical bases of sectionalism and criticized Turner and his disciples for projecting their own biases in suggesting that the South was somehow sectional and the North national.[2] As important, they and

3

other scholars insisted that Turner's approach ignored other important analytical variables, such as class, ethnicity, and culture. "What was fundamentally wrong with" sectionalism, Richard Hofstadter has written, "was not that it lacked validity, but that it lacked the importance with which [Turner and others] so solemnly tried to invest it."[3]

Today, there is a renewed interest in sectionalism, and scholars have advanced a multivariate approach to determine its existence and to measure its influence.[4] Not only do they stress ethnicity and culture, but some of them have also argued that section must be defined on the basis of ecologically adapted modes of production.[5] This approach emphasizes the ways in which the people of a section—the South, for example—wrested their food, their energy, their income, and their personal liberty from the environment. Such an approach complements and builds upon the insights provided by an appreciation of geography, ethnicity, and culture. If the modes of production were the same as those elsewhere, then the South would not have been a section, and questions about whether it had a distinctive legal culture would be meaningless. On the other hand, if the modes had been too radically different, the South would not have been a section at all, but a foreign civilization. Somewhere between those poles of conformity and differentiation lies the concept of section.

One mode of production shaped the South's history. That was the plantation system of agriculture in which African slave labor cultivated tobacco and cotton. After the Civil War ended, slavery, agriculture, and the black work force continued to shape the South's fortunes, although tenant farming and sharecropping created new arrangements that perpetuated traditional ways of doing business. Only since World War II has the South begun to break significantly from this historical path, with massive out-migration of blacks (a development begun in the early twentieth century), urbanization, and industrialization. The Sunbelt South is less agrarian and more commercial, and as a result, it has become at once more like and more competitive with other sections for business and federal support dollars.[6]

Legal historians have contributed to the resurgence of interest in sectional analysis. They accept the responsibility of making explicit those assumptions about sectional differences in the legal culture that earlier scholars had casually treated as implicit. Equally significant, they recognize the important analytical advantage that a comparative sectional perspective provides on the rise of national legal culture. As James

Willard Hurst, the dean of American legal historians, observed in 1982, "It is only within recent years that students of legal history have begun to explore ways in which legal doctrine and uses of law may have shaped or responded to sectional experiences and patterns different from or in tension with interests taking place on a national scale."[7] Almost all of this new attention, however, has gone to private law and legal institutions, much to the neglect of constitutional law.[8] We know precious little about the operation of fundamental frames of government within each of the southern states, of the existence of distinctive constitutional traditions within the South, and of the relationship of the section to the nation's ruling document.[9] In short, the role of the Constitution and of constitutionalism in southern history remains, despite all of the ink spilled over the problem of southern distinctiveness, elusive.

Recent scholarship on the history of private law and legal institutions has laid bare the section's "ambivalent legacy," one in which the South's legal culture was at once distinctive from and yet similar to that of the rest of the nation.[10] Might the same thing be said of the history of public law in the South? The essays in this volume explore one part of this question—the relationship of the South to the federal Constitution. As was true of *Ambivalent Legacy,* a collection of essays on private-law development in the South edited by David J. Bodenhamer and James W. Ely, Jr., the essays in the present volume are an exploration designed to encourage additional work and, we think, to add another dimension to the general debate about the place of section and law in American history.

The organic laws of each of the southern states were also important. Daniel Elazar cogently argues that the section's state constitution makers had a strongly contractual bent.[11] Although all constitutions are by their nature contracts between the governed and the governors, state constitutions in most of the South, more fully than in other sections, circumscribed the authority of government through a rigorous separation of powers and sharp limits on its authority to tax and to extend its credit for public and private development.[12] This contractual tradition persists even today. On average, the South's state constitutions are nearly one-quarter longer than the ruling documents of states outside the section. The Alabama Constitution, with approximately 174,000 words, is the nation's longest, a distinction held by Louisiana until 1974, when its quarter-of-a-million-word constitution was reduced to about 34,000 words. The Georgia Constitution, with its many local amendments, was more a code than a fundamental charter of government until a new organic law in 1982 ended the practice of allowing local amendments.[13]

This contractual tradition also informed the relationship of the South to the federal Constitution. No other section in the nation's history, for example, embraced so fully the compact theory of the Union, which held that the states, and not the people as a whole, had formed the Union and that these same states could dissolve it. Secession and the Confederacy were the ultimate expressions of this strongly contractual constitutional tradition. In the era of Reconstruction, the Republican Congress turned this tradition against the once rebellious states by requiring them to recognize explicitly the inherent superiority of the Constitution. The North Carolina Constitution of 1868, for example, provided that "there is no right to secede. This State shall ever remain a member of the American Union," and "every citizen of this State owes paramount allegiance to the Constitution and Government of the United States."[14]

This volume treats only one aspect of the contractual tradition—the South's relationship to the federal Constitution. Matters of state constitutional development, as important and little understood as they are, have been left for another day. Each author has conceptualized section in ways that stress the sociolegal and ideological forces associated with the South's unique modes of production rather than merely cataloging the distinctive features of its culture of public law. The essays, when taken as a whole, point toward a legacy of ambivalence—a tradition of uncertainty—in which southern political and legal spokesmen frequently sought to be in the federal constitutional order without being of it.

Powerfully contradictory behavior has fostered this sense of uncertainty. To begin with, there is no doubt that a kind of provincial belligerency has characterized southern white attitudes toward the federal Constitution. When Governor George C. Wallace in 1963 attempted to block black students from entering the University of Alabama by standing in the doorway of the school's administration building, he symbolized the defiance of white southerners not only to blacks but to attempts by the federal government to aid them. A hundred years earlier, a Georgia newspaper editor summarized the sentiments that lay behind such actions: "Free society! We sicken at the name. What is [the North] but a conglomeration of greasy mechanics, filthy operatives, small-fisted farmers, and moon-struck theorists. . . . hardly fit for association with a gentleman's body servant."[15]

Such vituperative rhetoric often masked other equally significant attitudes. Take, for example, the question of who best represents the southern constitutional tradition. In the pre–Civil War South do we turn to George Washington, James Madison, and John Marshall? Or did Spencer Roane, John C. Calhoun, and Jefferson Davis symbolize the spirit of that earlier era? The discourse of history distinguishes between the two groups, regarding the former as constitutional nationalists and the latter as constitutional polemicists of states' rights. James Madison, a Virginian, gave birth to the Constitution; Jefferson Davis, a Mississippian, attempted to destroy the Union through secession and civil war. The problem is just as difficult, if not more so, for our own time, when biracial politics have become a fact of southern life. George C. Wallace in the 1960s epitomized the attitudes of many white southerners by proclaiming: "Segregation now—Segregation tomorrow—Segregation forever."[16] Martin Luther King, Jr., however, while locked in a Birmingham, Alabama, jail for acts of civil disobedience designed to break the constitutional support of racial segregation, urged southerners of both races to embrace a more cosmopolitan and egalitarian meaning of the Constitution. "What affects one directly affects all indirectly," King wrote. "Never again can we afford to live with the narrow, provincial 'outside agitator' idea. Anyone who lives in the United States can never be considered an outsider anywhere in this country."[17]

These contradictory patterns of behavior merge into common themes founded on the section's modes of production. Racism, states' rights, and individual liberty of course were not unique to the section, but as the essays in this volume suggest, an appreciation of the southern response to them illuminates the place of the South in the American constitutional tradition. Together they provided the South with a legacy of great tragedy and, as several of the authors suggest, also of great opportunity.

Racism has been endemic in America. Slavery existed throughout the colonies, not just in the South. The most enlightened public leaders of the day were certain that blacks were inferior to whites, even subhuman. Southerners, however, came to hold slaves in such numbers that the section's wealth, social fabric, and national political power depended upon the peculiar institution. Slavery became integral to the economic well-being of southerners even as its significance waned in the burgeoning commercial economy of the North. Southerners realized that racial slavery fostered a social calculus of great complexity and of

7

potentially fatal consequences for both master and slave. "Deep-rooted prejudices entertained by the white; ten thousand recollections, by the blacks, of the injuries they have sustained," wrote Thomas Jefferson, "[and] the real distinctions which nature has made will divide us into parties, and produce convulsions, which will probably never end but in the extermination of one or the other race."[18] Fear of the free black population and of a servile slave rebellion, when coupled with the economic imperative of slavery, drove southerners to seek protection of their system of racial control under the Constitution.

Southern delegates to the Philadelphia convention in 1787 took the initiative to protect their peculiar human property. Slavery, from their point of view, was peculiar not because it was "odd" but because it was largely confined to their section. They demanded and won from their northern counterparts important concessions. The framers did not directly endorse human bondage; the words "slave" and "slavery" nowhere appear in the Constitution. Slavery nonetheless insinuated itself indirectly through eight separate provisions, and James Madison concluded at the end of the proceedings that these compromises were so important that agreement on the Constitution would never have been reached without them.[19]

In retrospect, the South achieved a Pyrrhic victory. By gaining federal recognition for slavery, the section assumed a burden of racial control that structured its social, political, and constitutional behavior for the next century and a half. The South, among all the sections of the new nation, thoroughly embraced slavery and the equally distinctive proslavery constitutional theory that supported it.

Until recently, the constitutional law of race relations in the South, in the words of Daniel Boorstin, was "indwelling."[20] The southern consensus on race was so pervasive and constraining that the law merely ratified rather than channeled attitudes about first slaves and later free blacks. In the pre–Civil War years the requirement to defend slavery forced southerners to fashion constitutional arguments intended to preserve the peculiar institution from critics within and without the section. The proslavery defense was so extreme that southern civil liberties suffered and a sense of injustice infected the nation's entire constitutional system. Southerners censored the mails for antislavery literature; they gagged congressmen from debating the merits of antislavery petitions; and in a desperate effort to hasten the return of escaped slaves, they secured passage of the Fugitive Slave Act of 1850, which paid federal commissioners more to return a slave to his or her master than to free the slave. The southern view of race relations attained its apotheosis in *Dred Scott v. Sandford* (1857) when the Supreme Court declared that persons of African descent had "no rights" that white persons were bound to respect.[21]

Indwelling attitudes toward race continued to shape southern understanding of the Constitution even after the Civil War and Reconstruction. Southerners once again successfully appealed to the Supreme Court, this time to fashion a workable accommodation with the great Civil War amendments—the Thirteenth, Fourteenth, and Fifteenth. With the acquiescence of the justices, southerners foisted second-class citizenship on newly freed blacks through such devices as the all-white party primary, literacy tests, and de jure segregation. The most important and pervasive of the new constitutional expressions of racism was the doctrine of separate but equal, which the justices sustained in *Plessy v. Ferguson* (1896).[22] Although pre–Civil War northerners invented the practice of racial segregation by law, and even though westerners adopted it in dealing with the Chinese on the Pacific slope, southerners made separate but equal the most distinctive feature of post–Civil War race relations.[23]

In the twentieth century, the constitutional law that supported traditional patterns of southern race relations underwent radical change, the effects of which echoed throughout the nation. The Legal Defense Fund of the National Association for the Advancement of Colored People (NAACP) skillfully orchestrated a litigation strategy that turned the Constitution into a tool to service the needs of black people.[24] Although racism remained pervasive, its legal stature gradually eroded, leaving behind positive protections for blacks in the due-process and equal-protection clauses of the Fourteenth Amendment. The NAACP harnessed federal power, once used to undermine the concept of black freedom, to sustain that freedom. The case of *Brown v. Board of Education* (1954) became a constitutional landmark as important for the South as *Dred Scott v. Sandford* and *Plessy v. Ferguson* and as far-reaching as both of those decisions for defining race relations in public facilities throughout the entire nation.[25]

Change has come in other ways. New social arrangements have replaced traditional ones; old ideas have given way to new practices. States' rights and, ironically, in view of the history of slavery, a concern for individual liberty have composed the other major themes in the

9

South's history under the federal Constitution. The doctrine of states' rights provided the constitutional scaffolding that legitimated slavery, segregation, and the rights of the white majority. The persistent localism in southern constitutional thought derives from a belief that local democracy offers the best opportunity to secure a responsible political order more sensitive to individual ambition and worth than a federal government, distant and out of sight, could be. Yet time and again, the vision of such local autonomy has meant, given the South's persistent racism and agrarianism, oligarchic control by a ruling white elite rather than genuine democracy.

Nonetheless, southern constitutional theorists of the late eighteenth and early nineteenth centuries had more on their minds than race in boosting states' rights. Spokesmen such as John Taylor of Caroline, Thomas Jefferson, and John C. Calhoun understood that the agricultural modes of production that accompanied the South's rural character and dispersed population meant that local control over political decision making would foster their particular vision of republican government. Even today, for example, county government retains a vitality in the South found almost nowhere else in the nation.

Southern proponents of states' rights also advanced the doctrine as a means of securing individual liberty (albeit white liberty) against an encroaching national government. The earliest invocation of states' rights involved freedom of political expression, not protection of slavery, although the influence of the peculiar institution was never far from the surface of antebellum southern consciousness. Congress in 1798 passed the Alien and Sedition Acts, which Federalists employed to harass their political opponents, the Jeffersonian Republicans. Through these measures the Adams administration secured ten convictions of Republican newspaper editors and printers. Shortly thereafter, Thomas Jefferson and James Madison penned the Kentucky (1798, 1799) and Virginia (1798) Resolutions, which invoked a compact theory of the Constitution that maintained that each state had an equal right to protect individual citizens from the hostile actions of the central government by declaring federal laws unconstitutional.

This refrain echoed through the early Republic, finding expression in the Nullification Crisis of 1832 and the great debate over the return of fugitive slaves, and culminating in secession. By that time, however, as Arthur Bestor has shown, the doctrine of states' rights as a means of protecting individual liberty had greater credence in the North, where antislavery forces invoked it, than in the South, where the concept of state sovereignty, a doctrine of power, had superseded it.[26] Southern leaders no longer wanted the federal government to leave them alone, but instead they expected that it would act as their agent to secure the South's interests in the territories. The enormous pressures for racial control in the South turned states' rights into a constitutional defense of racism, supplanting the concept's earlier libertarian emphasis. Local control abetted white political domination, and states' rights theory offered a plausible constitutional rationale to explain why the federal government could not rectify local racial injustices.

After World War II, the appeal to states' rights by southern political leaders became all the more dramatic as the NAACP eroded the section's long-standing system of racial control. Between 1955 and 1960, for example, southern states adopted over two hundred statutes, resolutions, and constitutional amendments defending segregation and opposing implementation of the Supreme Court's historic ruling in *Brown*. These various appeals reiterated the doctrine of interposition first articulated by southerners more than a century and a half before.[27] Expressing the constitutional point of view behind this "massive resistance," ninety-six members of Congress from the southern states in March 1956 issued a manifesto defending separate but equal as settled constitutional law.

Under such circumstances, states' rights became largely a code word for racism and white political opportunism, a transition that robbed the doctrine of much of its inherent legitimacy within the American federal system. The historian Arthur Schlesinger, Sr., writing from the perspective of a liberal nationalist, reached an even harsher judgment: he observed more than half a century ago that the history of "state rights agitation . . . must always be studied in its relation to time and circumstances" and concluded that the "state rights doctrine has never had any real vitality independent of underlying conditions of vast social, economic or political significance."[28]

The Little Rock crisis of 1957 illustrates Schlesinger's point. Tensions existed there among local blacks, a white-dominated school board, fire-eating politicians, and the federal government. Although leaders of the white community opposed to desegregation of the Little Rock public schools complained of outside agitation, southerners, not northerners, spearheaded the attack on Jim Crow laws. Black parents initiated the

11

Little Rock school cases in an attempt to improve their children's educational opportunities. Federal district and circuit court judges, frequently native southerners, provided judicial authority that enabled blacks to overcome legal disabilities.

White political leaders in Arkansas played fast and loose with states' rights, and the doctrine retained utility to the extent to which it fitted their view of political orthodoxy. For example, Governor Orval Faubus's interference with the Little Rock school board was contrary to states' rights doctrines but was dictated by the results of a crucial election, in which two integrationists on the board had won "nearly two-to-one victories over segregationist candidates."[29] White supremacy, rather than states' rights, thwarted efforts by local blacks to achieve civil rights and contributed to the larger national crisis over racial equality. An understanding of the constitutional politics of desegregation may well turn constitutional theory on its head, at least with regard to race relations. Terms such as "strict construction," "activist court," "judicial restraint," and "original intent" ceased "to have meaning when used by opponents of equality who were never committed to abstract principles, but only to preserving segregation at any cost."[30]

The logic of local democracy that lay behind the states' rights doctrine nevertheless retains significant validity, and its consequences have been powerfully ironic for the segregationist politicians, such as former Governors Wallace and Faubus, who once preached it. The Voting Rights Act of 1965 and its subsequent amendments, for example, pushed the South toward meaningful local democracy. In several states county governments, once the backbone of white political control, have fallen into the hands of the blacks, and even George C. Wallace expediently courted newly powerful black voters he had once condemned to perpetual segregation. Greater black participation at the local level has also renewed the Republican party in the South, not as a vehicle for black political power, as in Reconstruction days, but as a movement with an almost exclusively white political following.

The following essays weave together these themes of racism, states' rights, and individual liberty in southern constitutional thought and practice. They deal with the antecedents of southern constitutionalism, with its main features during the slave regime, with its meaning in contemporary biracial society, and with some of its most notable judicial spokesmen. Although the essays do not address the issue of federalism directly, each one of them touches on this central feature of American constitutionalism. Their authors underscore how the South's persistent parochialism, itself a manifestation of the section's unique modes of production, has set the terms under which the South has participated in and contributed to the American constitutional tradition.

Has the South achieved a distinctive place in that tradition? On balance, these essays suggest that the answer is yes, and they also indicate that racism, states' rights, and individual liberty, when viewed in combination, help to explain why. But these essays also indicate that the relationship between the Constitution and the South, as with any section of the nation, has been uncertain, even problematic. The federal nature of the Republic and the supremacy of the Constitution has always refracted the distinctive qualities of the southern constitutional experience. The restraints and guarantees in the Constitution that affected the South also influenced the North and West. In this regard, the essays that follow reaffirm that the centralizing and homogenizing aspects of the federal Constitution have made the nation a whole, not just a collection of states and sections.

These essays are also valuable for what they do not cover. We know little about many of the most important constitutional relationships in the history of the South. Although we have excellent works on the constitutional background of slavery, we have no comprehensive history of Native Americans in the South under the Constitution, and we have largely ignored the important comparative dimension that an understanding of the attitudes of southern Native Americans toward fundamental law could contribute to an appreciation of our own constitutional tradition.[31] The constitutional history of women in the South is equally undeveloped and just as urgent.[32] Furthermore, although we have pioneering studies of the South's criminal justice system, we know little about how that system, in matters such as convict labor, peonage, and the death penalty, fitted into the federal constitutional order.[33] Nor do we have much of an understanding of the interaction between southern state constitutional development and the federal document, especially the important matter of how the section's state constitution makers treated such fundamental issues as separation of powers, checks and balances, and protection of individual liberties and rights.[34] Until we better understand these and other matters, the constitutional history of the South will remain not only uncertain but elusive.

13

Notes

1. Frederick Jackson Turner, *Sectionalism in American History* (New York, 1932); C. Vann Woodward, *American Counterpoint: Slavery and Racism in the North-South Dialogue* (Boston, 1964); David M. Potter, *The South and the Sectional Conflict* (Baton Rouge, 1968), esp. 34–86; Julius Turner, *Party and Constituency: Pressures on Congress,* rev. ed. (Baton Rouge, 1970); V. O. Key, Jr., *Politics, Parties and Pressure Groups* (New York, 1964).

2. David M. Potter, "The Historian's Use of Nationalism and Vice Versa," in Potter, *The South and the Sectional Conflict,* 34–40; Woodward, *American Counterpoint,* 107–39.

3. Richard Hofstadter, *The Progressive Historians: Turner, Parrington, and Beard* (New York, 1968), 103.

4. For an early discussion of these issues, see Howard Odum and Harry E. Moore, *American Regionalism: A Cultural Historical Approach to National Integration* (New York, 1938). On the more recent approaches to section, see John Shelton Reed, *One South: An Ethnic Approach to Regional Culture* (Baton Rouge, 1982), and *The Enduring South: Subcultural Persistence in Mass Society* (Lexington, Mass., 1982); and Harry N. Scheiber, "Xenophobia and Parochialism in the Early History of American Legal Process: From the Jacksonian Era to the Sagebrush Rebellion," *William and Mary Law Review* 23 (1982): esp. 625–27.

5. The phrase "mode of production" has its origin in Marxist scholarship, where it refers to both technology ("forces") and social and class relations. See, among many other works, Barry Hindess and Paul Q. Hirst, *Pre-capitalist Modes of Production* (London, 1973). Here we use the phrase loosely, and with revision, to indicate, first, a set of techniques adapted for the exploitation of particular environments and, second, a resulting social organization and constitutional order. That is, our framework rejects explicit Marxist assumptions about the relationship of modes of production to particular kinds of historical change while accepting the importance of them as means of identifying sections. See, for example, Richard F. Bensel, *Sectionalism and American Political Development, 1880–1980* (Madison, Wis., 1984), esp. 3–59; Donald Woorster, "New West, True West: Interpreting the Region's History," *Western Historical Quarterly* 18 (1987): 141–56; and Kermit L. Hall, "The 'Magic Mirror' and the Promise of Western Legal History," *Western Historical Quarterly* 18 (1987): 317–26.

6. Scheiber, "Xenophobia and Parochialism," 659–60.

7. James Willard Hurst, "The State of Legal History," *Reviews in American History* 10 (1982): 292.

8. Charles Sydnor, "The Southerner and the Laws," *Journal of Southern History* 6 (1940): 2–23. For examples of the growing debate about the sectional

nature of legal development, see David J. Bodenhamer and James W. Ely, Jr., eds., *Ambivalent Legacy: A Legal History of the South* (Jackson, Miss., 1984), esp. 3–29; James W. Ely, Jr., and David J. Bodenhamer, "Regionalism and American Legal History: The Southern Experience," *Vanderbilt Law Review* 39 (1986): 539–67; and Paul Finkelman, "Exploring Southern Legal History," *North Carolina Law Review* 64 (1985): 77–116.

9. See, for example, Fletcher M. Green, *Constitutional Development in the South Atlantic States, 1776–1860* (Chapel Hill, N.C., 1930); and in a related, yet different, vein, Ralph Wooster, *The People in Power: Courthouse and Statehouse in the Lower South, 1850–1860* (Knoxville, Tenn., 1969), and *Politicians, Planters, and Plain Folk: Courthouse and Statehouse in the Upper South* (Knoxville, Tenn., 1975). A good recent study of state constitutional development in the troubled 1870s is John Walker Mauer, "Southern State Constitutions in the 1870s: A Case Study of Texas" (Ph.D. diss., Rice University, 1983).

10. Bodenhamer and Ely, *Ambivalent Legacy.*

11. Daniel Elazar, "The Principles and Traditions Underlying State Constitutions," *Publius* 12 (1982): 17–18, 20–21.

12. Ibid., 20–21; Mauer, "Southern State Constitutions," 12–26.

13. Albert L. Sturm and Janice C. May, "State Constitutions and Constitutional Revision, 1984–85," *Book of the States* 26 (1986–87): 14–15.

14. North Carolina Constitution, 1868, art. I, sec. 4.

15. As quoted in Arthur C. Cole, *The Irrepressible Conflict, 1850–1865* (New York, 1934), viii.

16. As quoted in David Burner et al., *An American Portrait* (New York, 1985), 2:766.

17. Martin Luther King, "Letter from Birmingham City Jail, April 16, 1963," *Documents of United States Constitutional History,* ed. William M. Wiecek and Paul Finkelman (Bloomington, Ind., 1987), 776.

18. Thomas Jefferson, *Notes on the State of Virginia* (1781), 181.

19. William M. Wiecek, *The Sources of Antislavery Constitutionalism in America, 1760–1848* (Ithaca, N.Y., 1977), 82.

20. Daniel Boorstin, "The Perils of Indwelling Law," *The Rule of Law,* ed. Robert Paul Wolff (New York, 1971), 85.

21. 19 How. 393 (1857).

22. 163 U.S. 537 (1896).

23. Leon Litwack, *North of Slavery: The Negro in the Free States, 1790–1860* (Chicago, 1961).

24. Mark V. Tushnet, *The NAACP's Legal Strategy against Segregated Education, 1925–1950* (Chapel Hill, N.C., 1987).

25. *Brown v. Board of Education,* 347 U.S. 484 (1954).

26. Arthur Bestor, Jr., "State Sovereignty and Slavery: A Reinterpretation of

15

Proslavery Constitutional Doctrine, 1846–1860," *Journal of the Illinois State Historical Society* 54 (1961): 117–80.

27. James W. Ely, Jr., *The Crisis of Conservative Virginia: The Byrd Organization and the Politics of Massive Resistance* (Knoxville, Tenn., 1976).

28. Arthur M. Schlesinger, "The State Rights Faith," *New Viewpoints in American History,* ed. Schlesinger (New York, 1934), 234.

29. Tony Freyer, *The Little Rock Crisis: A Constitutional Interpretation* (Westport, Conn., 1984), 116.

30. Finkelman, "Exploring Southern Legal History," 101.

31. See, for example, Karl N. Llewellyn and E. A. Hoebel, *The Cheyenne Way: Conflict and Case Law in Primitive Jurisprudence* (Norman, Okla., 1941); John Phillip Reid, *A Law of Blood: The Primitive Law of the Cherokee Nation* (New York, 1970); and Rennard Strickland, *Fire and the Spirits: Cherokee Law from Clan to Court* (Norman, Okla., 1975).

32. For an example of what might be done, see Mari J. Matsuda, "The West and the Legal State of Women: Explanations of Frontier Feminism," *Journal of the West* 14 (1985): 47–56.

33. See, for example, Edward L. Ayers, *Vengeance and Justice: Crime and Punishment in the Nineteenth-Century South* (New York, 1984).

34. Green's *Constitutional Development in the South Atlantic States* remains after half a century the leading work, but see also Mauer, "Southern State Constitutions in the 1870s." For a particularly good example of the relationship between state and federal constitutional developments, see A. E. Dick Howard, *Commentaries on the Constitution of Virginia,* 2 vols. (Charlottesville, Va., 1974).

The South and the American Constitutional Tradition at the Bicentennial

Herman Belz

The renewal of two-party competition and biracial politics in the South in the past two decades signifies the possible reintegration of the region into the national political community. A parallel development in the same period has been criticism of judicial policy making and activism, which in recent years has taken the form of a national debate over the propriety and possibility of a jurisprudence of original intent. Although southerners have not joined this debate with a united voice, they more than any other sectional group have historically found themselves in situations where it has seemed necessary to question the national constitutional consensus. Accordingly, we can perhaps gain deeper insight into the nature of American constitutionalism by considering the issues and events that have defined the place of the South in the constitutional tradition.

Of course the fact that dominates any consideration of this subject is the Civil War. No amount of new information or historical revisionism can deny the constitutional disruption caused by the formation of the Confederacy and the waging of civil war among Americans. It is nevertheless pertinent to ask how or in what sense states that had helped to found the republic eventually came to reject the Constitution of the framers. Stretching our historical imagination to include a southern perspective, we might even consider, secession notwithstanding, whether in a deeper sense the states of the Confederacy did not repudiate the constitutional tradition but rather remained faithful to it, or at least one conception of it. Finally, we may inquire into the process by which southerners revived the constitutional tradition after the Civil War, if indeed we believe that constitutional government was resumed in the South during or after Reconstruction.

It is apparent that answers to these questions depend in part on the definition of key terms. Usually in southern studies there is some uncertainty about what the South is or what it means to be a southerner. Were George Washington, Thomas Jefferson, James Madison, and John Marshall southerners? What about Spencer Roane, John C. Calhoun, and Jefferson Davis? If the South is primarily a geographical area, they were all southerners. And if "America" similarly designates territorial boundaries, they were all Americans. Yet the discourse of American history distinguishes between the two groups of men, regarding the former as national leaders and the latter as southern politicians. America, we can perhaps agree, is more meaningfully described with reference to political principles and ideals than to geography. Is this true also of the South? If so, what were or are southern political principles, and how do they stand in relation to those of the American political tradition?

As problematic as the definition of the South is the meaning of the constitutional tradition. Constitutional and legal scholars are at present well aware of the uncertainty surrounding the elementary question: what is the Constitution?[1] Is it the document authored by the framers in 1787 and the amendments subsequently added? Is it the principles and values embodied in the text? Does the Constitution include principles and concepts found outside the document, in philosophical and jurisprudential writings and vocabularies that are "available" to actors in the political community? Is there such a thing as "the spirit of the Constitution"? Is constitutional law, from whatever materials formulated, equivalent to the Constitution? And are the actions of public officials, the cumulative experience contained in the practices and usages of actual government, part of the Constitution?[2]

The more sophisticated our understanding of politics, language, and law, the more difficult it is to accept the idea that the American Constitution is a fixed, permanent, and binding supreme law having a true, ascertainable meaning. If we are unable to say with certainty what the Constitution is, how can we possibly talk about a constitutional tradition against which the actions of politicians and government officials can be evaluated? Yet ambiguity has its limits, and among scholars, as with the public in general to a much greater extent, there is a tendency in relation to certain issues to think of the Constitution as having a single, objective, correct meaning. This is a reminder that constitutional government in the United States has historically depended on viewing the Constitution as having a fixed and discoverable meaning.

The idea of an objective, unchanging Constitution may be a fiction— perhaps a very useful and constructive fiction. I refrain from comment on that issue. I suggest, however, that in considering the South's relation to national political development there has too often been a tendency to posit a single, true constitutional tradition as a framework for analysis and standard of judgment. This tendency is seen, for example, in the view that the South, at some point before the Civil War isolating itself from the rest of the nation, rejected the constitutional tradition and re- mained outside the national political mainstream until forced back into it by the second Reconstruction of the mid-twentieth century.[3] Though it is appealing in its simplicity, there is reason to doubt the adequacy of this assessment.

Let us, as an analytical strategy, define the Constitution as the princi- ples, rules, institutions, and procedures prescribed in the text and amendments to the document, along with the ends and objects of gov- ernment that shaped the framers' original design. Although in no sense merely empty symbols, many constitutional provisions are in this view broad, capacious, and imprecise in meaning. The constitutional tradi- tion accordingly can be thought of as the range of arguably valid ap- proaches to running the Constitution and achieving the ends and pur- poses of the regime that have shaped the course of our political history. On this basis let us examine events as much as possible from the stand- point of contemporary constitutional actors, trying in David Potter's words to be faithful to the historian's obligation to understand the thought and action of the past, rather than to defend and justify it as a guide for future action.[4]

Inclusion within the constitutional tradition, like the attribution of national identity to a people, is a conferral or signification of legitimacy that possesses great political importance, so much so that it can become in a literal sense a fighting matter. The South knows this fact well, for twice in its history it has experienced crisis and upheaval arising from conflict between its firm conviction that its laws and institutions conformed to the Constitution and the belief of a national political majority that the Constitution prohibited policies deemed vital to southern interests. Slavery and then racial discrimination—both legal and constitutional in the positivistic sense of being sanctioned by acts of constitutional decision and interpretation over a long period of time—were the issues that in the mid-nineteenth century and a century later were the source of sectional conflict. On both occasions we may say that the progress of history, conforming to the truth of philosophy and the principles of the American regime, determined that southern institutions, once arguably constitutional in the sense of receiving the tacit or express approval of the people and their government, lay outside the range of legitimate constitutional choice. In the language of positivistic history,[5] we would say that the meaning of the Constitution changed as the balance of political forces in the nation changed, calling into question the South's standing in the constitutional tradition.

I

Consideration of the South and the constitutional tradition begins with the American founding. Political principles and ideas, rather than culture, race, religion or immemorial history, formed the basis of American nationality.[6] Expressed in the Declaration of Independence and the revolutionary state constitutions, these ideas, known to us as republican political philosophy, included the natural right of individuals to liberty and equality; the right of the people to govern themselves as free political communities through representative institutions under majority rule; and limitations on government through the separation and division of power and the rule of law, including a constitution as a permanent, paramount, and binding political law. Acting in the federal convention and the state ratification conventions, the American people revised and applied these principles in forming a more unified state system in 1787–88.

National union, republican liberty, and balanced and limited government were the essential principles of American constitutionalism. General and ambiguous in nature, they could be understood in different ways. Structurally embodied or expressly stated in the document, these concepts established the boundaries of a new political community. In a superficial sense the ambiguity of the principles encouraged conflict, but at a deeper level the effect was unifying, for groups and individuals, and subsequently political parties, pursued their goals within the framework established by the Constitution. People invoked the principles of union, liberty, and balanced and limited power as justifications for proposed courses of action and public policies. In the broadest sense a response to the social and material environment, the Constitution was a practical instrument for carrying on politics. At the same time, repeated reference to the text of the Constitution as the source and symbol of legitimate authority confirmed its intrinsic value, apart from the results of specific political controversies. People believed that it was important to follow the Constitution for its own sake or for the common good, rather than for self-interested or expedient political purposes. For a variety of reasons, not the least of which was the authority emanating from the act of foundation itself, the Constitution was rapidly accorded the highest public status: political actors knew that the people took the Constitution seriously, regarded it as supreme law, believed that it was powerful because it embodied sound principles of government and society's fundamental values. Indeed, the people venerated the Constitution. Aware of this popular prejudice in favor of the Constitution, political groups and individuals were constrained to act in conformity with its provisions. The Constitution thus became a binding and paramount political law shaping the course and content of policies and events.[7]

Application of this view of the Constitution in historical analysis implies a broader understanding of the constitutional tradition than is perhaps usual. It suggests the possibility of divergent interpretations of the constitutional tradition within a consensus of regime values. The South's participation in national politics, understandable in these terms through most of its history, makes its experience a valid expression of the constitutional tradition.

There can be no disputing the fact that the southern states and southern political leaders played a major role in forming the Union and writing the Constitution. An older historiographical tradition regarded Madison, Jefferson, Lee, Randolph, Rutledge, and other Founding Fathers from below the Mason-Dixon line as liberal nationalists, rather than as reactionary southerners of the "conscious minority" type that came to the fore in the antebellum era.[8] If politics, society, and economy in the revolutionary South were essentially the same as in the nineteenth century, however—if it is misleading to search for a particular historical moment when the South became distinctive, as has been sug-

21

gested—then this characterization is no longer valid.[9] If those who found a nation are by definition nationalists, those who oppose or subsequently reject that nation can by logical inference be considered antinationalists. Yet if the American nation is preeminently defined by ideas and ideals, there may be a sense in which it is possible to remain faithful to the national idea while opposing the specific administration of government that at a particular time institutionally represents it.

Southerners played an essential part in making the Constitution and giving the Union its distinctive character as a new form of federal government.[10] And like their compatriots in other states, southerners defined the principles of union, liberty, and limited government in relation to their own local circumstances and institutions.[11] Among these was the institution of slavery, and it is clear that protection of slavery was a leading motive and object of southern delegates to the Constitutional Convention. It is also apparent that northern delegates, whether or not they believed slavery an evil institution that might eventually disappear, were prepared to accept the protections and immunities demanded by southerners in relation thereto.

The South's standing in the constitutional polity ultimately was rendered problematic by its dependence upon slavery. An empirical or positivistic view of the matter, however, suggests that slavery was a basic feature of the existing social order in many states, which it was a purpose of the Constitution to recognize and protect. Moreover, the compromises of the Constitution on slavery did not mediate between sharply divided moral positions for and against the institution. At the most, they were made within what can be described as a consensus of toleration of slavery.[12] In 1787 slavery had been legally abolished in the four New England states and Pennsylvania. As emancipation was prospective rather than immediate in three of these states, and as New York and New Jersey had not enacted abolition measures, thousands of slaves were still resident in the North. On a strictly factual geographical basis, therefore, one could say that slavery was a national institution at the time of the Constitutional Convention. Whether or in what sense slavery could be said to be a constitutionally legitimate institution, or the United States a slaveholding republic, was a less empirical, more philosophically controversial group of questions that depended on how one interpreted the Constitution in relation to the principles of the regime. Whether states that recognized slavery were within the constitutional tradition was an even broader question that involved the very definition of the national idea.

If these questions were raised during the adoption of the Constitution, they did not require resolution. Exigencies of national union and the stability of republican government had priority. A generation later, however, when slavery erupted as a major issue at the time of Missouri's admission to the Union, these issues began to emerge as highly pertinent and perplexingly unsettled. And by this time traditions of constitutional interpretation had taken shape that profoundly affected the way they could be dealt with.

Foremost among approaches to interpreting the Constitution that had developed by 1820 was the compact theory of the Union, with its corollary of states' rights and strict construction of central government legislative power. Formulated by southern political leaders Thomas Jefferson, vice-president of the United States, and James Madison, member of the Virginia Assembly, the compact theory crystallized and confirmed what may be described as the most readily available and generally accepted understanding of the nature of the Union in the early years of the republic.

II

In the debate over ratification, Federalists stressed the division of authority between the state governments and the general government under the sovereignty of the people. Glossing over the conflicts that were bound to arise in a state system based on dual and concurrent distribution of power, they were content to allow the precise character of "the people of the United States"—and hence of the nature of the Union—to remain ambiguous. Consolidationist or central-supremacy theories of the Union were slow to emerge. Alexander Hamilton, the most ardent nationalist, never offered a systematic statement of Unionist theory; James Wilson, a leading nationalist, as a member of the Supreme Court reiterated the idea of popular sovereignty and divided governmental authority.[13] Moreover, because the Union was regarded as an experimental undertaking, arguments for its perpetuity in the first forty years of the government were not expressed to counter frequent threats of disunion that were provoked by conflicts between state and federal authority.[14]

23

In this formative era of constitutional interpretation the compact theory of the Union stood out as a persuasive and valid description of the nature of the American state system.

According to Madison and Jefferson, the Union was a compact made by the states, which as constituent parties retained the right to judge whether the central government had violated the compact. Exercising this right by what they considered the accepted practices for implementing compacts, the states, in Madison's language, could "interpose" their authority between citizens of a state and the central government to stop unconstitutional acts of the latter. In the Kentucky Resolutions of 1799 Jefferson asserted that "a Nullification" of all unauthorized acts of the federal government performed under color of the Constitution was "the rightful remedy" for them.[15]

Considering the studied ambiguity of the framers and the authors of *The Federalist* on the question of who made the Constitution, the compact theory must be regarded as an arguably valid statement of the nature of the Union. Attempts to resolve the issue on historical grounds have been as enduring as they have been unsuccessful, and this largely because the very description of the problem involves contested questions of political science and political philosophy. From the perspective of constitutional law, the most significant feature of the compact theory was the proposition that the states created the Constitution and the Union. This view is often considered historically and theoretically inadequate because it denies the actual agency of the people of the United States in making the Constitution—that is, popular sovereignty. As a matter of empirically observed historical fact, however, it would seem more accurate and realistic, considering that the states in the revolutionary era were more effectively organized as republican governments than was the Confederation, to interpret "the people of the United States" as referring to the people as citizens of separate though related political communities.

From the standpoint of political philosophy or the science of government, evaluation of the compact theory depends on how a "state" is defined. A state may be considered the territory occupied by a political community, its governmental institutions and officers, or the people forming the community. Madison, in his Virginia Legislative Committee Report of 1800, used the third of these definitions to explain how the states, through the ratification process, had made the Constitution. Walter Hartwell Bennett, perhaps the most careful student of the matter,

24

points out that nothing was more important to the compact theory than the fact that the Constitution was ratified by conventions assembled in and consisting of delegates chosen in the various states. Bennett observes that it was not naive to think of these conventions as constituent bodies of the states, adding, "Not much was ever really done toward explaining why they should not be so regarded."[16] Looked at from this point of view, the analysis of the nature of the Union in the compact theory satisfied the criterion of national democratic inclusiveness, for the state governments, each representing a part, together represented all of the people of the United States.[17]

Recent scholarship has shown that the concept of the people of the United States, referring to a single political community, was more a clever theoretical invention by the proponents of the Constitution in the ratification struggle than an abstraction from historical reality. It was more a legal fiction than an expression of political reality, a formal rather than a substantive truth.[18] There is general agreement, on the other hand, that social contract theory was widely employed in state making and constitution writing during the Revolution.[19] If the people as the constituent power in the states made state governments, there was no reason why in the same capacity they could not make a new Constitution for the Union.

Too often in constitutional analysis the character of the people of the United States as a single political community has been a matter of assumption, on which basis the states' rights argument about the nature of the Union is judged to be historically unsound. The more pertinent and realistic question is: in what respects can it be said that the people of the United States acted as a single political community, apart from their states? At the Constitutional Convention, for example, a nationalist proposal for a single general convention to ratify the Constitution, enabling the people to act as a unit, failed to receive a second.[20] The historian R. Kent Newmyer, writing of Justice Story's theory of the Union advanced in the 1830s as an answer to South Carolina nullification, observes that the nationalist argument for the popular origins of the Constitution was "in some respects as metaphysical as the states' rights school he criticized for its metaphysics—as when it made sovereignty unequivocally descend on the American people in 1776."[21] Doubt about the historical soundness of the nationalist theory of the origins of the Constitution is implied in the conclusion of another scholar that whereas the states' rights doctrine was continuously elaborated by succeeding generations,

25

nationalists were less consistent and more expedient, arguing "more forcibly as time went on that 'whatever is, is right.' "[22] Furthermore, we might recall Tocqueville's matter-of-fact observation in the 1830s that the Union was formed by the voluntary agreement of the states. Tocqueville, no friend of the South, said that the states in uniting did not forfeit their sovereignty, nor were their inhabitants reduced to the condition of being one and the same people. And if a state should choose to withdraw from the Union, Tocqueville speculated, it would be difficult to disprove its right to do so.[23] Although these observations do not necessarily validate the southern compact theory, they serve to remind us that the historical evidence supports rival versions of the constitutional tradition.[24]

In a sense the shaping of American constitutionalism in the early national period was mainly an affair among southerners. The Republican party, substantially southern in composition, ran the Constitution after 1800 according to "Country" principles that, with some modification, became established national political practices.[25] The Republican and later the Democratic party fashioned a constitutionalism based on executive leadership, popular participation, states' rights, state government activism, and national territorial expansion. At the same time constitutional-law controversies involving southerners produced doctrines of Unionism that evolved into conflicting constitutional traditions. On the basis of the compact theory Virginia and Maryland, between 1813 and 1821, challenged federal authority. They were not the only ones to do so, of course, the disunionist and interpositionist protests of the New England states during the War of 1812 showing that men of that region were as narrowly provincial—or as nationalistic—as southerners. The Maryland and Virginia cases were more important from the standpoint of constitutional law, however, for they provided the opportunity for fellow southerner John Marshall to explicate the theory of central-supremacy federalism that in later years, after the Civil War, would be accepted as the true description of the constitutional tradition.

As the compact theory ought to be viewed as an arguably sound explanation of the origin and nature of the Union, so the nationalist theory of Marshall ought to be considered an acceptable analysis that was perhaps not so different from the states' rights position as is usually assumed. To be sure, Marshall was a nationalist, though not a consolidationist like Hamilton and other Federalists.[26] In a political-cultural sense he recognized that common republican citizenship, existing before the Revolution, united Americans as a national people. However, this view did not characterize his more strictly constitutional nationalist theory, in which the nation was established with the ratification of the Constitution. The decisive element in Marshall's Unionism was the idea that the people, acting in their highest capacity as sovereign individuals rather than as citizens of the states, delegated their powers to a new government in the Constitution, thus creating a compound system partly unitary and partly federal.[27]

The transcendent national character of the sovereign people in Marshall's conception of the Union appears more a theoretical premise than a principle derived from actual experience. In refuting the compact theory advanced by the state in *McCulloch v. Maryland*, Marshall observed that the Constitution was "submitted to the people" for ratification, and they acted on it "by assembling in Convention." Marshall conceded as a factual matter what the compact theorists built much of their case on: that the Constitution had been ratified by the people acting in separate political communities. "It is true," he wrote, "they assembled in their several States." But Marshall discounted the significance of this fact. ". . . and where else should they have assembled?" he asked. "No political dreamer was ever wild enough to think of breaking down the lines which separate the States, and of compounding the American people into one common mass. Of consequence, when they act they act in their States. But the measures they adopt do not, on that account, cease to be the measures of the people themselves, or become the measures of the state governments."[28] That point, however, had never been contended in the states' rights argument and was not the issue. The question was whether the people in ratifying the Constitution had acted as separate political communities or as a single encompassing community. Marshall did not answer this question.[29]

Eleven years later, as events forced both northerners and southerners to clarify and insist on the differences in their conceptions of the Union, Daniel Webster asserted that the Constitution "pronounces that it is established by the people of the United States in the aggregate," not only by the states or the people of the states.[30] In Story's *Commentaries* (1833), centralizing Unionist theory progressed to the point where it was considered irrelevant, in determining the character of the government, that the Constitution was written by delegates chosen by states and ratified by the people in state conventions, or that state agency in some respects was built into the operation of the federal government.[31] As Newmyer has observed, Story's nationalism was based on a strictly sectional and paranoid perception of American history, as biased as the southern reading of the nation's founding documents.[32]

27

If we resist the tendency to describe Marshall's Unionism as the single true expression of the constitutional tradition, it is possible to see his position as having points of contact with the states' rights–compact theory. Although clearly favoring the central government, Marshall acknowledged that the states for some purposes were "distinct and perfect sovereignties." This concession permitted the inference that they might exercise their power in conflict with that of the national government. Of similar import, Marshall described the Union as a complex system that for some purposes acted as a single nation and for others consisted of distinct and independent sovereignties. Not required to resolve the inconsistency and potential contradiction inherent in the system of divided sovereignty, Marshall was content to say that Americans had always been united in some respects and had acted as distinct societies in others. In *Cohens v. Virginia* (1821), he said the federal government, exercising its constitutional powers, could legitimately control any person or government in U.S. territory. Did this mean that any exercise of central authority, however slight, must prevail in case of conflict with state authority? According to Robert K. Faulkner, Marshall resisted this conclusion, in effect accepting a power-sharing arrangement between states and nation, at least in regard to commercial regulation, similar to that explicated by the Supreme Court in the Taney period.[33]

Marshall's campaign for central-supremacy federalism might be seen as an uphill struggle against the widely popular states' rights–compact theory of the Union and the practice of resistance to national authority that had appeared in every section of the country. South Carolina historian George C. Rogers, Jr., implying that Marshall's nationalism had little effect, characterizes his doctrine of national power based on the sovereignty of the people as "only a legal fiction."[34] Nevertheless, at the time, Marshall's principles of national power caused apprehension among some southerners, who feared their practical effect if made the basis of policies inimical to slavery. If any lesson was needed, the Missouri controversy of 1819–21 provided an alarming augury of the potential danger from excessive federal power.

III

Momentous political and constitutional events in the period 1820 to 1860 raised in the most acute form the question of the South's relationship to the constitutional tradition. Competing conceptions of Unionism had arisen that were confined to no particular section, though perhaps contested among southerners more than among any other regional group. In the decades preceding the Civil War these theories became more or less sectionally identified. Southerners professed the states' rights–compact theory, elaborating it in two forms: Democratic dual federalism and the theory of the concurrent majority of John C. Calhoun. Marshall's central-supremacy federalism meanwhile was affirmed and sectionalized, most notably by Whigs Daniel Webster and Joseph Story. The existence of these several theories is evidence that the nature of the Union at the time was uncertain. Yet it was the nature of liberty in particular—or of liberty as the central element in the union idea—that became problematic in the antebellum period. It was in relation to this issue that southern constitutionalism would ultimately be judged.

From 1790 to 1820 American liberty assumed regional variations. In a sense controversies over the respective powers of the federal and state governments were disputes over the meaning of liberty, understood as the freedom of local communities and individuals to govern themselves. Liberty, the purpose of national unification, was thought to be the result of placing limitations on government rather than a substantive value positively to be realized in some ideal or universal sense through government action. This perception began to change at the time of the Missouri Compromise, however, when controversy arose over the nature of liberty in a specific constitutional sense.

The occasion for controversy was the proposed admission of Missouri into the Union as a slave state. Previous practice suggested a policy of admitting Missouri and organizing the rest of the Louisiana Purchase territory under the principle of local option, allowing territories and states to decide the slavery question.[35] Some northern Federalists now objected to this course on the ground that slavery was inconsistent with republican government.[36] As an expression of the consensus on slavery in the making of the Constitution, it had been an operative rule in national politics before this time that only those with a direct interest in slavery—that is, slaveholders—should make decisions concerning the institution.[37] The corollary was the well-known rule against federal regulation of slavery on the ground that it was a local institution. After 1820, as the meaning of liberty under the Constitution became the central issue in American politics, the force of these two unwritten stipulations concerning slavery steadily weakened. Southerners and northern-

29

ers, both professing fidelity to the Constitution and the intent of the framers, struggled to determine the course of national development. In doing so they entered upon a collision course that ultimately resolved fateful ambiguities in the constitutional tradition.

For many years liberal nationalist historiography excluded the antebellum South from the constitutional tradition, telling a story of nullifiers and reactionary sectionalists who stamped out freedom of speech, freedom of the press, and the right of dissent and substituted for the natural rights of men the rights and autonomy of communities.[38] This interpretation implicitly regarded the northern free-soil position as truly representing the revolutionary and constitutional tradition. It has been challenged in recent years, however, by studies that see the Old South as adhering to the principles of American republicanism.

Newer accounts of southern political history treat republicanism as a philosophy of local and individual self-government, based on personal liberty, independence, and equality in civic virtue, and expressed in written constitutions that divided and limited power in a balanced structure of government. In the postrevolutionary generation the republican principle was democratized by the expansion of the suffrage, which enlarged the political community, and by the elevation of individual liberty to preeminence over the communal equality of citizens. Equal liberty, with the accent on liberty, became the unifying American value.[39] Within this theoretical framework southern republican liberty developed in two modes. The first, corresponding to the concurrent-majority Unionism of John C. Calhoun, was an antiparty republicanism associated with South Carolina but found also in other southern states. The second strategy for preserving liberty, a corollary of Democratic dual federalism, depended on a two-party electoral system within the South and in the nation as a whole.

As envisioned in Calhoun's theory of the concurrent majority and as practiced in South Carolina and to a lesser extent in other southern states, republican liberty was an elitist doctrine of virtue- and honor-based individualism that rejected political partisanship and the rule of simple numerical majorities. Proponents of this kind of republicanism warned against the danger to liberty from the manipulation of politicians, which could deprive citizens of their independence and reduce them to slavery or a condition of dependence. As slaveholders, antiparty republicans in South Carolina and elsewhere were acutely aware of the nature of liberty and sensitive to exertions of power by the

central government—for example, in the formulation of tariff policy—
that could reduce them to political and economic dependency. Recent
studies conclude that antiparty southern republicans, instructed by the
slaveholding experience to appreciate true liberty, evoked the values
of independent virtue, the good of the community, and denial of personal ambition, values that were also critical in the political culture of
slavery.[40]

The second variety of southern republican liberty, more widespread,
flexible, and persistent because rooted in the democratic sensibility of
the age, was based on political partisanship. This strand of republicanism was not exclusively southern but rather was national in scope,
its leading theoretician being Martin Van Buren of New York. Insofar as
the establishment of a national two-party system was a conscious and
deliberate change in the structure of the polity, the South's contribution
to it is evidence of its constructive role in defining the constitutional
tradition.[41]

In party-based republicanism, as in the antiparty type, individual personal liberty was the highest value, to be defended against power in any
form that threatened to make slaves out of freemen by reducing them to
political or economic dependency. Again, the slaveholding experience,
by teaching white southerners to value liberty inestimably, was the
ground of republican politics. But differences over how, from a republican standpoint, changes in the socioeconomic environment should
be dealt with, as well as concern for the security of the Union, led most
southerners to adopt partisanship as a constitutional principle.[42] Party
battles between Whigs and Democrats turned on the promise of liberty
or threat of despotism—social and economic independence or the denial of it—thought to result from alternative responses to the fact of
economic development. Private associations such as banks, railroads,
and commercial and manufacturing corporations, as well as public institutions, were seen as capable of exercising power over individuals
that could threaten their liberty.[43]

Love of liberty and fear of despotism learned in local party struggles
were ultimately important in national politics, where amid rising antislavery sentiment after 1820 the threat of power used adversely to
southern interests was ever present. Territorial expansion in the 1840s
delivered the threat with unmistakable clarity. Republican ideas of independence and virtue, shaped in local controversies over economic development, became the basis of the politics of slavery that southerners

31

pursued in the national arena. Maintaining party lines, politicians competed in federal elections especially by promising to protect slavery, the foundation of southern society and the republican way of life. Reinforced by democratic changes in voting and representation that stimulated popular participation, the politics of slavery—or of rights-conscious republican liberty—guided the South in the course of action that, given the matching commitment of northern abolitionists and free-soilers to their section's conception of liberty, led to secession and civil war.[44]

Territorial expansion eventually brought about the demand of the Republican party that slavery be prohibited from entering the national domain. That demand in turn signified to southerners denationalization or delegitimization of their institutions, marking them as inferior to citizens of northern states in constitutional rights and immunities. Slavery restriction portended a form of control that southerners regarded as despotic and, with no sense of irony, identified as slavery. These perceptions and beliefs shaped the state-by-state response to Lincoln's election, by which southerners determined that they had to maintain their liberty outside the Union.

A Republican administration, committed to slavery restriction in the short run and promising abolition in the more distant future, immediately raised the prospect of emancipation. And emancipation, by elevating blacks or depressing whites to the same status of freemanship, spelled denial of the equal liberty that defined southern republicanism. In the words of historian J. Mills Thornton, "Who would attribute dignity to, and seek to maintain, a position to which even a Negro could aspire?"[45] Self-consciously following the example of the revolutionary fathers, southerners seceded in order to maintain liberty and self-government—the political purpose that defined constitutional government in America. Like all Americans, Michael Holt writes in his account of secession, southerners acted to prevent the despotism that signified slavery. To Americans in the late twentieth century, evidence showing white southern—and also white northern—fear of enslavement is literally unbelievable. It is perhaps a mistake, however, to read back into the nineteenth century the concern and sensitivity about race that has become widespread in the past thirty years. According to Holt, black slavery was not the preoccupation of the nation. "The slavery that was important to them," he states, "was an abstract status men hoped to escape, a status they equated with the end of republican government."[46] Southern liberty thus irresistibly confronted northern liberty. Defended from both sides, the republic was divided by civil war.[47]

"We quit the Union, not the Constitution," Virginians explained as they seceded in April 1861.[48] In more ways than one, the writing of the Confederate Constitution was a culminating act defining the South's relation to the constitutional tradition. The formal similarities between the federal and the Confederate constitutions have often been remarked. They are considered evidence, in a superficial and ironic sense, of the South's ambivalent position in the constitutional polity—an indication of the attraction/revulsion syndrome that characterized its attitude toward national principles and ideals. Having rejected the nation's organic law, the secessionists wrote a constitution borrowing unoriginally from the instrument they repudiated. Indeed, the most careful student of the subject makes the revisionist argument that the Confederate Constitution was most significant for its departures from the U.S. Constitution and the dissatisfaction with American constitutional practice that they implied.[49]

The Confederate document contained provisions for an executive budget and item veto; restriction of presidential removal power; limited recognition of a parliamentary, "cabinet-in-Congress" device to facilitate executive and legislative cooperation; a six-year term for president without reelection; provision for presidential disability; constitutional amendment exclusively by states; and invocation of God's favor. These changes, many of them already found in state constitutions, may be said to have introduced elements for consideration and possible inclusion in the American constitutional tradition. At the time, however, the provisions of the Confederate Constitution that stood out as most important confirmed the compact theory of the Union, impliedly approved secession by virtue of its state sovereignty language, and gave express recognition and protection to slavery. More significantly than procedural and organizational innovations, these substantive changes expressed dissatisfaction with the U.S. Constitution, or with the way it was likely to be interpreted by the incoming Republican administration.

Nevertheless, the purpose of the Confederate Constitution, according to the leading historian of the subject, was to uphold and perpetuate the fundamental principles of the American Constitution.[50] This judgment refutes the liberal nationalist view that the South rejected the constitutional tradition. Instead, it confirms the implicit conclusion of recent studies that southern republican liberty was within the constitutional tradition. With notable objectivity, the new southern history views southern Unionism, liberty, and local self-government as valid expressions of American constitutionalism. Moreover, writers of the southern republican school do not concede the Declaration of Independence to the antislavery forces or separate the Declaration from the Constitution as revisionist historians tended to do.[51] On the contrary, they describe secession as justified by the spirit of 1776 as well as the compact of 1787.[52] The product of positivistic historiography, the new southern political history has its source in the republican paradigm that has influenced early American history writing in the past two decades, and it reflects no evident ideological bias. Yet it raises provocative and politically significant questions about American constitutionalism that require analysis.

IV

The basic issue is whether southern republican liberty based on slavery was genuine constitutional liberty. Were the actions of the southern states as political communities, and the policies proposed by southern lawmakers and executive officers in the national government, valid and legitimate exercises of constitutional power? Were southerners justified—were they correct—in asserting and defending their interests in the name of liberty and union under the Constitution? If the South rejected the constitutional tradition, did it do so only in secession? Or had it turned its back on the founding at some earlier point in time? These questions have usually been raised in considering Calhoun's place in American political thought. George Kateb, for example, observing that debate over the relationship of political equality and other values in American government has been more a household dispute than a competition of alien principles, asks whether Calhoun's contribution was yet another voice in the family quarrel, or rather was something else.[53] The effect of recent writing on antebellum politics is to broaden this question to include southern politicians in general.

The answer provided by historical scholarship is that the South interjected its voice in a family quarrel. Accordingly, this scholarship sees the southern approach to union, liberty, and balanced and limited government as developing within the constitutional tradition. It would be difficult to deny that slavery, an existing institution in most of the states, was accepted as constitutional in 1787 and compatible with republican government as it actually existed.[54] In 1860–61 eleven southern states seceded on the ground that northern states and the federal government had violated long-standing constitutional principles and rules governing slavery, and out of fear that a Republican administration would formally change the rules on slavery, denying southerners the rights of liberty, equality, and self-government. The fear proved self-fulfilling, as secession initiated events that within a few years in fact resulted in changing the constitutional rules on slavery. And from the standpoint of positivistic history this formal change, expressed in the Thirteenth Amendment, was not declaratory, nor was it considered as such by most people at the time. That is, it was understood not as merely declaring what had been the true meaning of the Constitution all along but rather as changing it.

Yet if it is the conclusion of history that slavery was constitutional, and southern republican liberty a valid strand within the constitutional tradition, what are the implications for the nature of American liberty and the meaning of the national idea? Are we to conclude that American liberty was a counterfeit thing, ultimately illegitimate because corrupted by the injustice of slavery? Of particular interest in this regard is the judgment of recent historians that southern republicans were acutely sensitive to the true nature of liberty because of the slaveholding experience. White southerners had a special grasp of the concept of liberty, writes William J. Cooper, Jr., a passion for it that was evident in the South's revolutionary ardor in 1776.[55] Edmund S. Morgan, describing colonial Virginians, states that the presence among them of slaves—persons totally subject to the will of others—"gave to those in control an immediate experience of what it could mean to be at the mercy of a tyrant." "Virginians may have had a special appreciation of the freedom dear to republicans," Morgan reasons, "because they saw every day what life without it could be like."[56] J. Mills Thornton asserts that because Alabamians knew slavery firsthand, they sought above all else to avoid it. For them, slavery was not a mere metaphor; because of their daily contact with genuine slavery, they were even more fanatically devoted to the worship of liberty and equality than other Americans in the Jacksonian era.[57] Kenneth Greenberg agrees that slaveowners were obsessively concerned with personal independence because of their knowledge, based on slavery, of the degrading effects of dependence. The experience of domination, he concludes, bred a devout commitment to freedom.[58]

These accounts, which imply a more positive view of southern re-

35

publicanism than Tocqueville's observation that under the influence of slavery the southern citizen "becomes a sort of domestic dictator from infancy," urgently raise the question of the meaning of liberty.[59] A different view of liberty emerges when we consider the matter from the perspective of the subject class of Negro slaves. Orlando Patterson, in his work *Slavery and Social Death*, argues that the struggle in which the slave was engaged throughout history "forced upon him a need that no other human beings have felt so acutely: the need for disenslavement, for disalienation, for negation of social death." "And so it was," writes Patterson, "that freedom came into the world. Before slavery people simply could not have conceived of the thing we call freedom." According to Patterson, men in premodern, nonslaveholding societies could not and did not value "the removal of restraint as an ideal."[60] Individuals yearned only for the security of being anchored in a network of power and authority. But this was not freedom, and to call it so, Patterson insists, is an abuse of language. Freedom "is not a faculty or a power to do something," he asserts; it is, rather, "the absence of the impediments in the way of doing it."[61]

In a sense Patterson's insight supports the southern republican liberty thesis. For if the institution of slavery defined and made clear the true meaning of freedom, those who enslaved, and others who observed the process, could rationally calculate and appreciate the inestimable value of liberty. Yet Patterson's point is that slaves loved liberty more and valued it higher than anyone else. Indeed, in his view masters learned about freedom from slaves.[62] For our inquiry into the nature of liberty under the Constitution, the lesson Patterson draws is sobering. "Beyond the socio-historical findings," he writes, "is the unsettling discovery that an ideal cherished in the West beyond all others emerged as a necessary consequence of the degradation of slavery and the effort to negate it. . . . The first men and women to struggle for freedom, the first to think of themselves as free in the only meaningful sense of the term, were freedmen. And without slavery there would have been no freedmen." Patterson poses the ultimate question raised by his study: "are we to esteem slavery for what it has wrought, or must we challenge our conception of freedom and the value we place upon it?"[63]

Although the historical accuracy of Patterson's conclusion about knowledge of human freedom is dubious, the point of view it represents, in relation to the contemporary controversy over race relations and affirmative action, is undoubtedly widespread. And the obvious implication of his position is that the Western concept of freedom should be questioned.[64] In the context of the present analysis, the conclusion would follow that southern liberty—and perhaps the very concept of American freedom itself—was illegitimate. Noting that the attempt to support freedom with slavery ended in the Civil War, Edmund S. Morgan speculates that the two institutions—freedom and slavery—were more closely related than the victorious Unionists thought. "Was the vision of a nation of equals flawed at the source by contempt for both the poor and the black?" he asks. "Is America still colonial Virginia writ large? More than a century after Appomattox the questions linger."[65]

What answers can be given to these questions? Provoked by the need to come to grips with the problem of slavery in the American republic, into what directions could a reconsideration of American liberty lead?

One direction, implied in Morgan's troubled query, would be repudiation of the liberal tradition. Heretofore the story of constitutional liberty and national progress has taken slavery into account without becoming preoccupied with it. This perspective may no longer be a permissible or available option, however, if racial consciousness, as a corollary of public policies of affirmative-action racial exceptionalism, continues to increase. As southern liberty in the liberal nationalist tradition was delegitimized and excluded from the national consensus, so the liberty of the American founding might be categorically discredited in a radical egalitarian view of our past. Usually we have asked: how different was the old South? In the future we may ask: how different was America from the old South? Or, as Morgan puts it, how much like the South was the rest of the nation?[66] If America was in essence southern, if slave-based republican liberty was simply an exaggeration of an American liberty so corrupted by racial and other exclusionist tendencies as to be fundamentally flawed, then the conclusion may follow that there is no history of American liberty worth studying. In that case, absolved of the legacy of the founding, Americans would be free to pursue a different conception of liberty.[67] Instead of being defined by republican principles and institutions, national identity would consist in the fact of continuous historical existence. Our history would be not an integrating account of expanding liberty but a disintegrating story of group consciousness and conflict.

Evaluation of the problem of slave-based liberty within the constitutional tradition poses a choice between two fundamentally opposed perspectives. From the standpoint of positive law—that is, the constitu-

37

tions, laws, and judicial decisions of the southern states and the U.S. Constitution as it was adopted, implemented, and accepted in public opinion from 1789 to 1860—slavery was a legal institution. According to this view, liberty that allowed some men to rule others without their consent, under the dispensation of the compact theory of the Union and the divided sovereignty of federalism, was constitutionally legitimate. If, however, the Constitution is not merely positive law, if it was intended to embody and guarantee natural rights under a universal standard of justice inherent in the law of nature, then slavery, the systematic rule by which some men control others in flagrant denial of natural rights and human equality, can never be regarded as legitimate, irrespective of the actions of government or the approval of public opinion. Historians, like the people whose actions they seek to understand, must choose between these perspectives in describing what the Constitution was or what it meant in a given historical situation. Most of the time historians adopt a positivistic outlook, accepting as the relevant horizon for analysis the conventions and opinions of the people and the actions and decisions of their government. Because the Constitution has not usually been regarded merely as a text to be read and applied in a positivistic manner, however, especially in times of national crisis, a more historically accurate analysis of American liberty takes as its point of departure the principles of the regime as expressed in the revolutionary founding.

This approach would assert that American liberty was sound in principle, although imperfectly realized. It would hold that liberty and equality of opportunity were the central ideas defining American nationality and that insofar as individuals enjoyed civil liberty they possessed equality. Proclaimed in the Declaration of Independence, these principles, in the nature of things and for specific historical reasons, could not be universally applied but had to be maintained as an ideal and realized on a prudential basis as circumstances permitted. In this view the Declaration of Independence is the nation's first founding document, a historical preface to the Constitution that supplies an aspirational and teleological element defining the philosophy of American government.[68]

To see how this view might be applied, we may consider Lincoln's analysis of the South and the constitutional tradition during the controversy over slavery. Lincoln agreed that slavery, where it existed, was constitutional. As he said in a speech in 1858, "We could not get our constitution unless we permitted them [i.e., southerners] to remain in slavery, we could not secure the good we did if we grasped for more." Having "by necessity submitted to that much," he reasoned, "it does not destroy the principle that is the charter of our liberties. Let that charter stand as our standard."[69] On another occasion Lincoln wrote: "I hold it to be a paramount duty of us in the free states, due to the Union of the states, and perhaps to liberty itself (paradox though it may seem) to let the slavery of the other states alone."[70] Although it was discussed in "covert language" and words that were "ambiguous, roundabout, and mystical," Lincoln acknowledged that slavery was mentioned in the Constitution.[71] And despite his devotion to the Declaration of Independence, he did not regard the Declaration as part of the Constitution. He recognized that although the equality of all men was "the great fundamental principle upon which our free institutions rest," and "negro slavery is violative of that principle," nevertheless, "by our frame of government" that principle "has not been made one of legal obligation."[72] Accordingly, he regarded the southern states, despite slavery, as republican governments in the sense of the Constitution.[73]

Nonetheless, the positivistic implications of these observations notwithstanding, Lincoln ultimately appealed to the liberty and equality of all men as asserted in the Declaration of Independence as the informing and animating principles of the regime, those which provided a moral standard for constitutional statecraft. He expressed this outlook in his references to equality as the ground for opposing slavery in the 1850s, and to liberty as the basis for opposing secession in 1861. The Constitution and the Union were essential to national prosperity, Lincoln reasoned, but they were not the primary cause. "There is something back of these," he wrote in January 1861, "entwining itself more closely about the human heart. That something"—"a philosophical cause"—"is the principle of 'Liberty to all'—the principle that clears the *path* for all—gives *hope* to all—and, by consequence, *enterprize,* and *industry* to all."[74]

In 1787 the American people were sufficiently united to form a sovereign, lawgiving government expressing their sense of nationality. Liberty was the fundamental purpose of the Constitution and formed the basis of national consensus. Agreement on slavery—to tolerate if not to approve and to protect it within limits—was also part of the consensus. In the course of time national unity broke down, in part because of the growth of slavery as an institution, in part because of changing conceptions of liberty and moral responsibility.[75] Tocqueville wrote in the

39

1830s that Americans formed one people in all cases specified in the Constitution, that is, in the matters that were subject to determination by majority rule.[76] Although in certain respects regulation of slavery was constitutionally stipulated, the general and unwritten constitutional rule was that power and responsibility over the institution belonged to the states. Liberty, on the other hand, as the basic purpose of the founding, was considered the legitimate interest and responsibility of all actors in the constitutional polity—individual citizens as well as local, state, and federal government officials.

The problem in 1860 was that whereas Republicans saw exclusion of slavery from the territories as a proper exercise of constitutional power dealing with the question of liberty, southerners saw it as an improper and unconstitutional interference with slavery and a restriction on their liberty and equality. The two sections interpreted the Constitution through the lenses of regional manners, morality, and political philosophy. After a certain point the document no longer withstood interpretation according to fundamentally opposed moral perspectives. The nation had to become unified again in a single way of life, in accordance with the principles of the regime. And the Constitution, an incomplete and imperfect document whether considered from the antislavery or the proslavery point of view, had to be amended. The ambiguity in the constitutional tradition that allowed rival forms of republican liberty to develop legitimately had to be resolved. Secession and civil war determined which version of American constitutional liberty would prevail.

V

Obvious as it was that the Confederate states were making war on the Constitution, in a legal sense their standing within or without the Union, and hence in the constitutional tradition, was by no means determined by this simple fact. Denying the legal validity and effect of secession, the U.S. government consistently held that the states were still in the Union, though with disorganized and disloyal governments. After the war, taking official Union government pronouncements on the illegality of secession at face value, former Confederates claimed the protection of the Constitution in seeking readmission of their states to Congress. The political ironies in this situation, as well as the passions aroused by Reconstruction measures that ambiguously tempered coercion with a measure of voluntary consent, have perhaps obscured the legal resolution of the wartime South's constitutional standing. Having recognized the belligerent status of the Confederate states in the *Prize Cases* in 1863, the Supreme Court went no further in acknowledging legal consequences of secession or legitimate independent standing for the Confederacy as a government. Concerning the separate states of the Confederacy, however, the Court held that actions taken during the war not in furtherance of the rebellion, but pertaining to valid civil purposes, were legal. In this limited sense the southern states, even under conditions of civil war, were found to be within the constitutional tradition.[77]

Consideration of the southern constitutional experience since the Civil War raises the same interpretive problem that appears in the antebellum period, with the difference that segregation and racial discrimination replace slavery as the source of questionable constitutional legitimacy. If the seceding states, at least in a de facto political sense, placed themselves outside the Constitution in their attempt to protect slavery, they were forced back under it by the results of the war. Yet whether the postwar South really conformed to national constitutional norms has remained a disputed question.

The time has long since passed when the constitutionality of Reconstruction measures, including the Thirteenth, Fourteenth, and Fifteenth amendments, could be questioned as a violation of the basic principle of consent.[78] Although the Supreme Court restricted the scope of centralizing civil rights statutes and constitutional provisions, it reflected public opinion in finding congressional Reconstruction to be constitutional.[79] The South, for its part, adjusted to the results of the war by adopting the Black Codes, for the first time conferring civil rights on blacks while keeping them in a subordinate position.[80] When Congress nullified the general policy of this legislation, the white South acquiesced in the rebuilding of expanded political communities under federal authority and based on black suffrage. For several years during Reconstruction control of these reformed state governments became the focus of renewed party competition in the South.

Regarding matters again from the standpoint of positivistic history, it would seem that once the former Confederate states resumed their place in the Union, state government and politics in the South, and the actions of southern lawmakers and executive officers in national politics, presumably were within the constitutional tradition. The meaning of union, liberty, and balanced and limited government had changed, as

41

had southern views of these principles. Most political histories of Reconstruction have implicitly assumed this perspective.[81] The principal objection to it as an account of constitutional history is that it ignores the violation of the Fourteenth and Fifteenth amendments that occurred during and after Reconstruction. Section 2 of the Fourteenth Amendment requires reduction in the population basis of a state's congressional representation in proportion to the ratio between the number of its male citizens whose right to vote is denied and the whole number of male citizens in the state. The Fifteenth Amendment guarantees a right not to be deprived of the suffrage on account of race or previous slavery. Through devices that were discriminatory in intent and in effect, southern states plainly abridged black citizens' right to vote and continued to do so well into the twentieth century. We may conclude that southern government and politics were in this sense unconstitutional, while we observe that enforcement of section 2 of the Fourteenth Amendment and determination of the unconstitutionality of southern electoral systems were the responsibility of federal lawmakers and judicial officers, who in several cases where the issue was raised refused to go behind the terms of southern constitutions and election laws to reach such a finding.[82]

The theme of continuing southern resistance to, or self-exclusion from, the national constitutional consensus appears in recent writing on the postwar South. It has been suggested, for example, that Reconstruction politics is the story of white southerners securing by the techniques of "political terrorism" what they could not achieve on the battlefields of the Civil War, namely, the freedom to order their society and in particular to maintain control over race relations.[83] Agreeing with this view, another scholar asserts that in the Reconstruction South "power *did* flow from the barrel of a gun."[84] Plainly, a political system based on force and violence rejects the assumption of peaceful resolution of conflict on which constitutionalism rests. It is not clear, however, that the same point cannot be directed at the North. The nature of the Union and the relationship of slavery to republican liberty having been resolved by a conflict of arms, the Civil War amendments to the Constitution might be regarded as having been imposed by accident and force, rather than by reflection and choice. And congressional Reconstruction policy, as a resolution of the issues of the war, might be considered a unilaterally imposed political settlement denying the principle of consent that was an essential element in the constitutional tradition. On the other hand, if

42

we grant the legitimacy of the constitutional amendments and Reconstruction statutes as an extension of the principles of the regime, we may nonetheless conclude that if southern laws and policies were unconstitutional, political and legal responsibility for the situation, especially in view of the extensive national powers conferred by the amendments, lay with the federal government. In contrast to the situation in the antebellum period, the ambiguous constitutional standing of the South in the reconstructed Union clearly implicated the national government.

Over southern politics from the end of Reconstruction to the mid-twentieth century hangs the heavy pall of racial segregation and discrimination. Segregation in southern public life was the result of state legislation and judicial decision, and from a positivistic point of view it was legal. But was it constitutional? There is little doubt that segregation and disfranchisement of Negroes, considered in their actual intention and social impact, in relation to the Civil War amendments to the Constitution properly understood in accordance with their original intent, were unlawful forms of discrimination that denied the equal protection of the laws. This view of the matter did not prevail in actual governmental practice, however, either in southern or in national politics during the late nineteenth and early twentieth centuries.

Confirming earlier judicial interpretation of the Fourteenth Amendment in similar cases, the Supreme Court in *Plessy v. Ferguson* (1896) upheld state-required racial segregation in railroad cars as constitutional.[85] The doctrine of separate but equal was thus deemed an acceptable gloss on the equal-protection clause of the Fourteenth Amendment. This understanding persisted until 1954, when the Supreme Court in *Brown v. Board of Education* decided that legally separate schools, and by implication other segregated public facilities, violated the Fourteenth Amendment even if they were equal or identical. By simply declaring in effect that *Plessy* was superseded, however—by failing to insist that it had been wrongly decided—the Court confirmed the view that segregation, until then, had been constitutional. On its face the decision supported the view that from Reconstruction until the mid-twentieth century southern government and politics conformed to constitutional tradition. Indeed, as a result of widespread criticism of the Court's opinion the issue became, in part, the "lawfulness of the segregation decisions," as a famous law review article put it. Recognizing the need to strengthen the argument against racial discrimination, Charles L. Black contended that segregation had been unconstitutional all along.[86] This claim no doubt expressed the feeling of a large segment of public opinion, but it did not accurately reflect the facts of constitutional history.

Like the analysis of slavery and the Constitution, evaluation of segregation can vary according to one's view of the requirements and permissible scope of the constitutional tradition. Insofar as segregation and discrimination rested on intimidation, force, and violence, they may be considered contrary to the method and morality of constitutionalism.[87] This was the perspective of V. O. Key's famous account of southern politics, which treated it as ultimately based on force, though sanctioned by the toleration of the rest of the nation.[88] From a more positivistic point of view, however, segregation and Negro disfranchisement were arguably within the constitutional tradition. The most careful study of suffrage reform in the late nineteenth-century South concludes, for example, that although a degree of fraud and intimidation was involved initially, the process of black disfranchisement on the whole proceeded by legal and constitutional means. Legislation regulating voting and the conduct of elections initiated and shaped the new structure of one-party politics based on a restricted electorate; it did not merely confirm changes in political behavior caused by extralegal forces. Indeed, legal and constitutional means were used because reliance on fraud and intimidation risked federal intervention.[89]

By the early twentieth century, segregation, discrimination, and single-party rule were confirmed in the "fundamental legal postulates of the society."[90] This view of the legitimacy of southern race relations is supported by recent scholarship showing segregation to be a moderate alternative to either total exclusion of blacks from the institutions of society or violent race war. Advanced by progressive modernizing groups in southern society, segregation appealed in large part because of its ambiguity and flexibility. It promised to preserve white supremacy while not categorically foreclosing development of the Negro race or denying educational and employment opportunities for individual blacks of talent and ability.[91] When the national government subsequently permitted the South's racially restrictive policies to continue without interruption or disapproval, the policies acquired constitutional legitimacy. Meanwhile, as the majority voice in the Democratic party, southerners played an important role in national politics. Taking advantage of the minority status of their party through most of the period from 1896 to 1932, they were able above all to prevent federal interference in race relations. Southern success in this respect illustrated the continuing relevance of the principle of the concurrent majority in the constitutional tradition.[92]

Protected within the structure of federalism and seemingly impervious to the pressure of outside forces in the first half of the twentieth century, southern politics and society changed rapidly after World War II. Commerce, industry, and urbanization increased at an accelerated pace, ending or alleviating the region's colonial economic condition and creating pressure for change in race relations. Meanwhile, in the political arena long-standing efforts of Negro civil rights organizations to break down discriminatory barriers began to pay off in a series of federal court decisions that weakened the structure of legal segregation. The *Brown* decision of 1954 at once culminated this preparatory phase of the civil rights movement and spurred more intense efforts leading to what has become known as the second Reconstruction.

Notwithstanding the judicial rulings and executive policies that anticipated the *Brown* decision, the overthrow of segregation marked a major break in historical continuity and constitutional development. How to rationalize the break constitutionally, as we have noted, was a major problem for the Supreme Court, which at one point in the litigation appeared inclined to rely on evidence of historical original intent to decide on the constitutionality of segregation. In the event, the Court based its finding on sociology and psychology, declaring the historical materials concerning the intent of the framers of the Fourteenth Amendment inconclusive. In a manner not unlike that employed by their secessionist forebears in 1860, it was southerners in particular who turned to history for justification in the modern struggle over civil rights. Accordingly, in the aftermath of *Brown* a revival of states' rights thinking, aimed at the defense of segregation, raised anew the question of the South's relation to the constitutional tradition.

Between 1955 and 1960, southern states adopted over two hundred statutes, resolutions, and constitutional amendments defending segregation and opposing implementation of the *Brown* ruling. Intended to interpose state authority between citizens of a state and the federal government as a means of challenging allegedly improper exercise of federal power, specific measures provided for local administration of pupil assignment according to ostensibly race-neutral criteria, repealed state compulsory education laws, cut off funds from school districts with integrated schools, and authorized private school tuition grants where public schools were closed to prevent integration.[93] Expressing the constitutional point of view behind this "massive resistance," ninety-six members of Congress from southern states in March 1956 issued a statement defending the doctrine of separate but equal as established legal principle (originally asserted, it was noted, in Massachusetts). Condemning the Supreme Court for using "naked judicial power" to abandon the separate-but-equal doctrine and substituting "personal political and social ideas for the established law of the land," the southern declaration of principle promised to use "all lawful means to bring about a reversal of this decision."[94]

In the opinion of many observers, massive resistance was evidence that the South, presented with an opportunity to "open a door" to its Negro citizens and accept responsibility for its past, reacted with violence, hatred, and suspicion.[95] Choosing to remain a "closed society," it restricted basic civil liberties, including freedom of speech, press, and association and the right of protest. Retrieving from the dustbin of history constitutional doctrines rendered invalid by the nation's political development since the Civil War, the South resorted to lawless means in its effort to maintain unlawful segregation and discrimination. In short, the South in this view rejected and remained outside the constitutional tradition.[96]

As a national political issue, massive resistance reached a climax in the conflict over school desegregation in Little Rock, Arkansas. Intervention of federal troops to assure desegregation in September 1957 was followed a year later by the Supreme Court's decision in *Cooper v. Aaron*, reaffirming the *Brown* holding and rejecting the state's contention that it was not bound by that case. An indication of the gravity of the situation from the federal point of view appeared in the Supreme Court's assertion of the novel doctrine of "judicial supremacy," contending that the justices' interpretation of the Constitution was "the supreme law of the land."[97] In the charged political atmosphere of the time what counted was the Court's urgent intervention, however, not the rationale that it offered for its decision. *Cooper v. Aaron* delivered a severe blow to the strategy of massive resistance by placing upon it the stigma of unconstitutionality and by giving impetus to federal desegregation efforts. Yet the Supreme Court's finding in the Little Rock case perhaps ought not necessarily to be regarded as a conclusive judgment on the South's standing in the constitutional polity at this time.

There is evidence to suggest that although massive resistance was in conflict with evolving national opinion on race relations, it expressed views of union, liberty, and balanced and limited government that can be considered within the tradition of constitutionalism. The most persuasive fact pointing to this conclusion is that defenders of segregation did not generally repudiate the rule of law by resorting to violence but rather engaged in constitutional politics to avoid desegregation.[98] Advocates of massive resistance used constitutional doctrines of state sovereignty and interposition to shape public opinion and prevent implementation of a Supreme Court ruling that they believed was wrongly decided. Strategists of resistance appear to have regarded interposition resolutions as lacking legal force. Their measures were seen as a political maneuver rather than a legal defense, a delaying tactic that might appeal to opinion outside the South on constitutional grounds rather than on an overtly racial basis.[99] The most thorough study of massive resistance, although unsympathetic to the architects of the policy on political and moral grounds, concludes that interposition was "a genuine reaffirmation of states' rights on a broader plane" going beyond the protection of white supremacy.[100] A recent account of the Little Rock crisis finds that state and local officials approached the desegregation issue as a matter of deference to constitutional symbolism and the rule of law. "Prior to and during the crisis of 1957–1959," writes legal historian Tony Freyer, "the school board, white moderates, segregationists, the federal government, and Governor Faubus—virtually everyone including the NAACP and its black constituents—publicly based their response to *Brown* totally or in part on the idea of a government of law, not men."[101]

This is not to deny that white southerners were motivated by hostility to racial integration and tried to create conditions in which the federal government would be unable to enforce the desegregation decree.[102] It would have been better if southern state governments had "opened the door," accepted their historic responsibility, and subordinated political passion and racial prejudice to the moral principle of racial equality. Freyer's study of Little Rock laments that this step was not taken and that desegregation became entangled in a morass of political considerations that invited confrontation.[103] Whether white southerners could be expected to have a moral response agreeable to northern opinion is debatable, however. And absent such a response it was better that the desegregation issue should be politicized through rule-of-law techniques than that it should be allowed to degenerate into counterrevolutionary violence. Indeed, avoidance of a violent outcome is evidence that southern politics and government in this period remained within the constitutional tradition. It is important to recall, moreover, that however morally repugnant the separate-but-equal doctrine now appears, at the time it was thought to be an arguably valid interpretation of the Fourteenth Amendment.

Temporarily effective in slowing the pace of school desegregation, massive resistance was transformed into a containment policy in the 1960s as the civil rights movement gained political momentum and the support of the federal government. Civil rights legislation enacted by Congress between 1964 and 1968 defined and prohibited unlawful discrimination in public facilities and accommodations, public education, private employment, voting rights, and private housing. Southern white politicians and public opinion opposed these measures but, having been defeated by superior political force, accepted them peacefully if resentfully.

Compared to Reconstruction or the consolidation of white supremacy in the late nineteenth century, southern white reaction to national enforcement of civil rights from 1954 to 1968 was remarkably restrained and nonviolent. Notwithstanding the searing emotional impact and psychological injury resulting from isolated violent confrontations, a recent study concludes that relatively little violence was employed against the civil rights movement.[104] The White Citizens' Council, for example, the grassroots organization that led the opposition to desegregation, rejected lawlessness and was committed to strictly legal means of defiance. The council refrained from and discouraged criminal acts to try to stop racial integration.[105] Where opposition to desegregation did turn violent, local leaders were revealed to be militant, alienated, Nazi-like activists concerned with issues going beyond white supremacy. The conception of political action behind most of the violent confrontations was clearly outside the peaceful, legalistic constitutional tradition to which most white southerners subscribed.[106]

Reflection on the South and the constitutional tradition after the second Reconstruction requires consideration of the role of blacks in the expanded political communities of state and nation. The civil rights movement itself in the late 1950s and early 1960s was in essential respects a southern movement. Seeking the application of national constitutional rights to override local law and policy, southern black civil rights organizations tried to change the federal-state balance and expand the scope of individual liberty protected by national authority. Clearly acting within the constitutional tradition, they proposed to give a new meaning to the concepts of liberty, union, and limited and balanced government. Far more questionable were civil rights demonstrations and protests that used violence or the threat of violence. Insofar as civil rights groups sought to attain their ends through mob action in the streets, they may be regarded as having transgressed the limits of the constitutional tradition. The case is similar with the black urban riots that occurred from 1964 to 1968. Although in a sense it may be true that constitutionalism is civil disobedience institutionalized,[107] and that individual acts in defiance of law have a place in a constitutional regime, nevertheless it would be difficult to deny that the black ghetto riots, historically and politically an outgrowth of the civil rights movement, assumed a level of criminal disorder that repudiated the constitutional tradition.

Since the second Reconstruction, two-party competition and biracial politics in the South have largely replaced single-party rule dedicated to maintaining white supremacy.[108] The number of black elected officials has increased dramatically, and in some places black candidates appeal to a white minority holding the balance of power. If from the standpoint of civil rights reformers the South was outside the constitutional tradition in the era of segregation, its acceptance of equal rights in the 1960s must be seen as restoring it to membership in the national community. This does not mean, of course, that racial considerations have been eliminated from southern or national politics. Indeed, one might argue that consciousness of race in policy making has increased. Instead of being confined to whites, however, racial politics is practiced by blacks as well and to some extent is endorsed by the federal government. The 1982 amendment to the Voting Rights Act, for example, which prohibited states and localities from according less opportunity to minorities than to others in electing "representatives of their choice," has been interpreted in a way that encourages racial bloc voting. The result seems to point to racially proportional representation, on the apparent theory that blacks can only be represented by blacks.[109] This new approach to equality is part of the larger national civil rights policy of affirmative action, which in some measure evaluates rights claims and allocates social resources according to racial criteria. If this trend appears to perpetuate the racial thinking and policy making that the equal-rights

49

principle was intended to overcome, supporters of black preferential treatment defend it as less unfair to whites than white preference was to blacks.[110]

To the student of history the persistence of racial favoritism in public policy can hardly be surprising. It would be remarkable, in a pluralistic political culture based on interest-group conflict, if blacks upon gaining a degree of power should not express their historic resentment against white racism by practicing their own brand of racial politics. For those who lived through the desegregation era the more interesting fact is that race-conscious policies could be so strongly condemned and appear so remote from the objectives of the civil rights movement thirty years ago.[111] In any event, in the present controversy over civil rights policy, critics of affirmative action and racial preference, appealing to the color-blind principle of the Fourteenth Amendment and the Civil Rights Act of 1964, find themselves denounced as opponents of constitutional rights. Surely their position is arguably correct and within the constitutional tradition, however, just as the argument for racial qualification and preference might be considered to be. For purposes of the present analysis the point of recent developments might be to caution us against too summary a judgment excluding the South from the constitutional consensus. When the director of the NAACP quotes proslavery features of the original Constitution as authority for a national policy of racial quotas, he provides ironic support for the view that the South acted within the constitutional tradition, as defined in the language and ideas of legal and historical positivism.[112]

The concepts of liberty, union and balanced and limited government, and the constitutional forms through which they are expressed, have always been subject to interpretive variation according to the manners and moral outlook of the groups and regions that constitute the nation. This variation is made possible because of the breadth, generality, and consequent ambiguity of the principles of the regime. The point of our constitutionalism has been to keep constitutional forms, procedures, and institutions from becoming so closely identified with a specific moral point of view or way of life as to become simply instruments of political warfare, destroying the impartiality of government.[113]

To those who are certain that their specific conception of liberty and equality conforms to some transcendent ideal and is exclusively prescribed by the Constitution, the constitutional tradition as I have presented it may appear unsatisfactorily broad and inclusive. It differs a great deal, for example, from the theory of the "perfect Constitution" of contemporary judicial liberalism, according to which the Constitution, properly construed, guarantees the values of equality, compassion, and respect that are deemed essential to citizenship in a liberal democratic government.[114] The American constitutional tradition aims lower and seeks less. In a nation of vast territorial extent and broad cultural diversity, its end is individual and local liberty, not some vision of justice and virtue according to which people will be made good.

Southerners helped found the nation and write the Constitution and were prominent in defining and elaborating the constitutional tradition. Eventually their understanding of the Constitution and their tendency to confuse it with their distinctive way of life—a tendency, it should be noted, that was not peculiar to them—led to rejection of the Union. Although the matter is surely debatable, a fair historical assessment would probably lay the failure of constitutionalism to the country as a whole, however, not just to southerners. After the Civil War the South resumed its place in the national community, adjusting its view of union, liberty, and balanced and limited government to the requirements imposed by the destruction of slavery. The distinctive feature of the South's adjustment to new conditions was racial classification and discrimination that the nation as a whole approved and for which it must be held responsible. When at length a change in the national standard of political morality in the mid-twentieth century required changes in constitutional law, the South, vainly appealing to history and precedent, adjusted once again. Reconstructed a second time in the 1960s, the South at the Bicentennial, in the new era of biracial politics, continues to play a significant role in shaping the constitutional tradition.

Notes

1. Walter F. Murphy, James E. Fleming, and William F. Harris II, *American Constitutional Interpretation* (Mineola, N.Y., 1986), 81–183.

2. In addition to ibid., see the discussion of these matters in Edward S. Corwin, "Constitution v. Constitutional Theory," in *American Constitutional History: Essays by Edward S. Corwin*, ed. Alpheus T. Mason and Gerald Garvey (New York, 1964), 157–79; Corwin, "Some Lessons from the Constitution of 1787," and "The Constitution as Instrument and Symbol," both in *Corwin on*

the Constitution, ed. Richard Loss (Ithaca, N.Y., 1981), 1:157–67 and 168–79, respectively; and Charles A. Miller, *The Supreme Court and the Uses of History* (Cambridge, Mass., 1969), 149–201.

3. Cf. Robert F. Durden, *The Self-Inflicted Wound: Southern Politics in the Nineteenth Century* (Lexington, Ky., 1985); and Frank Smith, *Look Away from Dixie* (Baton Rouge, 1965), 4, 16, 89–90.

4. David M. Potter, *The South and the Sectional Conflict* (Baton Rouge, 1968), 28.

5. Positivistic history is the method of analysis, premised on the separation of facts from values, that takes thought and action more or less at face value as understandable, significant, and true in relation to circumstances of time, place, and historical context broadly considered, rather than in relation to absolute or transcendent moral or philosophical principles.

6. Yehoshua Arieli, *Individualism and Nationalism in American Ideology* (Baltimore, 1966); Samuel P. Huntington, *American Politics: Promise of Disharmony* (Cambridge, Mass., 1981).

7. Cf. Martin E. Spencer, "Politics and Rhetorics," *Social Research* 37 (1970): 597–623, and "Rule of Law in America," *Southern Quarterly* 14 (1976): 333–49; Rozanne Rothman, *Acts and Enactments: The Constitutional Convention of 1787* (Philadelphia, 1974); and Donald S. Lutz, "The Purposes of American State Constitutions," *Publius* 12 (1982): 30. As the Constitution presumes the existence of states with their own constitutions, the American constitutional tradition can be defined as the record of state constitutional change and development. For discussion of this approach, see Daniel J. Elazar, "The Principles and Traditions Underlying State Constitutions," *Publius* 12 (1982): 11–25; Albert L. Sturm, "The Development of American State Constitutions," *Publius* 12 (1982): 57–98; and Elmer E. Cornwell, Jr., "The American Constitutional Tradition: Its Impact and Development," and Morton Keller, "The Politics of State Constitutional Revision, 1820–1930," both in *The Constitutional Convention as an Amending Device*, ed. Kermit L. Hall, Harold M. Hyman, and Leon V. Sigal, (Washington, D.C., 1981), 1–36, 87–112.

8. Benjamin F. Wright, "The Southern Political Tradition," in *Theory and Practice in American Politics*, ed. William H. Nelson (Chicago, 1964), 83–100; Manning J. Dauer, "Recent Southern Political Thought," *Journal of Politics* 10 (1948): 327–53.

9. John Richard Alden, *The First South* (Baton Rouge, 1961), 5; William J. Cooper, Jr., *Liberty and Slavery: Southern Politics to 1860* (New York, 1983), 48.

10. Michael P. Zuckert, "Federalism and the Founding: Toward a Reinterpretation of the Constitutional Convention," *Review of Politics* 48 (1986): 166–210; Martin Diamond, "What the Framers Meant by Federalism," in *A Nation of States*, ed. Robert A. Goldwin (Chicago, 1963), 25–42.

11. Cf. Cooper, *Liberty and Slavery*, 47–69.

12. William M. Wiecek, *The Sources of Antislavery Constitutionalism in America, 1760–1848* (Ithaca, N.Y., 1977), 63–83.

13. Clinton Rossiter, *Alexander Hamilton and the Constitution* (New York, 1964), 194; Elizabeth Kelly Bauer, *Commentaries on the Constitution 1790–1860* (New York, 1952), 213–14.

14. Kenneth M. Stampp, *The Imperiled Union: Essays on the Background of the Civil War* (New York, 1980), 20–22.

15. William McDonald, ed., *Select Documents Illustrative of the History of the United States, 1776–1861* (New York, 1915), 159.

16. Walter Hartwell Bennett, *American Theories of Federalism* (University, Ala., 1964), 167.

17. Robert K. Faulkner, *The Jurisprudence of John Marshall* (1968; Westport, Conn., 1980), 102.

18. Cf. Gordon Wood, *The Creation of the American Republic, 1776–1787* (Chapel Hill, N.C., 1969).

19. Thad W. Tate, "The Social Contract in America, 1774–1787: Revolutionary Theory as a Conservative Instrument," *William and Mary Quarterly* 22 (1965): 375–91; Donald S. Lutz, *Popular Consent and Popular Control: Whig Political Theory in the Early State Constitutions* (Baton Rouge, 1980), 225–38.

20. Max Farrand, ed., *The Records of the Federal Convention of 1787*, 4 vols. (New Haven, Conn., 1911–37), 2:93.

21. R. Kent Newmyer, *Supreme Court Justice Joseph Story: Statesman of the Old Republic* (Chapel Hill, N.C., 1985), 184.

22. Bauer, *Commentaries on the Constitution*, 260.

23. Alexis de Tocqueville, *Democracy in America*, 2 vols., Bradley ed. (New York, 1954), 1:403.

24. For an excellent survey of the problem, see Harry V. Jaffa, " 'Partly Federal, Partly National': On the Political Theory of the Civil War," in Goldwin, *A Nation of States*, 2nd ed. (1973), 109–37.

25. John M. Murrin, "The Great Inversion, or Court versus Country: A Comparison of the Revolution Settlements in England (1688–1721) and America (1776–1816)," in *Three British Revolutions: 1641, 1688, 1776*, ed. J. G. A. Pocock (Princeton, N.J., 1980), 406–29.

26. William W. Crosskey, "John Marshall," in *Mr. Justice*, ed. Allison Dunham and Philip B. Kurland, rev. ed. (Chicago, 1964), 3–26.

27. Faulkner, *The Jurisprudence of John Marshall*, 97–113.

28. 4 Wheat. 402, 403 (1819).

29. Bennett, *American Theories of Federalism*, 169.

30. McDonald, *Select Documents*, 257. Webster thus used very nearly the language employed by counsel for Maryland, in *McCulloch v. Maryland*, to describe the nationalist position, which language, however, was not adopted by John Marshall. Walter Jones, counsel for Maryland, stated: "To suppose

that the mere proposition of this fundamental law" [i.e., the Constitution] threw the American people into one aggregate mass, would be to assume what the instrument itself does not profess to establish." 4 Wheat. at 363.

31. Bauer, *Commentaries on the Constitution*, 285.

32. Newmyer, *Supreme Court Justice Joseph Story*, 178.

33. Cohens v. Virginia, 6 Wheat. 264 (1821); Faulkner, *The Jurisprudence of John Marshall*, 105–8.

34. George C. Rogers, Jr., "A Southern Political Tradition," in *Why the South Will Survive*, by Fifteen Southerners (Athens, Ga., 1981), 85.

35. Donald L. Robinson, *Slavery in the Structure of American Politics, 1765– 1820* (New York, 1971), 421.

36. Ibid., 422; Charles O. Lerche, Jr., "The Guarantee of a Republican Form of Government and the Admission of New States," *Journal of Politics* 16 (1949): 578–604. The provision in the Constitution that was cited as relevant was art. IV, sec. 4, stating: "The United States shall guarantee to every State in this Union a republican form of government."

37. Robinson, *Slavery in the Structure of American Politics*, 421.

38. Charles G. Sellers, Jr., "The Travail of Slavery," in *The Southerner as American*, ed. Sellers (Chapel Hill, N.C., 1960), 42; Clement Eaton, *The Free-dom-of-Thought Struggle in the Old South*, rev. ed. (New York, 1964); Dauer, "Recent Southern Political Thought," 327–53; T. Harry Williams, *Romance and Realism in Southern Politics* (Athens, Ga., 1961); Robert J. Harris, "The South: Research for What?" in *Perspectives on the South: Agenda for Research*, ed. Edgar T. Thompson (Durham, N.C., 1967), 40–51.

39. Rowland T. Berthoff, "Conventional Mentality: Free Blacks, Women, and Business Corporations as Unequal Persons, 1820–1870," *Journal of American History*, forthcoming.

40. Kenneth S. Greenberg, *Masters and Statesmen: The Political Culture of American Slavery* (Baltimore, 1985); Rogers, "A Southern Political Tradition," 85–88.

41. Cf. James W. Ceaser, *Presidential Selection: Theory and Development* (Princeton, N.J., 1979), 123–69.

42. Ibid., 131–49.

43. J. Mills Thornton III, *Politics and Power in a Slave Society: Alabama, 1800– 1860* (Baton Rouge, 1978); Harry L. Watson, *Jacksonian Politics and Community Conflict: The Emergence of the Second American Party System in Cumberland County, North Carolina* (Baton Rouge, 1981).

44. Cooper, *Liberty and Slavery*, 177–282.

45. Thornton, *Politics and Power*, 449.

46. Michael F. Holt, *The Political Crisis of the 1850s* (New York, 1978), 258.

47. Rowland Berthoff, "Writing a History of Things Left Out," *Reviews in American History* 14 (1986): 12.

48. Cooper, *Liberty and Slavery*, 282.

49. Charles R. Lee, Jr., *The Confederate Constitutions* (1963; Westport, Conn., 1974).

50. Ibid., 62.

51. Avery Craven, "The Civil War and the Democratic Process," *Abraham Lincoln Quarterly* 4 (1947): 269–92, and "The 1840s and the Democratic Process," *Journal of Southern History* 16 (1950): 137–47. Both essays are reprinted in Craven, *An Historian and the Civil War* (Chicago, 1964).

52. It is worth noting, furthermore, that the major recent work on the antebellum South that dissents from the republican-liberty interpretation analyzes secession as a Madisonian-liberal political movement, treating it as a legitimate option within the constitutional tradition. See James Oakes, "From Republicanism to Liberalism: Ideological Change and the Crisis of the Old South," *American Quarterly* 37 (1985): 551–71.

53. George Kateb, "The Majority Principle: Calhoun and His Antecedents," *Political Science Quarterly* 84 (1969): 583–605. Kateb says that Calhoun's concurrent-majority theory was understandable in light of previous political thought but was irrelevant to slavery because slavery was so gross an evil that it could not be discussed in the framework of that theory. Ralph Lerner, "Calhoun's New Science of Politics," *American Political Science Review* 57 (1963): 918–32, sees Calhoun as within the family quarrel, as does Margaret Coit Elwell, "The Continuing Relevance of John C. Calhoun," *Continuity*, no. 9 (1984): 73–86. Calhoun's theory has been viewed as a relevant anticipation of interest-group politics, but on the whole his attachment to slavery and his state-sovereignty teaching have disqualified him as a reliable source of American constitutionalism.

54. Major L. Wilson, *Space, Time, and Freedom: The Quest for Nationality and the Irrepressible Conflict, 1815–1861* (Westport, Conn., 1974), 189–91.

55. Cooper, *Liberty and Slavery*, 30, 38.

56. Edmund S. Morgan, *American Slavery/American Freedom: The Ordeal of Colonial Virginia* (New York, 1975), 376.

57. Thornton, *Politics and Power*, 25, 221.

58. Greenberg, *Masters and Statesmen*, x, 88.

59. Tocqueville, *Democracy in America*, 1:410. It will be noted furthermore that the view of the southern political mind presented in recent writing on southern republicanism also stands in sharp contrast to the description of deeply conflicted guilt feelings, attributed to southerners as liberal democrats and as Christians, that is found in the liberal nationalist interpretation of Charles G. Sellers, Jr., in *The Southerner as American*.

60. Orlando Patterson, *Slavery and Social Death: A Comparative Study* (Cambridge, Mass., 1982), 340.

61. Ibid., quoting Maurice Cranston.

62. Ibid., 340–41. Owners of slaves, Patterson states, were "quick to recognize this new value," that is, the political value of freedom as the absence of restraint, and exploited it by making manumission a behavioral incentive and an integral part of slave systems. By providing a major incentive for slaves, he says, manumission reinforced the master-slave relationship; he adds that no slaveholding class ever lost in the process of disenslavement.

63. Ibid., 341–42.

64. For discussion of the origins of this issue, see James Farr, " 'So Vile and Miserable an Estate': The Problem of Slavery in Locke's Political Thought," *Political Theory* 14 (1986): 263–89.

65. Morgan, *American Slavery/American Freedom*, 387.

66. Ibid., 386.

67. For a candid statement of the new conception of liberty advocated by those who regard American liberal democracy as inherently and fundamentally flawed because of its dependence upon racism, see Jennifer L. Hochschild, *The New American Dilemma: Liberal Democracy and School Desegregation* (New Haven, Conn., 1984). The author's thesis is that progress in achieving equality in race relations can be attained only by "substantial, authoritatively imposed change" that rejects the method of incremental change through popular democratic control. The rule of "authoritative leaders who see what is necessary to turn the semblance of democracy into real democracy" is to be preferred to traditional democratic self-government. Pp. 204–5.

68. Harry V. Jaffa, "What Were the 'Original Intentions' of the Framers of the Constitution of the United States?" *University of Puget Sound Law Review* 10 (1987): 351–95.

69. *The Collected Works of Abraham Lincoln*, ed. Roy P. Basler, Marion Dolores Pratt, and Lloyd A. Dunlap, 9 vols. (New Brunswick, N.J., 1953–55), 2:501.

70. Ibid., 1:348.

71. Ibid., 3:307, 4:22.

72. Ibid., 3:327.

73. Ibid., 1:347 (commenting that Texas was "already a free republican people on our own model") 4:440 (stating that the guarantee clause of the Constitution requires keeping the states in the Union to assure them a republican form of government).

74. Ibid., 4:168–69.

75. Thomas L. Haskell, "Capitalism and the Origins of the Humanitarian Sensibility," *American Historical Review* 90 (1985): 339–61, 547–66.

76. Tocqueville, *Democracy in America*, 1:428.

77. Ludwell H. Johnson III, "The Confederacy: What Was It? The View from the Federal Courts," *Civil War History* 32 (1986): 5–22.

78. But see Ludwell H. Johnson III, *Division and Reunion: America, 1848–1877* (New York, 1978), 241–42.

79. Texas v. White, 7 Wall. 700 (1869).

80. Cf. Dan T. Carter, *When the War Was Over: The Failure of Self-Reconstruction in the South, 1865–1867* (Baton Rouge, 1985), 217–21.

81. A recent example is Michael Perman, *The Road to Redemption: Southern Politics, 1869–1879* (Chapel Hill, N.C., 1984).

82. W. W. Willoughby, *The Constitutional Law of the United States* (New York, 1910), 551–55. On congressional enforcement of the Fourteenth Amendment, see George David Zuckerman, "A Consideration of the History and Present Status of Section 2 of the Fourteenth Amendment," *Fordham Law Review* 30 (1961): 93–135.

83. George C. Rable, *But There Was No Peace: The Role of Violence in the Politics of Reconstruction* (Athens, Ga., 1984).

84. James M. McPherson, "Redemption or Counterrevolution? The South in the 1870s," *Reviews in American History* 13 (1985): 549.

85. 163 U.S. 537 (1896). See Stephen J. Riegel, "The Persistent Career of Jim Crow: Lower Federal Courts and the 'Separate but Equal' Doctrine, 1865–1896," *American Journal of Legal History* 28 (1984): 17–40.

86. Charles L. Black, Jr., "The Lawfulness of the Segregation Decisions," *Yale Law Journal* 69 (1960): 421–30.

87. See Mary Frances Berry, *Black Resistance/White Law: A History of Constitutional Racism in America* (New York, 1971), 103, 238. Although the subtitle of Berry's book treats racism as constitutionally legitimate, references to repression based on "theoretically legal tactics" and proceeding "in the guise of constitutionalism" suggest that the author regards racial discrimination as in reality unconstitutional.

88. See V. O. Key, Jr., *Southern Politics in State and Nation* (New York, 1949), 1–11.

89. J. Morgan Kousser, *The Shaping of Southern Politics: Suffrage Restriction and the Establishment of the One-Party South, 1880–1910* (New Haven, Conn., 1974).

90. Ibid., 261–62. See also Joel Williamson, *The Crucible of Race: Black-White Relations in the American South since Emancipation* (New York, 1984), 229.

91. John W. Cell, *The Highest Stage of White Supremacy: The Origins of Segregation in South Africa and the American South* (Cambridge, 1982), 18–19, 176–80.

92. David M. Potter, *The South and the Concurrent Majority,* ed. Don E. Fehrenbacher and Carl N. Degler (Baton Rouge, 1972).

93. A corollary strategy undertaken by Alabama, Virginia, Florida, Arkansas, and Louisiana was to destroy the NAACP as an effective, functioning organization. Using their power to regulate foreign (out-of-state) corporations and the legal profession, these states tried to immobilize the NAACP so that it could not bring further desegregation suits. The Supreme Court struck down these state actions on the ground that they denied First Amendment rights of free speech, petition, and assembly of NAACP members. See Loren Miller, *The*

Petitioners: The Story of the Supreme Court of the United States and the Negro (Cleveland, 1966), 376–91.

94. Henry Steele Commager, ed., *Documents of American History,* 7th ed. (New York, 1964), 2:642.

95. Paul M. Gaston, "Sutpen's Door: The South since the *Brown* Decision," in *Two Decades of Change: The South since the Supreme Court Desegregation Decision,* ed. Ernest M. Lander, Jr., and Richard J. Calhoun (Columbia, S.C., 1975), 105–6.

96. Francis M. Wilhoit, *The Politics of Massive Resistance* (New York, 1973), 160; Numan V. Bartley, *The Rise of Massive Resistance: Race and Politics in the South during the 1950s* (Baton Rouge, 1969), 135.

97. 358 U.S. 1 (1958). Writing for the Court in an opinion signed by all the justices, Justice Brennan, purporting to rely on *Marbury v. Madison,* asserted "the basic principle that the federal judiciary is supreme in the exposition of the law of the Constitution." Stating that this principle "has ever since been respected by this Court and the Country as a permanent and indispensable feature of our constitutional system," Brennan concluded that "the interpretation of the Fourteenth Amendment enunciated by this Court in the *Brown* case is the supreme law of the land." Cf. Kenneth L. Karst, "Cooper v. Aaron," in *Encyclopedia of the American Constitution,* ed. Leonard W. Levy, Kenneth L. Karst, and Dennis J. Mahoney, 4 vols. (New York, 1986), 2:503; and Tony Freyer, *The Little Rock Crisis: A Constitutional Interpretation* (Westport, Conn., 1984), 152–63.

98. Albert P. Blaustein and Clarence Clyde Ferguson, Jr., *Desegregation and the Law: The Meaning and Effect of the School Segregation Cases,* 2d ed. (New York, 1962), 240–71.

99. James W. Ely, Jr., *The Crisis of Conservative Virginia: The Byrd Organization and the Politics of Massive Resistance* (Knoxville, Tenn., 1976), 93–102.

100. Bartley, *The Rise of Massive Resistance,* 133.

101. Freyer, *The Little Rock Crisis,* 172–73.

102. Ely, *The Crisis of Conservative Virginia,* 101.

103. Freyer, *The Little Rock Crisis,* 171–72.

104. Richard Maxwell Brown, "Southern Violence vs. the Civil Rights Movement, 1954–1968," *Perspectives on the American South* 1 (1981): 52.

105. Neil R. McMillen, *The Citizens' Council: Organized Resistance to the Second Reconstruction, 1954–64* (Urbana, Ill., 1971), 359.

106. Brown, "Southern Violence," 55–63. See also John Shelton Reed and Merle Black, "How Southerners Gave Up Jim Crow," *New Perspectives* 17 (1985): 15–19.

107. Harvey Wheeler, "Constitutionalism," in *Handbook of Political Science,* ed. Fred Greenstein and Nelson Polsby, vol. 5 (Reading, Mass., 1975), 6–7.

108. Cf. Jack Bass and Walter DeVries, *The Transformation of Southern Politics: Social Change and Political Consequence since 1945* (New York, 1976).

109. Cf. Timothy G. O'Rourke, "Voting Rights Act Amendments of 1982: The New Bailout Provision and Virginia," *Virginia Law Review* 69 (1983): 765–804.

110. Eleanor Holmes Norton interview, "The Pursuit of Equality," unpublished MS, Maryland Public Television, 1987, 25.

111. But see Richard Kluger, *Simple Justice: The History of Brown v. Board of Education and Black America's Struggle for Equality* (New York, 1975), 643, for insight into the depth of Negro feelings of resentment, which, in retrospect, it seems naive to think could have been assuaged or dissipated by the attainment of racially impartial equal rights.

112. "Is Affirmative Action Constitutional?" *Regulation* 9 (1985): 13–14, remarks of Benjamin Hooks; Hooks to the editor, *New York Times*, November 27, 1985, A22.

113. Cf. Robert Eden, "Tocqueville on Political Realignment and Constitutional Forms," *Review of Politics* 48 (1986): 349–73.

114. Cf. Henry P. Monoghan, "Our Perfect Constitution," *New York University Law Review* 56 (1981): 353–96.

Part Two

The Origins of Southern Constitutionalism

The colonial background of American constitutionalism—particularly with respect to the southern colonies—has been generally ignored by scholars. The chapters by David Thomas Konig and Herbert A. Johnson that follow here seek to reclaim this lost ground.

Each author asserts that there are important ties between the constitutional tradition of the colonial era and postrevolutionary developments. Konig explores the emergence of procedural due process in Virginia's county courts and stresses the pervasive localism that characterized the administration of justice. Johnson examines the compact theory of government as it evolved in South Carolina and emphasizes innovations regarding judicial review and criminal procedure. These authors demonstrate that notions of limited government and concern for the protection of liberty and property long preceded the first state constitution and the federal Constitution.

61

Country Justice:
The Rural Roots
of Constitutionalism
in Colonial Virginia

David Thomas Konig

Any inquiry into the colonial origins of the American constitutional tradition must overcome the powerful—and prevailing—notion that there are no meaningful links. The conventional wisdom remains, as Stanley Katz criticized it at Oxford in 1981, an array of "intellectual arguments for disregarding the [colonial] past as irrelevant to the national history of American law."[1] Even as Katz laid down his challenge to scholars to find such links, however, signs began to appear that the search had shifted its approach into lines that someday would permit us to identify continuities between the two periods. These inquiries ignored major cases and took up a new line of investigation that few people remembered as having been suggested by Julius Goebel in 1938. Goebel, whose sharp pen lacerated many able scholars who tried to follow his lead, nonetheless ought to be credited with making the earliest sustained argument throughout a corpus of scholarly work for studying the "relentless advance of . . . glacial jurisprudence" that steadily overwhelmed "the erstwhile leading cases with their gaudy background."[2]

Only in the last decade, long after Goebel's death, are scholars once again pursuing his suggestion. They are doing so by abandoning as fruitless the anachronistic search for landmark decisions or sweeping statements that would reveal the way in which a sovereign power shares, limits, or divides authority. Instead, they have begun to examine what Jack Greene, in a recent essay reviewing some of these contributions, called the "context and legitimacy" of law. Put simply, these scholars have shifted the inquiry downward—away from Parliament, the central courts at London, and the Privy Council—and into the conditions of legal activity on the local level, where colonists put into action their implicitly declared doctrines about the contours of legal power.[3]

In the present essay, I want to continue along these lines in the hope of pushing the inquiry forward. I propose to do so by looking at the Constitution within an actual and practical context that gave it existence, that is, from a background of provincial legal practices and within a framework of shared local assumptions concerning the proper exercise of legal authority. My method will be to examine in meticulous—even archaeological—detail the procedures that lawyers, litigants, and judges developed in rural Virginia, a state deeply divided over the Constitution, and one whose participants in the framing process included James Madison, George Washington, George Mason, Patrick Henry, and Edmund Randolph. Many of these details will appear arcane and quaint, rustic and irrelevant to our modern industrial society. But I hope that such details are not irrelevant to our inquiry into constitutional origins; in the method and minutiae of rural jurisprudence, I submit, will be found some of the essential mechanisms of justice that Virginians came to regard as the basic or fundamental components constituting a free society—in other words, what they called their "constitution."

The legal system of colonial Virginia was, first and foremost, a local system whose chief officials, the justices of the peace, resided in and among their county communities. At the same time—and perhaps more important—these men were amateur justices. Their lives revolved around the cycle of planting and marketing tobacco, not the administration of justice.[4] Brought up and trained to plant and market tobacco, they came to the bench with little or no legal training. Yet legal training was not a requirement for the county bench. The qualifications for magistracy in Virginia basically followed those set out in Dalton's *Countrey Justice*, which listed a number of sterling personal virtues but said of legal expertise only that justices "ought to be Men of competent Knowledge in the Laws of their Country."[5] Virginia statute prescribed less demanding standards, namely, that justices ought to be "the most able, honest and judicious persons of the county."[6] By practice, the most significant qualification was status: above all, the "gentlemen justices" were, as an English treatise described them, men of "ample Fortunes."[7]

Many justices took their responsibilities seriously, but membership in the county commission did not assure close attention to the business of the court. Attendance was erratic, and justices wandered into the courtroom not in any *en banc* manner but *seriatim:* the four needed to constitute the court entered together, but they would be joined intermittently by their colleagues. At a York County Court term in 1741, a session typical of countless others, Thomas Nelson and four others convened the court, to see Daniel Moore walk in soon after by himself, John Blair after a half dozen matters had been settled, and Samuel Reade after nearly three dozen orders and adjudications.[8] A disapproving correspondent wrote to the *Virginia Gazette* in 1770, "The usual hour of adjournment from one court day is to ten o'clock, the court in course; but perhaps if those who constitute and should attend the courts, meet by one o'clock, it may be called, through the colony, a very early meeting; and as two hours more are generally spent in *how do you's,* and seeing *who and who are together,* this brings almost the constant setting of the courts down to three or four o'clock."[9]

Satire and sharp criticism had little effect. Complaints from higher authority, such as the repeated urgings and threats of the governors, did little to improve performance.[10] Proceedings at the Henrico County Court, for example, were typical in 1713 for being "very often delayed for want of a sufficient number of Justices to expedite the same,"[11] and throughout the first third of the eighteenth century, as court business increased, justices frequently avoided the onerous burdens of coming to court. Governors responded by increasing the size of the county commissions, but the larger number of justices did not create continuity or add expertise. Although enough justices attended to permit business to go forward, the lack of consistent attendance from term to term limited their familiarity with cases that had been continued and lessened the effectiveness of the bench.[12]

The status of the justices may have accorded them some symbolic benefits at court day—deferential treatment amid the assembled throngs of county residents attending—but it scarcely sufficed to allow them extensive control of the court over which they presided. In the first place, their legal learning was scant; in eighteenth-century York County, for example, only three justices had been trained in England. Even had

65

they trained at the Inns of Court, they would not have acquired the knowledge of routine legal matters that constituted the bulk of court responsibilities. The Maryland barrister Charles Carroll of Carrollton spent four years at the Inns of Court but afterward admitted that he needed someone "to instruct me in the law" once he returned to the colonies; otherwise, he would be helpless at "the practical part of the law."[13] That should have been no surprise. Virginia councilor Robert Carter III described his own experience at the Inns as primarily "the life of a London blade."[14]

Few other county justices received anything that approached legal training. In an age when legal knowledge was obtained mainly by observation and apprenticeship, only firsthand acquaintance through actual participation could educate a person in the operations of the legal system. Yet few justices undertook to serve in lesser offices before assuming a seat on the bench. In York County, for example, justices of the peace brought little courtroom experience with them to the county commission. On becoming justices of the peace, most had been vestrymen or had served a small number of times on juries (usually grand juries), but such experience gave little useful knowledge for someone who was to administer and adjudicate in court. By the first decade of the eighteenth century in York, few justices came to office with firsthand experience in judicial administration, criminal procedure, or civil process. Accustomed to the advantages of wealth in Virginia society and politics, they expected appointment to the county bench and had little reason to prepare for it. If any one characteristic typified their background qualifications, it was birth: by midcentury, half of York's justices of the peace were sons of justices.

Enterprising Virginians knew that justices came to office lacking precise information about their powers and responsibilities. To fill that need, booksellers imported English manuals and even supplied them with a domestic product, George Webb's *Office and Authority of a Justice of Peace*, first published in Williamsburg in 1736.[15] Yet Dalton's *Countrey Justice* and Webb's *Justice of Peace* (the two most popular handbooks) gave little help in the courtroom. Webb's ubiquitous compilation offers many hints about the limits of magisterial competence in eighteenth-century Virginia. By what it includes and excludes, however, it reveals how justices of the peace conceived their role and defined their place in the legal system. The entries Webb compiled seem designed for a system in which justices of the peace discharged their authority mainly when sitting out of session as rural administrators and conservators of the peace. Webb's major concern was criminal matters, for a single justice had to know which offenses were petty enough for him to handle summarily, which had to be heard by the county court, and which, as possible felonies, required an examining court to determine if the case had to go to the General Court.[16]

Webb's manual had little to say about the business that came before the county courts, and less about the adjudication of civil disputes. If we can go by what he included as a guide to the extent of participation by justices in civil litigation, they were primarily concerned with getting cases into the courtroom (see the extensive treatment of "Attachment") and then up to the General Court (see "Appeals"). What happened in between, we might surmise, was the concern of others (a point I will return to later). In fact, Webb gave less attention to petit jury trials than to trials by ordeal or battle. Virtually useless when it came to adjudication, this most common of manuals concentrated on the details of rural police powers and flattered the justices' sense of place and tradition by supplying antiquarian information that appealed to their self-image as paternal agents of the monarch. It included, for instance, information on how they were to handle deodands and what to do with someone who had had carnal knowledge of the queen.[17]

Whatever authority the single justice wielded over slaves and the poorest of whites from his plantation parlor, however, the justice in the courtroom was a very different figure. Few loose papers survive for the county courts of colonial Virginia, and as a result we have no truly empirical inquiry into the mass of routine activities that constituted the actual operation of a county courtroom. Once undertaken in those papers that do survive, however,[18] such an inquiry reveals a rather passive role for the county magistracy. The most common of courtroom activities concerned the administrative oversight of property matters such as the probate and administration of decedents' estates and the recording of deeds. The justices were supposed to give careful attention to such matters, but in actual practice they did little more than administer oaths to individuals, either before appointing them or upon presentation of their reports—an important symbolic role, but nonetheless an empty one in actual oversight or influence. From the absence of their signatures on these reports, and from the speed with which they were processed on court day, it is clear that such important matters were being handled elsewhere, by nonmagisterial court officials and lay participants. I will return to that area later, but for the moment it is important to see that local instrumentalities of justice generally operated without the discretionary intervention of the bench. They came to stand as customary practices that had so hardened into settled habit that they might be expected as the due exercise of legal procedure—in other words, as the due process of law.

The justices appear to have exerted somewhat more authority in adjudication, but there, too, their role was circumscribed and reactive rather than broad and discretionary. In the first place, the appearance of clever and sedulous attorneys transformed the seventeenth-century courtroom, where justices had ruled with an unchallenged hand,[19] into an arena where untrained justices often sat exasperated and chagrined by legal cunning beyond their ability to challenge. To one critic, litigation proceeded "according to the art or influence of the lawyers and attornies before the judges, who by their education are but indifferently qualified for that service."[20] Landon Carter, a Richmond County magnate who ruled his vast private holdings with undeniably patriarchal authority, had only indifferent success when he attempted to act as a patriarch in the courtroom. In 1772 he suffered what he confessed was "a most singular insult" from an attorney while sitting as justice at the Richmond County Court. Carter, when asked if certain testimony ought to be admitted, answered on nonlegal grounds and was promptly taken to task by attorney Richard Parker. When Carter called Parker "impudent," the lawyer returned the remark and provoked the outraged Carter to threaten Parker with time in the stocks. To Carter's embarrassment, the court ignored his anger; although the two men made mutual apologies, Carter confided to his diary that the attorney had been the "hero" of the episode.[21]

This example, though perhaps probative of nothing by itself, nonetheless typifies a much broader pattern in which attorneys succeeded in dominating courtroom activity. They frequently made motions that the justices had little competence to deny. Carter, a year before his humiliation by Parker, had complained in his diary that he had spent three days in court "chiefly in obliging the Lawyers to say anything out of the causes they are engaged in, and making the most absurd motions imaginable."[22] The ability to deal with legal motions depended on a familiarity with the "practical part of the law" that few justices achieved. As noted, Carter had been forced to accept "a most gross affront" from Parker when the justice inexpertly "interposed as to the rules of pleading."[23] Not surprisingly, then, when St. George Tucker reflected on the actual power of the county elite before the Revolution, he called them "a race of *harmless aristocrats.*"[24]

If the bench lacked the skill to deny motions and control the progress of litigation, who possessed it? Why does an examination of mid-eighteenth-century county court order books[25] reveal hardly any examples of motions rejected in open court? Was it simply because the court accepted every motion made? Hardly. The reason, I submit, is that the decision was made elsewhere, in an area of legal procedure that has not been examined. The face-to-face activities of the courtroom, as recorded in the order books of each county, are the most easily recovered historical data on legal activity in colonial Virginia, but, it must be emphasized, they are scarcely the entirety. Order books, the backbone of the existing historiography, recorded only those *final* orders approved on court day. Behind these stands a largely unexamined process by which lesser officials conducted a variety of activities and actually passed on interlocutory orders. These aspects of the legal system were vital to the operation of the courts, for it was in them that skill in the "practical part of the law" best showed itself, and there, significantly, the justices of the peace had little or no role.

Perhaps the most important of these activities took place the day before the court opened its session. Known as "the rules," this was the time set aside for the clerk to hear and enter motions on the docket he prepared for the coming term. Normally, this procedure occurred on the day before term, but it is possible that the clerk heard the motions at his office well before that, while the court was "in vacation" between terms. No justice of the peace took part as the clerk entered the motions that each party was to make when its case came up in open court.

The clerk, who was the only trained professional among all court officials, was in the best position to make these interlocutory "office judgments" at the rules. Known as "side-bar rules" in England (where they were moved for at the side bar of the court), these activities were within the authority of the clerks as settled matters of practice. Although statutory modification in Virginia confirmed the common law by allowing the court to review these motions, and although by court procedure they were repeated in open court, it is clear that practice in most Virginia counties replicated that of the English courts by making the activities of the rules settled procedural matters. Although justices always held final authority to overrule a clerk upon objection by a party, such interventions were rare.[26] Motions were made, oaths taken, and writs served according to "the usual process,"[27] while clerks acted "of course" and even handled the mechanics of confirming defaults and confessions of judgment in their offices before having them passed on mechanically by the full court.[28]

Such preliminary activities must not be underestimated or thought of merely as the filing of papers. Litigants might test the strength of their pleas and probe their opponents' defenses in the forum of the rules. Order books, as historians have examined them term by term, fail to reveal the pattern of pleading that litigants followed in eighteenth-century Virginia; they reveal only a seemingly endless flow of continuances, with an occasional dismissal. The impression they give, therefore, is a misleading one: from this glacial progression of continuances, it might appear that courtroom activity was little more than ritualistic—the perfunctory entering of an action preparatory to an out-of-court settlement.

A computer reorganization of this material into the sequential progression of individual cases reveals much more, however. Such a reconstruction of the progress of thousands of cases through the docket uncovers consistent patterns of civil process and persistent practices of litigation. Cases, it appears, went through what became common patterns of clever pleading and counterpleading. The imparlance, which offered a chance to delay a case, did not bring parties together in common agreement but more often served as a preliminary to obtaining a lawyer and framing an effective plea. At the rules, for example, plaintiffs could see if an opponent had secured a lawyer and what plea he had entered. Alternatively, defendants could examine the rules docket and see what defenses other defendants would be making; if a given plea suited their needs, they might make the same one for themselves. Lawyers, making themselves available by their obvious presence on the courthouse steps, stood ready to give advice and gain clients. If a case was hopeless, parties learned the situation at the rules, where the county clerk presided over the proceedings and negotiations. When he finally entered in the order book that a case had been "dismissed," therefore, it stood only as the last step in a long process of demand, delay, reaction, and countermeasure. Each step was a calculation within a well-known context of assumption and expectation.

Central to this system, of course, were skilled clerks. They, alone of all court officials, had in every case undergone extensive legal training.

They obtained it in the office of the colony secretary, who directed a sort of school for court clerks. Each clerk, therefore, apprenticed for the secretary; by copying form after form, each one learned the nuances of pleading in a way that justices of the peace did not. If a county clerkship was not open when the trainee sought a position, he could work as a deputy clerk until a post opened up by the death of a sitting clerk or by the creation of a new county.[29] To his new position he took with him a form book, copied in his own hand, in which he had recorded all the proper pleadings.[30]

The county clerks brought to local justice the legal knowledge of pleading, the consistency, and the predictability that the bench did not offer. They, not the "gentlemen justices," examined the record of probate and inventory appraisal, and they also went over guardians' accounts presented to the court.[31] The clerks—or their deputies—drafted documents and stood as witnesses to them. In every case they received a fee for their trouble and skill. If a will, probate inventory, or indenture was to be legally drafted and efficacious in the eyes of that particular court, it had to have approval of the clerk; only he really took the time to peruse the documents and enter them as properly recorded.

The clerk's record was law, and it stood unimpeachable once recorded and not challenged. Although the first justice in the commission was supposed to examine and approve all records at the close of every term, it was impossible for any justice to recall every detail sworn to. Moreover, clerks often waited years before making up a final record after a term. Although statute required two justices to inspect the county's records yearly to ensure prompt and full recording, years might elapse before such an inspection, and only the clerk might be able to locate papers amid the "great disorder" that prevailed in many counties.[32]

County clerks, then, could build their offices into authoritative, independent, and—not coincidentally—lucrative positions. They served for life, and in many instances passed their offices to sons or nephews. Appointed by the colony secretary of state and not the county magistrates,[33] they possessed an independence that few other local officials enjoyed. In turn, they wielded patronage of their own by choosing their deputies. Moreover, they were permitted by law to practice law in counties other than their own,[34] a profitable privilege, indeed, and a most effective avenue to legal success. Because of their intimate knowledge of pleading and their connections to other county clerks, they formed a potent legal fraternity.

71

The clerk was not the only person below the level of magistrate whose discretionary authority and considerable responsibility spread the actual exercise of judicial authority broadly among the populace and engaged a significant portion of the county community in judicial operations.[35] Though the power of issuing execution, including that of ordering the imprisonment of a debtor, rested in the hands of the clerk, on occasion this power descended to his deputies.[36] Similarly, deputy sheriffs normally served process for sheriffs, who, chosen from among the bench, were too elevated socially to traipse about the county in search of defendants or judgment debtors. Altogether, these nonmagistrates created, through the informal patterns of court communication and execution, a significant structure of organization that distributed authority widely throughout the community. By their position at crucial points of control in the judicial system, they greatly weakened the hierarchical ideal of justice and replaced it with a set of settled procedural expectations, understood by the community and exercised by familiar individuals.[37]

The breadth of popular engagement in the legal process extended beyond formally appointed officials. A substantial segment of the male freeholding population was called on to furnish services on juries and jurylike bodies. The personnel of the trial jury (relatively random by today's methods of selection) was in truth a consistent body of men whose repeated appearance gave to the fact-finding process of the jury trial a quasi-professional consistency. In York County, many men served on dozens—some on hundreds—of juries. Their way of thinking about law and their knowledge of local matters are vital to recognize at a time when "memory jurisprudence" was the preeminent fund of legal reference.

Moreover, attention to the jury in its role as fact finder in civil suits has led historians to overlook other jurylike activities that created a widespread system of citizen engagement in the legal system. "Enquiry juries" performed a significant role as fact finders in the award of damages after confessed judgments (many of which, it should be pointed out, were the result of office judgments made, to all practical intents, before the county clerk and only ratified in open court by the justices). The enquiry jury for damages was a thriving institution in colonial Virginia, inseparable from the legal process and no less hallowed than the trial jury. Patrick Henry's famous oration in the Parson's Cause, it must be remembered, was to such an enquiry jury. Its great virtue to

Henry and to countless other Virginians was that it might effectively nullify the legal decision of the bench and render damages consistent with the community's accustomed notions of legal obligation and in conformity with practical expectation. Following a default, or office, judgment, the enquiry jury circumvented the power of the bench and placed adjudication under the authority of the clerk and the judgment of the community. By the middle of the eighteenth century in York County, the petit and enquiry juries had become common facts of judicial life, fundamental to every procedural expectation of local practice. In fact, they settled nearly as many litigated disputes as did the bench.[38]

County clerks, of course, did not possess the skills of the prothonotaries who performed these tasks in the English Court of Common Pleas or of the secondaries who did so for the Court of King's Bench. Virginia county clerks frequently entered judgments in language that fell far short of the precision of the proper legal terms of art. For example, they commonly used the term "dismissed" to describe an action that had been fully adjudicated, with final judgment and process issued. To an English barrister like Sir John Randolph, such "Ignorance of the Clerks" was scandalous, and in 1729 he insisted that it had to be changed or "all Judgments will be void." Randolph argued that the word "Dismissed is no Judgment and therefore no bar" if the plaintiff tried to sue again on the same obligation. Technically, of course, he was correct, and the clerk of the General Court complied. The Judges of the General Court, however, ignored Randolph's argument and continued to tolerate such informality among the counties.[39]

Reluctant to rule county practices defective, the General Court consistently overlooked the informalities of country justice if the anomalous recording did not affect anyone's right. It revealed its approval of local inattention to strict common-law rules, for instance, in its attitude toward appeals made upon allegedly defective declarations. An appellant might argue that a declaration was defective for not making all the necessary averments; without them, the jury's verdict went beyond the strict bounds of common-law pleading that restricted the submission of evidence to those allegations pleaded. The General Court reacted unsympathetically to such arguments: if a plaintiff proved beyond the averments, then justice was better served.[40] Only if a defective declaration touched substantive law would the General Court rule it legally improper—if, for example, it joined as a plaintiff a party who had a lesser estate than that being sued for by the other plaintiffs. Such a practice would have conferred title where inappropriate and would have affected substantive law in a manner that the General Court refused to concede.[41]

Few appellate cases survive, but the forty-two available eighteenth-century examples amply indicate a pattern by which the General Court at Williamsburg indulged the localities in their own particular conduct of justice as long as the informalities were not so bad that a jury did not have enough clear factual matter to decide. Equitable intervention by the General Court into county cases, for example, was only "very sparingly done where there has been a Verdict & the Merits of the Cause fairly tried," according to Edward Barradall in 1735. At Virginia county courts, he continued, "the strict Rules of Law are not very rigidly adhered to either by Judges or Juries."[42] As today, the "harmless error" of a lower court would not call for appellate reversal.

Where does this survey of rural justice lead us? Put more broadly but pertinently to our examination of constitutional origins, what is the connection between rural county clerks and the Constitution? The link, I submit, is in a body of belief central to eighteenth-century jurisprudence, namely, to the way in which eighteenth-century Americans created and adhered to the notion of procedural due process. What we have seen so far, on the microcosmic level of the lowest courts in Virginia, are the following: a weakened, or diminished, structure of hierarchy, which in turn contributed to a second fact, a limiting of judicial discretion; a broad distribution of judicial responsibility through widespread and consistent citizen engagement; the placing of considerable judicial authority in the hands of nonmagisterial county officers, who became responsible for the manner in which adjudication proceeded; a vigorous though not professionally trained bar, whose members stayed within certain well-known patterns of pleading; and a tolerant stance by the central court at Williamsburg, the General Court, toward a bewildering variety of local informality as long as such practices did not violate property rights by preventing the community from making its judgment in a fair trial.

Altogether, these practices created a system in which the citizens of Virginia could expect justice to proceed in a manner consistent with their particular, entrenched ideas of how justice would proceed. For colonial Virginians, the *way* in which justice was obtained stood central in their jurisprudence. As someone identified only as "Common Sense" wrote to the *Virginia Gazette* in 1745, "Law is a dead Letter, and lives only in the due Administration thereof."[43]

"Due administration," of course, was due process. To colonial Virginians, laws were but paper barriers against tyranny unless they were executed in a manner consistent with justice. Tyranny, eighteenth-century republicans argued, might just as easily use a legal system improperly as reject it entirely. England in the 1730s saw numerous attacks on the Whig oligarchy (which, after all, acted through Parliament, a "free" institution that was supposed to guarantee liberty); Parliament had succeeded in establishing what was otherwise a solecism: "legal tyranny." Liberty was not guaranteed by written laws or even by established institutions, the opposition argued, but through specific procedural liberties such as those fought for in the seventeenth century.[44]

Virginians knew all this well. "Common Sense" had argued precisely that point in his letter to the *Gazette.* Even a conquering tyrant, "an Usurper, who murder'd our King, by Force of Arms, could never alter the steady Course of Justice, in our Courts of Law, or destroy the Certainty thereof." Such a tyrant would impose his own judges, who would "determine, as Bribery, Faction, or Interest directs; the Law, which should protect us, will be warped, and made to authorize our Destruction: In such Cases, the Lawyers only can make the Defence, urging the known Rules of Law, detecting the fallacy, reporting and publishing such unjust Proceedings, bringing such Judgments to publick Censure, and by such Means, exposing such Judges to publick rage."[45] Those most familiar with how their own courts operated understood and skillfully applied such "known Rules of Law." Only they could assure that maxim vital to early modern Anglo-American jurisprudence: *cursus Curiae est lex Curiae* ("the practice of the court is the law of the court").[46]

For the localistically inclined Virginians, government had to preserve their own courts' procedural practices. It was typical of the eighteenth-century common-law thinking that they could not conceive of separating procedural precedents from substantive rights. When it came time to create a federal judicial system, they justified the continuation of their own forms of justice by reference to their own historical past and tenaciously opposed the creation of a powerful federal judiciary with a uniform common law.

For Richard Henry Lee, the battle continued the opposition he had begun by refusing to attend the Philadelphia convention. Taking his case directly to the people, he set out his objections in his *Letters from the*

Federal Farmer to the Republican (New York, 1787). Echoing the long tradition of distrust for words and paper guarantees, he cautioned, "It is not a few democratic phrases, or a few well formed features, that will prove its [the Constitution's] merits; or a few small omissions that will produce its rejection among men of sense; they will require what are the essential powers in a community, and what are the nominal ones; where and how the essential powers shall be lodged to secure government, and to secure true liberty." Among Lee's criticisms, that of "Common Sense" in 1745 recurred: "Men who govern, will in doubtful cases, construe laws and constitutions most favourably for increasing their own powers."[47]

Virginians took careful note of the possibility that there might someday be a federal common law with a system of uniform federal rules of procedure, and the importance of their own unwritten but firmly understood procedure recurred throughout the Virginia ratifying convention in the summer of 1788. When article III, section 2, clause 2, came up for discussion, it focused the leading lights of Virginia politics directly on this issue. It did not matter, Patrick Henry argued, what precise words the Constitution used in describing the federal judiciary. Specific guarantees meant little as long as their terms might be construed or applied in a manner repugnant to expectation and settled local practice. "What is meant by such words in common parlance?" Henry asked of the reference to appeals on "law and fact." If, as he and others feared, this clause permitted federal judges to review facts submitted to local juries, the entire system of jury trial as Virginians knew it would be undermined. "Poor people do not understand technical terms," Henry argued. He later took up the same point, insisting that the Constitution "cannot be understood, in many parts, even by the supporters of it." The jury, for example, was to consist of men from the "vicinage"—but how, Henry asked, would federal courts apply that term in order to be consistent with Virginia's particular practices?[48]

To George Mason, the analogy of county courts to state courts offered a useful argument for opposing a federal system of inferior courts and for preventing a uniform federal procedure. County writs, of course, ran only where issued. Their execution by local officials and the resulting adjudication by neighbors familiar with procedure and law remained an ideal of justice. "Have Hanover and Henrico the same objects?" he asked; "can an officer in either of these counties serve a process in the other?" Of course not, he knew, for James Madison had just conceded the same point, with reference to the same fears, only a moment earlier, "observing that the county courts were perfectly independent of each other, where the same inconvenience might arise" if process ran among them.[49]

William Grayson, soon to be one of Virginia's first senators, insisted that expectation, born of custom, was essential to justice. Virginians were deeply concerned about the fate of their debts to English merchants in 1788, and Grayson pointed out that contract law included within it the expectations of both creditors and debtors regarding the courts and procedures that would enforce obligations. Virginians had grown accustomed to a relatively slow process of recovery—much slower in some counties than others, significantly, owing to different process practices.[50] Adding that Virginians preferred such slowness and could not count on it among federal courts, Grayson explained that debts before 1776 were contracted with specific expectations concerning process and remedies. Virginia debtors would recall these as inseparable components of contract law, along with other adjustments such as the award of interest arrangements or brokerage fees. Grayson explained, "I presume, when the contracts were made, the creditors had an idea of the state judiciaries only. The procrastination and delays of our courts were probably in contemplation by both parties. They could have no idea of the establishment of new tribunals to affect them. *Trial by jury* must have been in the contemplation of both parties, and the *venue* is in favor of the defendant. From these premises it is clearly discernible that it would be wrong to change the nature of the contracts."[51] Procedure, then, unavoidably affected law, and local practice had to be maintained for that reason. Suitors would not, under the anticipated dual system of courts, know the venue in which they might have to sue, and the certain basis of law would be destroyed.

These debates revealed an intense preoccupation with what Julius Goebel identified as the concern "as to what the legal substratum of the new government was to be—a matter vital to the functioning of the federal judiciary." No state constitution had provided explicitly for such protections, as he explained, because "due process had developed at the hands of the courts with particular reference to settled procedural expectations."[52]

The constitutional protections of due process, then, could not be guaranteed by written enactments, especially in an age of legislative supremacy. For that reason, some Virginians doubted that even an explicit bill of rights would suffice to restrain abuses. To George Nicholas, a bill of rights "was no security." Distrusting any document by itself, he warned, "It is but a paper check."[53]

Revolutionary Virginians, with a powerful legal tradition emphasizing popular engagement in law and politics, naturally demanded that the instrumentalities of justice remain in the hands of the people who implicitly understood their purposes and practices. Not only the making of laws, but also the implementation and exercise of them, was necessary to render any constitutional protection meaningful and to assure a proper demarcation of judicial authority between a central government and the states. In its eighteenth-century history, the Virginia legal system had successfully worked out such arrangements between the inferior county courts and the superior court at Williamsburg. Basic legal principles stood supreme in provincial jurisprudence, while the rural localities implemented them along the lines and through the procedures understood by the people. Well before the revolutionary crisis, capital and countryside had struck an effective working balance, one that informed a strong constitutional tradition in Virginia after Independence.

Notes

The author is grateful for the advice and comments of W. Hamilton Bryson, Frank L. Dewey, Jack P. Greene, William E. Nelson, and Robert C. Palmer.

1. Published as Stanley N. Katz, "The Problem of Colonial Legal History," in *Colonial British America: Essays in the New History of the Early Modern Era*, ed. Jack P. Greene and J. R. Pole (Baltimore, 1984), 468.

2. Julius Goebel, "Constitutional History and Constitutional Law," *Columbia Law Review* 38 (1938): 555.

3. Jack P. Greene, "From the Perspective of Law: Context and Legitimacy in the Origins of the American Revolution," *South Atlantic Quarterly* 85 (1986): 56–77.

4. On the demanding tasks of managing a tobacco plantation, see T. H. Breen, *Tobacco Culture: The Mentality of the Great Tidewater Planters on the Eve of Revolution* (Princeton, N.J., 1985), esp. chap. 8.

5. Michael Dalton, *Countrey Justice* (London, 1619), as cited in George Webb, *The Office and Authority of a Justice of Peace* (Williamsburg, Va., 1736).

6. William Waller Hening, comp., *The Statutes at Large: Being a Collection of All the Laws of Virginia, from the First Session of the Legislature, in the Year 1619*, 13 vols. (New York, 1809–23), 2:69.

7. T. Barlow, *The Justice of Peace: A Treatise Containing the Power and Duty of That Magistrate* (London, 1745), vii–viii, as cited in Norma Landau, *The Justices of the Peace, 1679–1760* (Berkeley, Calif., 1984), 1. For specific figures on the wealth of justices in one county, see Darret B. Rutman and Anita H. Rutman, *A Place in Time: Middlesex County, Virginia, 1650–1750* (New York, 1984), 147.

8. York County Orders, June 15, 1741, Colonial Williamsburg Foundation.

9. *Virginia Gazette* (Rind), April 26, 1770.

10. See the proclamation by Gov. Alexander Spotswood in 1711, made public and recorded in May. York County Orders, May 21, 1711.

11. Henrico County Orders, June 1713, Virginia State Library, Richmond. See also Goochland County Orders, March 19, 1729, Virginia State Library.

12. For a sample period (1741–43) at the York County Court, 28 percent of all cases brought to issue and adjudged by the bench (twenty-one of seventy-five) took more than one term. A fuller quantitative examination of York cases from 1648 to 1774 forms the basis of David Thomas Konig, *The Course of the Law in Colonial Virginia: Local Justice and Government in Tidewater Virginia, 1607–1774, with Special Reference to York County* (forthcoming).

13. Carroll had attended because his imperious father resented dependence on local attorneys whose familiarity with such matters "imposed on" him. Alan McKinley Smith, "Virginia Lawyers, 1680–1776: The Birth of an American Profession" (Ph.D. diss., Johns Hopkins University, 1967), 74, 185.

14. As cited in Frank L. Dewey, *Thomas Jefferson, Lawyer* (Charlottesville, Va., 1986), 18.

15. Richard Starke's *Office and Authority of a Justice of the Peace,* also printed at Williamsburg, appeared only in 1774.

16. Webb, *Justice of Peace,* 5–10, 144–51.

17. Ibid., 11–13, 22–29, 120–26, 128, 194, 343. More useful on litigation, in that it briefly explained the major forms of action, was *Conductor Generalis,* first published in New York in 1711. However, there exists little evidence that it had much use anywhere in colonial Virginia. William Hamilton Bryson, *Census of Law Books in Colonial Virginia* (Charlottesville, Va., 1978). For manuals in general use in the colonies, see John A. Conley, "Doing It by the Book: Justice of the Peace Manuals and English Law in Eighteenth Century America," *Journal of Legal History* 6 (1985): 257–98.

18. For this particular question, the counties of Essex and Northampton have been chosen. York, other data from which are used in this essay, has no loose file papers in existence from before 1774. For more detail, see Konig, *Course of the Law,* chap. 5, "The Implications of Procedure."

19. Konig, *Course of the Law,* chap. 2, "The Sot-weed Gentry in Power."

20. John Daly Burk, *History of Virginia,* 4 vols. (Petersburg, Va., 1804–16), 3:154.

21. Jack P. Greene, ed., *A Diary of Colonel Landon Carter of Sabine Hall, 1752–1778*, 2 vols. (Charlottesville, Va., 1965), 2:726–27.

22. Ibid., 1:585.

23. Ibid., 2:726.

24. Tucker to William Wirt, September 25, 1815, "William Wirt's Life of Patrick Henry," *William and Mary Quarterly*, 1st ser., 22 (1914): 253. Describing the contemporary English situation, William Shenstone remarked more piquantly, "A Justice and his Clerk is now little more than a blind man and his dog. The profound ignorance of the former, together with the canine impudence of the latter, will, but rarely, be found wanting to vindicate the comparison. . . . The Justice is as much dependent on his clerk for superior insight and implicit guidance, as the blind fellow on his cur that leads him in a string." *Essays on Men and Manners* (1764), as quoted in Sidney Webb and Beatrice Webb, *English Local Government: The Parish and the County* (London, 1906), 1:348.

25. On this particular question, the order books of York, Middlesex, Lancaster, Westmoreland, King George, and Prince George counties were examined, Virginia State Library.

26. Pleading at the rules was set out for actions at the General Court by statute in 1727. Hening, *Statutes*, 4:186–87. Conway Robinson, in *The Practice in the Courts of Law and Equity in Virginia*, 2 vols. (Richmond, Va., 1832), 1:139, states that rules pleading did not become mandatory at the county courts until 1785 (citing Hening, *Statutes*, 12:33). He is correct insofar as their being made mandatory is concerned. The act of 1785 changed county court procedures by providing for two different types of terms (monthly and quarterly) and by requiring rules pleading at the former; it also reserved to the bench, at its quarterly meetings, the power to set aside such office judgments. The act did not, however, extend rules pleading to the counties for the first time. County courts generally followed the basic contours of practice at the General Court, and many of them—in particular, York, the major focus of this study—had adopted such a system much earlier in the eighteenth century. Joseph H. Smith describes what seems to be a very similar system in Prince George's and Charles counties in Maryland. Joseph H. Smith and Philip A. Crowl, eds., *Court Records of Prince George's County, Maryland, 1696–1699* (Washington, D.C., 1964), lxxxiv–lxxxix.

27. York County Orders, August 18, 1729.

28. See acknowledgment of these practices in R. T. Barton, ed., *The Reports by Sir John Randolph and by Edward Barradall of Decisions of the General Court of Virginia, 1728–1741* (Boston, 1909), B45, B229–230 (hereafter cited as *VCD*). Barton's pagination adds the letter "R" to Randolph's reports, a "B" to Barradall's.

29. On this system of training and placement, see Junius Rodes Fishburne,

"The Office of Secretary of State in Colonial Virginia" (Ph.D. diss., Tulane University, 1971), 375–81. I am indebted to John M. Hemphill II for this reference.

30. There exists an example of such a volume in the clerk's office of Augusta County and another (for Charlotte County) in the collection of the Virginia Historical Society, Richmond.

31. Inventories might even be directed to the clerk himself rather than to the court. See, for example, those for the 1720s in the Essex County Ended Suits, file box 3, Virginia State Library.

32. The two Middlesex County justices who reported such "disorder" in 1767 also reported that various categories of records had not been examined and approved since 1758, 1762, 1763, and 1766. Middlesex County Orders, May 5, 1767. Statute had required this inspection since 1745 (Hening, *Statutes,* 5:344), although it is clear that such inspections were only occasionally made. One reason that this neglect has escaped historical notice is the manner in which loose papers were translated onto the order books. A search through the order books would not reveal that the clerks bundled their loose papers for later recording into the order books and noted on the wrapping of such bundles when such papers were recorded and inspected. The wrappers were then thrown away, but a few very scattered examples survive, and a comparison of the dates of court term with recording date with magisterial examination date reveals the process to be rather drawn out. One such wrapper for 1712 can be found in the loose papers of the Essex County Ended Suits, file box 1.

33. This power of appointment was effectively attached to the secretary's office by John Carter in the 1720s, although it seems to have been used before. Fishburne, "Secretary of State," 346, 358.

34. Hening, *Statutes,* 2:81 (1662).

35. On citizen engagement in the administration of justice, see Konig, *Course of the Law,* chap. 4, "Yeoman Service: The Emergence of Civic Participation, 1676–1730."

36. See the *capias ad satisfaciendum* issued by deputy clerk Richard Tunstall in Essex County Ended Suits, file box 2.

37. On the ways by which lesser officials reduce hierarchical control of courts and exert power at various "control points" today, see Herbert Jacob, "Courts as Organizations," in *Empirical Theories about Courts,* ed. Keith O. Boyum and Lynn Mather (New York, 1983), 191–215.

38. For the sample period of 1741–43 at York, almost 23 percent of the 258 ended cases were decided in this manner (49, or 19 percent, by petit jury, and 10, or 3.9 percent, by enquiry jury). By comparison, the bench heard and adjudicated 75 cases, or 29 percent of all cases in which issue was joined.

39. Randolph made his argument in 1729 in Abbott v. Abbott, *VCD,* R21–R22. Nine years later, Edward Barradall noted that the practice had not

changed. Palmer v. Word, *VCD*, B289–B294. York's clerk, Thomas Everard, continued to use the term "dismissed" when a plaintiff lost an action, whereas Edward Thacker in Middlesex recorded that the plaintiff had to "pay according to law with costs" in such a situation.

40. Smith v. Brown (1729), *VCD*, R1–R7.

41. Meekins and Vadin v. Burwell and Holdcroft (1729), *VCD*, B15–B19.

42. Lutwige v. French (1735), *VCD*, B183.

43. *Virginia Gazette* (Parks), October 3–10, 1745.

44. J. A. W. Gunn, *Beyond Liberty and Property: The Process of Self-Recognition in Eighteenth-Century Political Thought* (Montreal, 1983), 16, 25, 230–36.

45. *Virginia Gazette* (Parks), October 3–10, 1745.

46. Croke, J., in Burrowes, et al. v. High Commission, 81 Engl. Rep. 42 (K.B. 1615).

47. Paul Leicester Ford, ed., *Pamphlets on the Constitution of the United States, Published during Its Discussion by the People, 1787–1788* (Brooklyn, N.Y., 1888), 291, 313.

48. Jonathan Elliot, ed., *The Debates in the Several State Conventions, on the Adoption of the Federal Constitution*, 5 vols. (Philadelphia, 1836–59), 3:540, 579.

49. Ibid., 3:583–84.

50. In Westmoreland County, for example, it was not unusual for a case to take two years before reaching final adjudication; in adjacent King George, the average case took between six and nine months.

51. Elliot, *Debates*, 3:274, 566.

52. Julius Goebel, Jr., *History of the Supreme Court of the United States: Antecedents and Beginnings to 1801* (New York, 1971), 101, 296.

53. Elliot, *Debates*, 3:445, 450–51.

The Palmetto and the Oak: Law and Constitution in Early South Carolina, 1670–1800

Herbert A. Johnson

raceful palmetto trees adorn the state flag and the great seal of the state of South Carolina, proud symbols of the affection of a people saved by a palmetto log fort in the Charleston harbor during the grim first months of the American Revolution. Less obvious on the great seal, and usually missing from the state flag, is an irregular mass at the foot of the palmetto tree. Sigillographers tell us that the object is a fallen oak tree, reminiscent of the defeat of the British oaken warships by the fort at Sullivan's Island.

South Carolina's great seal is an allegorical representation of the victory of the American cause over the might of Great Britain. Yet I find Virginia's seal a much more forceful treatment that stresses the disruption in government attendant upon the Revolution. The fallen body of the English king lies prostrate at the feet of victorious Liberty, who has placed one foot on the chest of the monarch. His crown, thrown from his head, lies at a distance from his body. British monarchical institutions died when American republicanism triumphed. Not so with South Carolina's seal. The palmetto's roots twine around the trunk of the fallen oak, ready to absorb nutrients and take new life from the remains of the dead tree. To me, this is a very positive allegorical presentation of the institutional continuities in South Carolina law and constitutionalism from the colonial period to the years after Independence. Now a palmetto is not an oak, but both are trees; and law and constitutional thought in England and South Carolina demonstrate both strong continuities and significant differences.

Constitutional Thought in Early South Carolina

America's move toward revolution from 1774 to 1776 occurred at a time when a century of tradition enshrined Whig constitutionalism in the minds of South Carolinians. The Fundamental Constitutions, that strange document said to have emanated from the pen of John Locke, was early determined inappropriate for the conditions of the young colony; but at the same time it was treasured as a constitutional curb upon the power of the proprietors or their resident governor. The mode of election of deputies to the proprietorial legislature was to be in accordance with the guidelines established by the Fundamental Constitutions. And taxes were to be raised only with the consent of the people; even if consent was forthcoming, a provision of taxation might be defective if it had not been passed in accordance with the Fundamental Constitutions.[1] In November 1670 Lord Ashley wrote Governor Joseph West, "We shall take care that no body in Carolina shall be oppressed in his just rights and lyberties,"[2] and South Carolinians found security in this assurance as set forth in the Fundamental Constitutions. At the same time they desired more effective government within the colony; by 1693 they petitioned for the establishment of government by means of a charter rather than under the Fundamental Constitutions.[3]

Religious toleration was a continuing constitutional issue throughout the proprietorial period. Shortly after settlement the governor of Carolina demanded that inhabitants sign a registry reflecting their religious beliefs. They protested and "verie modestlie tould [the Governor] . . . that they desired that the lawes for governing them should proceede from that patterne which the Lords had prescribed for them."[4] The matter of religious conformity festered in the colony's politics until passage of a 1704 colonial act requiring that each candidate for public office take a test oath. This act effectively excluded all dissenters from colonial government and precipitated what became known as the Exclusion Act crisis of 1704–6.

In the latter year the colonial act was disallowed by the crown, and the proprietors were ordered to strike it from the colonial statute book.[5]

However, in the interim a strong protest had been filed, supported by a pamphlet authored by South Carolinian John Ash but published under the name of Daniel Defoe. Citing charter rights, the pamphlet asserted that the Exclusion Act deprived South Carolinians of a charter-based right to hold public office. That right was secured by the fact that English subjects had been settled in the Carolinas well before Charles II granted the land to the proprietors, and the royal grant reserved all rights, titles, and interests hitherto possessed by Englishmen there residing. The pamphlet, entitled *Party-Tyranny; or, An Occasional Bill in Miniature, as Now Practiced in Carolina,*[6] leaves little doubt that South Carolinians relied upon the Fundamental Constitutions as the compact of government—the *Pacta Conventa,* they called it. The Constitutions were the "Sacred and unalterable Conditions, on which they Consent to be Governed and Directed, and to which they submit." Upon the breach of these "Capitulations of Government," the people, by right of nature and the constitution, came under the immediate direction and government of the English king. When the proprietors, or those acting upon their behalf as deputies within the colonies, acted in a way that was destructive of the constitution from which they drew their power, then "that Power is *Ipso Facto* dissolved, and resolves of Course into the Original Power, from whence it was derived."[7] Proprietary government in Carolina, from the colonists' viewpoint at least, was based upon a solemn compact derived from the royal grant to the proprietors as well as the Fundamental Constitutions and the Barbadoes Concessions.

Defoe's *Party-Tyranny* goes further than merely advancing a compact theory of government. It asserts that the reservations in the royal charter to the proprietors, guaranteeing the rights of Englishmen to those settling within the Carolinas, were not a matter of mere royal grace. Quite the contrary, this provision was made under the compelling need to protect the "Native right of the Freeman, inhabitants of Carolina settled" in the province at Chowan, North Carolina, before the date of the first Carolina charter. In other words, the inherent rights of Englishmen already settled *required* that the king reserve their rights as native-born Englishmen while granting governmental powers to the Carolina proprietors. No unilateral act of the crown, absent the consent of the early settlers, could divest the inherent rights of Englishmen. Indeed, the failure of the colonists' initial protest to the proprietors was what triggered the publication of the pamphlet, designed to be a "publick Appeal to the World for the Justice of their Application to the Parliament of England."[8]

Although it is unclear how effective Defoe's pamphlet was in persuading the proprietors and Board of Trade of the unconstitutionality of the Exclusion Act, we know that the Carolinian attack resulted in a retreat by the governmental authorities. At the instance of the crown the proprietors disallowed the Exclusion Act passed by the Carolina assembly, postponing for a decade the inevitable clash between proprietorial pretensions and colonial demands for government by consent of the governed. Neglect and nonsupport during the Yamassee War, coupled with the threat of impending Spanish invasion in 1719, resulted in a second and final challenge to the authority of the Lords Proprietors. Declaring that the actions of the proprietors in forsaking their colony had "unhinged the frame of government," the South Carolinians through their assembly declared the proprietary to be forfeited and placed themselves under the immediate direction of the crown.[9] Six years later, the surrender of authority still a matter of negotiation in England, they supplied a constitutional justification for their actions.

In *The Liberty and Property of British Subjects Asserted,* John Norris on behalf of the inhabitants of South Carolina disclaimed any desire to meddle with the property interests of the Lords Proprietors. On the other hand, they were determined to "keep them within the strictest limits of the Charter" in regard to their governmental authority. Contending that "Compact . . . is the sole Foundation of such [persons] as owe their Power to Patents only, which is all our natural Lords can pretend to claim by," Norris hinted broadly that such right might well be the basis of all forms of government.[10] The proprietors had broken their contract with the inhabitants by denying them assistance and protection; indeed, when danger threatened the proprietors were quite willing to permit the crown to assume the burden of defense. Citing manorial law and custom, Norris noted that when lords failed to perform their duties, the law released their tenants from quitrents. The duty of lords and tenants was reciprocal, and among the most sacred duties of a lord was that of protection. By the form of compact entered into by the Lords Proprietors, and by the English feudal laws of lord and tenant, the failure of the proprietors to defend their colonists was a breach that entitled the

Carolinians to throw aside their allegiance to the proprietors and attach themselves to their protector, the king.[11]

Later generations of Carolinians were to alter the focus of their affections from the Fundamental Constitutions to the proprietorial charter. In the course of the 1765 Stamp Act crisis, the Commons House of Assembly resolved that "His majesty's liege subjects of this province are entitled to all the inherent rights and liberties of his natural-born subjects within the kingdom of Great Britain. That the inhabitants of this province appear also confirmed in all of the rights aforementioned, not only by their charter, but by an act of parliament."[12] The British statute mentioned was most likely the 1729 parliamentary approval of the crown's purchase of seven-eighths of the proprietorial estate in the Carolinas and the assumption of all governmental authority over the two provinces. One might have assumed that upon the termination of proprietary authority, the charter rights would have been extinguished. Yet upon further reflection it is clear that Carolinians were on firm ground in urging the continuance of their privileges and immunities under the charter. First, the crown had purchased the property and jurisdictional power of the proprietors; it had not proceeded by *quo warranto* to divest the proprietors of those interests. It might thus be argued that the crown succeeded to the right, title, and interest of the proprietors, and in its dealings with the inhabitants of South Carolina, it was bound by the ancient charter and perhaps by the Fundamental Constitutions. Second, even if the termination of the proprietary power to govern could be seen as a rupture in the contractual relationship between proprietor and inhabitant, it nevertheless remained the case that the settlers of South Carolina had certain vested rights, predicated upon their charter and proprietorial concessions. Those rights—the inherent rights of Englishmen guaranteed in the reservations of the charter regarding the settlers at Chowan—could not be taken without the consent of the inhabitants of South Carolina.

It remained to William Henry Drayton to elaborate upon the charter privileges of South Carolinians and to expound even more fully upon their rights. His "Freeman" letter of 1774 was a powerful argument for the equality of Englishmen, wherever they resided, and their equal standing before the law and in relationship to the king and British Parliament. The king's prerogatives, Drayton argued, were constitutionally no greater in the colonies than they were at home. Neither could Parliament exercise authority over the colonies that it could not exert at home. Magna Carta could not be suspended in the colonies, as the British ministry and Parliament had attempted to do in Massachusetts Bay with the Intolerable Acts.[13] Commented Drayton, "The Americans being descended from the same ancestors with the people of England, and owing fealty to the same Crown, are therefore equally with them, entitled to the common law of England formed by their common ancestors."[14] That common law, so applicable to South Carolina, included Magna Carta, the Petition of Rights, the Bill of Rights of William and Mary, and the 1701 Act of Settlement. Upon this broad base of English constitutional law Drayton predicated the legality of colonial opposition to the pretensions of the king and his Parliament.

Equally significant for students of South Carolina constitutionalism is Chief Justice Drayton's April 23, 1776, charge to the grand jury at Charleston. Drayton reasoned that in accepting the 1719 overthrow of proprietary government by the Carolinians, the king of England conceded their right to overthrow a government that operated to their destruction. He had accepted them into his care, simultaneously conceding their right to revolt to preserve their inalienable rights.[15] One might paraphrase Drayton's position as, "The Commons House giveth the government of South Carolina to the King, and the Commons House can take it away again, blessed be the name of the Commons House of Assembly."

Technically, Drayton was incorrect in depicting the 1719 overthrow of the proprietors as a defense of inalienable rights of Englishmen. The weight of the evidence would indicate that the crisis was precipitated by a lack of protection in the face of Indian and anticipated Spanish attack. Shortly before the December 1719 overthrow of the proprietors' government, there had been a constitutional objection to the enlargement of the membership of the council without consent of the inhabitants and contrary to the charter, but the most memorable victory for the rights of Englishmen and charter privileges had been the exclusion controversy of 1703–6.

In the larger sense, Drayton was quite accurate in stating constitutional theory as it had developed in South Carolina. Charter rights combined with the limitations of the Fundamental Constitutions to protect the inherent rights of Englishmen settled in the province. Furthermore, the overthrow of the proprietors had resulted in a tender of allegiance to the king and an acceptance of his government and protection. Government in South Carolina could easily be interpreted as a compact between the governed and the ruler—a sovereignty required to be strong enough to protect the people against external dangers and civil disorder and yet limited by constitution, law, and custom to protect their rights as Englishmen.

Drayton's view of the English common law is also a natural outgrowth of South Carolina's ready acceptance of English precedents into provincial law. Although such a reception of English common law and statutes was not unique to South Carolina, among the mainland colonies South Carolina was unusual in its early acceptance of large segments of English law and in its affection for the legal institutions of the mother country. Drayton as "Freeman" viewed the entitlement to English common law as a matter of consanguinity and allegiance to the English crown. Distinctions between Englishmen resident in England and Englishmen resident in the colonies were odious. For this reason he challenged the system of colonial appeals being heard by the Privy Council rather than the House of Lords, the constitutional court of last resort in common-law matters.

The English Law "Birthright" and Its Reception

English law was brought to colonial America by a variety of methods, collectively resulting in what legal historians have come to call "reception." In the case of uninhabited territory settled by English subjects, it was the general rule that the law of England as it existed at the time of settlement was applicable to the province. Should the territory be conquered by English arms from the possession of another European nation, the law and customs of England as they existed on the date the legislature first convened formed part of the province's law, to be supplemented by such statutes as might be passed by the new legislature. Parliamentary statutes passed after the date of settlement, in one case, and after the date legislative powers were granted, in the other, did not apply to the colonies unless they contained express provisions making them applicable to one or all of the dominions of the king.

As a settled colony South Carolina was entitled to English law as it existed in 1670. Colonial legal history would be a dull subject if the method of reception could be so simply dismissed. From the beginning it had been recognized that local conditions might make certain provisions of English law inapplicable to the colony, even if they were enacted prior to the date of settlement. Colonial lawyers and judges were thus free to pick and choose those portions of English law that might be accepted as controlling in South Carolina. This process of reception followed the custom and usages of the courts, and consequently one cannot be at all definite about the influence of English law in South Carolina without exhaustive study of all the manuscript court records of the province.[16] Fortunately, at various times in the history of the American colonies, it became necessary that these informal receptions of English law through usage should be formally recognized by colonial statute. South Carolina took such a step in 1712, enacting a lengthy reception statute prepared by Chief Justice Nicholas Trott.[17]

The 1712 reception statute is remarkable not only for its contents, but for what it was intended to accomplish:

1. It recognized those English statutes enacted after 1670 that were part of the law of South Carolina, received either through past usage or by their specific mention in the 1712 statute.

2. It selected from the entire body of English statutory law— stretching back to Magna Carta—those statutes that were to be continued as a part of South Carolina law, and it provided that all other English statutes were declared inapplicable to South Carolina conditions and hence not in force in the province.

By my count 137 English statutes were declared operative in South Carolina from among the vast body of legislation passed by the English Parliament after 1215 and before 1670. The reception into South Carolina law of 29 statutes enacted after 1670 was either accomplished, or given statutory recognition, by the 1712 enactment.

We are frequently told by those who fail to study the preamble to the statute that South Carolina received English law *in toto* into its jurisprudence in 1712. Now though I will freely admit that one can find a great deal of law in 137 English statutes, and most of the important acts in constitutional history and private law were included in the list of received statutes, nevertheless it seems clear to me that a wholesale importation of English statutes was precisely what the 1712 act was intended to prevent.

At that early date there was a demand for precision in the statement of exactly what English legislation formed a part of the law of provincial South Carolina. All other statutes were not law in the colony, unless subsequently enacted by the assembly. Because of the 1712 reception statute, we can say with some degree of certainty what English law applied in South Carolina at that date. Unfortunately, there are no later general reception acts in South Carolina, so that we are left to speculate from the court records concerning the reception by custom of subsequent English parliamentary statutes. When South Carolina declared its independence and wrote a state constitution, it failed to insert a provision concerning the reception of English law.

This reception by statute, which I believe is unique for such an early period in a colony's history, left South Carolinians with a substantial body of English legislation as part of their provincial law. J. Nelson Frierson, formerly dean of the University of South Carolina Law School, referred to the 1712 reception act as "the definite point at which the system of laws of South Carolina . . . branched off from the trunk of the great tree of the English common law system."[18] The dean apparently shared my affection for horticultural metaphors, even though he did not identify the English tree as an oak.

Throughout the colonial period there are isolated examples of the reception of specific English statutes by act of the South Carolina assembly. There were also, undoubtedly, more frequent borrowings from English statutes and case law by the usages and customs of South Carolina courts. Within the scope of my work, I have found some evidence that with the growth of South Carolina in population and economic diversity, the colony began to place even greater reliance upon English precedent as an important source of provincial law. A 1743 chancery decree on the estate of James Goodbee demonstrates a recourse to English case law concerning decedent estates. These same South Carolina chancery manuscripts show the use of trusts to transfer remainder interests in slaves. Under English law, it was impossible to convey a future interest in personal property, owing no doubt to the fact that the grantee of personal property takes full possession and has ostensible authority to sell or dispose of it. Similarly in South Carolina, the transfer of a slave to one person for his or her life, with the remainder interest in any other party, resulted in full ownership vesting in the first grantee.[19] To prevent this result, Carolinians, like Englishmen, conveyed the personal property to a trustee for the lifetime use of the first taker, with instructions to transfer the remainder in fee to the intended holder of the future interest.

The application of these fairly complex rules of English law in early

91

South Carolina suggests that the law and customs of the mother country had a continuing and growing influence in South Carolina jurisprudence throughout the colonial period. The work of the courts tends to reinforce this impression. Rules of the Court of Common Pleas required attorneys to be suitably garbed in robes, bands, and wigs; the court constable had a staff of authority, emblazoned with the provincial coat of arms and the royal coat of arms.[20] And attorneys were required, before their admission to practice, to have been in regular attendance at one of the English Inns of Court for at least five years.[21] To the best of my knowledge, no other American colony put such a requirement for English training upon its colonial bar.

Despite widespread acceptance of English precedent and implementation of English practices in the training and garb of the bench and bar, South Carolina remained within the mainstream of constitutional thought in revolutionary America. The arrival of seventeen hundred British regular troops in September 1757 raised the issue of the Mutiny Act's applicability; colonial leaders in the Commons House were strong in their contentions that it did not apply and in asserting the traditional rights of Englishmen. William Henry Drayton in 1774 challenged the constitutionality of treason trials in England for offenses committed in the American colonies. In this connection he cited long-accepted constitutional principles requiring trial by a jury of the vicinage.[22] We have already noted the high constitutional principles set forth in the Commons House resolution concerning the hated Stamp Act; and South Carolina had a long-standing tradition of lower-house opposition to the pretentions of colonial governors.

Judicial Review and Assembly Powers

Emerging legislative power of the Commons House of Assembly initiated a constitutional debate over the exercise of what modern lawyers call judicial review. The proprietorial charter and gubernatorial instructions required that all colonial acts not be repugnant to the law of England. This rule required judges to consider colonial legislation in light of its variations from English parliamentary statutes and provided them with an opportunity to declare colonial laws null and void.

The first major case arose in 1735 and 1736 and dealt with a South Carolina act punishing counterfeiting by death without benefit of clergy.

In *Rex v. Mellichamp* the defendant was convicted of the crime and moved to stay the execution of judgment, contending that the act was void for repugnancy. Deciding this motion, Chief Justice Robert Wright held that all British subjects possessed the rights of Englishmen, even if resident in South Carolina. Consequently, Mellichamp might not be subjected to harsher criminal sanctions than were available under existing English law. In effect he nullified the South Carolina act, leaving his colleague Justice Lamboll to dissent upon the basis of legislative autonomy and the powers of the Commons House of Assembly.[23]

A decade later the same colonial law came before Chief Justice Benjamin Whittaker, and again the convicted defendant objected to sentencing by raising the constitutional issue presented in *Mellichamp*. Perhaps embarrassed by his pro-assembly political leanings, Whittaker issued an ambiguous order, staying execution of the judgment and declaring that there was an imperfection in the act under which the indictment was drawn and that no such offense was prohibited by a colonial act. On the one hand the decision might be construed as merely following the *Mellichamp* precedent and supporting the invalidity of the colonial act there considered. However, it could also be seen as being based upon some unidentified flaw in the indictment.[24]

The question of judicial review on the basis of repugnancy was raised more directly in the 1759 case of *Watson's Executrix v. Williams' Administrator*. The defendant demurred to the prosecution assertion that the colonial act permitting actions against administrators, and expanding plaintiff's remedies beyond those set forth in English law, was repugnant and hence void. Arguing this position, James Rattray set forth an extremely restrictive view of colonial legislative authority. In his opinion the law of England should not merely constitute a standard for colonial legislation; rather, it should occupy the field, leaving only the interstices subject to colonial regulation. He was willing to concede that in some circumstances colonial conditions might justify departure from English law, but these were to be limited to cases of necessity and to be sharply restricted in manner.

By way of contrast the replying argument of James Grindlay pointed out that Rattray's view of colonial legislative competence froze South Carolina law in the form of English law in 1669. Such a view would result in great inconvenience and limit the ability of the Commons House to act in the public welfare by suitable alterations in law. It fell to Chief Justice Michie to decide between these radically differing viewpoints concerning colonial enactments. His opinion points out that repugnancy did not invalidate any colonial law that varied from the English norm. English statutes did not apply throughout the empire unless express provision was made to that effect in the parliamentary enactment. Where variances did exist, colonial laws had received a review by the Privy Council; presumably, that body's concurrence in the colonial act negated any challenge to its validity. In short, Michie came down solidly in favor of colonial legislative power.[25]

Judicial review as debated in eighteenth-century South Carolina might be a forgotten chapter in history were it not for the subsequent development of the doctrine in American judicial history. Yet its occurrence in the colonial context emphasizes the importance that lawyers attached to the integrity of English law as the birthright of all British subjects. Rejection of Rattray's statutory theories cannot be viewed as the death knell of judicial review in the province. The very fact that royal judges had taken the step of comparing colonial legislation with the "higher law" of parliamentary enactment laid an important foundation for American constitutionalism.

Criminal Procedure

The 1731 Jury Act of South Carolina contained a number of significant constitutional provisions. Most famous was the system for impartial jury selection. This arrangement required the use of a six-drawered box provided with three locks, the keys to which were in the possession of separate officials. Selection of names of jurymen was to be made by a child less than ten years of age, who would publicly withdraw slips of paper containing their names from each drawer in turn until the jury was determined. Concern for the objectivity of jurymen contrasted markedly with the practice in contemporary England, where sheriffs had notorious influence on the selection of jurors and presided over the selection process with a heavy hand.[26]

William S. McAninch correctly identifies the 1731 Jury Act as one of the major extensions of the right to counsel in colonial America. It allowed representation by counsel in virtually all felony cases, as well as professional assistance in treason cases (a right received into South Carolina in 1712 by reception of the 1696 English Treasons Act). Other colonies, specifically Pennsylvania and Delaware, had extended the privilege more selectively, ignoring property-related felony offenses but including within the right to counsel most violent crimes and all capital offenses. Supporting this right to counsel was the Jury Act's requirement that an accused person be provided with a copy of the indictment at least three days before the commencement of trial; this procedural right, designed to prevent surprise, extended to all treason and felony cases. In England the right to receive a copy of the indictment in other than treason cases was not recognized until the nineteenth century. The language of the Jury Act also implies that South Carolina defendants, unlike their English contemporaries in the dock, were permitted compulsory process to secure witnesses on their behalf and were also permitted to introduce sworn testimony from such witnesses.[27]

The origins of the 1731 Jury Act are obscure, but it has been suggested that it was a product of the struggle between the Commons House of Assembly and the courts over the availability of habeas corpus in legislative contempt cases.[28] This power contest came to a head in 1733 when two Greenville settlers ignored the house's order to testify. After their imprisonment Chief Justice Robert Wright ordered their release under the provisions of the English Habeas Corpus Act of 1679 (received into South Carolina law). In response the house passed an act suspending the privilege of habeas corpus in these situations, and the council held that Wright had wrongly ordered the release of the prisoners. Ultimately the house had the last word by refusing to pay the chief justice's salary, but the legislative act permitting suspension of habeas corpus was disallowed by the king in Privy Council.[29] Although the 1731 Jury Act preceded these events, it is plausible to explain it as a legislative means of neutralizing the threat of criminal prosecution against members of the Commons House. Given the constitutional issues raised concerning judicial review just four years later, it is clear that extreme political tension between the Commons House and the Court of Common Pleas generated an outburst of new constitutional thought and some radically new legislation.

Protection of the Law

If we concede that South Carolina by 1776 had adopted the learning as well as the trappings of English law and practice, we must nevertheless observe that the provincial leadership overlooked one of the fundamental lessons of English legal history. Since the time of Henry II, English royal justice had been brought to the countryside by itinerant justices carrying royal commissions to try both civil and criminal cases by the common law of England. Royal authority was represented on the local level by this routine of judicial administration, undermining baronial power and winning allegiance to the king and support for his courts as arbitrators of local disputes. Despite the ancient English example, South Carolina continued to maintain its court system at Charleston well after the settlement of the back country, precipitating the Regulator Movement of 1764–67. Forced to take the law into their own hands after suffering at the hands of an assortment of murderers, rapists, and thieves, back-country leaders formed a voluntary association for protection of their lives and property, and for the punishment of criminals.[30] Better read in provincial history, they might have reminded their low-country neighbors that the 1719 revolution was in part justified by the lack of proprietorial protection. Governmental authority, like the dignity of law, depends in the final analysis upon the power of the government to protect its people against external invasions and internal civil disorder. The Regulators were closer to orthodox Carolina constitutional theory than either they or their low-country opponents could know or appreciate.

An adequate court system was not fully established in the back country before the American Revolution. The Circuit Court Act of 1768 had been disallowed by the crown, but the revised act passed the following year provided for a *nisi prius* system of courts in each of the seven districts. Writs and other forms of process were issued out of the Charleston office of the central law courts, and after trials in the district court towns the jury verdicts and pleadings were returned to Charleston for entries of judgment. Back-country leaders were disappointed at the failure to provide country courts for the trial of minor cases, but even more they deplored the delay in implementing the 1769 act while courthouses and jails were constructed. Not until 1773 was low-country justice available in back-country South Carolina, and a recent study of the operation of the circuit court at Camden would indicate that the *nisi prius* court was not particularly active before the American Revolution.[31]

Postrevolutionary Trends

Except for the chaotic years immediately following the British evacuation in 1783, South Carolina law seems to have continued to develop

96

along lines established under British rule. Bay's *Reports* contain numerous citations to British authorities, even in some cases decided in 1777 and 1779, well beyond the dates when other American states had declared English precedents inapplicable. In 1778 the old arrangement of the governor and council constituting the chancery court was abandoned, and three judges of equity elected by the legislature were constituted the new chancery court. True to the colonial pattern, the law courts of common pleas and general sessions, presided over by the same judges, continued to administer common-law justice in South Carolina. Of course, those judges now rode circuit regularly, meeting at Charleston or Columbia at the end of their tours to decide adjourned matters *en banc*. To most observers, it would have appeared that business was being resumed, as usual, after the unpleasant and disastrous events of the years 1780 to 1783.

Most of the significant changes in the law and constitution occur slowly, and after 1776 one can see the beginnings of later trends in South Carolina law. A number of early cases concern the exercise of eminent domain and the constitutional problems presented by the seizure of private property for public purposes. In 1792 the Common Pleas court held in *Bowman v. Middleton* that it was unconstitutional for the colonial assembly to pass a statute adjusting boundary lines between conflicting claimants. Such an action was condemned as being "against common right, as well as against Magna Carta, . . . [and it was illegal and unconstitutional] to take away the freehold of one man and vest it in another, . . . without any compensation, or even a trial by the jury of the county, to determine the right in question. . . . the act was, therefore, ipso facto, void."[32] Somewhat later, the same court upheld the right of the state legislature to exercise eminent domain for the purpose of opening a public street. Neither Magna Carta nor the 1790 South Carolina Constitution was found violated by the exercise of this power, for by these documents all citizens held their real estate subject to the paramount authority of the sovereign to take it as required for public use. Quite significantly, the court of common pleas divided equally— two judges for and two against—on the need to compensate the private owner so deprived of his property.[33] Clearly, within two decades after independence South Carolina judges were struggling with the constitutional requirements of substantive due process. There was great concern for the security of private property, as we can see in the construction of wartime confiscation statutes. Absent a conviction or attainder of treason, a Loyalist's widow could not be deprived of her dower rights in Carolina realty.[34] Slaves captured by an American marauding party into British Florida during the war were considered illegally taken from their owners, and restitution was ordered in the case of an owner who became an American citizen after the war.[35]

The judges also took notice of the disruption in business activity that had been occasioned by the War for Independence. In *Brewton's Estate v. Cannon's Estate*, they recognized that a "variety of distresses" had been occasioned by the war.[36] These distresses had altered the situation of the country, so that as a matter of law it was not proper to presume that bonds, because they were dated twenty years before, had been paid. This very presumption of payment was being urged in Virginia against the claims of British merchants attempting to collect prerevolutionary debts. Clearly, South Carolina judges preferred the strict performance of contractual undertakings to the satisfactions of revenge against British merchants or Loyalist refugees.

This conservatism is also evident in South Carolina legislation of the postwar period. James Ely has noted that the statutes are "keenly property-conscious" but strongly mercantilist in their orientation. The state began to support internal improvement projects: the construction of bridges and roads, channeling rivers for navigation, and the regulation of port pilots. Continuing colonial practices of granting patents for inventions, the legislature provided a fourteen-year monopoly for inventors under the terms of a 1784 statute. Four canal companies were incorporated in the three-year period 1786–88, each having perpetual existence, toll-making authority, and the power of eminent domain.[37]

Transition from colony to independent state and subsequent inclusion in a federal union seem to have had a moderate impact upon South Carolina's constitution. The old constitutional issues, based to a degree upon the uncertain law of the British imperial system, were no longer pertinent. But the constitutional theories that gave them birth continued to exist in South Carolina. Charter rights and the privileges of Englishmen continued to have credence in the rhetoric of revolutionary statesmen and leaders in the early national period. Issues concerning the relative powers of the legislature and the judiciary remained alive, although the rise of legislative power after the revolution made outright clashes most unlikely. A rapidly expanding economy, destined to reach its zenith within the half century after Independence, made the most substantial impact upon private-law matters. But for the most part the state continued to be ruled by low-country politicians and to cling strongly to its English heritage and colonial system of representation. Republican South Carolina lawyers shed their colonial wigs and robes, but it was eminently clear that the palmetto owed a great deal to early protection and later nourishment from the English oak.

Notes

1. "List and Abstract of Papers in the State Paper Office, London, Relating to South Carolina," *Collections of the Historical Society of South Carolina*, vol. 1 (1857), 98, 115, 123.

2. Printed in *Collections of the Historical Society of South Carolina*, vol. 5 (1897), 209.

3. B. R. Carroll, ed., *Historical Collections of South Carolina*, 2 vols. (New York, 1836), 2:326.

4. William Owen to Robert Blayney, March 22, 1670/71, *Collections of the Historical Society of South Carolina*, 5:303.

5. Christopher C. Crittenden, "The Surrender of the Charter of Carolina," *North Carolina Historical Review* 1 (1924): 385.

6. Daniel Defoe, *Party-Tyranny; or, An Occasional Bill in Miniature, as Now Practiced in Carolina*, in *Narratives of Early South Carolina, 1650–1708*, ed. Alexander S. Salley, Jr. (New York, 1911). On Ash, see David McCord Williams, "'Mr. Ash': A Footnote in Constitutional History," *South Carolina Historical Magazine* 63 (1962): 228.

7. Defoe, *Party-Tyranny*, 226.

8. Ibid., 229, 232, 247. It is not without constitutional significance that they saw their recourse to lie by way of petition to Parliament, rather than an application to the king in Privy Council. The distinction was to gain in importance as the century progressed.

9. Assembly resolve quoted in Joseph W. Barnwell, "Dual Governments in South Carolina," *Collections of the Historical Society of South Carolina*, 5:vii, ix. See also M. Eugene Sirmans, *Colonial South Carolina, 1663–1763* (Chapel Hill, N.C., 1966), 125–27; and Carroll, *Historical Collections*, 1:228.

10. [John Norris], *The Liberty and Property of British Subjects Asserted: In a Letter from an Assemblyman in Carolina, to His Friend in London* (London, 1726), 23, 24. The copy used is a photostat in the South Caroliniana Library, University of South Carolina, Columbia, taken from an original in the John Carter Brown Library, Brown University, Providence, R.I.

11. Ibid., 24, 30. Norris observed that "when there is likely to be any Danger or Expence in defending us, then we are the King's Subjects; but when there is any thing to be got by us, then we belong to our *natural Lords* again."

Ibid., 26. He also cited two proprietorial threats—to sell the colony to the South Seas Company, in which the Stuart Pretender was interested, and to send Swiss mercenaries to America to subdue Carolinian discontent. Ibid., 23–24, 27–28.

12. Carroll, *Historical Collections,* 1:526; the 1729 British statute authorizing surrender of the proprietary title, with savings clauses applicable to rights of South Carolina residents, is 2 Geo. 2, c. 34 (1729).

13. Anne King Gregorie, ed., *Records of the Court of Chancery of South Carolina, 1671–1779,* American Legal Records Series, vol. 6 (Washington, D.C. 1950), 12–13; Robert W. Gibbes, *Documentary History of the American Revolution,* 3 vols. (New York, 1855–57), 1:17, 24, 29, 31–36.

14. Gibbes, *Documentary History,* 1:16.

15. Ibid., 2:278, 286.

16. The literature on reception is extensive. See Herbert A. Johnson, *Essays in New York Colonial Legal History* (Westport, Conn., 1981), 226–28, for bibliographical citations; a consideration of reception by usage is at ibid., 193–212.

17. Thomas Cooper and David J. McCord, eds., *The Statutes at Large of South Carolina* (Columbia, S.C., 1836–41), 2:401–12.

18. Introduction to Gregorie, *Records of the Court of Chancery,* 27.

19. In this 1743 case the executrix and her second husband had invaded the corpus of the modest and heavily indebted estate for the maintenance of the decedent's infant son. The South Carolina Court of Chancery cited an anonymous case in the English King's Bench Court, decided in 1682, which held that maintenance of a child was the responsibility of the surviving parent; on the other hand, *Barlow v. Grant* in the High Court of Chancery in 1684 held that the size of the legacy left to an infant would determine whether the executors were justified in invading corpus for the child's support and maintenance. On the basis of these two precedents, the South Carolina chancery disallowed the executor's accounts, decreeing that the decedent's debts were of first priority. Once they were discharged an infant's legacy might be used for his support, but only the income would be available for that purpose. Gregorie, *Records of the Court of Chancery,* 395; Barlow v. Grant, 1 Vernon 255, 23 Engl. Rep. 451 (Ch., 1684); Anonymous, 2 Ventris 353, 86 Engl. Rep. 481 (K.B., 1682); Court of Chancery, Bundle 1736–1760, no. 6, South Carolina Department of Archives and History, Columbia.

20. Gregorie, *Records of the Court of Chancery,* 359–60; Court of Chancery, Bundle 1721–1735, no. 10, South Carolina Department of Archives and History.

21. Gregorie, *Records of the Court of Chancery,* 15. In Chancery the English distinction between solicitor and counselor was maintained; after 1770 the same attorney could not practice in both categories. Ibid., 15, 579.

22. Jack P. Greene, "The South Carolina Quartering Dispute, 1757–1758,"

South Carolina Historical Magazine 60 (1959): 193–94, 203; Sirmans, *Colonial South Carolina,* 321; Henry G. Conner, "The Constitutional Right to a Trial by a Jury of the Vicinage," *University of Pennsylvania Law Review* 58 (1908): 208.

23. Robert Cook, "Judicial Review and Legislative Power," in *South Carolina Legal History,* ed. Herbert A. Johnson (Spartanburg, S.C., 1980), 86–89.

24. Ibid., 89–91.

25. Ibid., 91–94.

26. William S. McAninch, "Criminal Procedure and the South Carolina Jury Act of 1731," in Johnson, *South Carolina Legal History,* 181, 183–88.

27. Ibid., 182–83, 188–93.

28. Ibid., 197.

29. Sirmans, *Colonial South Carolina,* 181–82; Carroll, *Historical Collections,* 1:297–99; Robert Johnson to Duke of Newcastle, May 4, 1733, State Papers Abstracts, *Collections of the Historical Society of South Carolina,* vol. 2 (1858), 262.

30. Richard M. Brown, *The South Carolina Regulators* (Cambridge, Mass., 1963); Charles Woodmason, *The Carolina Backcountry on the Eve of the Revolution,* ed. Richard J. Hooker (Chapel Hill, N.C., 1953), 166–70, 185–87, 214–15, 220, 230–32. For details of the Circuit Court Act of 1769 and its operation, see Carl J. Vipperman, "The Justice of Revolution: The South Carolina Judicial System, 1721–1772," and JoAnne McCormick, "Civil Procedure in the Camden Circuit Court, 1772–1790," both in Johnson, *South Carolina Legal History,* 226–40, 241–54.

31. "List and Abstract of Papers in the State Paper Office, London, Relating to South Carolina," *Collections of the Historical Society of South Carolina,* 2:192; William M. Dabney and Marion Dargan, *William Henry Drayton and the American Revolution* (Albuquerque, N.M., 1962), 53–54; Thomas H. Pope, *The History of Newberry County, South Carolina,* vol. 1 (Columbia, S.C., 1973), 28–29, 31–32.

32. 1 Bay 252, 254–55 (1792).

33. Lindsay v. Commissioners, 2 Bay 38, 62 (1796).

34. Mongin v. Baker and Stevens, 1 Bay 73, 80 (1787).

35. Turnbull v. Ross, 1 Bay 20, 20–23 (1785).

36. 1 Bay 482, 483 (1795); the case of *Ware v. Hylton,* decided in 1796 by the U.S. Supreme Court (3 Dall. 199), was then pending on appeal from the Virginia federal circuit court.

37. James W. Ely, Jr., "American Independence and the Law: A Study of Post-Revolutionary South Carolina Legislation," *Vanderbilt Law Review* 26 (1973): 939–71.

Part Three

Constitutionalism in the Nineteenth-Century South

A distinct southern constitutional position clearly emerged during the antebellum era. The increasingly acrimonious debate over slavery became the overriding constitutional issue. Consequently, the states' rights philosophy gained prominence as a constitutional buttress against federal interference with the peculiar institution. This development eclipsed but did not wholly displace the earlier tradition of southern nationalism.

The chapters of this section explore aspects of the states' rights controversy. R. Kent Newmyer's essay about John Marshall examines the violent reaction to the doctrine of implied powers as upheld in *McCulloch*. Although largely ignored for decades, Marshall's decision opened the way for the eventual appearance of a vigorous federal government. Paul Finkelman focuses on the southern treatment of free blacks from the North and the handling of extradition requests by governors. In Finkelman's view, the states' rights doctrine was vital to southerners but was employed only in an opportunistic fashion by northern leaders. William M. Wiecek, on the other hand, argues that southerners were inconsistent in their states' rights constitutionalism and favored the use of national power to safeguard slavery. He further maintains that much of southern constitutional history since the Civil War reflects attempts to reject legal values imposed from outside the region.

103

John Marshall and the Southern Constitutional Tradition

R. Kent Newmyer

John Marshall and the southern constitutional tradition are clearly inseparable, just as the dialectic between them is inseparable from the American constitutional tradition. Indeed, constitutional history during the formative period seems at times to be mainly a dialogue, and finally a passionate argument, between the chief justice and his Virginia neighbors. Only *Dartmouth College v. Woodward* (1819)[1] and *Gibbons v. Ogden* (1824),[2] of his great opinions, seem not to have either originated in Virginia or produced an explosive reaction there. The general course of this running war between Marshall and his southern critics is, of course, well known. I would like to traverse the battlefield yet one more time with the hope of providing a fresh focus, of clarifying causative factors and reassessing traditional interpretive emphasis: this while hoping to escape the pitfalls of historical anachronism and winner's history, both of which have plagued Marshall historiography.

My argument falls into four parts, the first of which treats the years 1801 to 1819. Despite the dramatic events of this period—the confrontation between Marshall and Jefferson in *Marbury v. Madison* (1803),[3] the Burr treason trial (1807),[4] the impeachment of Justice Chase in 1805, and *Fletcher v. Peck* (1810)[5]—the constitutional lines of battle were not clearly drawn between the Marshall Court and southern constitutionalists. This situation changed radically after Marshall's opinion in *McCulloch v. Maryland* (1819);[6] indeed, as I argue in my second sec-

105

tion, it changed because of that decision. The third section treats the joining of issues between Marshall and states' rights theorists in the 1820s. The final section aims to ascertain the lasting legacy of this confrontation.

The Pre-*McCulloch* Years

What most conditioned the relationship between Marshall and southern constitutionalists, especially those in Virginia, in the period before 1819—aside from the experimental nature of government itself—was the nationalism of Presidents Jefferson and Madison and the dominant wing of the Republican party.[7] The list of policies based on a broad construction of the Constitution was impressive indeed, the more so in light of the states' rights platform on which the Republican party was elected in 1800. Hamilton's much-maligned Bank of the United States, resting squarely on the doctrine of implied powers, continued with no diminution of power. Jefferson's acquisition of the Louisiana Territory in 1803 rested on a pragmatic, expansive approach to the Constitution that shocked even the Federalists and put the "broad constructionism" of the Supreme Court quite in the shade.[8] The Embargo of 1807, passed by a compliant Tenth Congress without substantive debate, brought the national government into a coercive contact with citizens to a degree not seen again in peacetime until the deployment of federal troops in the Little Rock school crisis in 1957.[9] Jefferson's use of the common-law doctrine of seditious libel to silence Federalist criticism, his personal intervention in the Burr treason trial, and his deployment of the navy to suppress the Barbury Pirates expanded both the power of the presidency and the authority of the federal government.[10] Climaxing the turn to nationalism by the former champions of states' rights was the War of 1812, ironically opposed by the Federalist party, which in 1812 briefly considered putting up John Marshall as its peace candidate.[11]

The defection of the Jeffersonian Republican party to nationalism puts the "nationalism" of the Marshall Court in new perspective. Jefferson's prediction in 1801 that the Court was a "battery" that would beat down and erase "all the works of Republicanism" seems dramatically overstated.[12] In fact, Marshall's leading opinions from this early period, starting with *Marbury v. Madison* (1803), show the chief justice to be as close, perhaps closer, to Republican (capital "R" and small "r") orthodoxy as

106

Jefferson and Madison. Given the politicalization of Congress and the presidency, *Marbury* was more an effort to rescue the Court from oblivion than to beat down or erase anything. What Marshall claimed for the Court in that opinion, moreover, was good Republican constitutional theory. True, President Jefferson did not appreciate the chief justice's stern lecture about his duty to obey the law. But the principle that law, not men, governed was an unquestioned republican axiom. So was the principle of checks and balances, which was strengthened by Marshall's effort to give the Court equality with the other branches—an equality that it neither had nor claimed in the 1790s and, in fact, would not fully realize until the 1820s. Certainly the idea that there were constitutional limits to congressional power was congenial to states' rights thinking at that time; and there was even reason to think that the Supreme Court, armed with judicial review, might be the logical enforcer of those limits.

Marshall's opinion in the Burr treason trial (1807) was, if anything, even more congruent with the Republican conception of limited government under law than was *Marbury,* though again the personal confrontation between Marshall and Jefferson obscures the fact.[13] The chief justice's issuance of a subpoena *duces tecum* to a sitting president was bold if not brassy and understandably raised Jefferson's hackles. But even if the president refused to appear before the circuit court, which he could hardly have been expected to do, Marshall made the point, so serviceable during Watergate, that even the president of the United States is answerable to the judicial process and the law of the land. Marshall's narrow definition of treason and the strict standards of proof he set forth also doomed treason as an implement of political oppression.

Marshall's opinion three years later in the Yazoo land case, *Fletcher v. Peck* (1810), appears at first glance to be much less congenial to states' rights constitutionalism.[14] For the first time in its history, the Court voided a state statute on constitutional grounds (rather than as a violation of a federal statute or treaty). Opposition was violent in Georgia, where the memory of *Chisholm v. Georgia* (1798) still rankled. In Virginia opposition came from John Randolph and the Tertium Quid faction of the Republican party, who viewed the Yazoo land scam as an insult to republican virtue.[15] Most objectionable was the fact that Marshall's opinion gave the constitutional go-ahead to Jefferson's and Madison's congressional bailout of the speculators, who were finally compensated in 1814. But the main point is that the practical outcome of *Fletcher* was perfectly congenial to the dominant wing of the Virginia Republican party. To hold state legislatures to their contractual word in land grants— the legal consequence of Marshall's opinion—was to stabilize and rationalize the land market, a result much in the interest of planters and speculators alike.

To summarize: I've argued that up to *Martin v. Hunter's Lessee* (1816),[16] at least, Marshall and his Court had not squared off with southern constitutionalists. States' rights purists like John Taylor of Caroline and John Randolph were as much concerned about the consolidating policies of Jefferson and Madison, of the presidency and Congress, as they were about the nationalism of the Marshall Court.[17] And for good reason: the decisions of the Marshall Court had not enlarged the power of Congress and might in fact have limited it; the Court had also opposed executive excesses. Nor was there anything in the policy implications of the Court's early decisions—or of Marshall's own economic predilections—to put it or him at odds with southern agrarian capitalism. As for slavery, Marshall and his Court were entirely orthodox and would remain so until the end. Objections to specific decisions there were during these years, but there is no evidence that states' rights theorists saw the Supreme Court or its chief justice as inveterate foes. *McCulloch v. Maryland* (1819) shattered this détente and set southern and American constitutional development on a new course.

McCulloch v. Maryland: **Constitutional Revolution Ltd.**

McCulloch was Marshall's greatest opinion and quite possibly the most far-reaching decision ever handed down by the Supreme Court. Ironically, it did not in its own day either strengthen the Union or win acceptance for Marshall's nationalist view of the Constitution—objectives generally assumed to have been successfully realized. *McCulloch's* immediate impact on history was rather to generate a powerful states' rights, anti-Court movement that dominated American constitutional and political history for thirty years during which Marshall's most cherished constititional principles fell into disuse. Why and how *McCulloch* should have had this impact on history is the problem I would like now to address, because it gets to the heart of the dialectic between the chief justice and southern constitutionalists and bears directly on our assessment of the lasting legacy of both.

What was it about Marshall's rendition of implied powers in *McCulloch* that set southern constitutionalism in motion and shaped its tone and substance? Doctrinal innovation was not the answer, for the simple reason that the doctrine of implied powers was not Marshall's creation. Congress had endorsed it in 1791 when it chartered the First Bank of the United States and again in 1816 with the Second Bank. Hamilton's memorandum to Washington in 1791 on the constitutionality of the bank included a definitive discussion of implied powers, one that Marshall borrowed word-for-word in his *McCulloch* opinion.[18] Also the court had acted on implied powers well before 1819, as for example in Marshall's exposition of judicial review in *Marbury.* Story employed the doctrine to justify wartime executive power in *Brown v. United States* (1814)[19] in words similar to Marshall's in *McCulloch.* Implied powers appeared to be a part of judging and governing, too: witness Jefferson's acquisition of Louisiana.

So why the outrage over *McCulloch?* The answer is that it was legally and historically unique. The case was legally unprecedented because the question of implied powers was fully before the Court for the first time and entirely dispositive. Hamilton had theorized about implied powers, but his theory was not law; Congress enacted the law but had not provided a constitutional justification for its action. Marshall's opinion did both at once: it settled the law and supplied the definitive constitutional justification for it. What Marshall did was to realize (in both senses of that word) the Court's unique institutional qualifications (as against Congress and the presidency) to speak authoritatively about the Constitution: its tried and proved deliberative procedures, its ability (thanks to Marshall) to speak in a single voice, the fact that its words are backed by the authority of the state, and, not the least important, the further fact that those words are printed and circulated widely among the lawyers and judges who are best located to educate society about constitutional law. The word of the Supreme Court, if one believed Marshall's logic, was inseparable from the Constitution itself, and its domain now clearly reached beyond the clarification of its own powers (which was the precedential meaning of *Marbury*) to those of the other branches as well. With *McCulloch* the Constitution became, as Charles Evans Hughes later put it, "what the judges say it is."[20] The Court appeared to be a permanently sitting Constitutional Convention with the power to adapt the work of the framers "to the various *crises* of human affairs," to use Marshall's phrase.[21] *McCulloch* completed *Marbury* and put the Court at the very center of the governing process—and this is what the southern states came to perceive and resent.

Marshall's opinion was controversial enough on its own terms; in the context of history it hit southern sensibilities like a firebomb. Part of the historical environment that explains the violent reaction to *McCulloch* was legal. I am referring to the running battle between the Marshall Court and Virginia over appellate jurisdiction under section 25 of the Judiciary Act of 1789, which conferred on the Supreme Court the right to hear appeals from the highest state courts on constitutional questions (which, readers will recall, could be heard at the state level in the first instance). The battle began with *Fairfax's Devisee v. Hunter's Lessee* (1813),[22] climaxed in *Martin v. Hunter's Lessee* (1816), and recurred with new intensity in *Cohens v. Virginia* (1821).[23] In *Fairfax* Story overruled a decision of the Virginia Court of Appeals, thereby voiding the Virginia Loyalist Confiscation Act of 1777 and, in effect, nullifying all state land grants based on that act. Virginia challenged the Court's jurisdiction under section 25, and in *Martin* Story upheld the constitutionality of that law in a sweeping defense of the Court's appellate jurisdiction.

The Court could not have ruled otherwise in *Martin* without putting itself out of business, but Story's opinion was provocative in the extreme.[24] It not only upheld section 25 but declared it to be constitutionally mandated, so that Congress had no choice but to pass it—*and presumably could not repeal it.* If that were not enough to goad Virginia jurists into action, Story went on to declare that the Court had the authority to interpret the common law of the state governing land, if that law was part of the legal issue raised at the state level. The gauntlet was down that Marshall picked up in *Cohens v. Virginia* in 1821.

Three historical events made the doctrinal and jurisdictional issues in *McCulloch* explosive. The first was the Panic of 1819 and the resulting depression, which hit the southern states particularly hard, leading them to blame the Second Bank of the United States for their suffering and Congress for chartering it. In the midst of the depression came the debates over the admission of Missouri as a slave state and the status of slavery in the territories. Both the panic and the debates focused southern attention on the dangers of congressional authority in the hands of a northern majority. If Congress could create a national bank by implied powers, it could also legislate federal internal improvements and protective tariffs. A northern majority in Congress armed with plenary powers by *McCulloch* also threatened slavery in the territories and even in the states where it already existed. Northern harangues against slaveholders during the Missouri debates gave an urgent tangibility to these fears, as did the Denmark Vesey conspiracy in Charleston in 1822, the third catalytic event of this period.[25]

History conspired in all these things to teach the southern states to think southern, to calculate the meaning of the Constitution and the advantage of union. At the center of these calculations was Marshall's exposition of national authority in *McCulloch,* especially as it dealt with the powers of Congress and the Court. Had the chief justice employed the broad authority of the Court that he claimed to strike down the bank and limit Congress by a strict construction of article I, section 8, he would have gone down as a southern hero rather than a national one. Instead, he underwrote the bank, which the South saw as an instrument of northern oppression, and in the process insinuated the dangerous doctrine of implied powers into the very text of the Constitution. The result was to arm Congress with a vast new authority just when the panic, the Missouri debates, and rumors of slave rebellion (not to mention the ongoing debate over federal internal improvements and protective tariffs) all alerted southern statesmen to the threat of a permanent northern congressional majority hostile to southern interests and institutions.

Judicial review, now clarified, expanded, and consolidated, assumed a sinister meaning it had not had in the earlier period; and here the lessons taught the South by *McCulloch* supplemented those taught by *Martin.* Both cases drove home the same point: when push came to shove, the Supreme Court of the United States was an arm of national authority. The hope that the Court might be a means of limiting the federal government was now dead and buried. If Congress and the president should cooperate (and the emerging party system worked to this end), and if the Court should underwrite their cooperation constitutionally (and the appointment process enhanced this possibility), then the system of checks and balances as a check on power was not what it was cracked up to be. What Marshall made clear to southern constitutionalists, in short, was that states' rights federalism, not separation of powers, was their main line of defense. What the southern states needed after *McCulloch,* what Calhoun supplied, was a practical working system by which the states could reclaim the authority to interpret the Constitution now claimed by the Court.

Constitutional Ferment in the 1820s

The decade of the 1820s was a major watershed in American history, the end of the colonial period in many ways and the beginning of the modern age. Politics went professional and the party system began to assume a permanent form. The contours of a new industrial order were clearly visible in the middle and northern states. Class lines began to take shape in the wake of economic change, and sectional self-consciousness grew exponentially in both the North and the South. Driven by fear of change and cultural myopia, intellectuals in both sections began to reshape the revolutionary heritage to justify sectional interests. Argumentation was the order of the day, and ideas took on new utility. "Writing is action," declared George Bancroft in 1826; "words have in the soberest sense, become things," echoed Story in 1833.[26]

Nowhere was this truth more apparent than in the realm of constitutional disputation between the Court of Chief Justice Marshall and the newly arisen phalanx of southern constitutionalists. To a remarkable degree it was *McCulloch* that called them into action and set the agenda for the subsequent debate. There was a new unity, too, in contrast to the earlier period, and a decided shift toward radicalism. Virginia nationalism, as symbolized by Washington, once a force to reckon with, was now in full retreat, along with the Enlightenment environment that sustained it. Moderate states' rightists in the Richmond Junto, who once defended the nationalism of Jefferson and Madison, now listened respectfully to John Taylor, whose radical agrarian constitutionalism they had once condemned as apocalyptic ranting.[27] Jefferson recanted his former nationalism by attacking Marshall and the Court.[28] Taylor responded to his new relevance by writing three states' rights treatises in three years, and the law faculties of the College of William and Mary and the University of Virginia soon added their bit; then came Thomas Cooper, president of South Carolina College, and John C. Calhoun, to mention only the most prominent. The stage was set for the debate over the Constitution between the North and the South that lasted to the Civil War and beyond.[29]

One of the most notable things about the constitutional debates of the

112

1820s, and one that speaks directly to the subject at hand, was the centrality of the Supreme Court. Opposition to specific decisions there had been before, but now for the first time in our history there was a long-lasting, broad-based attack on the Court itself. Chief Judge Spencer Roane of the Virginia Court of Appeals, legal voice of the Junto and Virginia's spokesman in the controversy over *Martin v. Hunter's Lessee,* led the way, along with Judge William Brockenbrough, in a series of newspaper articles attacking Marshall's *McCulloch* opinion. The chief justice, sensing the magnitude of the issue, responded in nine long essays signed "A Friend to the Union." What was remarkable about this exchange, aside from the manifest ability of Roane and the unmistakable genius of Marshall, was the fact recognized on both sides that the issue raised in *McCulloch* was not merely banking but the nature of constitutional union and the role of the Supreme Court in it.[30]

Jefferson also blamed the Court, and Marshall personally, for the South's troubles. To correct the matter he urged Justice William Johnson, whom he had appointed to the Court in 1804, to challenge the chief justice in open dissent, which he did.[31] John Taylor showed his strong displeasure with the Court and particularly *McCulloch* in *Construction Construed, and Constitutions Vindicated* (1820), though his main target remained Congress and political parties.[32] It was John C. Calhoun who would respond most directly to Marshall, as I shall argue shortly, but other intellectuals (including Judge John Bannister Gibson of the Supreme Court of Pennsylvania, in his dissent in *Eakin v. Raub,* 1825)[33] lashed out at the Court as well.

There was also widespread hostility to the Court among the states whose laws had been declared unconstitutional, and by 1832 there were eight of these. Outright resistance to judicial rulings was not uncommon, as with Kentucky in *Green v. Biddle* (1823),[34] Ohio in *Osborn v. Bank of the United States* (1824),[35] and Georgia in *Worcester v. Georgia* (1832),[36] to mention only the best known. Anti-Court sentiment was expressed in Congress, too, where a number of Court-curbing measures were considered. On the mild side was the proposal, prompted by *Green v. Biddle,* that no constitutional question be decided except by a majority of the whole Court, a requirement that Marshall, in fact, informally implemented after 1823. More extreme was the demand that all justices concur in any decision where the validity of a state or congressional act was at issue. Another plan required a minimum of five of seven justices on all constitutional questions. Yet another would have created a new supreme court to police the old one, this one composed of twenty-five judges, twenty-four of whom were to be state chief justices. Impeachment continued to be talked about throughout the 1820s, too. Most threatening of all, because it could be accomplished by a simple legislative majority, was the repeal of section 25 of the Judiciary Act of 1789.[37]

This pervasive antijudicial sentiment speaks to the fact that the Court had during the 1820s become a governmental power to reckon with—the logical focal point of the new constitutional dialectic between the North and the South. For this conclusion we need not rely on circumstantial evidence, either, strong as it is. Calhoun made the point bluntly in September 1831. Looking at the impending crisis in South Carolina and the previous decade of constitutional controversy, he concluded that "the question is in truth between the people & the Supreme Court. We contend, that the great conservative principle of our system is in the people of the States, as parties to the Constitutional compact, and our opponents that it is in the Supreme Court. This is the sum total of the whole difference."[38]

It is hard to miss the implications of Calhoun's observation: that Marshall and his Court had not just decided cases, or even doctrine, but had set forth a philosophy of the Constitution that the South was compelled to challenge. More difficult are the questions whether and to what extent the chief justice invented the constitutional nationalism he set forth so brilliantly in his opinions: whether and to what extent it was usurpatory. Jefferson condemned him for just such inventiveness,[39] and some Meeseian jurisprudes appear to agree. I would venture to say that the critics are largely wrong. This is not to deny the audacity of Marshall's judging, the creative liberties taken in certain cases: in *Marbury,* for example, when he blatantly ignored clear precedents contrary to the result he wanted to reach; or *Fletcher,* where he stretched article I, section 10, to the breaking point to make it reach public contracts. He knew how to pile inference on inference, as in *McCulloch;* how to obfuscate when convenient, as on exclusivism in *Gibbons;* how to obscure disagreement, as in *Sturgis v. Crowninshield* (1819).[40] As chief justice he maneuvered boldly within the confines of mandatory jurisdiction, as in the Georgia Indian cases. He knew when to hold (*Ogden v. Saunders,* 1827)[41] and when to fold (*Providence Bank v. Billings,* 1830),[42] as the song says.

Marshall was, then, a bold, canny, even inventive judge, though it should be remembered that even in the golden age, the deliberations of the Court were collective.[43] But even if one concedes Marshall's preponderant influence on constitutional questions, the point is that he did not invent the Constitution he expounded. The end product of Marshall's judging was in the largest sense what the framers intended: a flexible, muscular national government that would serve, not limit, the American people.[44] This is what the words of the document say when read for plain meaning, what a comparison with the Articles of Confederation indicates, what Marshall repeatedly asserted in his opinions. It is what Story spelled out in that remarkable chapter in book 3 of his *Commentaries on the Constitution* (1833) entitled "Rules of Interpretation," which is probably the most authoritative statement of intent ever made.[45] Most conclusive of all, this is what perceptive southern critics of Marshall themselves admitted. Henry St. George Tucker, son of St. George Tucker and professor of law at the University of Virginia, made the point when he admitted that the real problem was the Constitution itself.[46] The fatal mistake of the southern states was to abandon the Articles of Confederation, which Taylor now proclaimed to be the ultimate manifestation of republican wisdom.[47] What these southern conservatives realized—what historians have missed by focusing too much on the conservative motives of the framers of the Constitution and not enough on the document they framed—was that the Constitution of 1787 was a Trojan horse of radical social and economic transformation. John Marshall spoke this truth with a special fire in 1819; in that anxious age the South listened and heard.

John Marshall and His Southern Critics: The Lasting Legacy

And what difference did it make that Marshall and the Court and the South pitched into one another; and what was the historical legacy of that confrontation? The answer requires at least a couple of books, one for Marshall and one for his critics. For starters here are two sentences: In the campaign of history, Marshall lost the first battle but won the war. Southern constitutionalists won the first battle and lost the war. Let me rephrase: From the 1820s to the Civil War, in both law and politics, Marshall's constitutional nationalism retreated in the face of a resurgent states' rights constitutionalism. Appomattox ended southern dominance and destroyed whatever influence southern thinking might have had on

American jurisprudence after the war—and I contend that the South had much to offer. Grant's armies vindicated Marshall's Constitution; subsequent history made it relevant. *How* Marshall was relevant is yet another matter, as I will show after first considering the remarkable victory of southern constitutionalism in the years from *McCulloch* to the Civil War.

Let me deal first with the dynamic and controlling influence of southern states' rights constitutionalism on antebellum politics. It might appear that constitutionalism and politics were like oil and water, that the South's turn to formal constitutional remedies in the 1820s bespoke a lack of faith in its ability to bargain successfully in the political arena. Some, like John Taylor, did in fact explicitly condemn party as unrepublican and turn to constitutional principles as an alternative and preventative; so did northern conservatives like Joseph Story.[48]

If there was a tension between the formality of constitutionalism and the give-and-take pragmatism of American politics, there was also a deep symbiotic relationship, one that worked to the advantage of the southern states. In the 1820s both constitutional theorists and professional politicians addressed the same crisis: how to make the separate states and rival sections function as a nation. Indeed, in 1827, while Calhoun the theorist was pondering section 25 and reasoning toward nullification, Martin Van Buren, the quintessential new politician, was in Richmond negotiating the coalition between New York and Virginia that would be the basis of the newly emerging Democratic party.[49] President Jackson, it is true, threatened to use military force against the nullifiers, but he also responded politically to southern constitutional demands by ending national economic planning and by supporting slavery and moderate states' rights across the board.[50] Constitutional extremism, it would seem, was a good bargaining chit in the smoke-filled rooms.

I am suggesting that Jacksonian politics be seen as a victory for southern constitutionalism, that Marshall's constitutional nationalism, as a real force in the life of the nation, waned almost from the moment it was announced in *McCulloch*. Clearly, Jackson's election in 1828 signaled bad times ahead for Marshall's view of the Court and the Constitution, just as Nixon's in 1968 did for the doctrines of Chief Justice Warren. Like other strong presidents, Jackson believed that his word on the Constitution was just as valid as the Court's, a point he made forcefully in the Cherokee Indian case of *Worcester v. Georgia* (1832).[51] More important, he put men on the Court, six in all, who made constitutional law follow Jacksonian states' rights, proslavery priorities. The change was evident even while Marshall was chief justice; with Taney it became pervasive. This is not to deny continuities between the two Courts: a solicitude for property rights, a general commitment to economic progress. Marshall's great decisions, like *McCulloch* and *Gibbons,* were allowed to stand, too. Most important, the Taney Court did not surrender its power to decide, and in some areas, such as general commercial law and admiralty and maritime matters, it actually extended its reach.[52]

But the constitutional jurisprudence of the Taney Court differed substantially—Story would say fundamentally—from that of the Marshall Court.[53] Economic progress, yes, but the legal model for growth was that established by Taney in the *Charles River Bridge* case[54] and not Marshall and Story in *Dartmouth College.*[55] Implied powers as pronounced in *McCulloch* went into hibernation. The precedential meaning of *Gibbons* was obliterated in *Miln;*[56] and *Cooley v. Board of Wardens* (1851),[57] which did not even mention *Gibbons,* anticipated the modern age by enshrining process over doctrine.

This shift to result-oriented law was accompanied by the politicalization of the Court's mode of operation. Communal living among the justices ended in the 1830s as internal division and dissent increased. Caucusing among the justices on the Taney Court increased. Story saw the trend and despaired; Justice Catron, one of Jackson's appointees, saw it and, without flinching, declared that the workings of the Supreme Court were no different from those of the Senate.[58] Willy-nilly, the Court was doing what southern critics like Jefferson had insisted all along it should do: decide cases rather than the meaning of the Constitution.

Behind the Court's descent from the high Olympian ground taken by Marshall was the slavery issue, which ironically was the cutting edge of legal modernity. Slavery and abolition would finally drive the Court into a formal constitutional mode,[59] but before that happened these issues worked to undermine not only the doctrinal nationalism of the Marshall Court but doctrine itself and legal coherence as well. It was southern concern for slavery that forced Congress and the Court to put *McCulloch* on the shelf. Slavery forced the confusing doctrinal retreat from *Gibbons* that so distressed Story. In all constitutional questions involving the relationship of nation and state, obfuscation rather than clarification was the order of the day. Practicality rather than definitive law was the new

117

desideratum, and nowhere was this clearer than in those cases dealing directly with slavery: cases like *Groves v. Slaughter* (1841),[60] where the justices avoided confronting the constitutional issue of slavery and the commerce power, or the *Amistad* case,[61] where the Court took the narrowest possible constitutional ground, or *Strader v. Graham* (1851),[62] where it dodged the explosive conflict-of-law question presented by the facts.

The politicalization of the Taney Court—the southernization of constitutional law, one might say—came to a climax in *Dred Scott v. Sandford* (1857).[63] *Dred* carried to the Court all the political issues and passions of the 1850s, issues shrugged off by the political branches of the government. Those issues divided the justices just as they had divided politicians, and they also inspired the Court to the kind of political constituent-oriented calculations that had become the modus operandi of the Taney Court. Even as the justices fashioned law in terms of political results, they returned to formal constitutionalism with a vengeance. In this respect, *Dred* was the last shoot-out between Marshallian and southern constitutionalism. More precisely, it was Taney's definitive constitutional answer to Marshall's equally definitive position in *McCulloch*. *McCulloch* armed Congress with vast new powers that ultimately threatened slavery and slave society; *Dred* disarmed congressional authority over slavery by holding that the due-process clause of article V protected slave property in the territories and possibly in the free states as well. Taney had turned the tables: with Marshall the Constitution was mobilized to contain the states; with Taney it limited the national government. Taney did in 1857 what the South had hoped Marshall would do in 1819.

The Court's decision in *Dred Scott* helped bring on the Civil War, but Marshall's constitutional nationalism, especially in *McCulloch*, made *Dred Scott* necessary, if not inevitable. Did Marshall's judicial nationalism thus help cause the war? Did too much nationalism too soon put the Constitution and the Union in jeopardy? Put them at risk on the field of battle? How one answers the question influences one's interpretation of the Marshall legacy.

If the war complicates the process of historical judgment in this regard, it clarifies the process in other ways. Clearly, the war brought an abrupt end to the thirty-year reign of southern states' rights constitutionalism in American law and politics. Nullification and secession as constitutional devices were dead. So, unfortunately, was the tradition of constitutional and judicial realism that southern critics of Marshall had begun to fashion in the 1820s. They perceived that the Constitution of 1787, for all of its celebrated virtues, was not synonymous with life and liberty. It was the foundation of the Union—and also a manipulable human artifact in a constant power struggle among contending interest groups and coalitions. Southern legal realists also realized that justices of the Supreme Court could be among its chief manipulators. With the Taney Court, manipulation became the desideratum—indeed, the new constitutional norm.[64] Had this southern realism about the Constitution and the Court been incorporated into American jurisprudence after the Civil War as an antidote to legal formalism, perhaps the judicial excesses of the Gilded Age might have been curtailed and the gap between legal theory and reality diminished. Instead, the embryonic tradition of southern legal realism went down to defeat with the southern armies, was discarded as mere apologetics for slavery. The lessons of southern law, like the lessons of southern history, went unheeded just when they were most essential.

And John Marshall? Did not the war that doomed southern jurisprudence carry the chief justice to glory, and give his expansive version of the Constitution a new relevance? Nothing seems more plainly true: yet even here the meaning of relevance is elusive. Marshall's great nationalist opinions were liberally cited after the Civil War, first to protect property and curb "socialism," and then, in the twentieth century, to support national regulation and underwrite the modern corporate, welfare state. To prove relevance and greatness by counting citations, however, is problematic. The "grand style" of Marshall's opinions put them at a premium in the struggle between lawyers to persuade and in the effort of judges to legitimate. But history, not precedents, determines the deep structure of law; and the more precedents there are and the more often they fall on both sides of an issue, the less important they become. All this is to say that the modern state would surely have come without the Supreme Court's citations of *McCulloch* and *Gibbons,* just as for a long time it did not come *with* them.

Marshall would have been astonished, and probably appalled, by the behemoth state created over his constitutional signature. What he would have recognized in our own age and applauded is the Supreme Court's continued claim to determine what the Constitution means. And here in the institution of the Court, rather than in the substance of the law, lies his most original and lasting legacy. Here is where his great decisions counted most and lasted longest—not as precedents for the New Deal, or for that matter the Second Bank of the United States, but as building blocks in the emerging structure of the Court as it became not only the chief embodiment of the rule of law in America but a dynamic force in the system of democratic government. One hastens to say that even here in his greatest area of influence Marshall did not tailor from whole cloth. The raw material was there in article III of the Constitution, which gave the Court its "stately" jurisdiction, and in article VI, which made the Constitution and federal law supreme, and also in section 25 of the Judiciary Act, which provided for the Court's appellate jurisdiction from state courts in the most unequivocal language.

The logic of these provisions, even without exegesis, leads to a version of the Court's duties that goes far beyond Jefferson's minimalist notion that it should only settle disputes between parties. Still, it does not follow that judicial review as we know it would develop inevitably and automatically. Continuous disuse of the Supreme Court's powers after 1801 could easily have institutionalized weakness. And this is why Marshall's "being there," as Holmes put it,[65] was so important. It was equally important, however, that it was *Marshall* who was there and not Spencer Roane or John Bannister Gibson. Better than any man of his age, even including the framers, if one is willing to admit that men sometimes create what they know not, Marshall understood the constitutional potential for judicial governance. He had exactly the "right stuff," the unique personal and intellectual qualities, to turn potential into reality and to do so before time ran out: thus his immediate decision to abandon *seriatim* opinions, the most important single thing he did and the sine qua non of all that followed; thus his ability to persuade his brethren to follow along. Only by speaking in a single voice could the Court claim to expound the Constitution. By creating the possibility of a majority opinion, Marshall automatically established the dynamics of conference deliberation and created the unique leadership potential of the chief justiceship that he then went on to realize.

Marshall also demonstrated to his age and ours the possibilities of judging: how deciding could turn into governing; how opinions could be transformed into state papers. Yet as statements of law, even the greatest of these opinions were subject to change and even oblivion. What did not change was the model these opinions provided for what opinions can be. What was not challenged—not by southern constitutionalists on the Taney Court, not by strict- or broad-constructionist, conservative or liberal Courts; what Chief Justice William Rehnquist recently reaffirmed—

was Marshall's view of the Supreme Court as the most trustworthy interpreter of the Constitution and its most reliable guardian.

In elevating the Court, Marshall insinuated his own intellect, character,
and vision into the institution itself, so that it is hard to think of the chief
justiceship without thinking of Marshall, hard to think of the Supreme
Court without referring to its greatest chief justice. It is this conflation of
human and institutional character that marks this period of constitutional law as our "heroic age," if I might borrow a concept from Giambattista Vico.[66] Creating a nation's law, he tells us, is not only a rational
enterprise but a moral and ethical and perhaps a psychological one as
well. Giving law means little if it is not finally accepted by those to whom
it is given as of their own character and spirit. In this period of state
making, Marshall was both giver and legitimater, Solon and Prometheus.
By identifying himself with the Court, he supplied the legitimating link
between it and the Revolution, the sacred moment of national creation.
Marshall was to our law what Washington was to the nation. His legacy is
inseparable from the mythology that has surrounded him.

Notes

1. 4 Wheat. 518 (1819).
2. 9 Wheat. 1 (1824).
3. 1 Cranch 137 (1803).
4. U.S. v. Burr. 25 F. Cas. (Va. 1807) (No. 14,694).
5. 6 Cranch 87 (1810).
6. 4 Wheat. 316 (1819).
7. For a brief insightful discussion, see Richard Hofstadter, *The American
Political Tradition* (New York, 1984), chap. 2, "Thomas Jefferson: The Aristocrat
as Democrat."
8. The Federalists' opposition to the acquisition of Louisiana, which
stemmed from fear of southern expansionism, led them to seriously consider a
nullification doctrine as a means of asserting states' rights. James M. Banner,
Jr., *To the Hartford Convention: The Federalists and the Origins of Party Politics in
Massachusetts, 1789–1815* (New York, 1969), 111–19. For a discussion of John
Quincy Adams's constitutional objections to the acquisition of Louisiana, see
Linda K. Kerber, *Federalists in Dissent: Imagery and Ideology in Jeffersonian America* (Ithaca, N.Y., 1970), 41–42.
9. Leonard Levy, *Jefferson and Civil Liberties: The Darker Side* (Cambridge,
Mass., 1963), 139. For an extended discussion of the coercive nature of the
embargo, see ibid., chap. 6.

10. Levy discusses Jefferson's use of seditious libel and his role in the Burr trial in ibid., chaps. 3–4.

11. Albert J. Beveridge, *The Life of John Marshall,* 4 vols. (Boston, 1919), 4:31–34.

12. Jefferson to John Dickinson, December 19, 1801, *The Writings of Thomas Jefferson,* 20 vols. (Washington, D.C., 1903), 10:301–3; Richard E. Ellis, *The Jeffersonian Crisis: Courts and Politics in the Young Republic* (New York, 1971).

13. This famous trial is treated in Levy, *Jefferson and Civil Liberties,* chap. 4; Beveridge, *The Life of John Marshall,* 3:274–545; and George L. Haskins and Herbert A. Johnson, *Foundations of Power: John Marshall, 1801–15,* vol. 2 of *The Oliver Wendell Holmes Devise History of the Supreme Court of the United States* (New York, 1981), chap. 8.

14. The political and legal aspects of the case are treated in C. Peter Magrath, *Yazoo: Law and Politics in the Early Republic: The Case of Fletcher v. Peck* (Providence, R.I., 1966).

15. Ibid., 39–49.

16. 1 Wheat. 304 (1816).

17. Robert E. Shalhope, *John Taylor of Caroline: Pastoral Republican* (Columbia, S.C., 1980), 124–25; Robert Dawidoff, *The Education of John Randolph* (New York, 1979), chap. 5; Magrath, *Yazoo,* chap. 3; C. William Hill, Jr., *The Political Theory of John Taylor of Caroline* (Rutherford, N.J., 1977), 289, 291–92; Charles D. Lowery, *James Barbour: A Jeffersonian Republican* (University, Ala., 1984), 57, 82.

18. Hamilton to Washington, February 23, 1791, *The Works of Alexander Hamilton,* ed. Henry Cabot Lodge, 12 vols. (New York, 1903), 3:445–93.

19. 8 Cranch 169 (1814).

20. Charles Evans Hughes, speech at Elmira, N.Y., May 3, 1907, *Addresses of Charles Evans Hughes,* ed. Jacob G. Schurman, 2d ed. (New York, 1916), 185.

21. 4 Wheat. at 415.

22. 7 Cranch 603 (1813).

23. 6 Wheat. 264 (1821).

24. R. Kent Newmyer, *Supreme Court Justice Joseph Story: Statesman of the Old Republic* (Chapel Hill, N.C., 1985), 106–14.

25. Richard H. Brown, "The Missouri Crisis, Slavery, and the Politics of Jacksonianism," *South Atlantic Quarterly* 65 (1966): 55–72; William W. Freehling, *Prelude to Civil War: The Nullification Controversy in South Carolina, 1816–1836* (New York, 1965).

26. Bancroft to Jared Sparks, December 5, 1826, *Correspondence of George Bancroft and Jared Sparks, 1823–1832 . . . ,* ed. J. S. Bassett, Smith College Studies in History, vol. 2, no. 2 (1917), 122; Story to Joseph Hopkinson, November 27, 1833, Hopkinson Papers, Pennsylvania Historical Society, Philadelphia.

27. Lowery, *Barbour,* 133; Hill, *Taylor,* 285–86.

28. The posthumous publication of the *Memoirs, Correspondence, and Private Papers of Thomas Jefferson* . . . , ed. Thomas Jefferson Randolph, 4 vols. (London, 1829), revealed Jefferson's deep-seated hatred of the Marshall Court. For a full discussion, see Newmyer, *Story,* 160–61.

29. John Taylor, *Construction Construed, and Constitutions Vindicated* (Richmond, Va., 1820), *Tyranny Unmasked* (Washington, D.C., 1822), and *New Views of the Constitution of the United States* (Washington, D.C., 1823). The debate as it is manifested in various commentaries on the Constitution is treated in Elizabeth Kelly Bauer, *Commentaries on the Constitution, 1790–1860* (New York, 1952). Also see Newmyer, *Story,* 181–95.

30. Gerald Gunther, ed., *John Marshall's Defense of McCulloch v. Maryland* (Stanford, Calif., 1969).

31. Jefferson to Johnson, June 12, 1823, *Writings,* 15:439–52; Donald G. Morgan, *Justice William Johnson, the First Dissenter: The Career and Philosophy of a Jeffersonian Judge* (Columbia, S.C., 1954).

32. Hill, *Taylor,* 173.

33. 12 Serg. & Rawle (Pa.) 330 (1825).

34. 8 Wheat. 1 (1823).

35. 9 Wheat. 738 (1824).

36. 6 Pet. 515 (1832).

37. Newmyer, *Story,* 198–202.

38. Calhoun to Virgil Maxcy, September 1, 1831, *The Papers of John C. Calhoun,* ed. Clyde N. Wilson (Columbia, S.C., 1978), 11:464.

39. Jefferson to William Johnson, June 12, 1823, *Writings,* 15:439–52.

40. 4 Wheat. 122 (1819). Marshall's maneuvers in *Marbury* are discussed in Susan Low Bloch and Maeva Marcus, "John Marshall's Selective Use of History in *Marbury v. Madison," Wisconsin Law Review,* (1986), 301–37.

41. 12 Wheat. 213 (1827).

42. 4 Pet. 516 (1830).

43. Donald M. Roper, "Judicial Unanimity and the Marshall Court: A Road to Reappraisal," *American Journal of Legal History* 9 (1965): 118–34.

44. Marshall's positive, promotional view of constitutional government is spelled out in his letter to John Q. Adams, October 3, 1831, Adams Papers, Massachusetts Historical Society.

45. Newmyer, *Story,* 191–92.

46. Robert J. Brugger, *Beverly Tucker: Heart over Head in the Old South* (Baltimore, 1978), 85.

47. Shalhope, *Taylor,* 157–58, 165.

48. Shalhope, *Taylor,* 168–69, 175; Newmyer, *Story,* 37, 38, 53, 55, 63, 161–62, 313, 403.

49. Robert Remini, *The Election of Andrew Jackson* (New York, 1963), 53–61.

50. Robert Remini, *Andrew Jackson and the Course of American Democracy* (New York, 1984), chaps. 1, 2.

51. 6 Pet. 515 (1832).

52. On commercial law, see Swift v. Tyson, 16 Pet. 1 (1842); regarding admiralty, see Propeller Genesee Chief v. Fitzhugh, 12 How. 443 (1851).

53. Newmyer, *Story*, 217–36.

54. 11 Pet. 420 (1837).

55. 4 Wheat. 518 (1819).

56. New York v. Miln, 11 Peters 102 (1837).

57. 12 How. 299 (1851).

58. Catron to Andrew Jackson, February 5, 1838, as paraphrased in Carl B. Swisher, *The Taney Period, 1836–64* (New York, 1974), 64.

59. William Nelson, "The Impact of the Antislavery Movement upon Styles of Judicial Reasoning in Nineteenth Century America," *Harvard Law Review* 87 (1974): 513–66.

60. 15 Pet. 449 (1841).

61. U.S. v. The . . . Amistad, 15 Pet. 518 (1841).

62. 10 How. 82 (1851).

63. 19 How. 393 (1857).

64. Newmyer, *Story*, chap. 6.

65. Oliver Wendell Holmes, Jr., "John Marshall," in Holmes, *Collected Legal Papers* (New York, 1920), 267–68.

66. *The New Science of Giambattista Vico*, trans. Thomas G. Bergin and Max H. Fisch (Ithaca, N.Y., 1984), 343.

States' Rights North and South in Antebellum America

Paul Finkelman

I n 1934 Arthur Schlesinger, Sr., asserted that the history of "state rights agitation . . . must always be studied in its relation to time and circumstances." Schlesinger argued that the "state rights doctrine has never had any real vitality independent of underlying conditions of vast social, economic or political significance." He compared the doctrine to a storm shelter, opportunistically used when a tornado approached and abandoned when the danger had passed.[1]

At first glance, Schlesinger's analysis seems plausible. States in every region of antebellum America, at one time or another, sought protection through claims of states' rights, and the ubiquitous nature of the doctrine does make its use appear to have been opportunistic. The New England Federalists opposed the War of 1812 with states' rights arguments when only a few years earlier they had advocated a strong national government. Jefferson and Madison, who had secretly authored states' rights resolutions in response to the Sedition Act of 1798, both modified their commitment to the ideology when they reached the presidency.

But despite the apparent flexibility of the philosophy—and its utility for all sections—careful analysis suggests that the use of states' rights arguments in the antebellum period was not opportunistic. Rather, claims of states' rights were part of the larger matrix of constitutional argument that developed between 1789 and the firing on Fort Sumter.

The antebellum experience demonstrates that states' rights had a profound resonance for pre–Civil War Americans. In a large nation it is natural for some argument of this type to develop when local and regional interests clash with national priorities. For this reason alone states' rights was an acceptable political theory in both the North and the South. The nature of the Union itself, as a republic of states with different interests, needs, and institutions, fostered similar arguments. In pre–Civil War America the place of the states in the Union—their relationship to each other and to the national government—had not been fully determined. Thus states' rights was an evolving concept that was legitimate to political discourse on both sides of the Mason-Dixon line. The doctrine was a useful "shelter" precisely because, within certain limits, it was acceptable to the majority of Americans.

Sectionalism nevertheless affected the use of states' rights arguments. The antebellum South perceived a threat to its institutions from the North and the federal government. Southern states' rights arguments were therefore common and often quite extreme. Northerners also asserted states' rights positions, but these stances seem to have been staked out for tactical purposes, with limited conviction behind them.

Defining States' Rights

"States' rights" is a broad term with many connotations. For antebellum America there were four general applications of states' rights arguments: (1) independent or concurrent state power; (2) the denial of interstate cooperation and comity; (3) state noncooperation with, interference with, interposition with, or nullification of federal law; and (4) the assertion of a state's right to secede from the Union. During the antebellum period all of these states' rights positions were taken by some states.

Independent State Power

At the least controversial level states' rights simply meant the right of a state to pursue its own interests independent of, or concurrently with, the federal government. States claimed concurrent jurisdiction over taxation, navigation, commerce, and economic regulation, unless there was an explicit federal legislative or constitutional prohibition. The Supreme Court upheld many of these claims. Thus a state could require the use of local pilots to bring ships into a harbor but could not grant a monopoly for shipping in interstate commerce.[2] A state could build canals and charge tolls for their use, thereby legitimately affecting interstate commerce, but could not build a bridge that would block interstate traffic.[3] Although constitutionally prohibited from levying duties on goods from other states, a state could prohibit altogether certain articles of commerce.[4] At times, the Court welcomed state laws that supplemented federal statutes in order to further their enforcement.[5] However, a state could not complicate the enforcement of a federal statute with supplementary legislation.[6] Nor could a state impose a tax on a federal agency, because as John Marshall reminded Maryland authorities, "the power to tax involves the power to destroy."[7] Decisions on commerce and taxation may have vexed losing parties, but they were generally accepted.[8] Few Americans made strong states' rights arguments against rational standards for commercial regulation enforced by the Supreme Court.[9]

State Secession

At the other extreme of the states' rights spectrum was the claim that a state had a right to leave the Union voluntarily. New England Federalists advocated secession during the War of 1812. This position garnered little sympathy there, however, and was abandoned with the end of the war. Secession was never again seriously advocated in the North. Garrisonian abolitionists demanded "No Union with Slaveowners" more to attract attention than to gain support for secession: Garrisonian support for the Union after Fort Sumter shows that the slogan was a rhetorical tool in the war against slavery and not indicative of an actual goal.

For many southerners, on the other hand, the idea of secession—and ultimately the desire for it—was a powerful intellectual and political force. The concept of secession helps differentiate northern and southern constitutional thought, development, and action. Arthur Bestor has cogently argued, "Secession was the *alternative* to, not the proposed *outcome* of, the constitutional program that proslavery forces advocated, in the name of state sovereignty, during the controversy over slavery in the territories."[10] But what is significant is that the South viewed secession as a viable—indeed, an inevitable—alternative, whereas the North did not. From the very beginning of the nation the South believed in a right to secede if the national government threatened slavery. The peculiar institution led the South to have a peculiar commitment to the Union.

Even before the Union was solidified, southerners suggested that they might secede. During the drafting of the Articles of Confederation South Carolina's Thomas Lynch declared, "If it is debated, whether their slaves are their property, there is an end of the confederation."[11] Throughout the Philadelphia convention the southerners claimed that without substantial protection for slavery they would not join the Union. North Carolina's William Davie threatened that his state would "never confederate" unless slaves were counted for representation. Charles Cotesworth Pinckney claimed that a prohibition of the African slave trade would be "an exclusion of S. Carola from the Union."[12] Only southerners talked of leaving the convention or of not accepting the Constitution if they did not get their way.

After 1820 "Southerners repeatedly threatened to secede." During the Nullification Crisis of 1832–33 South Carolina took the theory to the brink of reality. In 1850 southern disunion conventions were thwarted only by the Compromise. After 1854 southerners warned that a Republican victory would lead to secession, and in 1860–61 they acted on their threat. Northerners reacted to this turn of events with surprise, because "the simple fact was that the disunion alarm had been sounded so often that only a few were willing to heed it any longer."[13]

The result of secession, as many had long predicted, was civil war. That is no doubt why most Americans—North and South—resisted carrying states' rights arguments to their ultimate logic. However, in the antebellum period two other manifestations of states' rights, leading to but not reaching secession, were acceptable. These were interstate noncooperation and the denial of interstate comity and state opposition to federal law. There were a number of areas of public policy, almost all of them related to slavery, in which states on both sides of the Mason-Dixon line applied these theories.[14] Some of these, such as the personal liberty laws of the North in response to the federal Fugitive Slave Acts and the problem of comity and the interstate transit of slaves, have been examined in great detail.[15] Less studied, but equally important for an understanding of antebellum states' rights, are the southern treatment of northern free blacks and the responses of southern and northern governors to requests for extraditions of persons charged with slavery-related crimes. Both subjects reveal the manner in which states' rights arguments were used in the North and South. They also demonstrate, not surprisingly, that states' rights was far more important to the South than the North.

Slaves, Free Blacks, and Interstate Noncooperation

The nature of the federal Union dictated that the states should go out of their way to respect each other's laws and institutions. Harmony within the Union did not simply require peaceful relations between the national government and the states. It also required that the states treat each other with dignity and understanding. As one judge argued on the eve of the Civil War:

> The relations of the different States of the Union towards each other are of a much closer and more positive nature than those between foreign nations towards each other. For many purposes they are one nation; war between them is legally impossible; and this comity, impliedly recognized by the law of nations, ripens, in the compact cementing these States, into an express conventional obligation, which is not to be enforced by an appeal to arms, but to be recognized and enforced by the judicial tribunals.[16]

This need for mutual respect was understood in the 1780s. The Philadelphia framers were acutely aware of the need to provide mechanisms for avoiding interstate conflicts and for resolving them if they did arise. Resolution of interstate conflicts could be accomplished by federal legislation or resort to theoretically impartial federal courts. Article IV of the Constitution was designed to avoid such conflicts.

Article IV required that the states give "Full Faith and Credit" to the laws and judicial decisions of other states and that states grant the same privileges and immunities to citizens of other states that they would give to their own citizens. Under this article a fugitive from justice was to be returned to the scene of the crime on request of the state governor, and fugitive slaves were to be returned on the claim of their owners. Except for this last clause, article IV did not directly deal with slavery. Nevertheless, the existence of slavery in some states, and the prohibition of it in others, undermined the harmony in the Union that article IV was designed to produce.[17]

129

Interstate Comity: Privileges and Immunities and the Rights of Northern Free Blacks in the South

The privileges-and-immunities clause required, at a minimum, that citizens of other states be treated with dignity and respect. This is one area of law in which southern states were markedly unwilling to fulfill any constitutional obligations to the North if the citizens in question were free blacks.[18]

The privileges-and-immunities clause of the Constitution evolved from a similar clause in the Articles of Confederation, which provided: "The better to secure and perpetuate mutual friendship and intercourse among the people of the different states in this union, the free inhabitants of each of these states, paupers, vagabonds and fugitives from Justice excepted, shall be entitled to all privileges and immunities of free citizens in the several states; and the people of each state shall have free ingress and regress to and from any other state."[19] When asked to approve the articles, South Carolina proposed inserting the word "white" in front of "free inhabitants." In the Congress only one other state, probably Georgia, supported this position.[20] No one raised the issue when the clause was discussed in Philadelphia. By this time Massachusetts, New Hampshire, Pennsylvania, Connecticut, and Rhode Island had taken steps to end slavery.[21] In a number of states free blacks could vote, own property, and exercise other rights of citizens.[22] Thus, when the privileges-and-immunities clause was adopted, it must have been clear to southern delegates that free blacks might be included in the word "citizen." As a House committee concluded in 1842: "The Constitution of the United States, therefore, at its adoption, found the colored man of Massachusetts a citizen of Massachusetts, and entitled him, as such, to all the privileges and immunities of a citizen of the Several States."[23]

Despite the obvious obligation to respect the rights of black citizens from the North, southern states invariably refused to do so. Most southern states prohibited the in-migration of free blacks. Although a blatant rejection of the privileges-and-immunities clause, this prohibition was of minor importance, since few northern blacks wished to move to the South. However, many free blacks working in the merchant marine entered the slave states for short periods of time when their ships landed in southern ports, and other free blacks went South for temporary employment. These blacks often faced harsh punishments under draconican laws known as the Negro Seamen's Acts. The nine slave states along the coast from Virginia to Texas subjected free black sailors to various forms of harassment. Seven of the states imprisoned black sailors upon their arrival. Ship captains bringing free black sailors into these states would be charged for the cost of their maintenance in the jails; if the bill was not paid the black sailor would be sold into temporary or permanent slavery to whoever would pay the debt. These statutes applied to blacks on foreign as well as domestic ships.[24]

The Negro Seamen's Acts first came before the courts in 1822, when Charleston authorities imprisoned Henry Elkison, a British subject. Elkison applied to U.S. Supreme Court Justice William Johnson for a writ of habeas corpus. Johnson, who was riding circuit at the time, found the act "unconstitutional and void, and that every arrest made under it subjects the parties making it to an action of trespass." However, Johnson decided that he lacked the power to issue a writ of habeas corpus. Instead, he issued a writ of homine replegiando, although he doubted it would have any effect on Elkison's imprisonment.[25]

The southern position on black seamen rested on a complex amalgam of states' rights and racism. In *Elkison*, attorney Benjamin F. Hunt argued that under its police powers South Carolina could protect itself from free blacks, because to do otherwise would make the state "guilty of an act, tending to self-destruction." Hunt admitted that Congress had "an exclusive right" to regulate commerce, but he denied that South Carolina's law infringed on congressional power. Rather, he compared his state's law to a New York law allowing the quarantine of vessels and individuals. For South Carolina, the "contagion" feared was not the spread of disease but the spread of free blacks.[26]

Hunt boldly claimed that slave states were exempt from certain constitutional provisions because the federal government could not interfere with any law that might affect the domestic institutions of the state. South Carolina's right to regulate free blacks from other states "was one, which from its nature, under the peculiar circumstances of her slave population, she could not and has not surrendered to the Federal Government."[27]

Nor could other states expect favorable treatment. Hunt callously asserted that South Carolina had only "require[d] . . . free persons of colour, when they arrive, to take up their abode in a very airy and healthy part of the city, until the vessel in which they came is ready to depart." This was surely an odd way to describe the city jail, but it did underscore South Carolina's unwillingness to accept that blacks might be citizens in Great Britain or the North. Under South Carolina law free blacks could not sue for writs of habeas corpus or homine replegiando but were "only entitled to the writ of *ravishment of ward,* sued out by guardian."[28] Thus, no matter what status a black might have in another state or country, South Carolina would ignore that status. States' rights overrode any constitutional powers of Congress or obligations to other states.

The South Carolina law also threatened international relations: Elkison, after all, was a British subject. However, South Carolina was unconcerned by any international ramifications of the law. Hunt argued that a treaty between Great Britain and the United States "does not interfere with the perfect right of the State" to enact a black seamen's law because the "treaty making power, can make no stipulation which shall impair the rights, which by the constitution are reserved 'to the States respectively, or to the people.' "[29]

The greatest danger from South Carolina's defense of its law was to the Union itself. Hunt's co-counsel, Isaac E. Holmes, shocked Justice Johnson by declaring that "if a dissolution of the Union must be the alternative, he was ready to meet it."[30] This position reflected a willingness of southerners to threaten secession in response to perceived assaults on their states' rights. Skillfully, Johnson turned this argument inside out, concluding that South Carolina's law was unconstitutional because "it is altogether irreconcilable with the powers of the general government; . . . it necessarily compromits the public peace, and tends to embroil us with, if not separate us from, our sister states; in short, . . . it leads to a dissolution of the Union and implies a direct attack upon the sovereignty of the United States."[31]

Despite Johnson's ruling, South Carolina's Negro Seamen's Act remained on the books until secession, and eight other states enacted similar laws.[32] In 1839 the Massachusetts legislature formally condemned the black seamen's acts and demanded their repeal, declaring that it was the "paramount duty of the state to protect its citizens in the enjoyment and exercise of all their rights."[33] In 1842 over 150 Bostonians asked Congress to prevent the imprisonment of northern black seamen. The petitioners, including many conservative businessmen, asked Congress to "render effectual in their behalf the privileges of citizenship secured by the Constitution of the United States." A House committee vainly recommended favorable action on the petition.[34] In 1844 Massachusetts sent Samuel Hoar to Charleston and Henry Hubbard to New Orleans as official state commissioners to negotiate a compromise on the issue. The missions were fiascoes. Hoar spent a night in Charleston before officials told him they could not guarantee his safety. The South Carolina legislature declared that Hoar was an "emissary sent . . . with the avowed purpose of interfering with" South Carolina's "institutions, and disturbing her peace" and gratuitously requested that the governor expel Hoar from the state. By the time this resolution was passed he had already left the state. In Louisiana Hubbard found an even less congenial atmosphere. Faced with the real prospect of being lynched, Hubbard left New Orleans on the same day he arrived. Subsequent communications from Massachusetts to these states were fruitless, and similar attempts by Maine to achieve a compromise also failed.[35]

South Carolina was the only state to flout a federal official overtly on this issue, but it was hardly the only state to adopt states' rights arguments in defense of restrictions on free black seamen. After the abortive Hoar and Hubbard missions, Georgia jumped to the defense of South Carolina and Louisiana. In an analysis that anticipated Chief Justice Roger B. Taney's *Dred Scott* opinion, the Georgia legislature asserted that all the states, "in the exercise of their sovereign rights," could determine for themselves who was a citizen and who was not. The southern states "did not regard" free blacks as citizens, a fact "of which the authorities of Massachusetts could not have been ignorant at the time of her aggressions." The legislature declared that "the people of South Carolina, Louisiana, Georgia, as well as all the States, claim the right of thinking for themselves." In doing so, they would choose to reject any claims of citizenship, and obligations of comity, toward free blacks from other states.[36]

For the South, states' rights and state sovereignty meant more than just the right of a state to determine citizenship for itself; it also meant the right to dictate to other states who could be a citizen, within the meaning of the U.S. Constitution. In other words, the South defined states' rights as the right of a state to decline to recognize the status of citizens from other states. Ironically, starting in the 1830s northern states adopted what was almost a mirror image of this policy. By treating slaves from the South as if they were free persons, northern states used states' rights to broaden the privileges of citizenship to include all persons.[37]

133

Interstate Comity: Rendition of Fugitives from Justice

Tied to the rejection of black citizenship was the refusal of some southern governors to approve the extradition of whites accused of kidnapping free blacks. Similarly, some free-state governors refused to extradite persons accused of helping slaves escape. Governors in both sections used states' rights arguments to explain their actions. There was, nevertheless, a striking difference in the ways these arguments were applied.

Northerners used states' rights arguments where they were convenient, but without any real conviction. Thus northern governors and legislatures were willing to turn to the president, the Congress, or the federal courts to vindicate their policies. With the exception of one case argued late in the antebellum period,[38] southerners rarely turned to the national government to solve interstate disputes. To have done so would have meant acknowledging the supremacy of the national government—something that ran counter to southern states' right theory. Southern states' rights responses also differed from those of the North in their appeal to other states. For example, during a lengthy dispute with New York, Virginia appealed for support from other slave states. Resolutions from South Carolina, Maryland, Kentucky, and elsewhere followed. Northern states never sought or presented such a united front against the South.

Throughout the antebellum period claims of states' rights, complicated by slavery and race, undermined the Constitution's extradition clause. Like the privileges-and-immunities clause, the constitutional obligation for the extradition of accused criminals was found in article IV, which declared: "A Person charged in any State with Treason, Felony, or other Crime, who shall flee from Justice, and be found in another State, shall on Demand of the executive Authority of the State from which he fled, be delivered up, to be removed to the State having Jurisdiction of the Crime."[39]

Virginia-Pennsylvania Extradition Controversy

The extradition clause implied a *pro forma* procedure between state governors. However, the process did not always work smoothly. The first conflict over extradition arose in 1791, when Governor Beverly Randolph of Virginia refused to extradite three Virginians charged with kidnapping a free black in Pennsylvania.[40]

Randolph turned Pennsylvania governor Thomas Mifflin's request for the extradition of the kidnappers over to Virginia's attorney general, James Innis. Innis rejected the extradition requisition on technical and procedural grounds. But he also raised an important states' rights argument. He noted that the kidnapping of a free black, under Virginia law, amounted only to a trespass "as between the parties" and "but to the breach of the peace" between the state and the defendants. Innis implied that Virginia did not have to recognize a felony in Pennsylvania unless it was also considered a felony in Virginia. He also concluded that "every free man in Virginia is entitled to the unmolested enjoyment of his liberty" unless deprived of it by federal law, the Constitution, or Virginia law. Since the kidnappers had not run afoul of any of these sources of law, they could not be returned to Pennsylvania. Instead, Innis suggested that the kidnappers be tried in Pennsylvania *prior* to their extradition; "if found guilty, and their personal presence should be necessary for their punishment, it will be then time enough to make a demand of them."[41]

Unsatisfied with this response, Mifflin brought the issue before President Washington, who eventually turned the matter over to Congress. In February 1793 Congress responded with "An Act respecting Fugitives from Justice, and Persons Escaping from the Service of Their Masters."[42] This law provided procedures for the extradition of accused and convicted criminals and for the return of fugitive slaves.

Noncooperation, North and South

From 1793 until the 1830s the criminal extradition process raised few interstate problems. However, after the mid-1830s the extradition of fugitives from justice, complicated by slavery, created sectional tensions. The most prominent cases involved northern governors who refused to extradite abolitionists and fugitive slaves to the South. However, southern governors also refused to cooperate in extradition cases. A brief examination of southern noncooperation will illuminate the protracted controversies and states' rights issues that developed out of northern noncooperation.

135

As already noted, Governor Randolph refused to extradite alleged kidnappers in 1791. In 1845–46 Virginia refused Ohio's requisition for a group of Virginians who had kidnapped white abolitionists in Ohio and had forcibly taken them to Virginia, where they were tried for allegedly trying to steal slaves.[43] In the 1840s and 1850s governors in Missouri refused to extradite whites accused of kidnapping free blacks in Illinois and enslaving them in Missouri.[44] Similarly, in the 1850s Virginia authorities refused to aid in the capture and extradition of men who kidnapped free blacks in Ohio.[45]

Northern governors and legislatures protested these results. The complaints of Pennsylvania's governor in the 1790s went to Virginia officials and to President Washington. The Illinois governor wrote long letters of protest to his Missouri counterpart when the latter refused to extradite the kidnappers.[46] Northern officials were often as concerned about the return of kidnapped blacks as they were about prosecuting the kidnappers. In 1840 New York adopted legislation empowering the governor to appoint agents to seek out and rescue kidnapped blacks.[47] Even Illinois, a state not noted for its sympathetic approach to black rights, adopted legislation authorizing the governor to appoint agents to secure the liberty of kidnapped blacks.[48] Between 1850 and 1860 Ohio spent over two thousand dollars and hired counsel in three states in a partially successful effort to help members of the Polly family regain their freedom after they were kidnapped and taken to Kentucky and Virginia.[49]

Northern political leaders were often disappointed in their negotiations over the return of kidnappers or kidnapped free blacks. They did not, however, resort to threats or fulminations when kidnap victims were not returned and extradition requisitions were rejected. Such a response would have been out of character with the style of northern politics: threats of retaliation or disunion were incompatible with northern support for a perpetual union and a relatively strong national government. In addition, northerners understood that quiet negotiations could be more productive than denunciation.[50] This behavior was in marked contrast to southern responses to northern refusals to extradite accused "slave stealers."

Between 1837 and 1845 Georgia, Louisiana, and Virginia attempted to extradite from Maine and New York free black sailors, fugitive slaves, and whites who were charged with slavery-related crimes. These attempts, frustrated by the governors of Maine and New York, led to con-

136

troversies that reached national politics. In the late 1850s the problem reemerged in a dispute between Ohio and Kentucky that reached the Supreme Court.[51] In these controversies northerners often took states' rights positions, whereas southerners often cloaked themselves in the rhetoric of nationalism. The ironies were not lost on Governor William H. Seward of New York, who told the governor of Virginia: "I must be permitted to express, with all due deference, my belief that if this question had arisen in any case not supposed to involve a peculiar interest of Virginia, that state would have been very unwilling to maintain a construction of the Constitution, which, if it is not altogether misunderstood on my part, is incompatible with the true dignity and sovereignty of the states."[52]

The Maine-Georgia Controversy

In May 1837 two Maine seamen, Daniel Philbrook and Edward Kelleran, helped a slave named Atticus escape from Georgia to Maine. Atticus's owner immediately went to Maine, found Atticus, and brought him back to Savannah. Georgia's governor was not so lucky in his attempts to have Philbrook and Kelleran returned for prosecution. In June Philbrook and Kelleran were indicted for "feloniously inveigling, stealing, and carrying away, a negro man slave."[53] For the next three years the governors of the two states sparred over the fate of the Maine sailors. The case dragged on in a war of resolutions between the states until 1842.

Successive Maine governors, Robert Dunlap, Edward Kent, and John Fairfield, relied on a constricted reading of the Constitution's extradition clause to argue that Philbrook and Kelleran had not "fled" from Georgia but had returned "homeward by the usual route and in the usual time," where they continued to reside openly, and that because they had not been under indictment when they returned home, neither man was "a person charged" with a crime when he left Georgia. The Maine governors denied that their actions resulted from "the nature of the property alleged to have been stolen," but they also made it clear that "the crime of simple larceny in stealing a man, alleged to be a slave," was not one recognized by Maine. Finally, the governors made strong states' rights arguments, asserting their right, as state executives, to protect their cit-

137

izens from "a foreign tribunal" and "unknown judges." Although Kent acknowledged that "the absolute sovereignty of the State is qualified and impaired" by the Constitution and that interstate relations were not analogous to "the intercourse between independent sovereignties," he nevertheless remained unwilling to extradite the two seamen.[54]

The responses of successive Georgia governors, William Schley, George Gilmer, and Charles McDonald, were also similar. Schley expressed his "utter astonishment" at Maine's position, pointedly asking, "Is the Governor of Maine better qualified to determine what constitutes felony in *Georgia*, than the Governor and judicial authorities of Georgia?" Similarly, Gilmer disputed the narrow interpretation of the words "flee from justice" and accused the Maine governor of deliberately violating his obligations to the U.S. Constitution. Gilmer asserted that extradition was never asked "as a matter of favor, to be granted according to" a governor's "discretion," but was rather a "demand" to be "made as a matter of right," and that the Constitution's extradition clause "gives no room for the exercise of will or caprice of the Governor, or his yielding to public opinion or feelings around him."[55]

Even more important, however, was Maine's refusal to fulfill its constitutional obligations because the offense at issue involved stealing a slave. Gilmer warned that this selective implementation of the Constitution would lead to retaliation. If Maine continued "to protect persons from punishment who take from the citizens of Georgia their slave property," then Georgia "must necessarily protect the rights of its citizens from the danger to which their slave property will be thus exposed from Mainers coming from Maine into her ports." Gilmer added ominously, "I shall not attempt to trace out the consequences to which such a state of things must lead."[56]

Georgia's legislature believed that Maine was violating "common courtesy," "justice, policy, patriotism," and the state's "imperative duty" to "comply with the laws of and Constitution of the country." Such actions "must inevitably lead to a speedy dissolution of the Union." Georgia considered retaliation but, in 1838, saw few options. It "would be clearly unconstitutional" for Georgia to close its "ports against the citizens of Maine," "declare a non-intercourse with her citizens," "seize upon the persons" of Maine's "citizens," or "levy upon their property." The legislature hoped to avoid a "violation of the Federal Compact," which would lead to "civil conflict." But the legislature also thought that "this dreadful alternative" would "inevitably" be "resorted to as a matter of self-defense" if "the unhallowed example of the Governor of Maine be followed by the authorities of the other States of the North."[57]

Georgia considered imposing "a quarantine upon all vessels" from Maine, "in consequence of viewing the doctrine of abolition as a moral and political pestilence, which if not checked will spread devastation and ruin over the land." The legislature resisted this impulse, however, and settled for condemning the actions of Maine's governor as "*dangerous* to the rights of the people of Georgia" and "*directly* in *violation* of the *plain letter* of the Constitution." The resolutions declared that Georgia had joined the Union "for the *better* protection of *her own*" rights, and when this protection was lost "by the *faithlessness*" of another state, then Georgia was "no longer *bound by any obligations to the common compact*" and was free "to seek and provide protection for her own people in her own way." If Maine did not return Philbrook and Kelleran, the resolution directed Georgia's governor to call a statewide convention "to devise the course of her [Georgia's] future policy, and provide all necessary safeguards for the protection of her people."[58]

In September 1839 Gilmer received a resolution from the South Carolina legislature, affirming its belief in the "solemn duty of every member of this confederacy to protect and defend the national compact and to insist on a strict and faithful observance of all its provisions by every sovereign party thereto." South Carolina had received "no official information of the facts in the case." Nevertheless, the Palmetto State was quick to come to the aid of another slave state. This communication must have gratified Georgia's political leadership, which up to this time had been enormously frustrated by the refusal of officials in Maine to extradite the two sailors.[59]

Perhaps it was this support from South Carolina that led Georgia to depart from a pattern of southern states' rights behavior by appealing to the national government. In December 1839 the Georgia legislature called on Congress to empower federal judges to issue arrest warrants for fugitives from justice upon applications of state governors and to authorize federal marshals to arrest fugitives and return them to the state seeking them. Governor McDonald asked Georgia's congressional delegation to submit the resolutions to Congress.[60]

This task made Georgia's congressmen uncomfortable. They doubted that Congress had the power to alter the process outlined in the Constitution, by which governors were to act on extradition cases. The congressmen reminded their governor that "the Federal Government is one of limited jurisdiction" that could "exercise no power . . . not expressly granted by the Constitution." The Georgia congressmen inadvertently conceded the point of the Maine governors, that the extradition clause was "merely directory to the States." The congressmen believed that the Constitution gave "no power to Congress to act in the matter and therefore no power to make any law to enforce it." They were also fearful of placing Georgia's "great sovereign and constitutional right . . . under the absolute control and decision" of a federal judge. Under the proposed scheme, laws that were "absolutely essential to protect the sacred rights" of Georgia's "citizens in their slave property" would be enforced by federal courts. Would Georgia "consent to place such power in the hands of a Judge, yea, perhaps of a Jury, whose judgment might, and probably would be swayed by his, or their, own prejudices, or controlled by the strong feelings and prejudices of all in and around the Court?" The Georgia congressmen suggested that the refusal of a governor to approve an extradition request would be a "just cause of war," but they were unwilling to submit the problem to the national legislature or the courts.[61] Though Georgia's representatives in the House demurred, Wilson Lumpkin, one of Georgia's senators, did in fact present the resolution to the Senate; it was printed and sent to the Judiciary Committee, which buried it.[62] Lumpkin may have acted because as a senator he felt an obligation to respond to the requests of the state legislature that elected him to his office.

The Maine-Georgia controversy indicated the potential for disruption that criminal extradition could pose for the Union. While proclaiming support for the Constitution, three Maine governors refused to abide by one of its demands. Similarly, Georgia professed its unending love for the Union and the Constitution[63] while declaring that it would separate itself from both, over what was arguably a trivial incident. In response to northern states' rights arguments, that is, Georgia threatened secession. Equally significant was the response of the Georgia congressional delegation. Unwilling to place the issue before Congress, the representatives suggested that the answer to the problem might be war. This kind of response typifies one distinction between northern and southern uses of the states' rights doctrine. Southerners were quick to threaten secession (or even civil war) and to tie secession to other states' rights arguments.

No northern politicians made such threats or even considered secession as an alternative to interstate or state-federal disputes.

New York and Its Southern Neighbors

The Maine-Georgia controversy was followed by similar ones between New York and Louisiana, Virginia, and Georgia. The controversies resulted from Governor William H. Seward's refusal to extradite fugitive slaves, free blacks, and whites accused of slavery-related crimes.

The New York-Louisiana controversy was short-lived. In 1839 the governor of Louisiana sought the extradition of a black for stealing clothing, a trunk, and twenty dollars. Seward thought this was "a suspicious looking case" and believed it was "probably another way of arresting a fugitive from *service.*" Seward refused to issue the arrest warrant, and Louisiana let the matter drop.[64]

The New York-Virginia controversy, on the other hand, festered for seven years. In 1839 three free black sailors helped a slave escape from Norfolk to New York City. The slave's owner immediately went to New York and successfully recovered his property. The governor of Virginia then demanded the extradition of the three black sailors. Seward refused to comply with this request, in part for technical reasons and in part because he refused to recognize the crime of "slave stealing." For the next four years the governors and legislators in both states asserted claims of state sovereignty, states' rights, and constitutional obligation in letters, speeches, resolutions, and statutes.

In 1839 Virginia's lieutenant governor, Henry L. Hopkins, argued that the sovereignty of the states required that New York respect Virginia's extradition requisition. To do otherwise would be "inconsistent with the true relations, rights, and duties of the States, and . . . disturb the general harmony of the country." Hopkins asserted that no one outside of Virginia "can rightfully interfere" with the "municipal regulations" of the state. He warned Seward that *"Virginia knows her rights and will at all times maintain them."*[65]

Seward responded by declaring that he did "not question the constitutional right of a state to make such a penal code as it shall deem necessary or expedient." He readily "admitted the sovereignty of the several states," on which Hopkins had so "strenuously insist[ed]." Seward declared that "no person can maintain more firmly than I do the

141

principle that the states are sovereign and independent." With a touch of irony he pointed out, "I have at least believed that my non-compliance with the requisition made upon me in the present case would be regarded as maintaining the equal sovereignty and independence of this state, and by necessary consequence those of all the other states."[66]

Like the Georgia-Maine controversy, this one led to threats of secession. In December 1839 Virginia's governor, David Campbell, accused Seward of following "the fanatic doctrines" of the abolitionists that "jeopardize the tranquility and hazard the dissolution of the Union." He warned, "It is impossible that the Union can continue long" if the North ignored southern law.[67] In January 1840 Seward expressed regret "that a construction of the constitution manifestly necessary to maintain the sovereignty of this State, and the personal rights of her citizens, should be regarded by the Executive of Virginia as justifying, in any contingency, a menace of secession for the Union."[68]

The controversy between the two states soon passed beyond letters, speeches, and resolutions. In May 1840, in a show of support for Seward, the New York legislature passed two personal liberty laws. The first guaranteed a jury trial to all persons seized as fugitive slaves in New York; the second authorized the governor to appoint agents and spend state money to help rescue kidnapped free blacks.[69] Neither law was directed at Virginia, but both indicated New York's resolve to maintain the integrity of its legal system in the face of southern demands. New York asserted its states' rights to protect its inhabitants.

In 1841 Virginia escalated the controversy by sending letters to all other slave states, asking for their support against New York. By this means Virginia sought to make a dispute between two states into a sectional schism. Seward soon received condemnatory resolutions from Mississippi, Alabama, and South Carolina, but New York, meanwhile, made no attempt to enlist the support of the North.[70]

Even more ominous was Virginia's adoption of a law that placed restrictions on all New York ships or New Yorkers sailing to Virginia. The law was passed in February 1841 but would not go into effect until May 1842. Virginia's governor was empowered to suspend the law if New York turned over the three black sailors and also repealed its 1840 jury trial law.[71]

Virginia's law was extraordinary. It undermined states' rights and federalism by holding one state hostage to what Seward described as "onerous and offensive" laws. In March 1841 Seward, taking the high road of federalism and constitutional law, asserted that New York would continue to honor constitutionally sound extradition requests from Virginia. He asserted "that measures of retaliation, injury and reprisal, are deemed equally unworthy the dignity of this State and inconsistent with its federal relations." Instead, Seward declared that the laws and Constitution of the United States provided "ample remedies for any injuries the citizens of this State may suffer from the unconstitutional proceedings on the part of Virginia."[72]

In a letter to yet another Virginia governor, in April 1841, Seward admitted that Virginia was "sovereign within her territory, in the enactment of her own laws," but denied that Virginia "could extend her legislative power" to dictate the actions of a governor of New York. Seward blamed Virginia's leaders for exaggerating the controversy by calling it "a flagrant invasion of the rights of that Commonwealth" that would justify secession. Seward accused Virginia of violating New York's sovereignty by offering "large pecuniary rewards" to anyone who would "seize, within the jurisdiction of New York and in violation of its laws, and convey to Virginia" the three free blacks. Seward pointed out that his Virginia counterpart "addressed public circular letters to" the slave states "inviting them to make common cause against New York." In addition, the Virginia legislature passed "an act attempting to impose invidious restrictions and onerous impositions upon" New York citizens in order to compel the governor to change his mind and the legislature to repeal a statute. Seward concluded by asserting that "there is no good reason to believe that the interests of the citizens of this State are less carefully regarded by its Legislature, than the supposed interests of the citizens of Virginia are by the General Assembly of that Commonwealth."[73] This analysis, in short, blamed Virginia for violating New York's state rights.

In October Seward attacked Virginia's inspection law, which would go into effect in 1842. Seward thought the law clearly violated the U.S. Constitution. He indignantly denounced the notion that Virginia could dictate to New York what laws that state should pass and what actions its executive should take. He noted that if Virginia could "make discriminating regulations" of commerce, "New York and any other state may exercise like powers." This, Seward asserted, "would produce anarchy and end in dissolution" of the Union. This was not a threat of secession but an argument against the constitutionality of Virginia's law. Seward concluded that "inasmuch as the parties are equals, if a reconciliation is to be accomplished, Virginia ought to make the first advance."[74]

In his 1842 annual message Seward recommended that the state challenge Virginia's inspection law in the Supreme Court. He also noted that a similar controversy had arisen between New York and Georgia. Like Virginia, Georgia had also passed legislation that discriminated against northern ships. In February South Carolina notified New York that, in sympathy with Virginia, it too had passed restrictive legislation directed at New York ships. In August Seward unsuccessfully requested authority from the Democratically controlled legislature to test the Virginia law in federal court. At the end of the year Seward left office, with no resolution of the issues. The new Democratic governor repudiated most of Seward's positions but did not take any steps to extradite the three sailors. Meanwhile, attempts to repeal the jury trial law failed. Defenders of the existing statute argued that a repeal would be a humiliation and a capitulation to Virginia, which had been so unfriendly to New York. The Democrats ignored these arguments, and the House passed a repeal measure in 1843, though the legislature adjourned before the Democratic majority in the Senate could act.[75] There were no further attempts at repeal, and the law remained on the books.

The Southern States' Rights Dilemma

Although Seward used states' rights arguments against both Virginia and Georgia, he was willing to abandon them when necessary. Thus he sought permission from his legislature to challenge in federal court the Virginia and Georgia inspection laws. He suggested to his Virginia counterpart that the problem of extradition might be solved by a constitutional amendment. Moreover, he also made use of nationalist arguments to attack the inspection laws. These arguments reveal what we already know about Seward and most other northern leaders: they fundamentally supported the Constitution and the Union, as would be made clear in the years 1861 to 1865.

For southerners, the extradition conflicts posed both practical and theoretical problems. Virginia tried two methods of retaliation. In 1841 New York sought the extradition of an indicted forger named Robert Curry. Virginia's governor, Thomas Gilmer, did not deny the "regularity of the requisition" but refused to honor it until Seward returned the three black sailors.[76] Gilmer's retaliation was ineffective for two reasons. First, Virginia had no interest in harboring a fugitive forger. There was no political reason to do so. More important, however, by declining to return Curry, Gilmer in effect acknowledged the force of Seward's position that governors had discretion in extradition cases. Shortly after he took office Gilmer's successor, John M. Patton, ordered Curry returned to New York.[77] However, by this time the damage to Virginia's theoretical position had been done.

Virginia and Georgia also tried to retaliate against New York and northern shippers. But such legislation, as Seward had pointed out, could be a two-edged sword. Even without northern retaliation, Virginia and Georgia faced more disadvantages from the disruption of commerce than any advantages they might have gained from preventing the escape of slaves.

In the mid-1840s Georgia and Virginia abandoned their efforts at retaliation.[78] Neither state wished to take the issues involved to the Supreme Court, because this step would have violated their sense of state sovereignty and states' rights. Seward, on the other hand, was anxious to challenge Virginia's inspection law, but he never had the opportunity to do so. His willingness to litigate the issue suggests that his commitment to states' rights differed from that of his southern counterparts: he was willing to abide by a Supreme Court decision. Seward probably expected the Court to deny the constitutionality of Virginia's inspection law, a decision that would have benefited his state; any cost to states' rights theory would have been marginal to New York, because it was unlikely that New York would have wanted to restrict interstate commerce. On the other hand, if Virginia had taken New York to court and won, Virginia would have then set the precedent that the Supreme Court could order state governors to act. This outcome was intolerable to most states' rights proponents.

Kentucky v. Dennison

In 1860 the staunchly states' right governor of Kentucky did take such a case to the Supreme Court, in *Kentucky v. Dennison* (1861).[79] In this case two successive governors of Ohio, Salmon P. Chase and William Dennison, refused to extradite a free black, Willis Lago, who was wanted for "stealing" a slave in Kentucky. The Ohio attorney general thought the indictment was faulty and invalid in Ohio "or wheresoever else the common law prevails." Equally important, what Lago did was not a crime in Ohio "or by the common law."[80]

Governor Beriah Magoffin of Kentucky found this position unpersuasive. Magoffin noted that the Constitution "was the work of slaveholders" and that in 1787 "non-slaveholding states were then the *exception, not the rule.*" Though he did not use the term directly, Magoffin argued that the original intent of the framers was to provide for extradition of people who helped slaves escape. He avoided any discussion of states' rights and state sovereignty. Instead, he accused Ohio of bad faith, violating comity, and "ingratitude" for the time "when Kentuckians ran with alacrity to the rescue of your people against the assaults of Brittish [sic] invaders and their more savage allies."[81] When Dennison refused to change his mind, Magoffin asked the U.S. Supreme Court to order Dennison to extradite Lago.

Kentucky v. Dennison presented a profound dilemma for the Taney Court. The Court in 1861 contained five southerners and two northern doughfaces. It was an overwhelmingly proslavery court, led by a chief justice who "had become privately a bitter sectionalist, seething with anger at 'Northern insult' and 'Northern aggression.' "[82] But though he was sympathetic to Kentucky's position, Taney refused to issue the writ of mandamus directed at Dennison. If he had done so, Taney would have set a precedent that Congress or the Supreme Court had the power to order state executives to act. With a number of states having already declared that they were no longer in the Union, and others threatening to secede, Taney was unwilling to give the Lincoln administration a two-edged sword that could be turned against the South.

Thus a fanatically proslavery chief justice sustained the use of states' rights theory by antislavery governors in Maine, New York, and Ohio. Ironically, this decision was rendered at the precise moment when antislavery politicians were abandoning states' rights for an aggressive nationalism. The leaders of this new antislavery nationalism included Seward and Chase. These men had few regrets about abandoning their states' rights positions: they had been useful rhetorical tools, but they were easily jettisoned.

Executive Discretion and States' Rights

From 1793 until the 1830s the criminal extradition aspects of the 1793 law had raised few interstate problems. However, starting in the 1830s the theory of executive discretion arose, and governors sometimes refused to honor extradition requests from other states. Executive discretion developed out of extradition requisitions that were complicated by slavery and sectional tensions. Once articulated, the theory was used in other cases. Ironically, it is one of the few antebellum states' rights legacies that remained a part of modern constitutional law well beyond the Civil War.[83]

Executive discretion was viable because under a federal system all states are equal. Thus Virginia could not truly make any demands on New York but could only request cooperation and hope for comity.[84] Even the national government lacked the power to force one state to act on a constitutionally protected claim of another state. In disputes between governors the Constitution made the federal government little more than a neutral observer. As Taney concluded in *Dennison*, "If the Governor of Ohio refuses to discharge this duty, there is no power delegated to the General Government, either through the Judicial Department or any other department, to use any coercive means to compel him."[85] In antebellum America, then, interstate disputes could only be negotiated; neither the national government nor a complaining state had the power to force another state to act.

The *Dennison* case revealed the underlying weakness of the states' rights arguments for the South. In *Dennison* Taney had to choose between protecting slavery and protecting states' rights. He chose to protect the latter, in the hope that this result would usually protect the former as well. But this solution did not really safeguard the South. Southern states' rights arguments stemmed from a fear of the national government's interfering with local institutions—the most important of which was slavery. Thus the South sought to preserve its states' rights against the national government.

The North, at least after 1820, never really feared the national government. Northerners were therefore quite willing to challenge southern laws in federal court. The South, fearing the effects of a strong national government, almost always resisted an appeal to the federal courts. Ironically, in *Dennison*, the one time a southern state brought the states' rights issue to the Supreme Court, the South was in the uncomfortable position of arguing for national supremacy. Oddly enough, the case did not raise the kind of state-federal issues the South feared. Instead, it raised an issue of state equality. The case was one that the South could not win. In protecting executive discretion the Supreme Court supported one of the few aspects of states' rights arguments that the North had subscribed to and that the South found onerous. But had Taney decided in favor of Kentucky, he would have given the national government power to invade the states. Either way, the South lost.

Because of *Dennison*, executive discretion in extradition remained a problematic legacy of antebellum states' right theory for over 125 years. Before 1987 courts consistently declared that in the rendition process "there is no discretion allowed, on inquiry into motives."[86] On the other hand, the courts allowed a number of exceptions to this rule, including bad faith, racial discrimination, or political motivations of the demanding state.[87] Most important, however, all courts recognized that if a governor refused to extradite someone, neither the federal courts, nor the state courts, nor the state legislatures could compel the governor to act. That was the civil rights heritage left by the three Maine governors, William H. Seward, Salmon P. Chase, and William Dennison, and, ironically, by Roger B. Taney.

The legacy of the antebellum extradition controversies remains alive. In 1987 the Supreme Court unanimously held that the federal courts could order a governor to extradite an alleged criminal. In an opinion that for the most part ignored the history of the extradition problem, Justice Thurgood Marshall declared that *"Kentucky v. Dennison* is the product of another time. . . . it may stand no longer."[88]

In his opinion Marshall argued that compliance with an extradition request "is a ministerial duty" that "precludes conflict with essentially discretionary elements of state governance, and eliminates the need for continuing federal supervision of state functions."[89] In overturning this long-standing precedent Marshall may have struck a blow for federal supremacy and the power of the Supreme Court. But it will take future cases to determine if Marshall's opinion is a wise one. It is not hard to imagine that in the future some defendant in a racially or politically motivated prosecution may regret Marshall's opinion and long for the good old days of gubernatorial discretion in the defense of civil rights.

Notes

1. Arthur M. Schlesinger, "The State Rights Fetish," in *New Viewpoints in American History,* ed. Schlesinger (New York, 1934), 234.

2. Cooley v. Board of Port Wardens of the Port of Philadelphia, 12 How. (53 U.S.) 199 (1851); Gibbons v. Ogden, 9 Wheat. (22 U.S.) 1 (1824); Maurice G. Baxter, *The Steamboat Monopoly: Gibbons v. Ogden, 1824* (New York, 1972). Monographic studies of particular Supreme Court cases that came out of the South may help illuminate the contours of a southern constitutional history.

3. Pennsylvania v. Wheeling and Belmont Bridge Co., 13 How. (54 U.S.) 518 (1852); Pennsylvania v. Wheeling and Belmont Bridge Co., 18 How. (59 U.S.) 421 (1856).

4. Cohens v. Virginia, 6 Wheat. 264 (1821) (upholding a conviction for selling federally approved lottery tickets in violation of Virginia law); Groves v. Slaughter, 15 Pet. 449 (1841) (declaring that a state, by appropriate legislation, could prohibit the importation of slaves as articles of commerce); The License Cases, 5 How. 504 (1847) (upholding a state tax on liquor produced in other states on the ground this was part of a state's inherent police power).

5. In Prigg v. Pennsylvania, 16 Pet. (U.S.) 539, 622 (1842) Justice Story asserted that state magistrates ought to enforce the Fugitive Slave Law of 1793. At 625 Story explicitly upheld the right of a state to pass supplementary legislation to aid the enforcement of this law. Story's opinion prohibited only state legislation that would have placed additional burdens on a master capturing a fugitive slave.

6. Ibid., 618. Here Story declared that "where Congress have exercised a power over a particular subject given them by the Constitution, it is not competent for State legislation to add to the provisions of Congress upon that subject." Story reiterates this point at 622–26.

7. McCulloch v. Maryland, 4 Wheat. (17 U.S.) 316 (1819), at 431.

8. The response to *McCulloch* is an exception. Many states and individuals expressed displeasure over this opinion, mostly because of opposition to the Bank of the United States. The annual statutes of the antebellum states contain numerous resolutions attacking banks in general, the Bank of the United States, and *McCulloch.* The search for a distinctive southern constitutional law might include a comparative survey of state legislative resolutions on the bank and other issues.

9. Thus there seems to have been no states' rights response to Story's nationalization of commercial law in Swift v. Tyson, 16 Pet. (U.S.) 1 (1841). Even Justice Peter Daniel, who was most concerned with states' rights, concurred in the opinion, in part because "cotton planters such as Daniel, as much as commercially oriented justices like Story, understood the importance of uni-

form commercial rules to the smooth operation of the antebellum credit system." Tony Freyer, *Harmony and Dissonance: The Swift and Erie Cases in American Federalism* (New York, 1981), 43.

10. Arthur Bestor, Jr., "State Sovereignty and Slavery: A Reinterpretation of Proslavery Constitutional Doctrine, 1846–1860," *Journal of the Illinois State Historical Society* 54 (1961): 119.

11. Worthington C. Ford, ed., *Journals of the Continental Congress, 1777–1789* (Washington, D.C., 1906), 6:1080, debate of July 30, 1776. As Bestor noted, the term "states' rights" did not appear in the American political vocabulary until 1798, and thus the concept of secession may have preceded the articulation of the concept of states' rights. "State Sovereignty and Slavery," 145.

12. Max Farrand, ed., *The Records of the Federal Convention of 1787,* 4 vols., rev. ed. (New Haven, Conn., 1966), 1:593, 2:371–75. The problem of slavery at the convention is dealt with in Paul Finkelman, "Slavery and the Constitutional Convention: Making a Covenant with Death," in *Beyond Confederation: Origins of the Constitution and American National Identity,* ed. Richard Beeman, Stephen Botein, and Edward C. Carter II (Chapel Hill, N.C., 1987), 188–225.

13. Kenneth Stampp, *And the War Came: The North and the Secession Crisis, 1860–1861* (Baton Rouge, 1950; reprint, 1970), 5, 8.

14. After 1820 there were two major antebellum examples of state resistance to federal law that were not immediately related to slavery. Georgia ignored the Supreme Court's ruling in Worcester v. Georgia, 6 Pet. (U.S.) 515 (1832), but the state's governor pardoned the plaintiffs in the case, thus mooting its states' rights opposition to the decision. This compromise was tied to the response of Georgia officials and President Jackson to the Nullification Crisis in South Carolina. Alfred H. Kelly, Winfred A. Harbison, and Herman Belz, *The American Constitution,* 4th ed. (New York, 1983), 212–13. More famous was South Carolina's nullification of a federal tariff in 1832. However, William W. Freehling in *Prelude to Civil War: The Nullification Controversy in South Carolina, 1816–1836* (New York, 1965) persuasively argues that the Nullification controversy was directly tied to South Carolina's self-conscious development as a slave society. Although slavery was not the immediate issue in the crisis, it was certainly the underlying cause.

15. Thomas D. Morris, *Free Men All: The Personal Liberty Laws of the North, 1780–1861* (Baltimore, 1974); Paul Finkelman, *An Imperfect Union: Slavery, Federalism, and Comity* (Chapel Hill, N.C., 1981).

16. Lemmon v. The People, 20 N.Y. 562, 642 (1860) (Clerke, J., dissenting).

17. The northern states allowing slave transit were New Jersey, Indiana, Illinois, and California. The precedent-setting case in the North was Commonwealth v. Aves, 18 Pick. (Mass.) 193 (1836), which adopted the English precedent, Somerset v. Stewart, 20 Howell St. Tr. 1 (1772). This subject is discussed in detail in Finkelman, *An Imperfect Union.*

18. Southern treatment of northern whites was mixed. Though many northerners visited the South with no difficulty, some northerners were prosecuted for antislavery-related activities on the basis of dubious evidence. Treatment of convicted northerners was often brutal, even by the standards of the antebellum South. For example, Jonathan Walker was branded for helping slaves escape. Walker, *The Trial and Imprisonment of Jonathan Walker, at Pensacola, Florida, for Aiding Slaves to Escape from Bondage* (Boston, 1845). Captain Daniel Drayton received a long prison sentence for a similar crime. Drayton, *Personal Memoir of Daniel Drayton, for Four Years and Four Months a Prisoner (for Charity's Sake) in Washington Jail* (Boston, 1855). William Chaplin was able to leave a Maryland prison only after posting a cash bail of $25,000, raised through a massive campaign by northern abolitionists. Chaplin had attempted to help two slaves escape. *The Case of William L. Chaplin* (Boston, 1851). Most southerners, other than slave catchers and kidnappers, were cordially treated in the North. John Hope Franklin, *A Southern Odyssey: Travelers in the Antebellum North* (Baton Rouge, 1975).

19. Articles of Confederation, art. IV.

20. Donald L. Robinson, *Slavery in the Structure of American Politics, 1765–1820* (New York, 1971), 153–54.

21. The abolition of slavery in the North is discussed in Arthur Zilversmit, *The First Emancipation* (Chicago, 1967).

22. Blacks could vote in most of New England, as well as New York, Pennsylvania, and North Carolina, at the time of ratification. The rights of blacks during this period were detailed by Justice Benjamin Curtis in his dissent in Dred Scott v. Sandford, 19 How. (60 U.S.) 393 (1857).

23. House of Representatives, *Free Colored Seamen—Majority and Minority Reports*, 27th Cong., 3d sess., January 20, 1843, H. Doc. 80, 2 (Serial 426).

24. There is almost no secondary literature on the Negro Seamen's Acts. The South Carolina law is discussed in Philip M. Hamer, "Great Britain, the United States, and the Negro Seamen Acts, 1822–1848," and "British Consuls and the Negro Seamen Acts, 1850–1860," *Journal of Southern History* 1 (1935): 3–28, 138–68; Donald G. Morgan, *Justice William Johnson, The First Dissenter: The Career and Philosophy of a Jeffersonian Judge* (Columbia, S.C., 1954), 194–206, William M. Wiecek, *The Sources of Antislavery Constitutionalism in America, 1760–1848* (Ithaca, N.Y., 1977), 132–40; and Freehling, *Prelude to Civil War*, 113–15. A history of the Negro Seamen's Acts, which has never been written, would add much to our understanding of the development and implementation of southern constitutional theory.

25. Elkison v. Deliesseline, 8 F. Cas. 493, 496 (C.C.D.S.C. 1823) (No. 4366). Because Elkison was a British subject, this case raised issues of foreign policy and the supremacy of federal treaties. The position of South Carolina was hostile to both interstate relations and state-federal relations.

26. *The Argument of Benj. Faneuil Hunt, in the Case of the Arrest of the Person Claiming to be a British Seaman . . . before the Hon. Judge Johnson, Circuit Judge of the United States, for 6th Circuit* (Charleston, S.C., 1823), 12–13, 14.

27. Ibid., 4.

28. Ibid., 8, 20.

29. Ibid., 4.

30. 8 F. Cas. at 494; Morgan, *Justice William Johnson,* 193–94.

31. 8 F. Cas. at 494.

32. The South Carolina law in force in 1822 was amended a number of times throughout the antebellum period. See act of December 19, 1835, *Acts of South Carolina, 1835,* 34–39. See also Louisiana act of March 16, 1842; "Restrictions of Colored Seamen and Others," *A Codification of the Statute Law of Georgia* (Savannah, Ga., 1845), 834–36; "An Act to Amend the Quarantine Laws," chap. 30, *North Carolina Acts of 1830;* and "Free Colored Mariners," pt. 1, title XIII, art. 3, *The Code of Alabama,* ed. John J. Ormond, Arthur P. Bagby, and George Goldthwaite (Montgomery, Ala., 1852), 242–44.

33. Massachusetts General Court, House of Representatives, *Report of the Joint Committee on the Deliverance of Citizens, Liable to Be Sold as Slaves,* March 6, 1839, H. Doc. 38, 35–36.

34. House of Representatives, *Free Colored Seamen,* 6–9. The problem of the arrest of free black seamen was real and often tragic. Free blacks were imprisoned when they arrived in southern ports, sometimes under quarantine laws and sometimes under local statutes. For example, in 1840 the antislavery lawyer Ellis Gray Loring wrote to the mayor of New Orleans on behalf of Luke Thompson, "a young coloured man, a citizen of Maine," who was arrested in New Orleans and held as a fugitive slave. July 27, 1840, Loring Letterbook, Houghton Library, Harvard University, Cambridge, Mass. Similarly, in 1840 Governor Seward of New York was asked to intervene on behalf of a black sailor from upstate New York whose family was "in deep affliction" when they found out that their son was held as a fugitive slave in New Orleans. Starr Clark to Seward, April 15, 1840, Seward Papers, University of Rochester, Rochester, N.Y. In 1842 Lewis Tappan requested Seward's urgent intervention on behalf of John Lewis, a black from New York City who had been a cook on the *St. Louis,* a Boston-based ship. Lewis was then "in the chain gang" in New Orleans "and in peril of being sold as a slave." Louisiana law required that the "Governor of the State of which he claims to be a citizen" provide a certificate to that effect. The *St. Louis* was about to return to Louisiana, and the captain hoped to rescue Lewis but could not do so without Seward's help. Tappan to Seward, January 11, 1842, ibid. A number of similar cases are discussed in Massachusetts General Court, *Report of the Joint Committee on the Deliverance of Citizens, Liable to Be Sold as Slaves.*

Abolitionists hoped to use *Free Colored Seamen,* the 1843 House report, to their advantage. David Lee Child informed Wendell Phillips that for one cent apiece, extra copies of the report could be printed and mailed out under congressional frank: "Under the order of members they would be folded and sealed up by the servants of the House, and would go to *all* parts of the country, without liability to detention or destruction by postmasters or Lynch Committees." February 13, 1843, Blagden Papers, box 11, Houghton Library. Seven years later, however, Joshua Leavitt condemned Winthrop for moving for an adjournment of Congress to avoid a debate over "the demand for justice in regard to the imprisonment of our citizens in southern ports." Leavitt hoped that Congress would pass legislation preventing the imprisonment of black seamen and "an act to recover, at the expense of the United States, the liberty of citizens of one state unlawfully held in slavery in another state." Leavitt to Charles Sumner, December 18, 1850, Sumner Papers, box 15, Houghton Library.

35. South Carolina resolution of December 5, 1844, reprinted in *State Documents on Federal Relations,* ed. Herman V. Ames (1900; reprint New York, 1970), 238; Henry Wilson, *The Rise and Fall of the Slave Power in America,* 3 vols. (Boston, 1872), 576–86.

36. "Report from the Committee on the State of the Republic," assented to, December 19, 1845, *Acts of the State of Georgia, 1845,* 209–11, reprinted as Senate, *Resolutions of the Legislature of Georgia,* 29th Cong., 1st sess., S. Doc. 100 (Serial 473).

37. Finkelman, *An Imperfect Union.*

38. Kentucky v. Dennison, 24 How. (U.S.) 66 (1861).

39. U.S. Constitution, art. IV, sec. 2, cl. 2. This clause was almost identical to a similar provision in art. IV of the Articles of Confederation: "If any person guilty of, or charged with treason, felony, or other high misdemeanor in any State, shall flee from justice, and be found in any of the United States, he shall upon demand of the Governor or Executive power, of the State from which he fled, be delivered up and removed to the State having jurisdiction of his offence."

40. Almost simultaneously, Pennsylvania sought the extradition of three Virginians charged with murdering four Indians in Pennsylvania. Two of the murderers of the Indians were involved in the kidnapping as well. Virginia also refused to send these men back to Pennsylvania. This case is discussed in William R. Leslie, "A Study in the Origins of Interstate Rendition: The Big Beaver Creek Murders," *American Historical Review* 57 (1951): 63–76. Leslie argued that the 1793 act resulted from the murder of the Indians along the Big Beaver Creek. However, Governor Mifflin of Pennsylvania appears to have been far more concerned about the kidnapping. Mifflin to President Washington, July 18, 1791, *American State Papers: Miscellaneous,* 1:38–43; address of Governor Mifflin, August 24, 1791, and Mifflin to the governor of Virginia,

February 1, 1792, *Pennsylvania Archives, Fourth Series* 4 (1900): 173–81, 218–
22. See also Fred Somkin, "The Strange Career of Fugitivity in the History of
Interstate Extradition," *Utah Law Review,* 1984, 511–31; and I. T. Hoague,
"Extradition between States: Executive Discretion," *American Law Review* 13
(1879): 181–243.

41. Randolph to Innis, June 14, 1791, *Calendar of the State Papers of Virginia,*
5:326–28; House of Representatives, *Fugitives from Justice, Communicated to
Congress, on the 27th of October, 1791,* 2d Cong., 1st sess., no. 22, *American State
Papers: Miscellaneous,* 1:41.

42. Message of President Washington to the Senate and House of Representatives, October 27, 1791, *A Compilation of the Messages and Papers of the Presidents,* ed. James D. Richardson (Washington, D.C., 1897), 1:103; act of
February 12, 1793, chap. 7, 1 Stat. 302.

43. *Calendar of Virginia State Papers* (Richmond, Va., 1893), 11:10–14, 19–
23.

44. Austin King, governor of Missouri, to Augustus French, governor of
Illinois, June 30 and July 27, 1849, and French to King, July 20 and August
28, 1849, *Collections of the Illinois State Historical Society,* Vol. 7, *Governors' Letter-
Books, 1840–1853,* ed. Evarts B. Greene and Charles M. Thompson (Springfield, Ill., 1911), 207–9, 212–16; French to the governor of Missouri, February
17, 1852, ibid., 244–45.

45. In 1851 the free black relatives of Peyton Polly were kidnapped in Ohio
and taken to Kentucky. Some of the Polly family were sold there, and the rest
were taken to Virginia. The Pollys in Kentucky were eventually recovered
through the intervention of the Ohio government. After nearly ten years of
negotiation and litigation, including a case taken to the Virginia Court of
Appeals, the Pollys in that state remained enslaved. There is no printed history
of this case. Records of it are found in the papers of Ohio governors in the
Ohio Historical Society, Columbus. See also *Journal of the Senate of Ohio,* 1851,
530, 586, 825, 847; annual message of the governor of Ohio, January 5, 1852,
Executive Documents, Ohio, Fiftieth General Assembly (Columbus, Ohio, 1852),
vol. 16, pt. 1, pp. 19–20; Ratcliff v. Polly & als., 12 Gratt. (Va.) 528 (1855); and
"Joint Resolution Relative to the Kidnapping of the Polly Family," resolution of
March 10, 1860, 57 *Ohio Laws* 149 (1860).

46. See the sources cited in n. 43.

47. State of New York, *Communication from the Governor in Answer to a Resolution Relative to the Abduction or Enslavement of Citizens of This State,* January 31,
1857, Assembly Doc. 47. The document includes a copy of the act of May 14,
1840. In 1860 the state paid Henry Hubbard $240 under this law for expenses
and fees for traveling to Washington, D.C., where he obtained the release of a
free black from New York named George Armstrong. This sum included

Armstrong's railroad ticket to New York and new clothing for him. Governors' Blotter, 1860, entry of May 10, 1860, New York State Archives, Albany.

48. "An Act to Reclaim Persons Who May Have Been Decoyed or Kidnapped and Taken Away Beyond the Boundaries of This State," act of February 15, 1855, *Illinois Laws, 1855,* 186. On the treatment of blacks in Illinois, see Paul Finkelman, "Slavery, 'The More Perfect Union,' and the Prairie State," *Illinois Historical Journal* 80 (1987): 248–69.

49. See n. 44.

50. For example, Maryland officials initially refused to extradite Edward Prigg to stand trial in Pennsylvania for kidnapping. Prigg was extradited only after an elaborate compromise guaranteed that he could not be sent to prison until the U.S. Supreme Court had heard his case. Prigg v. Pennsylvania, 16 Pet. (U.S.) 539 (1842).

51. Kentucky v. Dennison, 24 How. (U.S.) 66 (1861).

52. Seward to Thomas W. Gilmer, governor of Virginia, November 9, 1840, *Message of the Governor of Virginia, Communicating a Correspondence between the Governors of Virginia and New York in Relation to Certain Fugitives from Justice* (Richmond, Va., 1840), 36.

53. Governor of Maine [Edward Kent], *Message to the Senate and House of Representatives of Maine* [Augusta, Me., 1839], 3–5.

54. Ibid., 6–17. See also "Message of the Governor of the State of Maine," *Maine Acts, 1840,* 240–43.

55. Governor of Maine, *Message to the Senate and House of Representatives,* 17–25.

56. Ibid., 25.

57. Ibid.

58. Ibid., 28–33.

59. Gov. Patrick Noble of South Carolina to Gilmer, September 4, 1839, Gilmer Papers, Re: Requisitions Maine, Georgia Archives, Atlanta.

60. "Resolutions of the General Assembly of Georgia," December 29, 1839, reprinted in Senate, 26th Cong., 1st sess., March 11, 1840, S. Doc. 273.

61. Congressmen Julius Alford, William C. Dawson, Richard W. Habersham, Thomas Butler King, Eugenius A. Nisbet, and Lott Warren to Gov. Charles McDonald, March 16, 1840, McDonald Papers, Re: Requisitions Maine, Georgia Archives. See also Ulrich B. Phillips, *Georgia and State Rights* (1902; Yellow Springs, Ohio, 1968), 139–40.

62. "Resolutions of the General Assembly of Georgia," December 29, 1839, reprinted in Senate, 26th Cong., 1st sess., March 11, 1840, S. Doc. 273.

63. The Georgia legislature asserted: "Resort to the *ultima ratio?* This . . . cannot be resorted to without a violation of the Federal Compact; and long, long may it be before the States of this Union shall be involved in civil

conflict." Quoted in Governor of Maine, *Message to the Senate and House of Representatives*, 31.

64. Seward to the secretary of state, n.d., Seward Papers, Extradition Files (Stephen Johnson). See also extradition papers of April 13, 1839, from governor of Louisiana to governor of New York, *in re* Stephen Johnson, and draft of Seward to the governor of Louisiana, July 29, 1839, ibid.

65. Hopkins to Seward, October 4, 1839, [David Campbell], *Annual Message of the Governor of the Commonwealth and Accompanying Documents* [Richmond, Va., 1839], House of Delegates Doc. 1, 31–34 (emphasis in the original).

66. Seward to Hopkins, October 24, 1839, [Campbell], *Annual Message*, 38–43. See also *Autobiography of William H. Seward* 3 vols. (New York, 1877), 1:438.

67. "Message of Governor Campbell," [Campbell], *Annual Message*, 1–7.

68. "Annual Message to the Legislature, January 7, 1840," *Messages from the Governors of the State of New York*, ed. Charles Z. Lincoln (Albany, N.Y., 1909), 3:778.

69. "An Act to Extend the Right of Trial by Jury," act of May 6, 1840, *Laws of New York, 1840*, 174; "An Act More Effectually to Protect the Free Citizens of This State from Being Kidnapped or Reduced to Slavery," act of May 14, 1840, ibid., 319.

70. Lincoln, *Messages from Governors*, 3:810; "Resolutions in Relation to Fugitives from Justice," chap. 38, approved April 6, 1841, *Laws of Mississippi, 1841*, 155–56; "Preamble and Joint Resolutions of the General Assembly of the State of Alabama," approved April 27, 1841, *Acts of Alabama, 1841*, 19; "Joint Resolution in Relation to a Controversy between the States of New York and Virginia," approved February 14, 1843, *Alabama Acts, 1842*, 225; "Report and Resolutions in Relation to the Constitutional Rights of Slaveholders," resolution no. 9, April 6, 1841, *Maryland Laws, 1841*; resolution of Missouri, approved February 16, 1841, *Missouri Laws, 1841*, 336–37; resolution of Louisiana, no. 110, approved March 16, 1842, *Louisiana Laws, 1842*, 288–90. Both the Louisiana and the Missouri resolutions attacked New York's jury trial law, as well as the Empire State's conduct toward Virginia. See also "An Act to Prevent the Citizens of New York from Carrying Slaves, or Persons Held to Service Out of This State . . . ," act of December 20, 1841, *South Carolina Laws, 1841*, 149–52. South Carolina ultimately sent a copy of this law to the Congress, and it is reprinted in House of Representatives, *South Carolina, Virginia, and New York Controversy*, 27th Cong., 2d sess., March 17, 1845, H. Doc. 135.

71. Message to the Senate, March 26, 1841, Lincoln, *Messages from Governors*, 3:910–11; "An Act to Prevent the Citizens of New York from Carrying Slaves Out of This Commonwealth . . . ," chap. 72, act of March 13, 1841, *Acts of Virginia, 1841*, 79–82; "An Act to Extend the Right of Trial by Jury," *Laws of New York, 1840*, 174–77.

72. Message to the Senate, March 26, 1841, Lincoln, *Messages from Governors*, 3:910–13.

73. Ibid., 922, 923, 924, 925, 927.

74. Seward to Gov. John Rutherford, October 8, 1841, Seward Papers.

75. Governor's annual message, January 4, 1842, Lincoln, *Messages from Governors*, 3:936–37; message to the legislature, February 11, 1842, ibid., 980–83; message to the legislature, April 12, 1842, ibid., 1029–32; message to the senate and assembly, August 16, 1842, ibid., 1033–37; House of Representatives, *South Carolina, Virginia, and New York Controversy,* 27th Cong., 2d sess., March 17, 1845, S. Doc. 135; "An Act to Better Secure and Protect the Citizens of Georgia in the Possession of Their Slaves," act of December 11, 1841, *Georgia Laws, 1841,* 125–28.

76. Message to the senate, March 26, 1841, Lincoln, *Messages from Governors*, 3:910–11. See also "An Act to Prevent the Citizens of New York from Carrying Slaves Out of This Commonwealth . . . ," chap. 72, act of March 13, 1841, *Acts of Virginia, 1841,* 79–82; and "An Act to Extend the Right of Trial by Jury," *Laws of New York, 1840,* 174–77. (Gov. Thomas Gilmer of Virginia should not be confused with Gov. George Gilmer of Georgia.)

77. "Preamble and Resolution Relative to the Surrender of Fugitives from Justice," adopted March 20, 1841, *Acts of Virginia, 1841,* 157; Patton to Seward, March 22, 1841, Lincoln, *Messages from Governors,* 3:915–18.

78. The Virginia act was repealed by "An Act Amending the Act, Entitled, 'An Act to Prevent the Citizens of New York from Carrying Slaves Out of This Commonwealth, and to Prevent the Escape of Persons Charged with Commission of Any Offence,' Passed March 13th, 1841, and All Acts Amendatory Thereto," act of March 5, 1846, *Acts of Virginia, 1845–1846,* 67–68. A similar act passed by Georgia, "An Act the Better to Secure and Protect the Citizens of Georgia in the Possession of Their Slaves," act of December 11, 1841, *Acts of Georgia, 1841,* 125–28, was repealed "so far as relates to the Port of Savannah" a year later. "An Act to repeal an Act the Better to Secure and Protect the Citizens of Georgia . . . ," act of December 27, 1842, *Acts of Georgia, 1842,* 166. Savannah was the only port where this law would have been important.

79. 24 How. (65 U.S.) 66 (1861).

80. Atty. Gen. C. P. Wolcott to Dennison, April 14, 1860, Dennison Papers, Ohio Historical Society. This letter is reprinted in Kentucky v. Dennison, 24 How. at 67–70.

81. Magoffin to Dennison, June 4, 1860, Dennison Papers.

82. Don E. Fehrenbacher, *The Dred Scott Case: Its Significance in American Law and Politics* (New York, 1978), 311.

83. Hoague, "Extradition between States," 181–243.

84. This concept was implied by Chief Justice Taney in Strader v. Graham, 10 How. (U.S.) 82, 93–94 (1850). In that case Taney asserted that "every state

has an undoubted right to determine the *status,* or domestic and social condition, of the persons domiciled within its territory." Thus Taney concluded that Kentucky did not have to accept the law of Ohio in determining the status of slaves who might be free in Ohio but had returned to Kentucky. Ohio law, in other words, could have no force in Kentucky, except through comity.

85. 24 How. at 109–10.

86. Drew v. Thaw, 235 U.S. 432, 439 (1914).

87. 31 *Am. Jur.* 2d, 956, sec. 48. In the 1950s Governor Milliken of Michigan refused to approve the extradition of one of the Scottsboro Boys, who had escaped from prison in Alabama. More recently, Gov. Edmund G. Brown, Jr., of California refused to extradite American Indian activist Russell Means to stand trial for crimes he allegedly committed in South Dakota.

88. Puerto Rico v. Branstad, Governor of Iowa, et al., No. 85-2116, slip op. at 11 (U.S. Supreme Court, 1987).

89. Ibid., 8–9.

"Old Times There Are Not Forgotten": The Distinctiveness of the Southern Constitutional Experience

William M. Wiecek

Was southern constitutional experience different from that of the North? Intuition tells us that it was, and reflection on the experience of a slave society before and after abolition confirms as much. The pervasive influence of slavery produced distinctive emphases in southern constitutional thinking. After slavery disappeared, southern constitutional experience continued to go its separate way as whites tried to establish a new legal basis for race relations. The influence of slavery and race on law lingered long into the twentieth century and generated other differences in southern law.

Anyone who writes about the distinctiveness of southern constitutional thought must begin with the assumption that southern historical experience itself has been distinct.[1] For if it were not, why would its constitutional thinking be different? That assumption leads directly into the debated topic of southern exceptionalism. Before entering that thicket, however, let us heed C. Vann Woodward's caution about comparing the North and South. The South, he maintains, has been "plagued by comparisons and its history distorted by them. . . . The tradition of interregional comparison, following old patterns of sectional polemics, ha[s] mainly served to perpetuate stale provincialities and outdated quarrels."[2] Those who concur with Woodward on this point add to the detritus of interregional comparisons with reluctance. Nevertheless, because the topic of constitutional exceptionalism makes no sense without some introductory overview of its larger matrix, one more bit of debris piled on the heap of comparisons is a regrettable necessity.

Until recently, historians and other writers on the southern experience shared the assumption of contemporaries that the South somehow was different.[3] Most would have agreed with the substance, if not the vehemence, of the judgment rendered on the eve of secession by that inveterate South Carolina/Texas secessionist Louis T. Wigfall: "We are a peculiar people, sir! . . . We are an agricultural people. . . . We have no cities—we don't want them. . . . We want no manufactures; we desire no trading, no mechanical or manufacturing classes. . . . As long as we have our rice, our sugar, our tobacco, and our cotton, we can command wealth to purchase all we want."[4] Southerners did not consider themselves deviants: it was the North that had degenerated since national independence. "Free society!" snorted a Georgia editor in an oft-quoted secession editorial: "We sicken at the name. What is it but a conglomeration of greasy mechanics, filthy operatives, small-fisted farmers, and moon-struck theorists . . . hardly fit for association with a southern gentleman's body servant."[5]

This assumption of southern exceptionalism has come under critical scrutiny in the past generation. Some reject the idea that people of the South were that much different from other Americans.[6] The dean of southern historians, C. Vann Woodward, turned the tables on the exceptionalism thesis a generation ago by suggesting that if one of the sections was a deviant from the nineteenth-century norm, it was the North.[7] Howard Zinn, among others, reversed another commonplace by suggesting that it was not the South that had become more like the rest of the country; rather, it was the other way around, and perhaps always had been.[8] This scholarly dispute has not settled the question of southern exceptionalism, but it has led to a more sophisticated level of discourse on the question.

This is not the place to attempt a resolution of the broader issue. However, for the purpose of exploring the distinctiveness of southern constitutional thought, it is necessary to establish a point of departure concerning the general subject of southern exceptionalism. Mine was suggested by the theoretical sociological work of Ferdinand Tönnies, and particularly his distinction between societies based on *gemeinschaft* and those organized on the principle of *gesellschaft*.⁹ A *gemeinschaftliche* community is one organized around tradition, status, deference, and kinship. It is rural and stable, with folkways, custom, and mutual dependence more influential than external, formal behavioral constraints (such as laws). Masculine codes of honor and chivalric myths have been influential in such societies. A *gesellschaftliche* society is more "modern": it is urban, mobile, individualistic, commercial, industrial, bureaucratic, and organized around the principle of self-interest.

This broad dichotomy, applied to the free states and the slave states as of 1860, helps us perceive important differences between the regions. There is little disagreement among scholars on the objective indicia of these differences. They include the following: (1) The South was rural; the North was correspondingly more urbanized. (2) The South was an agricultural society, with nearly all its people engaged in agricultural production or related occupations, and with its exports exclusively agricultural; whereas the North was more industrialized, having a greater volume of manufacturing and commerce and an equal volume of agricultural production. (3) One of the most important consequences of this agricultural-industrial distinction was the North's more extensive transportation network (which was a true network, linking Chicago to the East via railroad lines and the entire upper Midwest to New York via the Erie Canal, as contrasted with the disconnected and unintegrated rail lines of the South, which served only to link interior agricultural regions with the coast). (4) The population of the North was 50 percent greater than that of the South. (5) The North's population was more heterogeneous in religion and national origin, whereas the South's population was sharply dichotomized, one-third being black (and 95 percent of those being slaves) and the whites (outside Louisiana and Texas) being overwhelmingly Protestant and descended from ancestors who came from the British Isles. (6) By every measure of wealth, the people of the South were poorer than the people of the North.¹⁰ These differences have persisted into modern times, though they are ever more attenuated.

Beyond these quantifiable differences, there are several more subjective distinctions. The people of the South (of both races) have been more inclined to a fundamentalist, evangelical, literal-interpretation form of the Protestant religious experience, whereas the Protestants of the North have been more influenced by religious reform movements and their secular offshoots, most notably abolitionism. Consequently, the whites of the South have been more inclined to religious, social, and political conservatism. The North has been more hospitable to education at all levels. All these various quantifiable and semiobjective differences are complemented by subjective attitudinal differences: like Wigfall and the Georgia editor, the people of both sections have perceived themselves to be different from each other in the past, and they continue to do so today.[11]

Given these real differences between the sections in the mid-nineteenth century, we are in a position to consider whether there were corresponding constitutional differences. That inquiry yields four general theses. First, to the extent that southern society, culture, and historical experience were distinct from the North's, that distinctiveness was reflected in southern laws, both public and private.

Second, the distinctiveness of southern society emerged in the late eighteenth century and continued to influence the development of public law in the South well into the twentieth century, long after the formal basis for differing constitutional systems was swept away by the Civil War and Reconstruction. However, the legal distinctiveness of the South has been masked from legal scholars for several reasons. Southern lawyers produced few legal treatises.[12] Some of its greatest lawyers—John Marshall, Bushrod Washington, William Johnson, William Wirt, Henry Clay—were nationalists whose careers were played out on a national stage and who largely shed sectional values. Southern constitutional thought after 1820 was diverted into political forums, while juridical forums became increasingly distracted by the sectional controversy, especially after 1850.[13]

Third, the principal driving force behind the distinctiveness of southern constitutional and legal thought (and of southern historical experience generally) was the fact that the South was until 1865 a slave society and after slavery's violent abolition a society organized around white supremacy, segregation, and racial oppression. This basic fact determined the emerging distinctiveness of southern law.

Fourth, secondary societal differences derived from the core fact of the South's commitment to slavery and segregation. Two of these secondary differentiating characteristics are relevant to southern constitutional development. First, the South's economic history and attitudes have been distinct from the North's. Though other matters help to account for this difference, slavery and the color line lurk in the background. Second,

162

violence has played a more prominent role in the South than elsewhere. Some of this violence, such as lynching after the Civil War, has been related directly to race; other facets of violence, especially attitudinal ones, are indirectly related. The resort to violence as a means of resolving political differences owes much to the fact that the South is the only region to have experienced Reconstruction, when alien values were imposed on its law from without, against the inclinations of the politically dominant majority of whites.

The Unique Constitutional Experience of a Slave Society

It is necessary here to sketch at some length the broad outlines of southern constitutional distinctiveness. There was no discernible, divergent southern constitutionalism before the 1790s, though a southern sectional bloc at the Philadelphia convention had succeeded in writing powerful guarantees for slaveholding interests into the Constitution. So successful were they that slavery assumed a central place in the American constitutional order, secured with constitutional guarantees accorded to no other political or social relation. Slavery was not an anomaly in the American legal system or extrinsic to it: rather, it was an essential component of it.[14] But the appearance of parties by 1795 demonstrated the power of sectional divisiveness. The worsening foreign-policy situation of the United States, exacerbated by party rivalry, evoked the debut statement of southern constitutional thought, the Virginia and Kentucky Resolutions of 1798–99. The triumph of Jefferson in 1800, followed by a quarter century of the Republican Ascendancy and the Virginia Dynasty, obviated the need for southern constitutional thinkers to develop the principles of the Resolutions of 1798–99 as an opposition posture. But the expansion of the U.S. Supreme Court's appellate authority over the decisions of state supreme courts provoked Chief Judge Spencer Roane of the Virginia Supreme Court of Appeals, abetted by Jefferson and the Richmond Junto, to a stubborn confrontation with Joseph Story and John Marshall over the nature of the federal Union.[15] Roane's "Hampden" and "Algernon Sydney" essays in the *Richmond Enquirer* (1819, 1821) extended the state-sovereignty ideas that had been broached two decades earlier.

The period of mature southern constitutional exceptionalism lasted from 1820 to 1865. It developed in three phases. In the first, which extended from 1820 until around 1835, southern constitutional thinking explicitly and self-consciously diverged from that of the rest of the nation. Southern thinkers and publicists developed a foundation structure of ideology, constructed of political theory and racist anthropology. They also invented and perfected political responses to what they perceived to be challenges to the security of their slave society. In the second phase, lasting from 1835 to 1860, southern political leaders followed John C. Calhoun in devising an elaborate constitutional program that expressed their vision of the origins and future of the American republic. And finally, in the third phase, 1860 to 1865, southern political leaders recognized that they would not be able to impose their constitutional vision on the rest of the country, nor would they be able to erect the securities for slavery they demanded within the American Union. Consequently, they withdrew from that Union and began their experiment with sectional independence, in a new nation with a constitutional structure that attempted to realize their ideals. This experiment was strangled in infancy, but southern constitutional exceptionalism survived the Confederacy, though in a modified form.

The first phase of overtly distinct southern constitutional thought began with the crises surrounding the admission of Missouri, from 1819 to 1821.[16] Southern leaders, without exception, saw in efforts to restrict the expansion of slavery into the Louisiana Purchase territory a lethal threat to slavery's future, not only to its opportunities for expansion into the American West but also to its security in the states where it already existed. (If it were admitted that slavery should not cross the Mississippi into what Jefferson called the "Empire of Liberty" because it was inconsistent with republican ideals and the Declaration of Independence, how could it persist in the extant slave states compatibly with the Constitution? Would not the ever-more-preponderant northern populace sooner or later take steps to constrict, then abolish, it?) Southerners quickly learned that their fears were not misplaced, thanks to Denmark Vesey's insurrection scheme in Charleston, South Carolina, in 1822. This suppressed slave uprising confirmed southern warnings that loose northern talk of slavery's incompatibility with the Declaration of Independence would be overheard by slaves, who would take the idea to heart, with unthinkable consequences.

To cope with this dreadful threat, southern thinkers returned to the origins of their distinctive constitutional theory, the ideas of the Virginia and Kentucky Resolutions. They devised a comprehensive ideological explanation of the American federal system, integrated racist assumptions into constitutional thought, and evolved a reflexive, defensive political program to shore up slavery's security at home.

First, John Taylor of Caroline and the Carolinians Thomas Cooper, Robert J. Turnbull, and Whitemarsh Seabrook warned of the dangers of what they called "Consolidation": a centripetal process whereby the national government unconstitutionally drew all powers unto itself, divesting the states of inherent and reserved sovereign powers. The federal government was not a sovereign, they insisted, but merely the creature of the people of the states, capable of exercising only those powers that they had delegated to it: defense and regulation of international commerce.

Integral to this concept of the Union was a revised vision of the place of black people in it. Southerners perceived more keenly than other Americans the anomaly of slavery and the ideals of the American Revolution. Being unable to disavow either, they were forced to reconcile the two, and they did so by hardening a racist ideology that denied blacks status as part of the American people because they were racially inferior and destined to a degraded status.[17] Gabriel Prosser's intended insurrection (Richmond, 1801), the Vesey scare, and Nat Turner's bloody uprising in southern Virginia (1831) confirmed white southerners' belief that there could be no place for blacks in American society other than as slaves. In the Virginia Constitutional Convention of 1829–30, Benjamin Watkins Leigh identified slavery as an integral element of the southern social, economic, and constitutional order requiring extraordinary protection in both state and nation.[18]

Carolinians, including Chancellor Henry W. Desaussure, Charles Cotesworth Pinckney, and Edwin C. Holland, defended slavery as a boon to blacks, an idea that South Carolina's governor, George McDuffie, celebrated as the positive-good thesis in 1835. "No human institution . . . is more manifestly consistent with the will of God, than human slavery," he proclaimed. "Domestic slavery, therefore, instead of being a political evil, is the cornerstone of our republican edifice."[19]

The public law of the slave states reflected this new exaltation of slavery and its concomitant degradation of blacks. The early tendency of southern courts to rule *in favorem libertatis* in cases of contested black freedom[20] gave way to a new spirit, captured unforgettably in Judge Thomas Ruffin's sombre words in *State v. Mann:* "The power of the master must be absolute, to render the submission of the slave perfect. . . . there is no remedy. This discipline belongs to the state of slavery. They cannot be disunited, without abrogating at once the rights of the master, and absolving the slave from his subjection. It constitutes the curse of slavery to both the bond and free portions of our population. But it is inherent in the relation of master and slave."[21] A comparable trend is discernible in statutory law, illustrated in the modification of Virginia's fairly liberal revolutionary-era emancipation measures[22] into the harsh and restrictive provisions of the 1837 Emancipated Slaves Act.[23] By 1835, whites had come to regard free blacks as an anomalous and dangerous group in a society structured to accommodate only two legally recognized classes of persons: those who were free and white and those who were black and enslaved.

The white political leadership of the South embodied these new attitudes into a political program that, viewed as a whole, constituted a coherent yet reactive response to the threat to slavery that they saw in free blacks, slave revolutionaries, white abolitionists, and West Indian emancipation. This program began with the Negro Seamen's Acts, enacted first in South Carolina in 1822 in response to the Vesey scare, and within a decade enacted by every southern coastal state. Defending these measures against Justice William Johnson's opinion holding them unconstitutional,[24] Robert J. Turnbull and Isaac E. Holmes proclaimed the states "free, sovereign, and independent, as to every object of internal polity," a status that they thought overrode any federal powers to regulate commerce or conclude treaties.[25] Southern leaders lashed out at proposals to send American delegates to the Panama Congress (1826) on the grounds that the conference would include delegates from the black republic of Haiti-Santo Domingo, whose independence was achieved in the bloody and successful slave uprising led by Toussaint L'Ouverture and Jean-Jacques Dessalines (1794–1804). They violently condemned the Ohio Resolutions, an 1823 proposal by Ohio and other northern states for federal financial support for colonization, seeing in it the beginning of a tendency of the federal government to "openly lend itself to a combination of fanatics for the destruction of everything valuable in the Southern country."[26]

The capstone of this political tendency was the Nullification movement of 1832. Though every other southern state repudiated and condemned this initiative, the Carolinians accomplished two things by it: they formally aired their constitutional theories, gaining practical experience in implementing the ideas that would stand them in good stead thirty years later; and they wrung concessions from the federal government on the ostensible subject of the dispute, the tariff. Disunionist inclinations were by no means a monopoly of southern thought: some New Englanders had toyed with the idea in 1803 and again in 1814, and they would recur to it later; the cis-Mississippi West was restive and separationist-minded until the Louisiana Purchase confirmed American control of the Mississippi. But it was left to the South to elevate disunion to the level of solemn constitutional theory. Though Nullification may have been a premature venture in 1832, its day lay in the future.

The effectiveness of southern constitutional thought in this first period, 1820–35, was seriously threatened by an old problem that had haunted southern political leadership since the mid-seventeenth century: the possibility that the division of the South on racial lines might be confused by a division on class lines, as poor whites perceived their interests to be inconsistent with those of the ruling elite and blacks remained *hors de combat.* Just as southern constitutional thought was coalescing in the 1820s, it was threatened by intrasectional and class divisions, which found public expression in the Virginia Constitutional Convention of 1829–30 and then, two years later, in debates in the Virginia General Assembly on a proposal for gradual, compensated emancipation in the Old Dominion. Neither event endangered the security of slavery: the slaveholding Tidewater emerged from the convention with its political power intact despite assaults from the tramontane regions, and emancipation was voted down in the General Assembly. In reaction to this double threat, Thomas R. Dew in 1832 published his *Review of the Debate in the Virginia Legislature, 1831–32,* a compendious defense of slavery on political, economic, and racial grounds. Dew's essay closed the early period of southern constitutional exceptionalism.

With this ideological groundwork in place, the South was able to move beyond a purely responsive reaction to events and to anticipate challenges to its interests. This effort was not always successful in the short run, and in the long run it led to the catastrophe of the Civil War. But in the quarter century of this aggressive phase of southern constitutionalism, the South articulated an alternative version of the American constitutional order. In retrospect, evaluated in the light of what the United States has become, it was at once reactionary and antidemocratic, on the one hand, and remarkably modern on the other. (That should be a disturbing thought.)

As troubling to southern repose as the twenties had been, the thirties were even worse. White southerners watched with dismay but not surprise as northern opponents of slavery abandoned gradualism and colonization in favor of immediatism. A phalanx of publicists and editors, activists and organizers, philanthropists and ministers, arose to condemn slavery. The Underground Railroad spread throughout the northern states. William Lloyd Garrison began publishing the *Liberator* in January 1831 and helped form the New England Anti-Slavery Society a year later. Organizational antislavery nodes were then established in New York City, Philadelphia, and northern Ohio. Great Britain forced emancipation on the British West Indies in 1833. In that same year, American abolitionists formed a powerful national organization, the American Anti-Slavery Society. The Union had obviously entered a new era: slavery was now gravely threatened from without as well as from within.

To meet this threat, southern political leaders capitalized on the control that they had established over the organs of the national government. When the resurgent abolition movement began a massive, nationwide propaganda offensive that was to consist of weekly mailings of antislavery periodicals throughout the South, southern political leaders and their northern Democratic allies responded in several ways. They sought to give local postmasters the right to exclude mailings banned by the laws of the recipient's state or to prohibit such mailings altogether, and they demanded extradition of northern abolitionists for trial in the southern states on charges of violating anti-incitement laws. When abolitionists turned their energies to petitioning Congress, southern leaders imposed gag rules in both houses that endured for nearly a decade (but that proved ineffectual and counterproductive in stifling criticism of slavery either within or outside the walls of Congress).

These political responses produced no durable doctrine, though they established a long-lived perception that the South was less hospitable to civil liberties than other sections of the country.[27] Southern leaders by the 1830s perceived that demography was against them: the free states already had a majority of representatives in the House, and that majority would widen indefinitely. Far from receding, the external threat to slavery only augmented. John C. Calhoun, the South's preeminent political thinker, determined to establish elementary and unshakable principles of union, first in a set of six resolutions that he offered in 1837, and then in a supplementary set offered a decade later in response to the controversy over the Wilmot Proviso.[28]

As embodied in the resolutions, Calhounite constitutionalism declared that the states acted as sovereigns in adopting the federal Constitution, by which they delegated specified powers to the federal government while retaining control over all their own "domestic institutions." It followed that any interference with those institutions (i.e., slavery), from whatsoever source it came—states, federal government, organizations, individuals—threatened the Union. The national government was the "agent" of the states and, as such, had to protect them from these external meddlings. Slavery was an "essential element" of the societies of the southern states. Congress adopted four of the 1837 resolutions embodying these points but declined to adopt two others, which claimed that efforts to abolish slavery in the District of Columbia or the territories were an attack on the institutions of the slave states and that the federal government could not discriminate among the states in the protection it extended their institutions, especially when it came to governing the territories or admitting new states. Calhoun tried again a decade later (and Congress again declined to endorse his ideas), making it explicit that in his judgment Congress could not discriminate among citizens of the free and slave states in access to the territories because they were the common property of all the states.

It would be a serious error, as Arthur Bestor demonstrated some twenty-five years ago, to infer from this Calhounite orthodoxy that the South was committed on principle to a constitutional ideal of state sovereignty. On the contrary: on all questions pertaining to slavery, the South after Calhoun's 1837 resolutions was highly "consolidationist," using national power to protect slavery in the states where it existed and, more important, to project it into the territories. Thus the South's antebellum constitutionalism was discriminating and opportunistic. As a staple-exporting agricultural region, the South embraced state sovereignty as a means of assuring that national power would not be used to benefit the commercial and industrializing regions of the nation. But as a slave society that controlled all but one institution of the federal government, it extolled national supremacy. Bestor correctly insisted that southern constitutionalism was a theory neither of rights nor of sovereignty but of power. Southerners used all means, including the agencies of the national government, to project slavery into the territories and the free states.[29]

This process might become clearer if we consider the two chief judicial monuments of southern constitutional thought, the *Dred Scott* case and *Ableman v. Booth*.[30] Chief Justice Roger B. Taney's *Dred Scott* opinion was doubly significant as an exemplar of southern constitutionalism. In the first half of his opinion, Taney labored to deny any possibility that blacks could be citizens of the United States or, if citizens of state X, that they could claim any rights in state Y. (The state-sovereignty premises of southern beliefs forced Taney to concede, with great reluctance, that a state might bestow citizenship on blacks if it were mad enough to want to do so.) In reaching this conclusion, Taney delivered his unforgettable dicta on blacks "as a subordinate and inferior class of beings . . . [who] had no rights which the white man was bound to respect."[31]

For his purposes, Taney felt it essential to impose the position of the framers of 1787, as he understood it, on the constitutional world of 1857. That step, in turn, led him to a literalist, inflexible position on interpreting the Constitution: no change in public opinion "should induce the court to give to the words of the constitution a more liberal construction . . . than they were intended to bear when the instrument was framed and adopted. . . . [The Constitution] must be construed now as it was understood at the time of its adoption. It is not only the same in words, but the same in meaning."[32] Taney's view has been repeatedly rejected in modern times, yet its spirit of reactionary judicial activism recurs today.

At three separate points in his *Dred Scott* opinion, Taney explicitly adopted tenets of Calhounite constitutional dogma, which by then had become orthodoxy for the South:

1. "The government of the United States has no right to interfere [with slavery] for any other purpose but that of protecting the rights of the [slave]owner."
2. Whatever territory the federal government acquires, "it acquires for the benefit of the people of the several states who created it [i.e., the federal government]. It is their trustee acting for them and charged with the duty of promoting the interests of the whole people of the Union."
3. "The only power conferred [on Congress with respect to the territories] is the power coupled with the duty of guarding and protecting the [slave]owner in his rights."[33]

To appreciate the significance of thus consecrating Calhoun's ideas into constitutional dogma, recall that in 1857 there were three general political-constitutional theories concerning the most urgent problem of the day, slavery in the territories: (1) that of the Republicans—free

170

soil—the power of Congress to exclude slavery from the territories, which in 1860 would command a legitimate political majority and for the first time since 1820 overthrow the Democratic/sectional control of the federal government; (2) that of the northern Democrats—popular sovereignty—which would leave the status of slavery in a territory to the voters there, and which might well have been the view of a majority of the voters of the North in 1857; and (3) that of the South—slavery national—which in 1860 would require the federal government to impose slavery on all the territories.[34] Taney's actions in *Dred Scott* destroyed the constitutional viability of the first two, which between them clearly commanded majority support among the American people at the time, and elevated the views of a sectional minority to the status of authoritative constitutional interpretation.

An even more vivid example of the nationalizing tendencies of slavery constitutionalism was provided by *Ableman v. Booth*. Unlike *Dred Scott, Ableman* remains good law today because it rests on a fundamentally sound idea: the maintenance of federal authority would be inconsistent with state judicial nullification and with a state habeas power having an arm long enough to release persons held by federal authority. Taney declared that "although the State of Wisconsin is sovereign within its territorial limits to a certain extent, yet that sovereignty is limited and restricted by the Constitution of the United States."[35] Such a notion was incompatible with a pure state-sovereignty constitutional outlook, yet it fitted in nicely with other slavery-nationalizing aspects of Taney's thought. In *Strader v. Graham* (1851), for example, he had held that the states had full authority over the status of persons within their jurisdictions, "except in so far as the powers of the states in this respect are restrained, or duties and obligations imposed on them, by the Constitution of the United States."[36] That sinister qualification might have meant nothing more than that the states could not liberate fugitive slaves, a truism. But it potentially might have cast doubt on the validity of gradual emancipation in the North or, less drastically, might have inhibited the power of the states to restrict the ingress of sojourners' slaves. Such proslavery ambiguities caused Taney no unease.

Taney also referred in *Ableman* to another doctrine that was to have a profound impact on American public law in the next century: dual sovereignty. He held that "the powers of the general government, and of the State, although both exist and are exercised within the same territorial limits, are yet separate and distinct sovereignties, acting separately and independently of each other, within their respective spheres."[37] This mischievous notion would impede state and federal regulation of economic matters early in the twentieth century but, more to the point, would form a bulwark of state power to suppress black people.

The third phase, and the culmination, of explicitly distinct southern constitutional thought came with secession and the historical experience of the Confederacy. The movement for southern independence drew on three traditions: disunion, state sovereignty, and interposition. Southerners had no monopoly on the disunionist impulse, as noted earlier. But it was they who most consistently threatened to secede from the union throughout the century, and with increasing frequency after 1830.

Disunion, however, requires a constitutional theory to justify it, and that was supplied by state sovereignty. Southerners were not consistent or purist in their use of state-sovereignty ideas, but they nevertheless carried them to their fullest exposition.[38] State sovereignty was a diagnostic tool, though, not a prescription or a therapy. For a guide to action, southern thinkers turned to the Virginia and Kentucky Resolutions. Interposition and Nullification as developed in the writings and speeches of John C. Calhoun became linked with an institution not confined to the South, the constitutional convention, to produce a mechanism designed, first, to protect the interests of the South within the Union but, as a last resort, to enable the individual states to leave it if necessary for their self-preservation. (Secession cut both ways, though, as Virginia learned when its western third seceded in 1861 to become the new state of West Virginia.)

The provisional and permanent constitutions of the Confederate States of America reflected the formal constitutional theories of the South, but imperfectly. The Confederate Constitution was explicit and emphatic on state sovereignty. Its preamble declared that the Confederacy was formed by the people of the several states, "each State acting in its sovereign and independent character." Article I was at pains to specify that all federal power was "delegated" by the people of the states. The framers of the Confederacy omitted the general-welfare clause of the preamble in the mother document, as well as the taxing and spending provisions from article I, section 8.[39] Fearing, as always, "consolidation," the framers denied the federal courts of the Confederacy diversity jurisdiction. Later, when they perceived that their counterpart of the old section 25 of the

1789 Judiciary Act conveyed a more extensive federal-question jurisdiction than the mother statute, they overreacted by repealing the section authorizing creation of a supreme court. As a result, the Confederacy never had a supreme court.[40] Thomas Hill Watts, attorney general of the Confederacy, summed up the approach of his government: "A strict construction of the [Confederate] Constitution is essential to preserve the rights of the States, the Sovereign parties to the Constitutional compact."[41]

The Confederate Constitution differed from the Constitution of 1787 in other ways, too. It explicitly extended to slavery all the securities that its framers had demanded when they were federal and state officials in the old Union: the federal government was prohibited from passing laws "denying or imparing the right of property in negro slaves"; the slave status of sojourners', transitory, and fugitive slaves was explicitly preserved; and slavery was protected in any territories to be acquired by the Confederacy. The framers embodied some favorite Democratic constitutional notions in the document, such as a limitation of taxation to revenue purposes and a prohibition of internal improvements. And they incorporated some structural innovations, such as the line-item veto and a one-term, six-year presidency.

Vice-President Alexander Stephens summed up the achievements of the Confederate Constitution in this way: "The new Constitution has put at rest forever all the agitating questions in relation to our peculiar institutions—African slavery as it exists among us—the proper status of the negro in our form of civilization. . . . Our new Government is founded . . . upon the great truth that the negro is not the equal of the white man. That slavery—subordination to the superior race, is his natural and normal condition."[42] Stephens identified nothing new or evanescent here. The basic character of the Confederacy's constitutional outlook had been present embryonically since 1800, and it was to survive the destruction of the new nation, lingering until the middle of the twentieth century. Harold D. Woodman has aptly characterized the phoenix emerging from its ashes as "an evolving bourgeois society in which a capitalist social structure was arising on the ruins of a premodern slave society. . . . While slavery, the institution that had been at the core of that non-modern ideology and social structure, had been forcibly extinguished, its culture and ideology lingered and gave the new society that emerged a peculiar, southern form."[43]

173

The Southern Constitutional Order
after Abolition

Out of defeat and devastation, the South had to rebuild its societies in 1865. The physical needs alone would have been staggering, but the South simultaneously had to work out a different basis of relations between the races to replace slavery. Equality was out of the question: Ulrich B. Phillips was indisputably correct that the central theme of southern history has been "a common resolve indomitably maintained—that it shall be and remain a white man's country."[44] The result of this determination in the ensuing century may be summed up thus: The white South first turned to explicit, legally sanctioned racial subordination as a surrogate for slavery. After the North forcibly denied southerners that option, they then turned to a more subtle regime of racial legal equality that masked economic oppression, segregation, and discrimination. From that they went on to impose disfranchisement and systematic social degradation through Jim Crow. At all times, the legal order was supplemented by extralegal violence.

Paul Finkelman has maintained that the postbellum South rested on a "segregationist constitutional theory."[45] This concept is misleading if it suggests that the New South was created around a comprehensive constitutional field theory, as it were, that governed both federal relations and the internal workings of the southern polities, comparable in its scope to the state-sovereignty and anti-consolidationist constitutionalism of the Old South. Ostensibly, the postwar southern legal order did not differ from that of other regions, and federal relations were dictated by the victor. The postbellum era was not characterized by an overtly distinctive southern constitutional outlook.

But something may be salvaged of the notion of a segregationist constitutionalism if we begin with the problem of individual legal status. The jurists and legislators of a slave society perceived something that their counterparts in the North did not: the abolition of slavery did not automatically entail upon the freed people a civil status with known rights and immunities. The jurisprudence of slave societies had been explicit on the idea that emancipation conferred absolutely nothing on its beneficiary but a restricted right of locomotion: that is, a right to move about at will (subject to things like curfews and durational residence limitations) without first having to get a master's permission. Chief Judge Joseph Lumpkin of Georgia had declared in 1853 that the status of the African in Georgia, whether bond or free, is such that he has no civil, social or political rights or capacity, whatever, except such as are bestowed on him by Statute. . . . the act of manumission confers no other right but that of freedom from the dominion of the master, and the limited liberty of locomotion; . . . it does not and cannot confer citizenship, nor any of the powers, civil or political, incident to citizenship; . . . the social and civil degradation, resulting from the taint of blood, adheres to the descendants of Ham in this country."[46]

Emancipation, as Taney had emphasized in *Dred Scott*, did not confer any immunities of citizenship or bundles of rights and obligations comparable to those enjoyed by white citizens. Those elements of civil status had to be conferred by positive law. They were inherent consequences of the natural law only for whites. Whatever the status of the freedmen was to be, it could be determined only by legislation. Without positive law, the freedman was a human close to being a legal nullity, a person not recognized by the law.

Northern jurists did not comprehend this basic truth about status in the laws of a slave society. Tutored by the abolitionists, they assumed that abolition would be followed by the automatic assumption of a legally recognized civil status for the freedmen. This status did not necessarily have to be equivalent to that of whites in all respects: there was ample room for racial discrimination, in the northern view. But it did have to include certain fundamental rights, immunities, and obligations, among them, at a minimum, the right to be free from violence and the correlative right to claim the protection of the state against such violence. This insistence harked back to Chief Justice John Marshall's statement in *Marbury v. Madison* that "the very essence of civil liberty certainly consists in the right of every individual to claim the protection of the laws, whenever he receives an injury. One of the first duties of government is to afford that protection."[47] Civil rights, in the nineteenth-century sense of that term, also included the right of access to courts and the processes of law, both as parties and as witnesses, and basic rights of civil capacity, including the right to establish legally recognized rights of marriage and parenthood, the right to own and dispose of property, and the right to make contracts. In free-state law, a slave was a human deprived of these rights by positive law; when the state of slavery sloughed off him, he automatically resumed these natural and inherent rights because of his human condition. His race was relevant only to the extent that it might mean that he could be subjected to certain lim-

175

ited disabilities by positive law—for example, he might not be permitted to vote or might be prohibited from marrying someone of the opposite race. (He was in fact thus circumscribed in many northern states at the time.) But these restrictions were incidental; race was not destiny.[48]

This divergence in the laws of the two sections had immediate consequences. Acting on their perception of legal reality, southern legislators in the Johnson governments of 1865–66 immediately turned to the task of conferring a legal status on the freedmen, which they accomplished by the Black Codes.[49] These statutes effected three things. First, they conferred a civil status on the freedmen, conveying by positive law most of the fundamental rights that northern jurisprudents assumed accrued automatically—but often with discriminatory limitations: a black could testify in court, but not against whites, for example. Second, the Black Codes carried forward into the post-emancipation era much of the race-control elements of the law of slavery. Freedmen in some states were prohibited from owning or carrying weapons; they were subject to unequal punishments under the criminal law and to discipline by the whip, that ancient symbol of slavery, by employers and masters; and under the criminal surety laws, they could be hired out to someone paying their fines.

Third, the Black Codes created *de novo* something lacking in the slave laws: a system of labor coercion. It had been a peculiarity of the slave laws that they failed to include any positive laws that accomplished the primary purpose of slavery: forced labor. For the exaction of labor out of their slaves, masters and mistresses were left to their own devices; the law did not intrude, except to the limited extent of sometimes providing a public whipper, a service presumably for enfeebled masters and some mistresses. Abolition left the South with a landless black peasantry of some four million souls whose labor was essential to the southern economy. According to prevalent racist theory among whites, blacks would not willingly work or submit to labor discipline. Any controls to get work out of blacks would have to be imposed from without, by law. So the Black Codes embodied extensive labor-control provisions. Mississippi's was typical: it permitted hiring out of black convicts and vagrants; required licenses from police boards for blacks to work as occasional labor; prohibited blacks from quitting jobs (enforced by forfeiture of all accrued wages); permitted the arrest of a black who quit his job (the statute termed him a "deserter"); created a system of apprenticeship limited to blacks; forbade enticement of laborers; and created an all-encompassing vagrancy status (including persons "with no lawful employment or business"), which permitted arrest and hiring out.[50]

The North was outraged by such laws. The *Chicago Tribune* editorialized about the Mississippi law: "We tell the white men of Mississippi that the men of the North will convert the State of Mississippi into a frog pond before they will allow such laws to disgrace one foot of soil in which the bones of our soldiers sleep and over which the flag of freedom waves."[51] These laws, along with the South's recalcitrance on all aspects of Reconstruction policy and the insanely arrogant attitude of congressional Democrats, convinced reluctant congressional Republicans that since southerners had defaulted on their responsibilities in providing an acceptable system of internal governance, Congress would have to do it for them. The result was the Civil Rights Act of 1866, which conferred all the benign elements of the Black Codes but significantly added this expression of the northern conception of equality before the law: all persons shall enjoy the "full and equal benefit of all laws and proceedings for the security of person and property, as is enjoyed by white citizens, and shall be subject to like punishment, pains, and penalties, and to none other."[52]

The Civil Rights Act was part of a revolutionary constitutional order imposed on the South from the outside, by conquerors who controlled a Congress from which southern representatives were excluded, and enforced by an army of occupation that included black troops. Moreover, this revolution-from-without accompanied a revolution-from-within. The war had literally decimated the prewar leadership cadre, with many of the men who would have guided southern society in the late 1860s dead, disabled, impoverished, or in exile. Most of the remainder of that leadership was at first disfranchised, whereas the ex-slaves were enfranchised after 1867. The bottom rail was on top, and the top rail had been chopped up for kindling, it seemed to southern whites. The South was undergoing a social revolution that would have been overwhelming in any event, even without constitutional complications. The principal consequence of this enforced new order was that it lacked legitimacy in the eyes of the southern majority, the whites. No such regime could survive. The new status and rights of freedmen were therefore especially fragile and vulnerable, liable to overthrow in the inevitable counter-revolution. They could last only as long as the North was willing to commit funds and soldiers to enforce them.

The white South first tried nightriding and terror to subvert the new order. Whatever lassitude had lulled northern concern for the freedmen was roused by this violence against Unionists and freedmen: the North forcefully and effectively suppressed the insurgency, augmenting the growing corpus of federal civil rights laws as it did so. Ultimately the white South was forced to resort to less obtrusive means to restore the white man's government.

First came the political components of the solution. The Compromise of 1877 assured, above all, that the North would not again intrude in the internal affairs of the southern states. That guarantee was part of a larger, unwritten understanding of how the federal system was to function in the postbellum world. The northern states claimed a suzerainty over the South: they, through their control of the federal government, would direct the foreign relations and the economic reintegration of the southern states with the rest of the nation. The North returned internal sovereignty to the southern states under the slogan of "self-government." That phrase connoted, among other things, a license for whites to reorganize race relations to their liking.

The Compromise of 1877 was accompanied by the "restoration of home rule," a political process by which the Republican governments established under military Reconstruction were overthrown and replaced by Conservative, Redeemer, and Bourbon regimes. The period of one-party rule began, and the South turned to the task of restoring white supremacy. Part of this process included the creation of a New South ideology organized around the ideals of "reconciliation," industrialization, and progress; it also included the systematic fabrication of the myth of the Lost Cause.[53]

The New South had to reestablish the place of blacks in the legal order; obviously, northern ideals of equality before the law would not do. White southerners first expanded the legal structure of Jim Crow. Segregation and racial discrimination had existed before the Civil War, but they assumed an enlarged importance after abolition, when they would have to serve as substitutes for the racial subordination that automatically accompanied slavery.[54] Law played a vital role in imposing Jim Crow, as white legislators translated custom and public policy into statutes.

Law was equally important in suppressing blacks into a status of economic involuntary servitude. Scholars have traced the transformation of the Black Codes into a system of comprehensive labor subordination encompassing enticement, emigrant-agent, contract enforcement, vagrancy, criminal surety, and convict labor laws.[55] Others have followed in detail the persistence of peonage;[56] and the effects of tenant farming, sharecropping, and the crop-lien system are staples in all economic histories of the region.

Having achieved the economic subordination of blacks, white legislators then turned to the next agenda item, stripping them of political power. This step was accomplished by the universal adoption throughout the South of the Mississippi Plan in the period 1890 through 1917. The white disfranchisers made no secret of what they were about. Carter Glass proclaimed in the Virginia disfranchising convention of 1901–2: "Discrimination! Why, that is precisely what we propose; that, exactly, is what this Convention was elected for—to discriminate to the very extremity of permissible action under the limitations of the Federal Constitution, with a view to the elimination of every negro voter who can be gotten rid of, legally."[57] The disfranchising effort was successful from the whites' point of view: by World War I, black voting had been virtually eliminated in the South.

The U.S. Supreme Court's reaction to this repression of blacks was curiously mixed. The Court validated racial segregation in public accommodations and public schooling and state-mandated segregation in private colleges and schools.[58] Similarly, the Court accepted the constitutionality of the Mississippi Plan and thus validated the disempowering of blacks.[59] The mood of formalism that then dominated the Court, along with its narrow reading of the Civil War amendments and Reconstruction civil rights legislation, assured southern whites that the judiciary would not stand in the way of segregation so long as there was a pretense of racial equality. Yet the Court was not wholly indifferent to the evils of involuntary servitude and Jim Crow.[60] It showed itself surprisingly firm in condemning peonage;[61] it moved vigorously against the more egregious evasions of the Fifteenth Amendment;[62] and it struck down overt residential segregation.[63] So the white South got mixed signals from the Supreme Court, but the basic element of the Compromise of 1877—the promise of no northern interference with the white South's free hand in restructuring race relations—remained intact.

Law and Economics below the Mason-Dixon Line

Slavery and race were the principal determinants of the South's distinctive constitutional tradition, but they were not the only ones. Lesser influences also shaped a distinctively southern approach to public law. Neither of the two discussed here was autonomous or unrelated to questions of slavery and race. The more important of them was the South's regional economic experience.

It is now a commonplace that the South has experienced a colonial economy into modern times. Until the twentieth century, it remained largely in the primary stage of economic development, exporting raw or semiprocessed materials, where the processing consisted of little more than reducing bulk. It experienced little indigenous capital formation. The South has always relied on a basic economic strategy of exploiting its people (of both races) and its natural resources in destructive ways that ravaged both people and land without in any way altering its regional economic colonial status. C. Vann Woodward and Harry Scheiber, among others, have traced the depressing story of this process since the Civil War.[64] Many early factors encouraged this colonial economic status: a subtropical climate suited to the production of export staples such as tobacco, indigo, rice, and cotton; rivers with fall lines far inland and gentle gradients, conducive to direct transatlantic trading connections with the British Isles; and the metropolis's mercantilist economic policy before Independence. But race and slavery would exert an enduring, malignant influence for most of three centuries to retard economic development while encouraging economic growth.

Edmund S. Morgan has suggested that Virginia's seventeenth-century ruling elite solved the emergent problem of class divisions in the tobacco colony by encouraging the growth of slavery, attempting to link the interests of the potentially revolutionary class of unmarried, landless whites with that of the gentry through racial solidarity.[65] This began a tradition in which race trumped class, but only imperfectly. Numerous recent studies have demonstrated the persistence of class divisions in the South into our time and the recurrent ability of the ruling classes to manipulate, co-opt, and/or coerce poorer whites by appeals to white supremacy.[66] From this class division, always overridden but never obliterated by race solidarity, much of the South's economic history flows—and that economic history, in turn, had some effect on the law's development.

One consequence of the South's class structure was the early establishment of its tradition of low taxes and low public services. Naturally, the white South wanted no educational services provided for the enslaved black population; indeed, in the antebellum period it was a felony to educate slaves. But the southern elite saw little to be gained by educating poor whites, either: increased literacy would only make the poor more discontented with their lot as dirt farmers and mill hands. Any increase in public services would require an increase in taxes, and a large part of those taxes would necessarily come out of the pockets of the upper classes and the corporations they were trying to entice. But low taxes are only half the story:[67] retarded economic development is the other half. With no sources of public funds to pay for public services and public institutions, the South lagged behind the rest of the nation in providing schools, asylums, universities, and a bureaucracy capable of running a government. In place of coercive taxes, the South has tended to rely on voluntaristic and charitable alternatives to public services that elsewhere are taken for granted. The consequences of this retardation, especially in public education, are incalculable. Illiteracy and ignorance beset the South as a legacy of this dual curse of slavery and low taxes. Southern poor laws comparably displayed a distaste for taxes, bureaucracy, and institutions. Hence, while the North was discovering asylum, the South continued to rely on a system of poor relief devised in Elizabethan times, clinging to centuries-old techniques of outrelief and apprenticeship.[68]

Though the South disdained coercive financial contributions to the state, it had no reluctance to coerce labor. Slavery was the extreme form of a forced exaction of labor, and the attitude that blacks could and should be forced to work outside the wage system persisted after emancipation in convict-labor and convict-lease systems, the chain gang, and the forms of involuntary servitude noted earlier. But whites were affected, too. In common with other American jurisdictions before Independence, the southern colonies exacted labor contributions from free persons for road upkeep. This policy persisted in some southern jurisdictions until the eve of the Civil War. The slave states drafted nonslaveholding whites as conscripts for slave patrols, requiring that they furnish weapons and mounts.

Tony A. Freyer has suggested that interpersonal relationships have permeated southern law, producing such attitudes as hostility to limited corporate liability and the use of accommodation notes.[69] This situation obviously comports with the attitudes and social relationships of a *gemeinschaftliche* society, but it has also had consequences for legal institutions. One was a heightened degree of hostility to banks and corporations that lingered longer in the South than elsewhere. Corporations represented impersonal, "soulless" entities, neither sensitive to honor

181

nor susceptible of shame. Judge Spencer Roane's suspicion of corporations expressed in the 1809 *Currie's Administrators* case typifies this attitude. Resisting rationalization of insurance premiums, he maintained that if the incorporators' "object is merely private or selfish, if it is detrimental to, or not promotive of, the public good, they have no adequate claim upon the legislature for the privilege" of incorporation.[70] Similarly, another Virginia judge, Peter V. Daniel, directed in his will that none of the proceeds of his estate were to be invested in the stock of banking corporations, holding to the end his distaste for banks.[71] This hostility was intensified if the corporation was "foreign," that is, chartered by another state. Before the Civil War, southern legislatures not only denounced the penetration of their economies by foreign corporations but actually erected barriers to exclude them or impede their operations. The Taney Court's first important corporation case, *Bank of Augusta v. Earle* (1839), was the result of just such an effort.[72]

Southern jurists clung to a monopoly model of economic development for a generation after it had been abandoned in the North in favor of a model that stressed competition.[73] Early in the nineteenth century northern judges, led by New York's chancellor and supreme court justice James Kent, promoted a monopoly model in decisions that sustained legislative grants of monopolies over travel routes and enjoined competition by competing lines.[74] They abandoned this preference at about the time of the *Charles River Bridge* decision (1837), which refused to read an implied monopoly grant into a corporate charter under the contracts clause of the federal Constitution.[75] Southern jurisdictions declined to extrapolate that holding into a generalized hostility to monopoly grants, express or implied, relying instead on the older rationale of upholding or implying monopoly privileges in return for service to the public.[76] The attraction of monopolies persisted in the South after the Civil War, producing, among other things, the renowned *Slaughterhouse Cases* of 1873. In his dissent there, Justice Joseph Bradley condemned the butchering monopoly as "one of those arbitrary and unjust laws made in the interest of a few scheming individuals, by which some of the Southern States have, within the past few years, been so deplorably oppressed and impoverished."[77] Bradley's angry words suggest how far the legal systems of the North and South diverged: the competition model had become so axiomatic to northern jurists (Bradley was from New Jersey) that it seemed part of the natural order of things, whereas

182

the South's preference for the alternative constituted a commitment to ignorance and penury.

Perhaps the single most egregious feature of southern law in the economic sphere was its consistent legislative preference for the interests of debtors. It would not be saying too much to identify this as a major theme of nineteenth-century southern legal history. This legislative preference is evident as early as the time of South Carolina's 1785 Pine Barrens Act. It continued through the postrevolutionary struggles over British and Loyalist debts and included such classic legal episodes as abolition of imprisonment for debt; creation of exemptions for homesteads, farming implements, tools of trade, and even the family Bible; the married women's property acts (like the homestead exemption, pioneered by southern states); and the stay and moratoria legislation that were characteristic of antebellum insolvency laws. All these constitute an invariant inclination in the South to favor the interests of debtors over those of creditors.

There should be nothing surprising about this debtor bias in southern law. Since the seventeenth century the South has been a debtor region, first to British and Scottish investors and factors and then to economic interests centered in Philadelphia and New York. An area suffering from chronic specie scarcity and capital outflow might naturally be expected to be sympathetic to the needs of debtors. But this pro-debtor bias of southern law did not directly reflect class antagonisms of southern society. The planter elite of eighteenth-century Virginia, its Jeffersons and Washingtons, were debtors, after all, and a reliance on indebtedness as a substitute for indigenous capital formation continued throughout the South through the nineteenth century.

The dark and bloody ground of early Kentucky legal history provides vivid examples of how statutory favoritism to debtors has influenced the development of southern law. One was the turmoil induced by an 1821 stay law. After the court of appeals, the highest court of the commonwealth, held the statute unconstitutional, the debtor interest in the legislature abolished the court itself, with the expectation that a new court would uphold the measure. For a period, both courts continued to function, until the creditor interest regained control of the legislature, abolished the new court, and thereby terminated the United States' unique experience with a judicial Avignon papacy.

Federal courts did not escape Kentucky's debtor controversies. In

1797 and again in 1812, the state legislature enacted the "Occupying Claimant" laws in an effort to cleanse the Augean stables of Kentucky land titles. These statutes provided that a successful claimant in a title dispute must compensate the ejected occupier for improvements the latter made; if he refused, the occupier might claim title on payment of the value of the land before the improvements. Kentuckians had long feared that federal courts might favor out-of-state creditor interests,[78] and the U.S. Supreme Court confirmed their fears by holding the measures unconstitutional under the contracts clause as a violation of the interstate compact with Virginia concluded at Kentucky statehood.[79] Kentuckians in response did not go quite so far as to demand the abolition of the Supreme Court, as they were contemporaneously doing with their own court of appeals. Rather, they contented themselves with the more modest measures of seeking repeal of section 25 of the 1789 Judiciary Act or abolition of judicial review by the Supreme Court.

Kentucky hostility added fuel to the southern and western fires of resentment at the Supreme Court, which culminated in an unsuccessful 1831 effort to repeal section 25. John C. Calhoun translated Kentucky's grievances into a component of his larger, emerging conception of the Union. He recommended a sectional veto on national legislation, which he thought would be achieved simply by section 25's repeal. "If the appellate power from the State courts to the U. States court provided for by the 25th Sec. did not exist," he wrote Virginia senator Littleton Tazewell in 1827, "the practical consequence would be, that each government [federal and state] would have a negative on the other, and thus possess the most effectual remedy, that can be conceived against encroachment. . . . how far can [section 25] be reconciled with the Sovereignty of the States, as to their rights?"[80] Thus did the rivulet of a state's social and economic policy flow into the river of southern legal sectionalism.

War and Reconstruction did not abate the South's partiality to debtor legislation or the influence of that attitude on larger constitutional developments. Far from it: the postwar South distanced itself further from legal trends elsewhere in its avidity for debt repudiation, which in Virginia went by the more euphemistic name of Readjustment. Second only to questions of race, railroads were the staple of state Reconstruction politics, as the states of the former Confederacy sought to rebuild their physical plants and their economies. Either having never experienced the prewar mania for public inducements to railroads or having suffered a war-induced amnesia on the matter, the southern states heavily committed their credit or their resources to encouraging railroads, seeing in them a panacea that would lead to the New South. As these hopes withered and public enthusiasm curdled in the economic downturn following the Panic of 1873, southern leaders noticed that railroad investment had inflated the public debt and sought to disburden themselves of it. The U.S. Supreme Court had already sternly warned the states against trying that sort of thing,[81] but the war, defeat, and occupation had not dulled southern legal ingenuity. (Indeed, a strong impressionistic argument can be made that adversity only stimulated it.) Southern attorneys seeking to uphold repudiation, especially as practiced by the Bourbon regime in Louisiana, turned to an old product of southern states' power ideology that had survived the war, the Eleventh Amendment. Surprisingly, the U.S. Supreme Court went along with the repudiationist reading of the amendment, permitting the states to shelter behind its protection of sovereign immunity as a defense against suits by outraged bondholders.[82]

Harry Scheiber has demonstrated that postbellum southern economic policy was premised on the delusion that the South's genuine economic ills were caused by external agents (the federal judiciary, northern investors) and could be relieved by such unlikely measures as attacks on the jurisdiction of the federal courts, prohibition of railroad rate discrimination, antidrummer legislation, laws prohibiting aliens from owning land, and other peripheral or symbolic matters.[83] In reality, the South's enduring problem of economic colonialism could best be addressed by attacks on the crop-lien system, racial oppression, and inadequate state taxes, policies that would have been anathema to the post-Reconstruction conservative leadership of the region.

The class cleavages of white southern society, present all along, began to emerge in the late nineteenth century as white elite southern political leadership ignored the real problems of the region and intensified the traditional and misguided policy of stimulating economic growth, not development, and of exploiting the region's people and resources through such destructive measures as encouraging child labor and virtually giving away coal, mineral, and timber resources to outside investors. Native white southern political and economic leaders willingly took on the role of what Trotsky called "compradors": native intermediaries who serve as agents for foreign businessmen.

This shortsighted and exploitative policy finally provoked political resistance from up-country whites who believed that their way of life was being destroyed and who saw the policy of white supremacy as the cover that it was for a hidden agenda of upper-class dominance over the poor of both races. The Populist movement was the product of this perception. Elite white leadership struck back, effectively, with the program of disfranchisement, eliminating not only all blacks but a significant number of poor whites from access to political power, self-help, and participation in republican political processes.[84] The years 1895 and 1896, epochal ones for American constitutional development, marked the complete triumph of the conservatives' program. The Mississippi Plan was being put into place and would be ratified by the U.S. Supreme Court in two years; Jim Crow received the court's blessing; the Court struck down the federal income tax and checked the federal police power; it exalted the labor injunction as a weapon that would smash union organization and gut workers' First Amendment rights.[85]

The second subsidiary theme relevant to the South's legal distinctiveness is the problem of violence in southern history. The concept of a "violent South," or, to borrow the title of John Hope Franklin's influential study, *The Militant South*,[86] is so widely accepted as almost to have attained the status of a cliché.[87] But a reconsideration of the relationship between violence and the laws can provide a corrective to some misconceptions prevalent about the violent South.

The people of the South, of both races, have been more prone to acts of interpersonal violence than Americans elsewhere.[88] Much in southern culture provides a matrix for violence: the influence of slavery (recall Jefferson's heartfelt worries expressed in *Notes on Virginia*), *Herrenvolk* democracy, the antidemocratic traditions of the South's elite leadership, the dominance/deference models of gender roles, the authoritarian and militaristic strain in southern public life, the traditions of a rural society where weapons are routinely wielded for hunting and where a rural gendarmerie has come into being only in the twentieth century. From this matrix, Wilbur Cash has drawn an ineradicable portrait of a society where violence combined with individualism to weaken the hold of law and social institutions and where as a result southerners casually resorted to self-help, violence, and homicide to resolve disputes.[89] Charles Sydnor's classic 1940 essay, "The Southerner and the Laws," maintained that the (white) southerner considered himself above or at least outside many of his state's positive laws because of the South's rural, plantation, slave-society character.[90]

But did the tradition of violence really conduce to a disregard of statutory and common law in the South? Does the former necessarily produce the latter? Did it, in fact, do so in the South's historical experience? We may concede the prevalence of violence and yet doubt that white southerners did have a cavalier, contemptuous attitude toward positive law. Consider the problem of vigilantism, superficially considered to be the product of a widespread popular predisposition to violence. In the popular mind, vigilantism is conflated with lynch law, but it is essential to recognize distinctions between the two. Both have been prevalent in the South, the former since the Regulator movements of South Carolina (1769) and North Carolina (1771),[91] the latter since Virginia judge Charles Lynch contributed his name to the activity by anti-Loyalist zeal shortly thereafter. But vigilantism in the South, as elsewhere, has been a political phenomenon, fundamentally democratic in nature, in which "the people," organized as a disciplined and purposive mob, have supplied or replaced the institutions of law and governance for limited periods, always because of their grievance that extant, often distant, legal institutions were inadequate to their peacekeeping function.

On the other hand, "lynch law," as it is oxymoronically called, is a popular outburst of violence that threatens rather than reinforces the rule of law. Admittedly, vigilantism and lynching overlap or shade into each other. But the Regulators and the San Francisco Committee of Vigilance (1854, 1856) were essentially different from Emmett Till's murderers and the Leo Frank lynch mob. And both should be distinguished from the phenomenon known as "whitecapping," also indigenous to the South, in which rural people resisted threats to their way of life from distant agents of "progress," such as industrialization. The first Klan was a special and unique case of political violence and will be considered later.

The above distinction serves purposes other than an idle taxonomy of concepts. The phenomenon of vigilantism, far from being a repudiation of law, is actually a hypertrophied reaffirmation of legal institutions and is characteristic of both *volksrecht* (e.g., the South Carolina Regulators or the San Francisco Vigilantes) and *volksgesetz* (e.g., the California and Colorado mining camp regulations, created in large measure by southern Forty-niners), which have been endemic to frontier areas in the United States and Canada. Lynching, on the other hand, strikes at law. The state would be well advised under certain circumstances to tolerate vigilantism, as British and American authorities tolerated mobs in the eighteenth century to the extent that "the people out of doors" took on not only a legitimate status but almost a crypto-governmental one. But the state must suppress lynching as group criminal activity.

Before leaving the subject of lynching, it would be useful to draw some historical distinctions. Before the Civil War, lynching was seldom lethal, and its victims were predominantly whites. "To ride Judge Lynch's horse," as the activity was described in Missouri and other border states, was to be ridden out of town on a rail. Usually the most violent consequence of a lynching was a degradation of one's dignity, as by a tarring and feathering. There were lethal lynchings before the Civil War—such as that of the Murrell Gang in Mississippi, where the victims were white, and the McIntosh burning in St. Louis, where the victim was black—but these were exceptions. The character of lynching changed after emancipation. It became lethal, with death sometimes coming after torture, and its victims were predominantly black. (Again, exceptions come to mind—Leo Frank, Italian immigrants in New Orleans—but they were just that, exceptions.)

One obvious legal explanation for this change presents itself. When slavery was abolished, so of necessity was the slave criminal code. Its limited reconstruction in the Black Codes served principally the economic purpose of labor coercion. Given northern determination to force the South to adopt something generally comporting with northern ideals of equality before the law, the South could recreate no overt substitute for the criminal-disciplinary measures of the old slave codes. If there was to be a functional substitute, it had to be by subterfuge (e.g., making rape a capital offense, with the unwritten understanding that the typical—indeed, virtually exclusive—prosecution would be of a black for rape of a white woman). But opportunities there were limited, and if whites were to control the behavior of blacks by lethal violence, it would have to be done outside the law; hence lynching.

Sydnor's oft-cited argument, that the white southerner considered himself beyond the statutory law when it suited him, requires comment. Sydnor thought it so obvious as not to need elaboration that "geographic distance kept the full force of the law from touching the Westerner; the social order diminished the force of law in the South."[92] He was in error in the first half of the statement. Distance from civilization in frontier areas served not to diminish law-abidingness but to stimulate it: the frontier was not lawless but rather scrupulously law-abiding (within the limits possible in an area where police forces were nonexistent or stretched thin). The second half of the statement may be salvaged, but only with qualifications and explanation. For some purposes, in the realm of interpersonal relations, the white southerner did in fact consider statutes precatory or admonitory rather than obligatory, especially when questions of race were involved. Why should this be so? The rural or frontier character of the South is not a satisfactory explanation; if it were, it would apply equally to the West.

Under the legal regime of slave societies in North America, two separate but parallel bodies of law coexisted: the ordinary civil law for whites and a special body of statutory law, with its separate enforcement mechanisms, for slaves. The slave codes were supplemented by informal systems of plantation justice, as well as by unwritten codes of racial etiquette (doffing the hat, saying "Yes, sir"). Emancipation abolished the slave codes, requiring that the laws for whites and the laws for blacks be more or less unified and integrated. But old habits of thought persisted. Because blacks were not equals in the eyes of whites, it was thought preposterous to pretend that the laws applied to them equally, whatever northerners might rhapsodize about equality before the law: hence the white southerner's disregard of certain statutory laws when it suited him. The ancient impulse of Western law, tracing back to Justinian, that likes should be treated alike, was seen as having no application to blacks, who were not likes. Therefore the white southerner felt no compunction about disregarding a law that would be absurd if applied literally. But Sydnor's *aperçu* should not be taken to mean that there is something inherently lawless in southern culture. Rather, it was the white man's de facto adjustment to a situation where the law seemed to command something meaningless.

Southern legal experience since 1867 has reflected the fact that the South is the only region to have undergone the experience of having its constitutions, values, and much of its legal order imposed from without, in apparent disregard or at least suspension of the American ideal of self-government. Reconstruction was a singular anomaly in American experience, and southern legal thought was influenced by that peculiarity. Probably the most important result of the partial abeyance of self-government during Reconstruction was that the white southerner acquired an apparently ineradicable reputation for being lawless, as he sought to overthrow a regime of laws that he had no hand in making and that he therefore considered illegitimate.

Guerilla resistance, in the form of the Klan and its ilk, was one expectable reaction to the imposition of northern legal values on the southern order. The Force Acts and suspension of the writ of habeas corpus in South Carolina effectively put an end to that sort of extralegal resistance. Then another immediately appeared. There were many people in the South—blacks, most native northerners who settled in the South, and some native southern whites—who wanted to accommodate to the new legal order, who wanted to adopt northern legal values and something resembling the northern economic order. And there were many who refused to accept this new legal order. Under such circumstances, internecine war was probably inevitable, and it promptly occurred in Arkansas (the "Brooks-Baxter War" of 1872–74) and in Louisiana (the election disorders of 1872–76).

Nightriding was related to this internecine tendency. The epitome of this form of violence was the Klan in its first incarnation (*floruit* 1866–71). To a great extent, the antiblack, anti-Unionist, anti-Republican violence of Reconstruction was political, having a clearly articulated political objective, the destruction of Republican power in the South and the restoration of what white Democrats considered self-government. Considered as descendants of the mobs of the previous century, the nightriders of the Reconstruction era were a rational political response to the tensions of Reconstruction. They reappeared in an echo some ninety years later, but by then, to borrow Marx's phrase, tragedy had degenerated into farce. Massive resistance also represented an effort to throw off legal values being imposed from without, but the old order had by that time decayed so far that revolution came relatively speedily and successfully. The second Reconstruction stuck.

Southern constitutional experience and outlook have differed from that of other regions. Forged in the smithy of a slave society, the public law of the South for a century and a half was a weapon used to preserve the white man's government, coercing the labor of blacks and disciplining their behavior toward whites. Public law also helped maintain the economic retardation of the South. Today this self-defeating distinctiveness has almost disappeared, leaving the South free to cultivate the positive aspects of its constitutional heritage and to share that heritage with the rest of the nation. An emphasis on regional and state autonomy as a counterpoise to the powers of a centralized national leviathan can stand the nation in good stead today, especially in the defense of individual freedom that the South's traditions so long repressed.

190

Notes

I thank Colleen B. Grzeskowiak for research assistance with this essay.

1. In this essay, "the South" includes the states of the Confederacy plus Delaware, Maryland, West Virginia, Kentucky, Missouri, and Oklahoma.

2. C. Vann Woodward, *Thinking Back: The Perils of Writing History* (Baton Rouge, 1986), 121, 123.

3. To cite only some representative classics: Jesse T. Carpenter, *The South as a Conscious Minority: A Study in Political Thought* (New York, 1930); Wilbur J. Cash, *The Mind of the South* (New York, 1941); Charles S. Sydnor, *The Development of Southern Sectionalism, 1819–1848* (Baton Rouge, 1948); Avery O. Craven, *The Growth of Southern Nationalism, 1848–1861* (Baton Rouge, 1953); Clement Eaton, *The Growth of Southern Civilization, 1790–1860* (New York, 1961); William R. Taylor, *Cavalier and Yankee: The Old South and American National Character* (Garden City, N.Y., 1963); Francis B. Simkins, *The Everlasting South* (Baton Rouge, 1963); and the essays collected in *The Idea of the South: Pursuit of a Central Theme*, ed. Frank E. Vandiver (Chicago, 1964).

4. Interview with Louis T. Wigfall, 1860, in William R. Russell, *My Diary North and South*, ed. Fletcher Pratt (New York, 1954), 99.

5. Quoted in Arthur C. Cole, *The Irrepressible Conflict, 1850–1865* (New York, 1934), viii.

6. Thomas P. Govan, "Was the Old South Different?" *Journal of Southern History* 21 (1955): 447–55; Charles G. Sellers, ed., *The Southerner as American* (Chapel Hill, N.C., 1960); Grady McWhiney, *Southerners and Other Americans* (New York, 1973); Richard N. Current, *Northernizing the South* (Athens, Ga., 1983); Edward Pessen, "How Different from Each Other Were the Antebellum North and South?" *American Historical Review* 85 (1980): 1119–49.

7. C. Vann Woodward, *The Burden of Southern History*, rev. ed. (Baton Rouge, 1968). See also Woodward, *Thinking Back*, 122: it was the North, not the South, that was "the center of national exceptionalism."

8. Howard Zinn, *The Southern Mystique* (New York, 1964).

9. Tönnies, a German sociologist, was born in 1855 and died in 1936. His principal work, *Gemeinschaft und Gesellschaft*, did not appear in English translation until 1957: *Community and Society*, trans. Charles P. Loomis (East Lansing, Mich., 1957).

10. This list is compiled from Carl N. Degler, *Place over Time: The Continuity of Southern Distinctiveness* (Baton Rouge, 1977), 10–25; Woodward, *Thinking Back,*; and James M. McPherson, "Antebellum Southern Exceptionalism: A New Look at an Old Question," *Civil War History* 29 (1983): 230–44.

11. John S. Reed, *The Enduring South: Subcultural Persistence in Mass Society* (Lexington, Mass., 1972), 9–32.

191

12. Before 1850, I know of only two that can plausibly be ranked with the work of James Wilson, Zephaniah Swift, Nathaniel Chipman, Nathan Dane, James Kent, Joseph Story, William A. Duer, Simon Greenleaf, and Isaac Redfield: St. George Tucker, *Blackstone's Commentaries, with Notes of Reference to the Constitution and Laws, of the Federal Government of the United States; and of the Commonwealth of Virginia* (Philadelphia, 1803), and Henry St. George Tucker's *Commentaries on the Laws of Virginia* (Winchester, Va., 1831). On the former, see Charles T. Cullen, *St. George Tucker and Law in Virginia, 1772–1804* (New York, 1987). The South was distinguished, however, by its statutory compilations. See William W. Hening, comp., *The Statutes at Large: Being a Collection of All the Laws of Virginia, from the First Session of the Legislature, in the Year 1619,* 13 vols. (Richmond, Va., 1809–23); and Thomas Cooper and David J. McCord, eds., *The Statutes at Large of South Carolina* (Columbia, S.C., 1836–41).

13. I deliberately bypass the question whether southern jurists were generally inferior to northern judges before the Civil War. Mark Tushnet has occasionally implied that they were: see, e.g., *The American Law of Slavery, 1810– 1860: Considerations of Humanity and Interest* (Princeton, N.J., 1981), 29, 42. Bertram Wyatt-Brown rejects that idea: *Southern Honor: Ethics and Behavior in the Old South* (New York, 1982), 263. My own view is: first, a bar that produced such luminaries as Spencer Roane, William Gaston, and Thomas Ruffin (to mention only state court judges) cannot have been wholly unworthy of notice; but second, no one is in a position to make such sweeping generalizations until we have many more studies of southern and northern jurists, with individual studies comparable to Levy's *Shaw* and Reid's *Doe,* and also prosopographical work on the southern bench. See Kermit L. Hall, "The Promises and Perils of Prosopography—Southern Style," *Vanderbilt Law Review* 32 (1979): 331–39.

14. For elaborations of this neo-Garrisonian view of the Constitution as a proslavery document, see Paul Finkelman, "Slavery and the Constitutional Convention: Making a Covenant with Death" in *Beyond Confederation: Origins of the Constitution and American National Identity,* ed. Richard Beeman et al. (Chapel Hill, N.C., 1987), 188–225; and William M. Wiecek, "The Blessings of Liberty: Slavery in the American Constitutional Order," in *The Constitution, Slavery, and Its Consequences,* ed. Robert Goldwin and Arthur Kaufman (Washington, D.C., in press), and "The Witch at the Christening: Slavery and the Constitution's Origins," in *The Constitution: A History of Its Framing and Ratification,* ed. Leonard W. Levy and Dennis J. Mahoney (New York, 1987), 167–84.

15. On resistance to the U.S. Supreme Court's appellate review authority over the decisions of state supreme courts, see Charles Warren, "Legislative and Judicial Attacks on the Supreme Court of the United States—A History of the Twenty-fifth Section of the Judiciary Act," *American Law Review* 47 (1913): 1–34, 161–89; and William M. Wiecek, "The 'Imperial Judiciary' in Historical

Perspective," *Yearbook of the Supreme Court Historical Society,* 1984, 61–89, esp. 64–68.

16. I have explored this development in some detail in William M. Wiecek, *The Sources of Antislavery Constitutionalism in America, 1760–1848* (Ithaca, N.Y., 1977), 106–49.

17. Duncan J. MacLeod, *Slavery, Race and the American Revolution* (Cambridge, 1974), chaps. 4–5.

18. Speech reproduced in *Democracy, Liberty, and Property: The State Constitutional Conventions of the 1820s,* ed. Merrill D. Peterson (Indianapolis, 1966), 341–43.

19. Gov. George McDuffie's message to the General Assembly, 1835, reprinted in *Journal of the General Assembly of . . . South Carolina . . . 1835,* 5–9.

20. E.g., the well-known cases of Harry v. Decker & Hopkins, Walker (1 Miss.) 36 (1818); Rankin v. Lydia, 2 A. K. Marsh. 468 (1820); Lunsford v. Coquillon, 14 Mart. (La.) 465 (1824)

21. State v. Mann, 2 Dev. (N.C.) 263 (1829).

22. "An Act to Authorize the Manumission of Slaves," 1782, Hening, *Statutes,* 11:39–40.

23. "An Act Amending the Laws concerning Emancipated Slaves, Free Negroes and Mulattoes," chap. 70, *Acts of the General Assembly of Virginia . . . 1836–37.*

24. Elkison v. Deliesseline, 8 F. Cas. 493 (C.C.D.S.C. 1823) (No. 4366); see also Justice Johnson's concurring opinion in Gibbons v. Ogden, 9 Wheat. (22 U.S.) 1, 27–33 (1824), on the same subject.

25. *Caroliniensis* (1824?), a pamphlet reprint of articles by Turnbull and Holmes in the *Charleston Mercury,* in the South Caroliniana Library, the University of South Carolina, Columbia.

26. Message of Gov. George M. Troup to Georgia legislature, 1825, reprinted in *State Documents on Federal Relations,* ed. Herman V. Ames (1900; reprint, New York, 1970), 208–9.

27. See the two classic studies by scholars from both sections: Clement Eaton, *The Freedom-of-Thought Struggle in the Old South,* rev. ed. (New York, 1964); and Russell D. Nye, *Fettered Freedom: Civil Liberties and the Slavery Controversy, 1830–1860,* rev. ed. (East Lansing, Mich., 1963).

28. Some historians (I among them) have tended to see the essence of Calhoun's thought in his two *summae, Discourse on Government* and *Disquisitions on Government,* both dictated shortly before his death. These two treatises actually had little effect on the development of southern constitutional doctrine, and some of their proposals, such as the dual presidency and the sectional veto, found little favor among southern thinkers. The 1837 and 1847 resolutions, on the other hand, represented the mainstream of southern thought and established constitutional dogma for the region.

193

29. Arthur Bestor, Jr., "State Sovereignty and Slavery: A Reinterpretation of Proslavery Constitutional Doctrine, 1846–1860," *Journal of the Illinois State Historical Society* 54 (1961): 117–80.

30. Respectively: 19 How. (60 U.S.) 393 (1857); 21 How. (62 U.S.) 506 (1859). On the former, Don E. Fehrenbacher, *The Dred Scott Case: Its Significance in American Law and Politics* (New York, 1978), is definitive.

31. 19 How. at 405, 407. Some scholars emphasize that, in context, these words refer to the status of blacks in 1776 and 1787: see, for example, Walter Ehrlich, *They Have No Rights: Dred Scott's Struggle for Freedom* (Westport, Conn., 1979). However, it is clear that Taney meant his characterizations to apply equally to 1857; see Fehrenbacher, *The Dred Scott Case*, 348.

32. 19 How. at 426.

33. 19 How. at 426, 448, 452.

34. See resolutions offered by Sen. Jefferson Davis of Mississippi, *Congressional Globe*, 36th Cong., 1st sess., February 2, 1860, 658.

35. 21 How. at 516.

36. 10 How. (51 U.S.) 83, 93 (1851).

37. 21 How. at 516.

38. See Alexander H. Stephens, *A Constitutional View of the Late War between the States*, 2 vols. (Philadelphia, 1868, 1870); "The Address of the People of South Carolina . . . to the People of the Slaveholding States" (1860), in *South Carolina Secedes*, comp. John A. May and Joan R. Faunt (Columbia, S.C., 1960), 82–92.

39. The definitive texts of the Confederate constitutions may be found in Charles R. Lee, Jr., *The Confederate Constitutions* (Chapel Hill, N.C., 1963). The author's helpful parallel-column comparison of the U.S. and Confederate constitutions throws into clear relief the contrasts between the documents.

40. William M. Robinson, *Justice in Grey: A History of the Judicial System of the Confederate States of America* (Cambridge, Mass., 1941), 436.

41. Opinion of May 16, 1862, in *The Opinions of the Confederate Attorneys General, 1861–1865*, comp. Rembert W. Patrick (Buffalo, N.Y., 1950), 94.

42. Speech reprinted in Edward McPherson, *Political History of the United States during the Great Rebellion, 1860–1865*, ed. Harold M. Hyman and Hans Trefousse (1865; reprint, New York, 1972), 103–4.

43. Harold D. Woodman, "Sequel to Slavery: The New History Views the Postbellum South," *Journal of Southern History* 43 (1977): 554.

44. Ulrich B. Phillips, "The Central Theme of Southern History," *American Historical Review* 34 (1928): 31.

45. Paul Finkelman, "Exploring Southern Legal History," *North Carolina Law Review* 64 (1985): 98.

46. Bryan v. Walton, 14 Ga. 185, 198 (1853).

47. 1 Cranch (5 U.S.) 137, 163 (1803).

48. See the discussion of the legal status of blacks in the free states in Paul Finkelman, "Prelude to the Fourteenth Amendment: Black Legal Rights in the Antebellum North," *Rutgers Law Journal* 17 (1986): 415–82.

49. The most thorough survey to date of this topic is Theodore B. Wilson, *The Black Codes of the South* (University, Ala., 1965).

50. *Laws of . . . Mississippi . . . 1865*, chaps. 4–6.

51. *Chicago Tribune*, December 1, 1865.

52. Civil Rights Act of 1866, chap. 31, sec. 1, 14 Stat. 27.

53. See in general Paul M. Gaston, *The New South Creed: A Study in Southern Mythmaking* (New York, 1970), chap. 1, "Birth of a Creed."

54. See the authors' introductions to C. Vann Woodward, *The Strange Career of Jim Crow*, 3d rev. ed. (New York, 1974), and Joel Williamson, *The Origins of Segregation* (Lexington, Mass., 1968), for reflections on the historiographic debate engendered by the 1955 publication of Woodward's *locus classicus*.

55. William Cohen, "Negro Involuntary Servitude in the South, 1865–1940: A Preliminary Analysis," *Journal of Southern History* 42 (1976): 31–60; Daniel Novak, *The Wheel of Servitude: Black Forced Labor after Slavery* (Lexington, Ky., 1978).

56. Pete Daniel, *The Shadow of Slavery: Peonage in the South, 1901–1969* (Urbana, Ill., 1972).

57. Quoted in A. E. Dick Howard, *Commentaries on the Constitution of Virginia* (Charlottesville, Va., 1974), 1:17.

58. Respectively: Plessy v. Ferguson, 163 U.S. 537 (1896); Cumming v. Richmond County Board of Education, 175 U.S. 528 (1899) (ruling that a board of education not only may segregate public schools but may even refuse to provide a high school for blacks though it provides one for whites); Berea College v. Kentucky, 211 U.S. 45 (1908).

59. Williams v. Mississippi, 170 U.S. 213 (1898).

60. See generally Benno Schmidt's revisionist treatment of this period in Alexander M. Bickel and Benno C. Schmidt, Jr., *The Judiciary and Responsible Government*, vol. 9 of *The Oliver Wendell Holmes Devise History of the Supreme Court of the United States* (New York, 1984), 729–990.

61. Bailey v. Alabama, 211 U.S. 452 (1908); Reynolds v. United States, 235 U.S. 133 (1914); but cf. Clyatt v. United States, 197 U.S. 207 (1905).

62. Guinn v. United States, 238 U.S. 347 (1915).

63. Buchanan v. Warley, 245 U.S. 60 (1917).

64. C. Vann Woodward, *Origins of the New South, 1877–1913*, vol. 9 of *A History of the South*, ed. Wendell Holmes Stephenson and E. Merton Coulter (Baton Rouge, 1971), esp. chap. 11, "The Colonial Economy"; Harry N. Scheiber, "Federalism, the Southern Regional Economy, and Public Policy since 1865," in *Ambivalent Legacy: A Legal History of the South*, ed. David J. Bodenhamer and James W. Ely, Jr. (Jackson, Miss., 1984), 69–105.

195

65. Edmund S. Morgan, *American Slavery/American Freedom: The Ordeal of Colonial Virginia* (New York, 1975).

66. Some of this literature is discussed in Barbara J. Fields, "Ideology and Race in American History," in *Region, Race, and Reconstruction: Essays in Honor of C. Vann Woodward,* ed. J. Morgan Kousser and James M. McPherson (New York, 1982), 143–77.

67. On this point, see James W. Ely, Jr., and David J. Bodenhamer, "Regionalism and American Legal History: The Southern Experience," *Vanderbilt Law Review* (1986): 553.

68. James W. Ely, Jr., " 'There Are Few Subjects in Political Economy of Greater Difficulty': The Poor Laws of the Antebellum South," *American Bar Foundation Research Journal,* 1985, 849–79.

69. Tony A. Freyer, "Law and the Antebellum Southern Economy: An Interpretation," in Bodenhamer and Ely, *Ambivalent Legacy,* 56–57.

70. Currie's Administrators v. The Mutual Assurance Society, 4 Hen. & Munf. (14 Va.) 315, 347–48 (1809).

71. John P. Frank, *Justice Daniel Dissenting* (Cambridge, Mass., 1964).

72. 13 Pet. (38 U.S.) 519.

73. On monopoly vs. competition models of economic development, see Stephen B. Presser and Jamil Zainaldin, *Law and American History: Cases and Materials* (St. Paul, Minn., 1980), 510–35.

74. See opinions of Kent, C. J., in Livingston v. Van Ingen, 9 Johns. 507 (N.Y. Court for Trial of Impeachments and Correction of Errors, 1812); and Kent, Ch., in Croton Turnpike Road Co. v. Ryder, 1 Johns. Ch. 611 (N.Y. Chancery, 1815).

75. Proprietors of Charles River Bridge v. Proprietors of Warren Bridge, 11 Pet. (36 U.S.) 420 (1837).

76. See the Virginia, Alabama, and Arkansas cases cited and discussed in Ely and Bodenhamer, "Regionalism and American Legal History," 554.

77. 16 Wall. (83 U.S.) 36, 120 (1873).

78. On Kentucky federal courts generally, see Richard E. Ellis, *The Jeffersonian Crisis: Courts and Politics in the Young Republic* (New York, 1971), chaps. 9–10; and Mary K. B. Tachau, *Federal Courts in the Early Republic: Kentucky, 1789–1816* (Princeton, N.J., 1978).

79. Green v. Biddle, 8 Wheat. (21 U.S.) 1 (1823).

80. Calhoun to Tazewell, August 25, 1827, Calhoun Papers, Manuscripts Division, Library of Congress, Washington, D.C., quoted in Gerald Gunther, *Constitutional Law* (Mineola, N.Y., 1985), 38.

81. Gelpcke v. Dubuque, 1 Wall. (68 U.S.) 175 (1864).

82. Louisiana ex. rel. Elliott v. Jumel, 107 U.S. 711 (1883); New Hampshire v. Louisiana, 108 U.S. 76 (1883); Hans v. Louisiana, 134 U.S. 1 (1890). On the role of the Eleventh Amendment generally, see John V. Orth, *The Judicial Power*

of the United States: The Eleventh Amendment in American History (New York, 1987).

83. Scheiber, "Federalism, the Southern Regional Economy, and Public Policy."

84. Woodward, *Origins of the New South;* J. Morgan Kousser, *The Shaping of Southern Politics: Suffrage Restriction and the Establishment of the One-Party South, 1880–1910* (New Haven, Conn., 1974).

85. The references are to, respectively, Williams v. Mississippi, 170 U.S. 213 (1898); Plessy v. Ferguson, 163 U.S. 537 (1896); Pollock v. Farmers Loan and Trust Co., 157 U.S. 429 (1895), and 158 U.S. 601 (1895); United States v. E. C. Knight Co., 156 U.S. 1 (1895); and In re Debs, 158 U.S. 564 (1895).

86. John Hope Franklin, *The Militant South, 1800–1861* (Cambridge, Mass., 1956).

87. James W. Ely and Terry Calvani, "Forward to Symposium on the Legal History of the South," *Vanderbilt Law Review* 32 (1979): 3.

88. Finkelman, "Exploring Southern Legal History," 102–3.

89. Cash, *Mind of the South.*

90. Charles S. Sydnor, "The Southerner and the Laws," *Journal of Southern History* 6 (1940): 2–23. Note, however, that Sydnor insisted that the southerner had a high level of respect for two other kinds of laws: (1) the U.S. Constitution and the Bible, considered as embodiments of a secular and a religious form of higher law; and (2) the unwritten "code of honor" so important in a *gemeinschaftliche* society.

91. Recall, however, that these two movements were diametrically opposed in their basic character. South Carolina's protested the absence or insufficiency of law and legal institutions in the Piedmont back country, whereas North Carolina's protested, in part, the activities of courts, sheriffs, lawyers, and judges in the up-country.

92. Sydnor, "The Southerner and the Laws," 12.

197

Part Four

Civil War and Reconstruction

The Civil War and Reconstruction cemented the unique place of the South in the federal Union. Southerners achieved, however fleetingly, a de facto independence from the federal government. Moreover, the crucible of defeat and the bitter Reconstruction experience markedly influenced southern thinking about constitutional issues.

This section considers the impact of the Civil War and Reconstruction in shaping southern constitutionalism. Donald Nieman analyzes the Confederate Constitution and challenges the view that it was a notably southern document. He concludes that the Constitution was rooted in republicanism and fit within the American constitutional tradition. Michael Les Benedict maintains that white southerners denied the legitimacy of the new state constitutions required by Congress as part of the Reconstruction process. Because these state constitutions rested upon black political support and encouraged redistributive economic programs, southerners pictured their efforts to undermine the Reconstruction constitutions as a struggle for liberty and free government. Both authors find evidence of considerable continuity in constitutional values despite the political turmoil of the era.

199

Republicanism, the Confederate Constitution, and the American Constitutional Tradition

Donald Nieman

    The scholarly literature on the Confederate Constitution is extensive, and most of it examines the extent to which the document embodied the states' rights vision of the Old South. This tendency is perhaps inevitable. States' rights and state sovereignty had been at the heart of the sectional conflict for decades and received a great deal of attention from the Confederate framers. Moreover, these matters are central to the perennial debate over Frank Owsley's assertion that states' rights doomed the Confederacy's bid for independence. Concern with states' rights, however, has led most scholars to emphasize the distinctively southern nature of the Confederate Constitution and to ignore how closely it reflected the constitutional concerns and practices of the nation as a whole. It has also inhibited careful consideration of the Confederate framers' most remarkable innovations—changes in the nature of the presidency and legislative-executive relations.[1]

In making these innovations, the Confederate framers were deeply influenced by republican ideology. Republicanism had emerged during the American Revolution, and although it underwent significant changes, it remained powerful in antebellum America. At mid-century it provided the vocabulary that Americans used to discuss politics and shaped the way they thought about political-constitutional issues. It deeply influenced the Confederate framers' approach to constitutional reform, especially the significant changes they made in the presidency. These were designed to preserve republicanism by mitigating the influence of party, checking partisan politics, placing tight restraints on self-serving politicians, and guaranteeing that those in government acted in the public interest. Because this vision and the means that the Confederate framers employed to achieve it were so deeply rooted in republican values, they did not merely reflect the views of the planter elite that dominated the Montgomery Congress. Evidence suggests that representatives of the up-country yeomanry, who were frequently the planters' bitter political adversaries, also acceded to these reforms. Moreover, the significant changes in the presidency made by the Confederate framers were not peculiarly southern: they mirrored constitutional theory and practice in other sections and were within the mainstream of American constitutional development.

The priority that the Confederates gave to constitution making—especially when faced with the prospect of war with the United States—must have struck foreigners as quintessentially American. When the Provisional Confederate Congress met in Montgomery on February 4, 1861, delegates immediately set to work framing a constitution. In less than a week, they drafted and ratified a provisional constitution and appointed a committee of twelve to write a permanent constitution. Committee members, like other delegates, venerated the U.S. Constitution and staunchly maintained that secession was the only means available to vindicate the South's constitutional rights. Not surprisingly, then, they used the 1787 Constitution as the basis of their work and limited themselves to modifying that document. The committee completed its work on February 26, and in the ensuing fortnight the entire Congress, working in secret session, debated, revised, and approved its draft.[2]

In committee and on the floor of Congress, a group led by Robert Barnwell Rhett of South Carolina vigorously pressed a distinctively southern states' rights agenda. This group achieved victory on a number of points. The preamble of the new Constitution clearly established the long-cherished southern principle of state sovereignty, stipulating that "the people of the Confederate States, each state acting in its sovereign and independent character," created the national government and delegated to it certain powers. The document restricted congressional power, eliminating the general-welfare clause and prohibiting enactment of protective tariffs and appropriations for internal improvements. It also

202

deprived the national courts of diversity jurisdiction and authorized state legislatures to impeach national officials operating within their jurisdiction (although reserving for the Confederate Senate the right to try such impeachment cases).[3]

Delegates did not, however, make the national government dependent upon the sovereign states, and they refrained from striking at the essential elements of national power. Aside from eliminating the general-welfare clause and restricting tariffs and internal improvements, they did not deny their Congress any of the legislative authority conferred on the U.S. Congress by the Constitution. Moreover, they refused to eliminate the necessary-and-proper clause, traditionally a fertile source of broad congressional power. Nor did the Confederate framers shy away from asserting national supremacy or conferring on the government means to enforce it. They stipulated that the Confederate Constitution and laws and treaties made under its authority were the supreme law of the land and authorized the national Supreme Court to hear appeals from state courts in cases involving the Constitution, treaties, or national laws. Finally, delegates established "a permanent federal government," refusing to include in the Constitution the right of secession. The Montgomery Congress, in sum, curbed national authority in certain specific areas, but created a government with broad, flexible authority and the means to meet challenges to the exercise of that authority.[4]

Congress was much bolder in dealing with the presidency and legislative-executive relations. Indeed, no less a figure than Robert Toombs, Jefferson Davis's chief rival for the presidency and one of the most influential members of the committee that drafted the permanent Constitution, suggested that these were the key changes that the Montgomery Congress made in the U.S. Constitution. "The formation of our Permanent Constitution, next to the preservation of our national existence is unquestionably our greatest work," he noted prior to ratification, "and in my judgment the most important amendments which will be proposed to the old Constitution are those which alter the relation . . . between the executive and legislative department of the government."[5]

Given the reverence of Toombs and his colleagues for the U.S. Constitution and their reluctance to alter fundamentally the balance of power between the states and the national government, the new Constitution's dramatic changes in the executive department are quite remarkable. The president of the Confederacy was to serve a six-year term but was ineligible for reelection. He could dismiss cabinet officers but might remove other executive department civil servants only for "dishonesty, incapacity, inefficiency, misconduct, or neglect of duty." If the Confederate Constitution reduced the president's control over patronage, it expanded his power in dealing with Congress. Appropriations bills that originated in Congress required two-thirds majorities to become law, whereas money bills that the president initiated needed only the approval of simple majorities. Thus the framers shifted the initiative in the crucial area of appropriations to the executive. Moreover, the Constitution gave the president the item veto—the right "to approve any appropriation and disapprove any other appropriation in the same bill"—and thus further strengthened the executive. Finally, it provided that Congress might authorize members of the president's cabinet to sit on the floor of either house and participate in debate. Although Congress did not implement this provision during the Confederacy's brief existence, it nevertheless represented a significant innovation.[6]

At first glance one might conclude that, despite their reverence for the U.S. Constitution, the founders of the Confederacy left the mainstream of the American constitutional tradition. Perhaps they moved backward into the future, claiming to preserve the traditions of the republican fathers while in fact striking out in bold new directions. Closer examination, however, reveals that no matter how far these innovations departed from American constitutional practice at the national level, they were deeply rooted in popular political-constitutional attitudes and state constitutional practice. Moreover, they anticipated the direction of constitutional change in post–Civil War America.

Confederate tinkering with the executive betrayed a suspicion of party and partisan politics that was central to political-constitutional discourse in nineteenth-century America. Civic virtue—the willingness to put the common good ahead of individual interests—was central to the ideology of republicanism that emerged from the Revolution. So, too, was a deep distrust of politicians and a conviction that persons who wielded governmental authority must be carefully watched lest they expand their power at the expense of liberty. Closely related to these attitudes among eighteenth-century republicans was suspicion of special privilege conferred by government.[7] During the political and ideological battles of the 1820s and 1830s this suspicion became an all-consuming passion. Democrats denounced anything that hinted of special privilege as an attempt to create an aristocracy inimical to liberty and republican government. Such appeals to egalitarianism and suspicion of special interests captured the imagination of the heirs of republican political culture. Indeed, they sounded with such resonance that Whigs constantly—although never completely successfully—struggled to defend their support for protective tariffs, banks, and government-supported internal improvements by claiming that they served the general welfare and raised the level of opportunity for all.[8]

These attitudes explain the powerful appeal and persistence of hostility to political parties. In the eighteenth-century Anglo-American political world, as Richard Hofstadter has demonstrated, party and faction were synonymous and suggested a group of self-interested individuals who pursued their own advantage at the expense of the common good. Because they believed that a republic would fall into civil war and tyranny if individuals eschewed the common good and factions emerged, politically conscious Americans of the revolutionary era viewed parties as a source of declension. Although factionalism was endemic to American politics during and after the Revolution, and well-organized political parties emerged during the 1790s, most people looked upon parties as a temporary evil. Indeed, even party chiefs like Jefferson, Madison, and Monroe clung to an antiparty ideal, believing that political leaders should not be swayed by the dictates of party and aspiring to end party division.[9]

Of course this vision was not realized. During the 1830s the second party system emerged, and such party leaders as Martin Van Buren developed a theoretical justification for political parties based upon democratic premises. They argued that party rivalry gave substance to democracy by offering voters a choice between competing visions of the public good and guaranteed the existence of an opposition that scrutinized the actions of those in power. This celebration of parties implicitly rejected the notion that there was one definition of the common good. Accepting pluralism, it rested instead on the assumption that American society was composed of competing groups that had different visions of the common good and that the vision acceptable to the majority should prevail.[10]

Politically conscious Americans were familiar with the justification for parties and were eager partisans. Yet even Democrats, who most lustily sang the praises of party, remained susceptible to the allure of antiparty ideas. Many questioned the pluralistic vision of parties as competing alliances of interest groups. They viewed their program—hostility to special privilege—as essential to serve the common good rather than as a means to promote the interests of certain groups. Democratic politicians, they contended, were paladins of liberty who used power to ensure that special interests did not gain control of government and use it to promote aristocracy and subvert liberty and equality. As heirs of revolutionary republicanism, however, they assumed that power threatened liberty and realized that a well-organized group that controlled government might easily use its position to destroy liberty. Consequently, they retained a latent suspicion of politicians and might easily be drawn to criticize parties as cabals of self-interested politicians. In an 1845 attack on political patronage, for example, Democratic theorist Theodore Sedgwick charged that parties and the hoards of appointed officials who were beholden to them posed a threat to the common weal. "Interested rather in the success of party than in the beneficial influence of its measures," he explained, "these government retainers frown upon anything which savors of insubordination, cherish passive obedience to party organization, and proclaim from every housetop that party organization and regular nominations are the vitality of patriotism." Indeed, as Michael Holt and J. Mills Thornton have shown, suspicion of party leaders remained alive and active among northern and southern Democrats during the 1850s.[11]

Antiparty attitudes appealed even more strongly to evangelicals and Whigs, groups that broadly overlapped. They viewed parties—like the Masonic Order or the Roman Catholic church—as powerful groups that threatened the social order. Their suspicion of party went even deeper, however. They viewed society organically: evangelicals believed that the creation of a moral community benefited all members of society, whereas Whigs were convinced that different economic groups had mutual interests. Assuming the existence of social harmony and a common weal, Whigs and evangelicals denounced political parties as self-serving agents of conflict that subverted this natural order. Although Whigs and evangelicals organized and participated in parties, they tended to view these organizations as necessary evils, associations of high-minded individuals who were compelled to organize to prevent self-serving opponents from subverting the common good.[12]

By 1860 southerners were perhaps more receptive to antiparty ideas than other Americans. The meteoric rise of the Republicans impressed upon southerners the evils of party: in their eyes the Republican party was bent upon using government to promote the interests of the North by riding roughshod over the rights of the South. As such, it was a chilling reminder of the dangers posed by political parties. For Robert

Smith, an Alabama delegate to the Montgomery Congress, the politics of the 1850s underscored the evils of party. "The chief executive officer of the nation had come to be the appointee of a mere self-constituted and irresponsible convention," he argued in 1861. "As a consequence, each four years heralded the advent of a politician thrown upon the surface by accidental causes and reflecting the latest heretical dogma of a section, rather than addressing himself to the good of the whole country." The *New Orleans Daily Picayune* concurred, explaining that although parties sometimes "contributed to the strength of the political system," they always contained the potential for harm. Indeed, when (as in the case of the Republicans) they were "organized for sectional purposes," they were "a public curse." "Party spirit is a prolific subject and the time is not inappropriate for its consideration," the *Picayune* noted two days after the Montgomery Congress convened. "Warned by the past, let us at the threshold of a new career be wary of undue party spirit and guard against its extravagances."[13]

The Confederate framers took the *Picayune's* warning to heart, especially as they considered changes in the presidency. The committee that drafted the permanent Constitution accepted, with apparently little discussion, Robert Barnwell Rhett's suggestion that the president serve for six years and be ineligible to succeed himself. In debate on the proposal in the Montgomery Congress, two delegates suggested a longer term, and Rhett himself contended that the president should be eligible for reelection six years after leaving office. Delegates rejected these amendments, however, and adopted the committee's original proposal with little debate. By removing the possibility of reelection, they clearly believed that they were lifting the president above party politics and freeing him to pursue the national interest. "Ineligibility would cure some of the evils that have grown out of irresponsible caucuses and party assemblages," explained Alabama delegate J. L. M. Curry. "A President ineligible is freed from the temptation of using his official influence to secure reelection. He is the executive of the whole people and not merely the head of a party." Robert Smith concurred. When presidents were eligible to serve more than one term and elections held every four years, "the measures of Government . . . received direction . . . not so much from the wisdom and for the good of the people as for the triumph of party." Extending the tenure of office and making the president ineligible for reelection, he cautiously predicted, might remedy this evil.[14]

This attempt to place the president above party did not mark a break with the American political-constitutional tradition. Ambivalence about the proper role of party was particularly noticeable in antebellum discussion of the presidency. As Richard Hofstadter and Ralph Ketcham have demonstrated, the first six presidents rejected the notion that the president was a party leader. Instead, they envisaged a patriot president who stood above party and worked only for the best interest of the nation as a whole. With the rise of the Democratic party this view came under attack, as Martin Van Buren and other Democratic loyalists argued that in a democracy the president was the leader of the party that the people put in power. As such, he was obliged to use his power and influence to transform party principles into policy and to reward the party faithful for their services.[15]

Nevertheless, the notion of a patriot president continued to be attractive. Zachary Taylor announced his candidacy in 1848 with the caveat that he would accept nomination to the presidency "provided it had been made entirely independent of party considerations." Although he subsequently accepted the Whig nomination, he explained that, if elected, he "would act independent of party domination" and "administer the government untrammeled by party schemes." Indeed, as candidate and president, he attempted to act as an independent leader who stood above party, did what was best for the nation, and, like Washington, restored unity to the republic.[16] Even Andrew Jackson, who was the leader of what many scholars regard as the first modern American political party, clearly articulated the ideal of the president as an independent leader who aggressively used executive authority to further the common good. In his repeated appeals for a constitutional amendment limiting the president to one term, he anticipated the mechanism that the Confederate framers later employed to free the president from the temptation to partisanship. Jackson contended that a president who was ineligible for reelection would not base decisions on political and partisan considerations and would act in the best interest of the nation. "In order . . . that he may approach the solemn responsibilities of the . . . office . . . uncommitted to any other course than the strict line of constitutional duty . . . ," he argued in his second annual message, "I . . . invite your attention to the propriety of . . . such an amendment . . . as will render him ineligible after one term."[17]

Fascination with limiting the president to a single term, moreover, remained powerful in the late nineteenth and early twentieth centuries.

Even during the secession crisis some strident northern critics of the South and the Confederacy applauded this Confederate change in the U.S. Constitution. "These innovations [the six-year presidential term and ineligibility for reelection] will commend themselves to the approval of all who have watched the mischiefs produced by the too speedy recurrence of elections, and by the manoeuvers of acting presidents for reelection," proclaimed *Harper's Weekly*. "They would gladly be adopted by people throughout the Union." In the century and a quarter since the Civil War, support for limiting the president to one six-year term has been persistent and widely shared. Presidents, political commentators, and party platforms have repeatedly advocated a single six-year presidential term. Members of Congress have introduced 124 constitutional amendments establishing a six-year term, the great majority of which have made the president ineligible for reelection. The persistent aim of these advocates, like that of the Confederate framers, has been to lift the president above politics. "What this amendment seeks," explained Sen. Mike Mansfield in his testimony on behalf of a 1971 amendment establishing a single six-year term, "is to place the Office of the Presidency in a position that transcends as much as possible partisan political considerations." Indeed, the cold war and the rise of the national security state have merely perpetuated fascination with the idea of a patriot president who, freed from political concerns, might concentrate fully on pursuing the national interest in a hostile world.[18]

Concern for lifting the president above politics also informed the Montgomery Congress's decision to restrict presidential control of patronage. In allowing the president to remove civil servants only for cause, the framers stripped the Confederate president of one of the most formidable tools that his Union counterpart used to keep Congress loyal to the administration. Because they viewed the president as a national leader rather than a party chief, this shift did not trouble delegates. If the president were to use patronage for party advantage, he not only would be acting from improper motives but would diminish his credibility as a truly national leader and would engender the partisanship that Confederate framers hoped to avoid. They were convinced that this change would restore efficiency to government and end the corruption of the spoils system that had threatened the antebellum republic. J. L. M. Curry asserted that the tendency of the patronage system in the United States was "to corrupt public opinion, to degrade public station, . . . and 'to raise up a host of hungry, greedy, and subservient partisans, ready for

209

every service, however base and corrupt.' " Curry was confident, however, that the Confederate Constitution would rid the slaveholders' republic of this curse.[19]

Like the one-term presidency, civil service reform had deep roots in antebellum political-constitutional culture. Politicians had defended the spoils system as a means of democratizing government and officeholding. Nevertheless, persistent criticism of the spoils system recalled warnings of classical republican theorists that patronage was a prime source of corruption that endangered the republic. Whigs were perhaps more concerned about civil service reform than Democrats, but even Democrats worried that patronage could be abused. Obsessed by the dangers of power and privilege, they frequently voiced concern that executive patronage power might be used to allow a privileged band of officeholders to feed at the public trough. The evils of patronage were sharply denounced with every revelation of corruption, incompetence, and inefficiency in the civil service. Such denunciations were particularly sharp and widespread in 1859–60, after sensational reports of widespread corruption in the Buchanan administration. Consequently, during the secession winter northern and southern editors excoriated the spoils system and loudly demanded civil service reform.[20]

The Confederate framers' determination to extirpate the spoils system, of course, also anticipated the direction of national developments in the half century following the Civil War. Civil service reform was perhaps the most celebrated political issue of the Gilded Age. Northern patricians, editors, and civil servants pressed for an end to the spoils system and achieved an important victory in 1883 with the Pendleton Act. During the remainder of the nineteenth century and well into the twentieth, the movement continued and spread to the state and local level. Indeed, for reformers of the Progressive Era, a stable, efficient, well-regulated society depended upon a professional, nonpartisan civil service.[21]

Although they were also members of Congress, the Confederate framers did not doubt that legislative control over finance must be subject to stricter scrutiny than it had been given under the Constitution of 1787. Alexander Stephens noted that he and the other delegates at Montgomery had been appalled by "the extravagance and profligacy of appropriations by the [U.S.] Congress for several years past." His colleague Robert Smith was even more blunt. Legislators too frequently tacked onto appropriations bills items that did not serve the common good but were designed to line the pockets of political cronies or serve the parochial interests of their constituents. Members of Congress supported their colleagues' pet appropriations, and the president had to sign omnibus appropriations bills heavily laden with pork in order to fund important programs. The U.S. Constitution, Smith noted, provided an inadequate check on such "reprehensible, not to say venal dispositions of the public money." As heirs of the republican tradition, southerners knew that this was not just a matter of a few misspent dollars. Honesty in the public arena was essential, according to the *Milledgeville* (Georgia) *Southern Recorder*, "to keep the body politic in a healthy condition."[22]

Because they believed that they had elevated the president above politics, members of the Montgomery Congress gave him sweeping powers over the purse. The Constitution limited legislators' opportunity to load bills with special-interest measures by stipulating that appropriations measures not submitted by the president must pass by two thirds majorities. Moreover, the Constitution reinforced the president's authority over the budget by giving him the item veto—the right to veto specific provisions of an appropriation bill without vetoing the entire measure. Stephens lauded these reforms as great improvements on the U.S. Constitution: "Our fathers had guarded the assessment of taxes by insisting that representation and taxation should go together . . . but our new constitution went a step further, and guarded not only the pockets of the people, but also the public money, after it was taken from their pockets." Addressing his constituents, Smith concurred: "By refusing to give a mere majority of the Congress unlimited control over the treasury . . . and by giving the President the power to veto very objectionable items in appropriations bills, we have . . . greatly purified our Government."[23]

The spirit of distrust for legislators that these provisions betrayed had deep roots in American political and constitutional thought. As Gordon Wood has demonstrated, the nationalists of the 1780s sought constitutional reform because they believed that state legislators posed a threat to individual rights. Indeed, Jefferson had warned of the potential for abuse by legislatures, remarking in his *Notes on Virginia* that "173 despots would surely be as oppressive as one." Suspicion of legislative authority remained alive in antebellum America. Democrats—eager to ensure that the people controlled government—respected legislative power but did not blindly worship it. They feared that self-serving individuals might capture the legislature and use it to pass measures that conferred special privilege or in other ways threatened liberty. Thus The-

211

odore Sedgwick, one of the most prominent Democratic writers, argued that legislators too readily capitulated to special interests. Constitutional reform, he contended, should aim at placing restrictions on legislatures that would inhibit such abuses. As supporters of active government, Whigs believed that legislative power was essential if government was to fulfill its obligation to promote economic development and moral reform. Nevertheless, they assumed that democracies frequently thrust demagogues into office and feared that unchecked legislative power could easily erode the protection of property rights essential for social progress.[24]

Suspicion of legislative authority was clearly expressed in the state constitutions and amendments adopted in the three decades preceding Sumter. Convinced that there was a direct relationship between legislative chicanery and the frequency of legislative sessions, reformers replaced the annual legislative sessions that had been the norm in the late eighteenth and early nineteenth centuries with biennial sessions. State constitutions also restricted legislative flexibility in making economic policy. In the 1820s and 1830s legislatures had eagerly chartered banks, issued bonds to support construction of state-owned internal improvements, and invested in and endorsed the bonds of private transportation companies. When the bubble of prosperity burst in 1837, widespread popular revulsion against these measures led to adoption of state constitutional provisions strictly limiting legislatures' authority to incur debt. A number of states placed an absolute limit on state debt, and others stipulated that legislation raising state debt above a specified amount must be approved by popular referenda or enacted by two successive legislatures. Other provisions restricted legislative authority to charter corporations, purchase stock in corporations, create banks, and pledge the credit of the state to corporations. Moreover, state constitutions strengthened executive power to prevent enactment of legislation contrary to the public interest. Whereas early state constitutions either denied the governor the right to veto legislation or permitted a simple majority of legislators to override a veto, those ratified after 1830 more often than not required a two-thirds vote to override.[25]

The Confederate Constitution's attempt to control enactment of partisan and special-interest legislation also anticipated late nineteenth-century developments. In 1873 the *Albany Law Journal* captured the spirit of Gilded Age constitutional reform in an article demanding further restrictions on legislative discretion. "The constitutional changes which have been made in many states have been extensive, but they have not been sufficient in that they do not . . . render the duties of the legislators more fixed and definite," the *Journal* charged. "Until this is done there will always be . . . usurpation and profligacy on the part of the legislators." During the remainder of the century state constitutional conventions heeded this admonition. Constitutions became much longer and more codelike as restrictions on legislative authority of the sort that had appeared in antebellum constitutions became more numerous and widespread.[26]

Late nineteenth-century state constitutional revision followed the Confederate Constitution most closely in strengthening the executive as a bulwark against legislative activism. In 1873 the *Central Law Journal* happily noted that "most if not all" state constitutions gave the governor veto power and urged that "in this day of hasty legislation" state chief executives should not be bashful in using it. By the turn of the century all but three states gave the governor the power to veto legislation, and among states with a gubernatorial veto, only four permitted a simple majority in the legislature to override a veto. Like the delegates to the Montgomery Congress, late nineteenth-century constitutional reformers were particularly intent upon preventing legislators from enacting appropriations measures that served parochial interests at the expense of the common good. They not only expanded the governor's authority to draft budgets and present them to the legislature but, following the lead of the Confederate framers, gave the governor the item veto as a means of protecting his budgets. Indeed, by the 1920s forty-seven states gave the governor authority to present a budget and thirty-seven gave the executive an item veto.[27]

The most remarkable change in executive-legislative relations made by the Confederate framers—that authorizing Congress to permit cabinet officers to participate in congressional debates—also reflected the framers' desire to eliminate partisan politics from policy making. Several delegates, notably Alexander Stephens, Robert Toombs, and Robert Smith, were admirers of the British parliamentary system. As a member of the committee that drafted the provisional Constitution in early February 1861, Stephens used his influence to secure key elements of the British system. He excluded from the provisional document the U.S. Constitution's prohibition against members of Congress holding other federal offices, opening the way for the provisional president to choose members of Congress to serve in the cabinet. Stephens also secured adoption of a provision that barred Congress from appropriating funds unless requested by the president or a cabinet minister. Such provisions, he believed, would give Confederate government the unity and central direction afforded by the British Constitution. A president who possessed broad budget authority and had influential members of Congress as cabinet officers would have the tools necessary to formulate and implement a coherent program. Stephens viewed inclusion of these provisions in the provisional Constitution as the first step toward writing them into the permanent Constitution. There, combined with a six-year single term for the president, they would help realize Stephens's dream: formulation of coherent policy that was dictated by reason and concern for the public interest rather than by partisan considerations.[28]

Members of the Montgomery Congress remained wedded to separation of powers, however, and rejected efforts to graft these elements of the British system onto the permanent Constitution. Because the provisional government was to last only one year, Congress agreed to omit the prohibition against members of Congress serving in the executive branch. This necessary expedient would allow experienced leaders like Toombs and Stephens to sit in Congress and participate in debate on the permanent Constitution while, at the same time, assisting the provisional president in organizing a government. But including this provision in the permanent Constitution was an entirely different matter. Even though Toombs was a member, the committee on the permanent Constitution prohibited members of Congress from holding executive department appointments, thereby dashing any hopes that cabinet ministers would be members of Congress. Instead, it gave Congress discretionary authority to permit cabinet members to sit in Congress and participate in debate (but not vote). When the entire Congress debated the committee's draft, Stephens and Toombs attempted to make this language mandatory but were unsuccessful. Congress was more favorable to the provision expanding the president's control over the budget. But even so, concerned that they needed the power to check a president who abused his budgetary authority, congressmen stipulated that Congress might by a two-thirds majority enact appropriations measures not requested by the president.[29]

The provision permitting cabinet ministers to sit in Congress, then, did not represent a break from the tradition of separation of powers. Members of the Montgomery Congress assumed that the legislative and executive branches must be separate and that each needed the means to check the other. They nonetheless admitted that smooth operation of the system required cooperation between the two branches. Moreover, they believed that the president, whom they had freed from the bonds of partisanship, must be able to convince Congress to enact programs that the public interest demanded. Rejecting political parties as a means of providing the president with influence in Congress, they sought to give him this influence through reasoned discussion. They believed that if cabinet ministers were able to explain presidential policies on the floor of Congress, they would be able to gain support for policies that were in the national interest.[30] Alexander Stephens suggested the close relationship between this provision and the framers' desire to mitigate the influence of party. The constitutional provision permitting cabinet ministers to sit in Congress, he informed a Savannah audience in March 1861, would help inhibit the fatal growth of party spirit by obviating the president's need to establish a partisan newspaper. "Our heads of department can speak for themselves and the administration . . . without resorting to the indirect and highly objectionable medium of a newspaper," he explained. "It is to be greatly hoped that under our system we shall never have what is known as a Government organ."[31]

Taken together, these changes in the presidency and in the executive-legislative relationship were decidedly undemocratic. The six-year single-term presidency enabled a president to act with less regard for public opinion than if he had to seek reelection at the end of four years. The item veto and budgetary provisions dramatically increased presidential and decreased congressional power over the purse. Thus the Confederate Constitution transferred power in a crucial area from representatives who were subject to frequent reelection to a president who was insulated from popular accountability. Although there is no indication that the delegates were conscious of the undemocratic implications of their constitutional reforms, many would have been happy with such an outcome. Not only were wealthy slaveholders far better represented in Montgomery than in antebellum state legislatures, but a number of outspoken conservatives like Stephens played a prominent role in the proceedings. Perhaps a hierarchical conception of society or concerns about the loyalty of the growing class of nonslaveholding southern whites influenced their behavior. Yet even if they consciously sought to temper democracy, the Confederate framers were not acting in a peculiarly southern manner. Many northern reformers who advocated constitutional reform to erode the influence of party—including Whigs in the

215

antebellum period as well as the "best men" and proponents of efficiency in the late nineteenth century—were driven by the desire to limit popular influence on policy.[32]

The conservatism of many of the framers probably reinforced the suspicion of partisan politics that republicanism had bequeathed to them. Nevertheless, one should not conclude that they were driven primarily by a commitment to limit democracy. Many conservatives outside Congress demanded root-and-branch reform of a political system that, they believed, encouraged "demagogues' appeal to popular caprices, and demagogues' surrender to popular clamors." The remedies they suggested were sweeping. "Nothing is stable—nothing reliable—and nothing secure and free from the caprices of demagogues," complained an Atlanta editor. "The people want peace and security and . . . are willing to elect a President and Vice-President for ten years; a Senator for the same term and their members of Congress for five years by the general ticket system." Others suggested ending popular election of the president. The delegates to the Montgomery convention rejected such suggestions, however. Though they lengthened the president's term by two years, they did not change the system of electing the president. Similarly, they refused to lengthen the terms of senators or representatives, establish more stringent standards for voting in national elections, or stipulate that House members be chosen in at-large elections. Their action thus stands in stark contrast to that of the Georgia secession convention, which drafted a new state constitution with significant antidemocratic provisions. The contrast suggests that the Confederate framers chose not to press for substantial restrictions on democracy. It also cautions against viewing the changes they made in the presidency simply as a product of their hostility toward democracy.[33]

Indeed, most delegates realized that sponsoring serious antidemocratic reform at Montgomery was unthinkable. They were deeply concerned about attracting to the Confederacy the states of the upper South (which at this time had not left the Union) and reluctant to alienate potential supporters in those sharply divided states. They realized that fundamental changes in the political order would be controversial and might tip the scales against secession in the upper South. They also shied away from such changes because they were intent on framing a constitution as quickly as possible in order to get on with the pressing business of creating a government and preparing for war. Basic changes in political institutions would, of necessity, entail lengthy debate and so

216

were out of the question. Robert Smith suggested that he and other delegates wanted to change the method of electing the president but realized the difficulties inherent in the project and drew back. "The task of reformation would . . . have been difficult," he noted, "and I doubt if you can by interposing machinery of any kind between the elector and the elected, prevent the candidate from . . . being . . . chosen immediately by the people so long as they retain the right to vote for the office; a right which in our Government cannot elsewhere be lodged without materially altering its form and essence."[34]

The framers' decision to refrain from substantial restrictions on popular control not only averted interminable debate at Montgomery but avoided widespread criticism of the Constitution when it was made public. Most southern white men were fiercely committed to preserving democracy, and a Constitution that they viewed as limiting popular control would have sparked fiery criticism of the new regime. One need only consider the wartime response to the Confederate Congress's decision to exempt from the draft one white man on every plantation with twenty or more slaves to realize that southerners would not quietly submit to measures that they perceived as undemocratic. Moreover, we should not assume that the hysteria accompanying the secession crisis had a chilling effect that made southerners fearful of political criticism. In fact, many southerners excoriated state secession conventions when they refused to authorize popular referenda on ratification of the Confederate Constitution.[35]

Despite southerners' willingness to lash out at measures conferring special privilege or eroding popular sovereignty, there is little evidence of substantive criticism of the Confederate Constitution itself. Opponents of immediate secession in northern Alabama vigorously protested the state convention's refusal to hold a referendum on the Constitution. Yet these dissenters—including a group in Frankfort, Alabama, who resolved that "our Congressional nominee, if elected, is to represent us in the United States Congress and not in the Congress of this so-called 'Southern Confederacy' "—registered no criticism of the Constitution in their resolutions of protest.[36] The editor of the Cooperationist *Huntsville* (Alabama) *Southern Advocate* was critical of delegates who voted against popular ratification, noting that "they are justly amenable to the condemnation of the people, should they again seek popular favor." However, he conceded that there "is no legitimate objection to the Constitution or to the new Government."[37] According to a convention delegate, all five of the members of the Alabama convention who voted against the Constitution had "expressed their approbation, and said if it [the Constitution] were submitted to the people that they . . . would vote for it."[38]

The response in northern Alabama was not unique. In Georgia a substantial minority of delegates resisted the undemocratic provisions of the state constitution drafted by the convention. Yet they had no doubts about the work of the Confederate framers; the Georgia convention ratified the Confederate Constitution by a vote of 276 to 0. In the Mississippi convention a substantial minority wanted to submit the document to the people. As one explained, "I shouldn't be so particular myself about submitting the Constitution to the popular vote; but four hundred of my people have informed me that if it isn't done they *won't stand it.*" However, these men did not object to the Constitution itself. "They do not take issue on the merits or demerits of the Constitution itself; only one of them has criticized it adversely," explained the Jackson correspondent of the *New York Tribune.* "They profess to be heartily in favor of it; and one speaker last evening asserted that nineteen-twentieths of the people of the State would vote for it."[39]

The few who did offer substantive criticism of the Constitution were not moved by concern for preserving democracy. In South Carolina, Robert Barnwell Rhett's *Charleston Mercury* skewered the document for its failure to end popular election of presidential electors. On the floor of the South Carolina convention a large minority led by wealthy planters attacked the Constitution because it failed to prohibit the admission of free states, preserved the U.S. Constitution's formula for determining representation, granted Congress unlimited power to levy indirect taxes, and prohibited the African slave trade. Because of this spirited reactionary opposition, there were more votes cast against the Constitution in the South Carolina convention (the vote was 138 to 21) than in any other convention. Criticism in Alabama and Mississippi, though not as widespread, followed the same lines. Two prominent Alabamians who opposed the Constitution objected to the prohibition of the African slave trade and the failure to limit membership in the Confederacy to slave states. They also charged that by mandating popular election of presidential electors every six years, the Constitution would lead to frequent conflict within the polity. In Copiah County, Mississippi, a public meeting urged the state convention to reject any constitution that prohibited the African slave trade: "We will never consent to any government, except on the express condition that each state may be the sole judge of their domestic institutions, coupled with the choice of sources from which their supply of labor may be maintained."[40]

Despite scattered criticism by states' rights zealots and outspoken opponents of democracy, it appears that the Constitution won widespread acceptance from a populace that was jealous of its prerogatives. The reason is that the framers reflected political values that had broad appeal. Suspicion of parties, politicians, and government, firmly rooted in American republicanism, shaped the action of the Confederate framers. Republican ideology, a loose and often contradictory set of attitudes and values, provided the idiom with which they discussed and the lenses through which they viewed political-constitutional issues. It drew them inexorably to reforms designed to reduce partisanship, restrain selfish politicians, and create a government capable of pursuing the common good. Because most southern white men shared these beliefs, there was much praise and little criticism of the Constitution in the hinterland. Moreover, these values were widespread among northerners. Consequently, numerous northern commentators who viewed the Confederacy as a moral pariah reluctantly admitted that the Confederate Constitution offered many improvements that the United States might profitably adopt.[41] Indeed, many of the Confederate Constitution's innovations were strikingly similar in both spirit and practice to constitutional changes in the North before and after the Civil War. The actual operation of the Confederate political system suggests that the framers' determination to curb parties was naive and contributed to governmental ineffectiveness.[42] Nevertheless, the spirit that animated Confederate constitutional reform, far from being distinctively southern, was well within the mainstream of the American constitutional tradition.

Notes

I have benefited immensely from discussions on the Confederate Constitution with Harold Hyman. Linda Nieman and Phil Paludan offered perceptive comments and suggestions on an earlier draft and forced me to clarify my arguments.

1. The standard work on the Confederate Constitution is Charles R. Lee, Jr., *The Confederate Constitutions* (Chapel Hill, N.C., 1963). Lee offers a careful discussion of constitution making at Montgomery that is thoroughly researched

and does not ignore changes in the executive. Nevertheless, he views states' rights issues as central to the framers' work and concludes that the Confederate Constitution must be understood primarily as a manifestation of southern states' rights constitutionalism. Other treatments that share this orientation include Jesse T. Carpenter, *The South as a Conscious Minority: A Study in Political Thought* (New York, 1930); William T. Leslie, "The Confederate Constitution," *Michigan Quarterly Review* 2 (1963): 153–65; H. C. Nixon and John T. Nixon, "The Confederate Constitution Today," *Georgia Review* 9 (1955): 369–76; and Albert N. Fitts, "The Confederate Convention: The Constitutional Debate," *Alabama Review* 2 (1949): 189–210 (hereafter cited as "Constitutional Debate"). Owsley's position, which is stated in his *States' Rights in the Confederacy* (Chicago, 1925), has been widely acclaimed as well as hotly criticized. For the most recent dissent from this position, see Richard E. Beringer, Herman Hattaway, Archer Jones, and William N. Still, Jr., *Why the South Lost the Civil War* (Athens, Ga., 1986), 203–35.

2. Lee, *The Confederate Constitutions;* Albert N. Fitts, "The Confederate Convention: The Provisional Constitution," *Alabama Review* 2 (1949): 83–101 (hereafter cited as "Provisional Constitution"); Fitts, "Constitutional Debate," 189–210.

3. Robert Barnwell Rhett, "The Confederate Constitution," *DeBow's Review* 39 (1869): 930–34; Lee, *The Confederate Constitutions*, 82–122. Appendix C of Lee's book prints the U.S. Constitution and the Confederate Constitution side by side and indicates changes made in the latter with italics.

4. Constitution of the Confederate States of America, preamble. See also Lee, *The Confederate Constitutions*, 82–122; and T. R. R. Cobb, "Notes on the Confederate Constitution," in "The Making of the Confederate Constitution," ed. A. L. Hull, *Publications of the Southern History Association* 9 (1905): 285–92. For a similar analysis of the framers' reluctance to undermine national power, see Emory M. Thomas, *The Confederate Nation, 1861–1865* (New York, 1979), 62–65.

5. As quoted in Fitts, "Constitutional Debate," 189.

6. For the changes discussed in this paragraph, see Constitution of the Confederate States of America, art. I, secs. 6, 7, 9; art. II, secs. 1, 2.

7. Bernard Bailyn, *The Ideological Origins of the American Revolution* (Cambridge, Mass., 1967), chaps. 2, 3, 6; Gordon Wood, *The Creation of the American Republic, 1776–1787* (Chapel Hill, N.C., 1969).

8. Rush Welter, *The Mind of America, 1820–1860* (New York, 1975), 77–128, 165–89; J. Mills Thornton III, *Politics and Power in a Slave Society: Alabama, 1800–1860* (Baton Rouge, 1978), 3–58; William J. Cooper, Jr., *Liberty and Slavery: Southern Politics to 1860* (New York, 1983), 113–19; Daniel Walker Howe, *The Political Culture of the American Whigs* (Chicago, 1979), 138–39; Glyndon Van Deusen, "Some Aspects of Whig Thought and Theory in the Jacksonian Period," *American Historical Review* 63 (1958): 305–22.

9. Richard Hofstadter, *The Idea of a Party System: The Rise of Legitimate Opposition in the United States, 1780–1840* (Berkeley, Calif., 1970). See also Wood, *Creation of the American Republic,* 58–59; and Ralph Ketcham, *Presidents above Party: The First American Presidency, 1789–1829* (Chapel Hill, N.C., 1984).

10. Hofstadter, *Idea of a Party System,* 212–71; Ketcham, *Presidents above Party,* 141–50; Michael Wallace, "Changing Concepts of Party in the United States, 1815–1828," *American Historical Review* 74 (1968): 453–91.

11. [Theodore Sedgwick], "Political Patronage," *United States Magazine and Democratic Review* 17 (1845): 165; Thornton, *Politics and Power,* 312–42; Michael Holt, *The Political Crisis of the 1850s* (New York, 1978), 130–38. See also Welter, *The Mind of America,* 165–89, esp. 177–78.

12. Howe, *American Whigs,* 50–55; Ronald P. Formisano, "Political Character, Antipartyism and the Second Party System," *American Quarterly* 21 (1969): 683–709.

13. Robert Smith, *An Address to the Citizens of Alabama on the Constitution and Laws of the Confederate States of America* (Mobile, Ala., 1861), 13; *New Orleans Daily Picayune,* February 6, 1861.

14. Rhett, "The Confederate Constitution," 930–34; Lee, *The Confederate Constitutions,* 104–5; J. L. M. Curry, "The Confederate States and Their Constitution," *Galaxy* 17 (1874): 402; Smith, *Address,* 13–14.

15. Hofstadter, *Idea of a Party System,* 91–102, 170–211; Ketcham, *Presidents above Parties,* 89–139.

16. Brainerd Dyer, *Zachary Taylor* (Baton Rouge, 1946), 277–87 (quotations from 278, 280); Holt, *Political Crisis of the 1850s,* 67–76.

17. James D. Richardson, comp., *The Messages and Papers of the Presidents, 1789–1902,* 10 vols. (Washington, D.C., 1903), 2:519.

18. "The Two Constitutions," *Harper's Weekly,* March 30, 1861, 194; Senate Judiciary Committee, *Hearing before the Subcommittee on Constitutional Amendments on S.J. Res. 77 to Amend the Constitution by Providing a Single Six-Year Term President,* 92d Cong., 1st sess., 1971, 8–12, 33 (quotation from 33).

19. Curry, "Confederate States," 402.

20. Welter, *The Mind of America,* 171, 235; Ari A. Hoogenboom, *Outlawing the Spoils: A History of the Civil Service Reform Movements, 1865–1883* (Urbana, Ill., 1961), 7–12; [Sedgwick], "Political Patronage," 163–75; David Meerse, "Buchanan, Corruption, and the Election of 1860," *Civil War History* 12 (1966): 116–31; Emerson D. Fite, *The Presidential Campaign of 1860* (New York, 1911), 132–41. For criticism of the spoils system in the wake of the Buchanan administration scandals, see *New York Herald; Milledgeville* (Ga.) *Southern Federal Union,* March 26, 1861; and *Milledgeville* (Ga.) *Southern Recorder,* February 19 and March 12, 1861.

21. Hoogenboom, *Outlawing the Spoils;* John G. Sproat, *The Best Men: Liberal Reformers in the Gilded Age* (New York, 1971), 257–71; Morton Keller, *Affairs of State: Public Life in Late Nineteenth Century America* (Cambridge, Mass., 1977),

272–75, 313–14; Robert Wiebe, *The Search for Order, 1877–1920* (New York, 1967), 60–61, 161, 168, 171.

22. Stephens, as quoted in the *Milledgeville Southern Federal Union*, April 2, 1861; Smith, *Address*, 7–8; *Milledgeville Southern Recorder*, February 19, 1861.

23. *Milledgeville Southern Federal Union*, April 2, 1861; Smith, *Address*, 10–11.

24. Wood, *Creation of the American Republic*, 257–467; Thomas Jefferson, *Notes on the State of Virginia*, in *The Portable Thomas Jefferson*, ed. Merrill D. Peterson (New York, 1975), 164; Welter, *The Mind of America*, 190–249; [Theodore Sedgwick], "Constitutional Reform," *United States Magazine and Democratic Review* 13 (1843): 563–82, "The Progress of Constitutional Reform in the United States," *United States Magazine and Democratic Review* 18 (1846): 243–56, and "History of Constitutional Reform in the United States," *United States Magazine and Democratic Review* 18 (1846): 403–20.

25. The standard collection of state constitutions is Francis N. Thorpe, ed., *The Federal and State Constitutions*, 7 vols. (Washington, D.C., 1909).

26. "Legislative Discretion," *Albany Law Journal*, May 31, 1873, 337; Simeon Baldwin, "Recent Changes in Our State Constitutions," *Journal of Social Science* 10 (1879): 136–51; Keller, *Affairs of State*, 319–21.

27. *Central Law Journal*, May 25, 1877, 483; Robert H. Wells, "The Item Veto and State Budget Reform," *American Political Science Quarterly* 18 (1924); 782–91; Frank W. Prescott, "The Executive Veto in the American States," *Western Political Quarterly* 3 (1950): 98–113, and "The Executive Veto in the Southern States," *Journal of Politics* 10 (1948): 659–75.

28. Lee, *The Confederate Constitutions*, 71, 97–100; Smith, *Address*, 9–10; Alexander H. Stephens, *A Constitutional View of the Late War between the States*, 2 vols. (Philadelphia, 1868, 1870), 2:338–39; Alexander Stephens to Linton Stephens, February 9 and 17, 1861, and Linton Stephens to Alexander Stephens, February 12, 1861, Alexander Hamilton Stephens Papers, Southern Historical Collection, University of North Carolina, Chapel Hill (microfilm; originals in Manhattanville College Library).

29. Lee, *The Confederate Constitutions*, 96–99; Fitts, "Provisional Constitution," 87–88, and "Constitutional Debate," 190–92; Alexander Stephens to Linton Stephens, February 17 and March 10, 1861, Stephens Papers.

30. Smith, *Address*, 9–11; Fitts, "Constitutional Debate," 190–91.

31. *Milledgeville Southern Federal Union*, April 2, 1861.

32. Lee, *The Confederate Constitutions*, 47–50; Ralph Wooster, *The People in Power: Courthouse and Statehouse in the Lower South, 1850–1860* (Knoxville, Tenn., 1969); Howe, *American Whigs;* Welter, *The Mind of America*, 105–28, 190–218; Sproat, *The Best Men;* Wiebe, *The Search for Order.*

33. *Augusta* (Ga.) *Chronicle and Sentinel*, February 24, 1861; *Gate City Guardian* (Atlanta), as quoted in the *Augusta Chronicle and Sentinel*, February 28 and

March 8, 1861; Michael P. Johnson, *Toward a Patriarchal Republic: The Secession of Georgia* (Baton Rouge, 1977), 79–187.

34. Lee, *The Confederate Constitutions*, 56; Wilfred Buck Yearns, *The Confederate Congress* (Athens, Ga., 1960), 24; Junius Hillyer to Howell Cobb, January 30, 1861, *The Correspondence of Robert Toombs, Alexander H. Stephens, and Howell Cobb*, ed. Ulrich Bonnell Phillips (Washington, D.C., 1913), 535; Thomas R. R. Cobb to Marion Cobb, February 3, 5, and 9, 1861, "The Correspondence of Thomas Reade Rootes Cobb, 1860–1862," *Publications of the Southern History Association* 11 (1907): 160, 163, 169; Smith, *Address*, 14.

35. A. B. Moore, *Conscription and Conflict in the Confederacy* (New York, 1924), 255–96; Lee, *The Confederate Constitutions*, 126–35; *New Orleans Daily Picayune*, March 15 and 16 and April 1, 1861; *Mobile Daily Advertiser* and *Copiah County* (Miss.) *News*, as quoted in the *Springfield* (Mass.) *Daily Republican*, March 23 and 25, 1861; *Huntsville* (Ala.) *Southern Advocate*, April 3, 1861.

36. *Tuscumbia North Alabamian*, as quoted in the *Chicago Daily Tribune*, March 29, 1861. See also the *Savannah Morning News*, as quoted in the *Augusta* (Ga.) *Daily Constitutionalist*, April 7, 1861.

37. *Huntsville Southern Advocate*, April 3, 1861.

38. Ibid., April 17, 1861.

39. Johnson, *Toward a Patriarchal Republic*, 154–78; *New York Daily Tribune*, April 4, 1861. There are other indications of absence of popular criticism of the Confederate Constitution. Substantial minorities in most of the state secession conventions were critical of the refusal to submit the Constitution to popular ratification. Nevertheless, not only was there little criticism of the document in these bodies, but only a handful of delegates voted against ratification. In Florida, as in Georgia, the vote was unanimous. Delegates ratified the Constitution in Texas by 126 to 2, in Louisiana by 102 to 7, in Alabama by 87 to 5, and in Mississippi by 78 to 7. Though there were more negative votes in South Carolina, they came from Conservatives rather than from delegates who thought that the Constitution was antidemocratic. See Lee, *The Confederate Constitutions*, 125–38. I have examined the following newspapers for coverage of events in the South between January and June 1861: *New Orleans Daily Picayune, Montgomery Advertiser, Augusta Chronicle and Sentinel, Augusta Constitutionalist, Milledgeville Southern Recorder, Milledgeville Southern Federal Union, Huntsville Southern Advocate, Athens Southern Banner, Chicago Daily Tribune, New York Daily Tribune, New York Daily World, New York Daily Herald*, and *Springfield Daily Republican*. This research produced no evidence that proponents of popular control found the Constitution wanting. Moreover, in the vast literature on dissent in the Confederacy I have found no indication of substantive criticism of the Constitution. Although a great deal more work needs to be done to determine popular response to the new document, at this point there is noth-

ing to suggest popular opposition to the constitutional changes made at Montgomery.

40. *Charleston Mercury,* as quoted in the *New York Daily Tribune,* March 19, 1861; Lee, *The Confederate Constitutions,* 134–36; *Montgomery Daily Advertiser,* March 24, 1861; *Copiah County News,* as quoted in the *Springfield Daily Republican,* March 25, 1861.

41. *Harper's Weekly,* March 30, 1861; *New York Herald,* March 17, 1861; *New York Daily World,* March 18, 1861; James Schouler, *History of the United States under the Constitution,* 7 vols. (New York, 1899), 6:55; Horace Davis, *American Constitutions: The Relations of the Three Departments as Adjusted by a Century* (Baltimore, 1885), 21–22.

42. Eric McKitrick, "Party Politics and the Union and Confederate War Efforts," in *The American Party Systems: Stages of Political Development,* ed. William N. Chambers and Walter Dean Burnham (New York, 1967), 117–51; Harold M. Hyman and William M. Wiecek, *Equal Justice under Law: Constitutional Development, 1835–1875* (New York, 1982), 226–28.

The Problem of
Constitutionalism
and Constitutional Liberty
in the Reconstruction South

Michael Les Benedict

During the bicentennial year of the framing of the American Constitution, Americans celebrated the document that articulates the fundamental law of the United States. But as much as we venerate the document, we ought to remember that it has no meaningful life of its own. Many nations have written constitutions, some of them guaranteeing more liberty than ours. Article 83 of the constitution of Poland, for example, instructs the government to "guarantee its citizens freedom of speech, of the press, . . . of meetings and assemblies," and even of "processions and demonstrations." Article 128 of the constitution of the USSR guarantees "the inviolability of the homes of citizens and privacy of correspondence." It is a community's commitment to constitutionalism and principles of constitutional liberty that gives meaning to a written constitution. In the absence of such commitments, a constitution is no more than what its name indicates, a document that sets up an institutional framework of government—that "constitutes" it. South Carolina's able Republican governor Daniel Chamberlain, driven from office in the violent "Red Shirt" election of 1876, learned the lesson well. Evaluating his experience twenty-five years later, he wrote, "Rights, to be secure, must, in the last resort, rest on stronger supports than constitutions, statutes, or enrolled parchments."[1]

During Reconstruction ten of the eleven Confederate states were required to frame new constitutions. Most had to do so twice—once under the prodding of President Abraham Lincoln or Andrew Johnson and again under the semicompulsion of the congressional Reconstruction Acts. The resulting constitutions established governments similar in structure to those of other states and not terribly different from those established by preceding state constitutions or those that followed. As Kenneth M. Stampp realized years ago, "They were neither original or unique."[2] Although several did concentrate a larger appointment power in the governor than was usual,[3] as a whole they established democratic procedures for electing government officials common to the states of the Union before Reconstruction and after. Yet with the exception of Virginia, every one of these states witnessed transfers of government power accompanied by the kind of fraud and violence we now associate with third-world nations. In three of them—Arkansas, Louisiana, and South Carolina—there were what can only be described as insurrections (more than one in Louisiana) and civil war.[4] Conditions in Texas were similar in character but not degree.[5] In Mississippi and Alabama, and perhaps also Florida, the transfer of power from Republicans to Conservatives involved brutal violence and intimidation that approached civil war but probably fell short of a proper definition of it.[6] Not only did violence accompany transfers of power in these states, but continued violence and fraud eliminated viable political opposition. In Georgia violence played a role in undermining the dominant party but probably was not determinative, and in North Carolina a similar campaign of violence led only to a partial transfer of power and did not destroy the opposition entirely.[7] In Tennessee the transfer of power was accomplished through an open violation of the law, sponsored by the governor of the state.[8] Only in Virginia were political contests relatively fairly and freely conducted, and bitter complaints about intimidation emanated even from there.[9]

Conflict beyond the bounds of constitutional democracy occurred within state legislatures as well. The most extreme abuse was the attempted Conservative coup in the Louisiana legislature in January 1875. The bitter election of 1874 resulted in an evenly balanced house of representatives. Control would turn on which of the claimants were given five contested seats. Before a regular vote could be taken on organizing the house, the Conservative candidate for speaker seized the chair and gavel, claiming election on the basis of the votes of the Democratic contestants. He then announced the election of a Conservative clerk and sergeant at arms. Suddenly men who had forced their way into the chamber turned down their lapels, displaying badges marked "assistant sergeant at arms," and threw the Republican house officers out of the room. Forcibly detaining enough Republicans to make a quorum, the Conservatives then decided the disputed contests in favor of their claimants, securing a majority of the house. Republicans persuaded the commander of the federal garrison, which had been billeted in New Orleans to keep peace between the parties, to intervene. In what came to be known as "DeTobriand's Purge" (a reference to "Pride's Purge" of Parliament, which made Oliver Cromwell dictator), the commander ousted the Conservative claimants to the contested seats, restoring the status quo ante.[10]

Nearly as bad was the Conservative purge in 1869 of black Republicans elected to the Georgia state legislature and the seating of their defeated white Conservative rivals, on the grounds that the Georgia state constitution did not expressly authorize blacks to hold office. That purge precipitated a crisis in Georgia politics and Congress that led directly to the collapse of the Republican party in the state.[11] In North Carolina Conservatives converted the simple majority of legislative seats they had won in the Ku Klux Klan–influenced election of 1870 to a two-thirds majority by refusing to seat Republicans elected from districts where the Republican governor had sent militia to protect voters. They then proceeded to convict and remove him on flimsy articles of impeachment.[12] Conservatives forced Mississippi Republican governor Adelbert Ames from office on similarly flimsy charges after they secured control of the state legislature in the violent election of 1875.[13] After winning overwhelming majorities in the Georgia state legislature in 1871, Conservatives forced the Republican governor to resign under threat of impeachment and then called a special election to fill the vacancy, rather than permitting the Republican lieutenant governor to finish out the term.[14]

Conservative violence and chicanery engendered Republican responses that also transgressed the limits of constitutional government. The most obvious abuses occurred in the various boards authorized to count and confirm election returns. Convinced that black southerners uniformly voted Republican, Republican returning boards were quick to accept evidence that deviant returns were the result of violence or fraud. They were probably right, but the returning boards did not demand the kind of evidence that would compel that conclusion, and they were constituted in such a way as to invite charges of partisanship.[15] In Georgia Republicans reacted to Conservative machinations by trying to persuade Congress arbitrarily to extend the term of the state legislature in new Reconstruction legislation.[16]

All of this occurred despite the trappings of constitutional government established by state constitutions. Plainly, southern white Conservatives did not concede those governments the legitimacy that a constitution is designed to impart, and Republicans were forced to measures that subverted commitment to constitutional values in response. Of course, one explanation is that most white southerners simply did not have a commitment to democratic and libertarian constitutional values. But that certainly is not how southern Conservatives characterized themselves and their struggle. Reconstruction itself was "the betrayal of constitutional liberty," they insisted, "a crime against the principles of free government."[17] It was the Republican governments that were tyrannical and undemocratic. Therefore Louisianans gave the name Liberty Monument to a memorial, located at Liberty Place, to those who unsuccessfully tried to overthrow the Republican state government in 1874.[18] It is time historians took seriously southerners' rhetoric and comprehended their resistance to Radical Reconstruction as a manifestation not merely of blind racism and greed but also of the failure of the Republican constitutions and governments to secure constitutional legitimacy in the eyes of a large part of the population from which Republicans expected obedience.

Perhaps it is fatuous to suppose that one could have established a constitutional system of government in the South that would have secured at the same time the allegiance of white and black southerners. Had northern Republicans been willing to sacrifice the interests of the freedmen or to rely primarily on national power to protect their rights, it probably would have been possible to establish a constitutional basis for government acceptable to southern whites. But northern Republicans were willing neither to leave freedmen's interests in the hands of southern whites nor to transfer primary responsibility for protecting their rights to the national government. Nor were they willing simply to exclude ex-Confederates from constitutional government by imposing massive disfranchisement. "We do not want oligarchies of professed Union men," they insisted.[19] "Our policy towards the mass of our enemies must be liberal. . . . otherwise you nourish alienation and encourage the elements of treason and war."[20] The federal system gave the states the responsibility for protecting people against private wrongs, and ultimately Republicans determined that the proper way to see that they fulfilled the responsibility was to establish systems of government in which blacks and whites shared power and to which they would recognize a common allegiance.[21]

It was skepticism about the possibility of establishing such a constitutional consensus that led more radical Republicans to urge long-term national supervision of the southern states as territories. "There are no symptoms that the people of these provinces will be prepared to participate in constitutional government for some years," Thaddeus Stevens said bluntly. Participating in territorial government under the watchful eye of Congress, southerners could "learn the principles of freedom."[22] Radicals urged radical land reform and the establishment of nationally supervised school systems. The idea was to establish a new social and economic system—"small farms, thrifty tillage, free schools, social independence, flourishing manufactures and the arts, respect for honest labor, and equality of political rights."[23] In such a society the consensus necessary for constitutional government might be established. Radicals understood, George W. Julian wrote later, "that no theories of democracy could avail unless adequately supported by a healthy public opinion. They saw that States must grow, and could not be suddenly constructed where materials were wanting."[24]

Republicans did not simply impose new governmental systems on the South. Many of the more conservative Republican congressmen urged their colleagues to make no specific provision for constitutional conventions at all. Simply refuse to recognize the southern states' restoration to normal relations in the Union until they voluntarily modified their constitutions to guarantee equal civil and political rights, they urged. "The formation of a State government must be the voluntary act of the people themselves."[25] In practical terms, conservative Republicans expected, this step would divide southern whites, with more moderate southerners urging the framing or amending of constitutions in a way that would satisfy Congress. Sooner or later they would be successful, and southern states would be restored with acceptable constitutions that had gained the support of a large proportion of the white population, as well as that of the black.

Ultimately, however, congressional Republicans rejected this advice. Radicals complained that it would give ex-rebels control over the pace

of Reconstruction. All worried that if southern whites remained recalcitrant, impatient northerners might repudiate the Republican party
and turn to Andrew Johnson and the Democrats to end the stalemate. As
a consequence, Republicans imposed a process for establishing new
state governments. Yet they still left a good deal to voluntary southern
action. Their Reconstruction legislation required southerners to vote on
whether to hold constitutional conventions in the first place, to elect
convention delegates, and then to ratify the constitutions proposed.
These requirements were consistent with the Republicans' constitutional
justification for their program: that the national government could hold
the South in "the grasp of war" until its citizens voluntarily agreed to
conditions of peace.[26] But they also corresponded to the procedure that
had become customary throughout the country for establishing fundamental law, an embodiment—theoretically problematical, it is true—of
the American conviction that government is based on a compact among
the governed.[27] In fact, as originally conceived, ratification would have
required the participation of an absolute majority of the registered voters
in the ratification elections, as well as in the elections to call the constitutional conventions in the first place. The effect of this requirement
was to increase the proportion of the population that would have to
approve the new constitutions and to obligate an absolute majority to
acquiesce in the new systems, on the principle that those given a fair
opportunity to participate in a canvass are bound by the result. However, Republicans also barred from registering and voting all men who
had sworn to uphold the constitution before the war and then joined the
rebellion.[28] Mistakenly believing that this rule would disfranchise a relatively few men who prior to the rebellion had held higher-level federal
offices, in fact Republicans thus disfranchised large numbers of minor
state and local officials as well.[29] Of course, people barred from participating in the process by which constitutions are established will
hardly feel bound to support them. There is also no way to know how
the participation of the disfranchised might have affected the results.[30]
Moreover, the purpose of the disfranchisement was to deprive potential
opponents of the new constitutions of their most experienced and senior
political leaders. It was natural that even those who were not disfranchised might believe that ratification under such circumstances
failed to reflect the considered will of the people.

Faced with the alternative of continued military supervision of government and the prospect of possibly more radical congressional action

in the future, a significant number of southern white leaders did come out for ratification of new state constitutions. A larger number, however, urged whites to register and then abstain from voting, in order to deny backers the participation of the absolute majority of the registered electorate required for ratification. Had Republicans been willing to risk adhering to this element of their program, southern whites might have successfully defeated the new constitutions when initially proposed, as they did in Alabama, the first state to hold a ratification election. This result would have given Republicans a second opportunity to follow the course advocated by their more conservative wing: allow white southerners to defeat proposed constitutions until the moderates among them gained the upper hand, providing a firm, white base for new constitutional systems.

However, with Andrew Johnson working successfully to maintain Conservative control of the provisional governments, southern Republicans pleaded with their national allies to drop the absolute-majority requirement. The other course left them at the mercy of ex-rebels. In fact, as long as Johnson kept them in control of day-to-day administration, southern Conservatives preferred staying under military supervision to adopting constitutions that would give black-supported Republicans a real chance at power. There was a good chance that southern Conservatives might outwait northerners, many Republicans feared, precipitating Democratic victories in the North.

Rather than risk it, Republicans dropped the requirement. A simple majority in a ratification election, no matter what the total vote, would suffice to establish a new state constitution. They even applied the new requirement retroactively to Alabama, restoring the state to normal relations in the Union even though its people had rejected its constitution according to the rules in place when they voted.[31] Such a proceeding proved that "the constitution they impose is not the constitution of the people of Alabama, but a constitution of the minority of the whole people, and that, a negro minority," Alabama Conservatives averred.[32] In Arkansas news that Republicans had repealed the absolute-majority requirement arrived on the second day of the two-week ratification election. There too opponents had worked, apparently successfully, to persuade voters to abstain. Over twenty years later, William M. Fishback remembered the outrage with which he and other Conservative leaders had received the news. "Such an election could not be in any sense regarded as fairly expressing the wishes of the people of the state," he insisted.[33] Throughout the South, whites refused to vote either in the elections to call conventions or in the ratification elections.[34]

The results were stark. Only in Virginia and North Carolina, among states for which the votes were published by race, did over 40 percent of the registered white voters even cast a ballot in the elections to hold conventions.[35] Evidence indicates the situation was much worse in the ratification elections. It suggests that in every state the vast majority of the votes sustaining the constitutions were cast by black southerners, although significant proportions of the white voters may have joined them in North Carolina and Georgia. The votes were not reported to Congress by race, but figures have been discovered for Louisiana parishes except New Orleans. In those parishes 40,409 of the 41,861 votes favoring ratification were cast by black voters.[36] A historian of Alabama Republicanism during Reconstruction has estimated that 62,000 of the approximately 68,000 votes in favor of that state's Reconstruction constitution were cast by freedmen.[37] Conservatives in Mobile, Alabama, published the names of those voting for ratification, listing 76 "White Renegades" among the 4,585 voters sustaining the constitution.[38] A racial division of such proportions over the fundamental law was bad enough. But because a constitution must ultimately win the acquiescence of its opponents in order to serve its legitimizing function, the failure of whites to vote at all was most ominous. The result was that Conservatives considered the ratification process a sham. Years later the Conservative North Carolina leader Zeb Vance remembered the disfranchisement best. But he lumped the disfranchised and those who had abstained together and repeated the conclusion that had undermined hopes for constitutional government in the South: "At least 40,000 citizens," he recalled, "by a pure fraud, . . . [were] deprived of the right to vote for the Constitution of their choice."[39]

Yet when one considers the constitutions themselves, what is striking is how similar they were to previous southern state constitutions. It was a time of constitutional ferment in the northern states. Constitutional conventions there would soon establish new forms of regulatory agencies, at the same time severely limiting the general authority of state legislatures, restricting local autonomy, and also transferring a variety of municipal powers to the states. Almost none of these changes were reflected in the southern constitutions, which in many ways were the last of the Jacksonian documents, expanding suffrage and treating state legislatures as direct representatives of the people, rather than threats to them.[40] Only in Arkansas, Florida, and North Carolina did the Republicans who dominated the state conventions eschew reliance on their earlier state charters. Mississippi's constitutional convention followed previous constitutional language establishing the executive branch and about half of the provisions on the judiciary, substantially altering the rest. In the other states, the framers followed earlier declarations of rights and articles establishing the legislative, executive, and judicial branches, to a large extent repeating previous language word for word. In Tennessee the 1834 constitution, amended by sections disfranchising rebels, abolishing slavery, and enfranchising freedmen, continued to serve as the state's fundamental law during Reconstruction. Although disfranchisement was agitated in nearly every convention, only four constitutions—those of Alabama, Arkansas, Louisiana, and Tennessee incorporated any such provisions.[11] Most also expanded significantly on earlier articles dealing with education and corporations and attended in more detail to state finance and taxation. Some—especially Virginia's—made detailed modifications in local government or established special bureaus to promote immigration or land distribution.

The difference that so enraged white southerners, of course, was the extension of civil and especially political rights to black southerners. Much of the new Alabama Constitution merely restated the state's previous constitutional provisions, Conservatives conceded. "But these are rendered delusive and useless by the diabolical ingenuity of other provisions, contrived . . . to insure . . . the ascendancy of the negro race."[42] To white southerners the black suffrage provisions themselves promised unconstitutional, tyrannical government. Without question, white southerners were bitterly, violently, and unreasoningly racist, and it is certainly possible to find those who with grim pleasure engaged in race war, pure and simple, who needed no justification to vent their racial hatred. But judging by what white southerners said *to each other* in public print and private communication, for most southerners racism interacted with deeply held principles of constitutional liberty in a manner that convinced them that they were the oppressed, not the oppressors; the victims, not the tyrants. As the resolutions of a Mississippi Conservative party convention indicated, they saw themselves engaged in a struggle to "vindicate alike the superiority of their race over the negro, and their political power to maintain constitutional liberty."[43]

This conviction grew out of basic understandings about government shared by most Americans—notions at the heart of what legal scholars have denominated "laissez-faire constitutionalism."[44] One of the most central of these is that the purpose of government is to promote the general welfare rather than the special interests of particular individuals or groups. Acts that violated this principle were denounced as "special legislation" or "class legislation." Not only did opponents fight such legislation in the political arena, but courts sometimes ruled that it violated various constitutional limitations on legislative power. Most twentieth-century Americans believe that the general community can derive benefits from legislation that helps particular groups. Therefore modern American government engages in a wide range of redistributive activities. But nineteenth-century Americans' notions of what might be in the general interest were far narrower. Whig and Republican promoters of active government might convince people that a protective tariff or railroad subsidies helped the community at large, but they fought a deep current of Jeffersonian and Jacksonian suspicion of the ability of the powerful to pervert government to their own ends.

Of course, in prevailing nineteenth-century opinion, autocratic or aristocratic governments always degenerated into machines for the enrichment of the few who controlled them. As Vernon L. Parrington summarized the common view (represented by Jefferson), "A class will serve class interests. Government by aristocracy is government in the interest of aristocracy."[45] But democratic governments were subject to similar risks. There were two ways in which government might be perverted into an engine of special privilege. First, the rich and powerful might exercise authority over a hoard of dependents, gaining an influence far out of proportion to their numbers. "Place power in the hands of those who have none, or a very trivial stake in the community, and you expose the poor and dependent to the influence and seductions of wealth," and the poor "will become subservient to the ambitions of the rich."[46] This was a fear that had long led advocates of republican government to favor property requirements for voting and to regard independent, yeoman landowners as the guarantors of republican liberty.[47] The second raised an opposite danger: demagogues, seeking power and plunder for themselves, might gain control of government by promising to pass legislation to improve the condition of the poor at the expense of the rest of society, in effect confiscating a part of the property of the prosperous for the benefit of the poor, the ignorant, and the venal.[48]

White Americans' racism, both North and South, interacted with these understandings. Even as they concluded in the 1820s and 1830s that all white men, in whatever economic circumstances, were independent enough to be entrusted with the ballot, they disfranchised black men on the grounds of their supine dependence on wealthy employers or, alternatively, their dangerous susceptibility to demagoguery because of their innate ignorance and cupidity.[49] Thus Pennsylvania's Democratic senator Charles Buckalew, a respected expert on legislative representation, warned Republicans against black suffrage: "By pouring into the ballot-boxes . . . a large mass of ignorant votes, and votes subjected to pecuniary or social influence, you will corrupt and degrade your elections."[50] And Ohio Democrat Durbin Ward warned of black voters, "It is preposterous to suppose they will be, during this generation, at least, anything more than pawns on the chess-board of politics—puppets in the hands of political wire-pullers."[51] Even the sympathetic commander of the Freedmen's Bureau, General Oliver Otis Howard, worried that unless the state or national governments undertook a massive education program, the freedmen "will become the tools of demagogues and a power for evil rather than for good."[52]

Thaddeus Stevens and other radical Republicans were more concerned about their dependence on ex-rebels. Enfranchisement alone could not secure the fruits of Union victory in the South, they warned. Unless Republicans secured the freedmen economic independence through confiscation and land reform, the southern aristocracy would simply control their votes.[53] In this matter their worries coincided with those of poorer southern whites. "Give them [freedmen] a vote now and what would inevitably result?" a southern columnist editorialized. "The rich landed proprietors, employing large numbers of ignorant laborers whom they could control . . . would hold the elections in their own hands. The poor white man, with his single vote, would be voiceless as the grave in the counsels and legislation of the state."[54]

Southern whites were quickly relieved of the prospect, or perhaps the hope, that the wealthy among them might control the black vote. As they watched native and immigrant whites—that is, whites who were native or immigrant to the South—begin to organize black voters (they never could conceive that black leaders played their own, independent role in this process), they realized with horror that the danger all ran in the opposite direction. "Political adventurers had taken the colored people in hand [and] . . . united them in an oath-bound political party."[55] A southern moderate reported to the influential Republican senator Henry Wilson how whites saw things: "Vast power is placed under the

235

control of ignorance and passion, and . . . bad men are preparing to use it recklessly for selfish and sinister purposes."[56] In family letters, the same correspondent exchanged concerns about "the small, low and mischievous white men who are endeavoring to ride into power on the negroes['] back."[57] It was an article of faith among the vast majority of southern whites that Republicans "make tools of the poor deluded creatures to advance their own purposes."[58]

Of course, in the opinion of most white southerners, such political managers were bad by definition. It was plain that the only way they could ride black votes to power was to appeal either to the freedmen's passions or to their interests, and to nineteenth-century Americans, with their firm conviction that government must act for the benefit of the whole community, neither was legitimate. President Andrew Johnson's denunciation of black suffrage indicates how southerners understood matters: black people were "enemies of free institutions," he insisted. "If the inferior race obtains the ascendancy over the other, it will govern with reference only to its own interests—for it will recognize no common interest."[59] One need hardly point out the hypocrisy of men who had supported slavery—the most extreme form of class legislation ever enacted in the United States—complaining that Republicans' success in winning black votes must "mean the . . . virtual enslavement of the white race."[60] But that does not mean they were insincere about the fears they expressed. On the contrary, who knew better the potential of state power to oppress?

As Michael Perman has shown, Republicans desperately sought to achieve legitimacy in the eyes of southern whites.[61] But political reality made that an impossible goal, given southern commitment to laissez-faire constitutionalism. The fact was that, like any politicians, Republicans had to respond to the demands of their constituents. Black southerners wanted access to public services that had been denied them as slaves—orphanages, asylums, hospitals, and especially educational institutions. The Republicans were in the position of having to serve a free population doubled in size by emancipation at the same time that emancipation had eliminated one of the largest prewar subjects of taxation, the slaves themselves. Worse, emancipation and the dislocation of war had lowered the value of the other major subject of tax revenue, plantation lands. Increased taxation of other property was inevitable, and even with higher taxes it is difficult to see how southern state governments could have maintained balanced budgets and paid for even basic social and educational services.

But what made this difficulty a matter of constitutional liberty to southern whites was the fact that parties promised to be divided largely along color lines, and therefore along class lines as well. As they considered the prospects under their new constitutions, southerners protested, "Taxation and representation are no longer to be united. They who own no property are to levy taxes and make all appropriations. The property-holders have to pay these taxes, without having any voice in levying them!"[62] Even the moderate James L. Orr, who would join the South Carolina Republican party, cautioned, "There will be presented the anomaly of a class of people wielding the political power of the State and levying taxes on the property of another class who will have in reality no political power." As an example, Orr pointed to black demands for state-supported public education. "Property holders will be compelled to build schools for this class who will not contribute a dollar for the education of their own children," he worried.[63] Conservatives were more strident. Thomas S. Gathright, who would later serve as Mississippi's superintendent of education under a Democratic administration, in 1870 lambasted public schools as "an unmitigated outrage upon the rights and liberties of the white people of the state."[64] "The appropriations to support free schools for the education of negro children, for the support of old negroes in the poor-houses, and the vicious in jails and penitentiaries . . . will be crushing and utterly ruinous," South Carolina Conservatives exclaimed. "The consequences will be, in effect, confiscation."[65] Mississippians echoed South Carolinians: constitutional "provisions, on the subject of 'Public Works,' 'Houses of Refuge,' etc. . . . are all designed to establish means to rob the people." Mississippi's new constitution amounted to "the licensing of . . . CONFISCATION by means of taxation."[66] Louisianans likewise insisted, "Negro suffrage would be tantamount to confiscation."[67]

As these southern protests indicate, the enfranchisement of southern blacks raised pressures in the Reconstruction South for the kinds of redistributive governmental policies that would not be acceptable to most Americans until after the turn of the century—in fact, perhaps not until the New Deal. The transfer of wealth inherent in Republican programs to provide public services to the freedmen violated the basic tenets of laissez-faire constitutionalism. The lament of a southern newspaper indicates how closely linked to this objection calls for white supremacy were: "Shall the white man be subordinated to the negro? Shall the property classes be robbed by the no-property herd?"[68]

This resentment may have been exacerbated by an apparent willingness of southern Republicans to use local government as a sort of government works program, another example of redistributive public policy. We need further research to learn whether Conservative complaints to this effect were based on fact, but at least one researcher sympathetic to the Republicans, looking closely at Charleston, South Carolina, has concluded that Republicans "created the impression among many voters, especially blacks, that the first priority of city government was to provide employment for the many destitute and unemployed."[69] At the same time, white Republican leaders were often ostracized and black activists blacklisted. As a consequence, many Republicans became dependent on government jobs as their sole means of support. It may well be that this dependence on government jobs led Republicans to pass the salary increases that Conservatives attacked so bitterly—salary increases necessary merely to compensate for the depreciating value of the state scrip in which they were paid.[70] But no matter how reasonable the explanation, most southern whites regarded Republicanism as a conspiracy among political adventurers, a "villainous scheme for transferring the earnings of the people to the pockets of the spoilsmen." "Taxation is robbery," they insisted, "when imposed for private gain."[71]

The situation would have been grim enough if Republican spending had been limited to expanding public services and meeting an increased payroll. But southern Republicans knew they had to devise programs whose benefits extended to white southerners, in order to establish the legitimacy of the governmental system they had enacted. They could not proceed in the one way sure to win white support—by imposing restraints on black freedom—so they tried to meet the goal by promoting economic prosperity, especially through the expansion of transportation facilities. But this attempt, too, cost money, stretching the already strained resources of the states. Republicans tried to escape from their dilemma by creating "contingent" debts, guarantees of loans to private enterprises for which they would become responsible only if the businesses failed. But the businesses did fail in the economic downturn of the 1870s, leaving the states with even greater obligations. Like third-world nations in recent years, the Republican governments found themselves in a cycle of raising taxes and refloating loans at ever-steeper discounts and higher interest rates to pay off currently due interest and principal. Worse, just like other states and the national government at the same time, the Reconstruction governments entered into their promotional efforts and their financing arrangements without having established systems that would enable them to differentiate worthy from unworthy projects or having instituted the controls over expenditure necessary to avoid fraud. The result was disastrous. Projects were funded, contracts let, and financial agents chosen on political rather than economic grounds, in a cycle that opened the way for widespread influence peddling and bribery. When the business ventures collapsed, southern taxpayers were left holding the bag. And the vast majority of those taxpayers were white, whereas the constituency of the party that had incurred the states' obligations was overwhelmingly black.[72] Horace Greeley saw the problem with unusual clarity:

> The old Slave governments of the South were . . . very rarely corrupt or prodigal. The planters paid most of the taxes; they decided who should be legislators; and they did not abide jobbers. . . . They had no public support of the poor; each subsisted, after a fashion, his own used-up slaves. The Poor Whites lived or died as they might; and, except for the Whites of two or three great cities, there were no public schools: and this made government cheap and taxes light. With Emancipation came a great change. There was an urgent demand for schools . . . , for the public support of paupers, White and Black . . . ; and so with many public institutions. Just when the people were poorest, they were required to bear the heaviest public expense, though only accustomed to the lightest. Dissatisfaction and complaint were inevitable.[73]

The Republican finance and internal improvement fiascoes of course confirmed southern whites' worst expectations. Reconstruction had, they were convinced, established exactly the sorts of governments they had feared. Taxes and state debt had risen dramatically, but there was little to show for it. In fact, because of the increase in the free population, spending per citizen had actually dropped since the war. Moreover, taxes had been shifted from slaves to land, so that the taxes levied on small farmers increased disproportionately to what they had paid before emancipation.[74] By 1874 the state auditor of Mississippi reported that one-fifth of all the land in the state was technically forfeit for taxes.[75] By 1873, 20 percent of Alabama's tax receipts went to pay off the interest on

239

its bonded debt. These payments accounted for all of the state's deficit.[76] The interest on Louisiana's debt accounted for 11½ mills of the state's 21½-mill property tax in 1874.[77]

Until new research into southern finances during Reconstruction is completed, one cannot judge just how heavy southern tax and debt burdens really were, although a historian presently undertaking that job has said that the debts did exceed the capacity of the weakened state economies to repay.[78] But it was not only the amount of the taxes that was at issue. "It is not taxation, nor even an increase of taxation, that the people of South Carolina object to," a sympathetic journalist reported, but rather "it is *taxation without representation, an unjust, tyrannical, arbitrary, overwhelming taxation,* producing revenues which never get any further than the already bursting pockets of knaves and dupes!"[79] Taxpayer protests did lead to retrenchment in southern Republican policies, but as a South Carolina Conservative insisted to reform Republican leader Carl Schurz, "The evils . . . are not of a transient character. They arise out of the very nature of things." The true problem was that "property is held almost entirely by the white race, political power is almost entirely with the African race."[80] That is, black southerners did not directly feel the tax consequences of the state policies they sustained. The militantly racist *Alexandria* (Louisiana) *Caucasian* thundered that for eight years "the negroes of the South [have] organized . . . [to obtain] class legislation over and over again for their exclusive benefit."[81] "This is the rule of the proletariat," Mississippi white-liners exclaimed; "it is naked communism—and negro communism at that."[82] As it prepared for the violent Mississippi election of 1875, the Democratic party organ headlined, "The Robbery and Oppression of the South, and Not Negro Rights, [Is] the Issue."[83]

Some revisionist historians of Reconstruction have perceived growing northern sympathy for white southerners to have been a manifestation of renascent northern racism.[84] But in fact southern complaints of black "class legislation" naturally resonated with northerners committed to laissez-faire constitutionalism, especially as they grew more concerned about potential "class legislation" in the North. What southern Conservatives described seemed uncomfortably similar to the corrupt machine politics developing in northern cities, where taxpayers were at the mercy "of greedy and irresponsible crowds controlled by adventurers as reckless as themselves, whose object is nothing but plunder"; where "the educated and wealthy [man] . . . felt himself as much disfran-

240

chised as if he had been excluded from the polls by law"; and where taxes took on the character of confiscation—"organized communism and destruction of property under the guise of taxation."[85] "Ten years ago the North was nearly united in . . . sympathy for the freedmen," the *New York Times* wrote. "Now . . . not a few believe that the rights of the whites have been infringed on."[86] E. L. Godkin, the editor of the *Nation*, was surely one of them. "Instead of establishing equal rights for all, we set up the government of a class," he lamented in 1871. By 1874 he was editorializing on "Socialism in South Carolina."[87]

In effect, the governmental system established in the South during Reconstruction pitted democracy against a concept of equal rights many Americans believed inherent in liberty. Benjamin F. Butler perceived the issue clearly and understood its implications for the North as well as the South. According to southern Conservatives, he told his largely working-class constituents, "republican government means, that the majority shall not rule unless the majority are the owners of the property of the State, that the majority shall not rule unless that majority is composed of the educated classes."[88] But southern Conservatives did not perceive themselves to be rejecting democracy. To them, a system in which ambitious men acquired power by making impossible or illicit promises to voters the southerners considered too ignorant or venal to regard the common good was not really democratic. On the contrary, it violated democracy by in effect giving bad men —"a few thousand white vampires" who controlled an "unbroken black line" of "political chattel"[89]—more votes than good men. Therefore white southerners could claim with all sincerity that the South would vote Democratic "if left to a *fair* ballot"—that is, a ballot that discounted black votes.[90] They insisted that "the carpet-bagger . . . has become, with the scalawag, through their influence with the negro, a sort of aristocrat or autocrat."[91] White southerners could calmly contemplate frauds from which they would have recoiled if elections had been "between intelligent voters" rather than being occasions "where whole hordes [are] hustled to the poles & voted."[92] Robert Toombs could promise to fashion a new Redeemer constitution "by which the people will rule and the nigger will never be heard of!"[93] Indeed, they could believe that "to rescue the government from Republican control involves the very salvation of Republican institutions."[94]

The Redeemer constitutions accurately reflected this southern white constitutionalism. More significant, they showed how congruent southern white concerns were with growing northern concerns, for these constitutions were very similar to those being framed in the North at the same time. The constitutions of the 1870s through the 1890s, North and South, reversed the trend toward broader suffrage, imposed strict limits on state legislative power, withheld state authority from a variety of areas, and withdrew power, by constitutional restrictions and gerrymander, from polities where the "dangerous classes" were large and politically potent.[95]

Thus we have the irony and the tragedy of Radical Reconstruction in the South. The irony was that Republicans sought to establish democratic constitutional government but in the process threatened constitutional liberty, as white southerners understood it. The written constitutions that created southern Reconstruction governments could not establish their legitimacy in the eyes of most southern whites, unless they corresponded to deeper, unwritten understandings of the essentials of constitutional government. To southern Conservatives, the war against those constitutions was a struggle not against liberty and democracy but for them. The tragedy was not only that southern whites were successful but that by the 1870s and 1880s their ideas were no longer just southern.

Notes

1. Daniel H. Chamberlain, "Reconstruction in South Carolina," *Atlantic Monthly* 87 (1901): 484.

2. Kenneth M. Stampp, *The Era of Reconstruction, 1865–1877* (New York, 1965), 170.

3. Charles William Ramsdell, *Reconstruction in Texas* (New York, 1910), 227; Cal Ledbetter, Jr., "The Constitution of 1868: Conqueror's Constitution or Constitutional Continuity?" *Arkansas Historical Quarterly* 44 (1985): 34–35.

4. In Arkansas the transfer of power precipitated civil war. Louisianans rose in open insurrection, temporarily overthrowing the Republican state government, in September 1874. From then until 1877 they forcefully took control of town and parish governments and offices, finally forcing Republicans to surrender power under threat of violence after the disputed election of 1876. In South Carolina Conservatives backed their claim to victory in the disputed election of 1876 with armed force; Republican rivals had to surrender to it when Pres. Rutherford B. Hayes informed them that he would not intervene to prevent violence. See John M. Harrell, *The Brooks and Baxter War: A History of the Reconstruction Period in Arkansas* (St. Louis, Mo., 1893); Joe Gray Taylor,

Louisiana Reconstructed, 1863–1877 (Baton Rouge, 1974), 267–313, 480–505; and Francis Butler Simkins and Robert H. Woody, *South Carolina during Reconstruction* (Chapel Hill, N.C., 1932), 514–41.

5. Conservatives captured control of the state legislature in 1872 in a campaign marked by some amount of violence. In advance of the gubernatorial election of 1873, they gutted the militia law by refusing appropriations, thus depriving the Republican governor of a force to protect Republican voters (or intimidate Democratic ones, depending on the politics of the observer). More important, they provided only one day for the election, in apparent contravention of the four-day requirement imposed by the state constitution. Consequently, the defeated Republicans refused to concede the legitimacy of the election and prepared to resist the claims of the Conservative governor-elect by both force and law. They conceded defeat when Pres. Ulysses S. Grant refused to send troops to maintain order, in effect refusing to protect the Republican claimants from the superior military force of the Conservatives. Ramsdell, *Reconstruction in Texas*, 313–17; John L. Waller, *Colossal Hamilton of Texas: A Biography of Andrew Jackson Hamilton, Militant Unionist and Reconstruction Governor* (El Paso, Tex., 1968), 136–39.

6. The historian of Mississippi Reconstruction entitled his chapter on the transfer of power "Revolution." William C. Harris, *The Day of the Carpetbagger: Republican Reconstruction in Mississippi* (Baton Rouge, 1979), 650–90. See also Harry P. Owens, "The Eufaula Riot of 1874," *Alabama Review* 16 (1963): 224–37; Loren Schweringer, *James T. Rapier and Reconstruction* (Chicago, 1978), 133–50; and Walter L. Fleming, *Civil War and Reconstruction in Alabama* (New York, 1905), 771–96. In Florida a campaign preceded by several years of violence led to a disputed result. Both sides contemplated the use of force, but the Conservatives won a court decision in which the Republicans decided to acquiesce. Jerrell H. Shofner, *Nor Is It Over Yet: Florida in the Era of Reconstruction, 1863–1877* (Gainesville, Fla., 1973), 225–42, 295–98, 309–39.

7. Elizabeth Studley Nathans, *Losing the Peace: Georgia Republicans and Reconstruction, 1865–1871* (Baton Rouge, 1968), 127–46; Horace W. Raper, *William W. Holden: North Carolina's Political Enigma* (Chapel Hill, N.C., 1985), 155–98; Allen W. Trelease, *White Terror: The Ku Klux Klan Conspiracy and Southern Reconstruction* (New York, 1971), 226–42.

8. Tennessee law disfranchised large numbers of ex-Confederates. The Republican governor, DeWitt Clinton Senter, running for reelection with Conservative support against a rival Republican, secured victory for himself and Conservative control of the state legislature by ordering registrars not to challenge the votes cast by those disfranchised. Thomas B. Alexander, *Political Reconstruction in Tennessee* (Nashville, Tenn., 1950), 217–26; James C. Parker, "Tennessee Gubernatorial Elections: I. 1869: The Victory of the Conservatives," *Tennessee Historical Quarterly* 33 (1974): 34–48.

243

9. Jack P. Maddex, *The Virginia Conservatives, 1867–1879: A Study in Reconstruction Politics* (Chapel Hill, N.C., 1970), 67–85; Caroline F. Putnam to Benjamin F. Butler, November 14, 1869, *National Anti-Slavery Standard* (New York), December 4, 1869, 1; Senate, *Address of the Republican State Convention, Held in Richmond, Virginia, on the 24th and 25th of November, 1869 . . .* , 41st Cong., 2d sess., S. Misc. Doc. 3; petition from Isaac P. Baldwin et al., January 11, 1870, Senate Judiciary Committee Papers, Record Group 46, National Archives, Washington, D.C.

10. Taylor, *Louisiana Reconstructed*, 304–7.

11. Congress responded after a critical delay by rescinding the state's restoration to normal relations in the Union. The Republican governor's attempt to recover from the disaster by postponing the next scheduled elections divided his own party, and the demoralized and divided Republicans were easily defeated. Nathans, *Losing the Peace*, 147–212.

12. Raper, *Holden*, 199–218.

13. Harris, *The Day of the Carpetbagger*, 691–98.

14. Nathans, *Losing the Peace*, 220–22.

15. For examples of the problems raised by partisan returning boards, see William Gillette, *Retreat from Reconstruction, 1869–1879* (Baton Rouge, 1979), 110–11, 121–23, 315, 324–29; Shofner, *Nor Is It Over Yet*, 285–87, 307–13; and Taylor, *Louisiana Reconstructed*, 241–46, 491–93.

16. Nathans, *Losing the Peace*, 185–89.

17. Zebulon B. Vance, "Reconstruction in North Carolina," in *Why the Solid South? or, Reconstruction and Its Results*, ed. Hilary A. Herbert et al. (Baltimore, 1890), 70.

18. James A. Renshaw, "Liberty Monument," *Louisiana Historical Quarterly* 3 (1920): 259–78.

19. Henry Winter Davis, "Lessons of the War," in Davis, *Speeches and Addresses Delivered in the Congress of the United States, and on Several Public Occasions* (New York, 1867), 580.

20. George S. Boutwell, "Reconstruction: Its True Basis," in Boutwell, *Speeches and Papers Relating to the Rebellion and the Overthrow of Slavery*, 2 vols. (Boston, 1867), 2:406. I have reversed the order of the sentences.

21. For a fuller discussion of this point, see Michael Les Benedict, "Preserving the Constitution: The Conservative Basis of Radical Reconstruction," *Journal of American History* 61 (1974): 65–90.

22. *Congressional Globe*, 39th Cong., 1st sess., December 18, 1865, 74.

23. George W. Julian, "Dangers and Duties of the Hour—Reconstruction and Suffrage," in Julian, *Speeches on Political Questions* (New York, 1872), 269–70.

24. George W. Julian, *Political Recollections, 1840–1872* (Chicago, 1884), 306. See Michael Les Benedict, *A Compromise of Principle: Congressional Republicans and Reconstruction, 1863–1869* (New York, 1975), 137.

25. John A. Bingham, in the *Congressional Globe,* 39th Cong., 2d sess., February 13, 1867, 1211. The conservative Republican Senate majority leader, William Pitt Fessenden, also tried to abort any Reconstruction measure spelling out how southerners must proceed. Benedict, *A Compromise of Principle,* 237–38.

26. Benedict, "Preserving the Constitution," 82–83.

27. Of course, the most apparent problem is that in the Lockean system all individuals must agree to enter into society; it is difficult to justify the ability of the majority to impose its will on those who refuse. The southern use of conventions to legitimize secession led to a reaction in the North against the view that they represented the organic people. But the more limited, legalistic view of conventions was fully articulated only in 1867, with the appearance of John A. Jameson's *The Constitutional Convention: Its History, Powers, and Mode of Proceeding* (Chicago, 1866). See Harold M. Hyman, *A More Perfect Union: The Impact of the Civil War and Reconstruction upon the Constitution* (New York, 1973), 41–49, 119–23.

28. Reconstruction Act, 14 Stat. 428–29; Supplementary Reconstruction Act, 15 Stat. 14–16.

29. The calculations on which William A. Russ based his conclusion that huge numbers of southerners were disfranchised are seriously deficient, in that they ignore the casualties inflicted by the war and attribute failure to register to vote during Reconstruction entirely to disfranchisement. Russ, "Registration and Disfranchisement under Radical Reconstruction," *Mississippi Valley Historical Review* 21 (1934): 163–80. Nonetheless, it is clear that many tens of thousands were ineligible to vote under the Reconstruction Acts. Gen. Edward R. S. Canby, commander of the second military district under the acts, estimated totals of 11,686 whites ineligible to vote in North Carolina and 8,244 in South Carolina, respectively 9 percent and 14 percent of the white electorate early in 1867. Senate, *Registered Voters in Rebel States,* 42d Cong., 2d sess., S. Exec. Doc. 53, 3–7. The army estimated that 10,500 Georgians were disfranchised, about 9 percent of the electorate. Ibid., 8.

30. One cannot tell the effect simply by seeing whether constitutions were ratified by a larger majority than the number disfranchised. The fact of disfranchisement may have affected strategy and *élan* in ways that multiplied its effect.

31. Benedict, *A Compromise of Principle,* 315–20.

32. Resolutions of Alabama Conservatives, as quoted in *Appleton's Annual Cyclopedia,* 1868, 15.

33. William M. Fishback, "Reconstruction in Arkansas," in Herbert et al., *Why the Solid South?* 297.

34. Michael Perman, *Reunion without Compromise: The South and Reconstruction, 1865–1868* (Cambridge, 1973), 304–48.

35. Edward McPherson, *Political History of the United States of America during the Period of Reconstruction* . . . (Washington, D.C., 1875), 374.

36. Donald W. Davis, "Ratification of the Constitution of 1868—Record of the Votes," *Louisiana History* 6 (1965): 301–5.

37. William M. Cash, "Alabama Republicans during Reconstruction: Personal Characteristics, Motivations, and Political Activity of Party Activists, 1867–1880" (Ph.D. diss., University of Alabama, 1973), 102.

38. Margaret Davidson Sizemore, "Frederick G. Bomberg of Mobile: An Illustrious Character, 1837–1928," *Alabama Review* 29 (1976): 111.

39. Vance, "Reconstruction in North Carolina," 77.

40. Harold M. Hyman and William M. Wiecek discuss constitutional trends in the nation in *Equal Justice under Law: Constitutional Development, 1835–1875* (New York, 1982), 356–57. Harris has recorded a similar judgment on the Mississippi Constitution. Harris, *The Day of the Carpetbagger,* 158–59. The Reconstruction constitutions may be consulted conveniently in *Sources and Documents of United States Constitutions,* ed. William F. Swindler, 10 vols. (Dobbs Ferry, N.Y., 1973–79).

41. As initially proposed, the constitutions of Virginia and Mississippi also included disfranchisement sections, but in deference to Conservative and moderate Republican opposition, national Republicans arranged for those sections to be voted on separately, and they were defeated. Maddex, *The Virginia Conservatives,* 67–85; Harris, *The Day of the Carpetbagger,* 199–217, 257.

42. Petition of John A. Winston et al., Petitions and Memorials File, 40th Cong., House of Representatives, Record Group 233, National Archives.

43. As quoted in *Appleton's Annual Cyclopedia,* 1868, 510.

44. For a fuller discussion of the following description of laissez-faire constitutionalism, see Michael Les Benedict, "Laissez-Faire and Liberty: A Re-Evaluation of the Origins of Laissez-Faire Constitutionalism," *Law and History Review* 3 (1985): 293–331.

45. Vernon L. Parrington, *Main Currents in American Thought,* 3 vols. (New York, 1927–30), 1:359.

46. Philip N. Nicholas, in *Proceedings and Debates of the Virginia State Convention of 1829–30* (Richmond, Va., 1830), 367.

47. Jack R. Pole, *Political Representation in England and the Origins of the American Republic* (London and New York, 1966), 31; Jack P. Greene, " 'Slavery or Independence': Some Reflections on the Relationship among Liberty, Black Bondage, and Equality in Revolutionary South Carolina," *South Carolina Historical Magazine* 80 (1979): 207; Edmund S. Morgan, "Slavery and Freedom: The American Paradox," *Journal of American History* 59 (1972): 5–29; Dickson D. Bruce, Jr., *The Rhetoric of Conservatism: The Virginia Convention of 1829–30 and the Conservative Tradition in the South* (San Marino, Calif., 1982), 75–76; Chilton Williamson, "American Suffrage and Sir William Blackstone," *Political Science Quarterly* 68 (1953): 552–57.

48. Benedict, "Laissez-Faire and Liberty," 306–7; Michael E. McGerr, *The Decline of Popular Politics: The American North, 1865–1928* (New York, 1986), 48.

49. Kirk H. Porter, *A History of Suffrage in the United States* (Chicago, 1918), 62–111.

50. *Congressional Globe*, 39th Cong., 1st sess., 1866, 83.

51. Durbin Ward, "Against the Fifteenth Amendment," in Ward, *Life, Speeches and Orations of Durbin Ward* (Columbus, Ohio, 1888), 166.

52. Oliver Otis Howard, *Report of the . . . Commissioner Bureau of Refugees, Freedmen, and Abandoned Lands to the Secretary of War, Oct. 20, 1869* (Washington, D.C., 1869), 13.

53. Thaddeus Stevens, in the *Congressional Globe*, 39th Cong., 1st sess., December 18, 1865, 74; George W. Julian, "Dangers and Duties of the Hour—Reconstruction and Suffrage," in Julian, *Speeches,* 268–69.

54. Juhl [Julius J. Fleming], in the *Charleston* (S.C.) *News and Courier,* July 22, 1865, reprinted in *The Juhl Letters to the Charleston Courier: A View of the South, 1865–1871,* ed. John Hammond Moore (Athens, Ga., 1974), 22.

55. James L. Kemper, *Letter from Governor Kemper on the Petersburg Charter* (Richmond, Va., 1874), 2.

56. William Henry Trescot to Wilson, September 8, 1867, in Gaillard Hunt, "Letter of William Henry Trescot," *American Historical Review* 15 (1910): 579.

57. E. A. Trescot to William Henry Trescot, April 7, 1867, typescript, William Henry Trescot Papers, Caroliniana Library, University of South Carolina, Columbia.

58. James M. Willcox to Susannah Willcox, July 20, 1868, J. M. Willcox Papers, Perkins Library, Duke University, Durham, N.C.

59. James D. Richardson, ed., *A Compilation of Messages and Papers of the Presidents of the United States,* 10 vols. (Washington, D.C., 1896–99), 6:478, 566.

60. Kemper, *Letter on the Petersburg Charter,* 3.

61. Michael Perman, *The Road to Redemption: Southern Politics, 1869–1879* (Chapel Hill, N.C., 1984).

62. Remonstrance of South Carolina Democrats, as quoted in *Appleton's Annual Cyclopedia,* 1868, 697.

63. As quoted in the *New York Times,* August 9, 1867, 2.

64. Gathright illustrated his charge with the example of schools in Noxumbee County, where it would cost $40,000 to build schoolhouses, "and not twenty-five white children in that county can be benefited, while the colored population pays almost no part of this tax." *Hinds County* (Miss.) *Gazette,* October 12, 1870, as quoted in Stuart Grayson Noble, *Forty Years of the Public Schools in Mississippi* (New York, 1918), 14.

65. Remonstrance of South Carolina Democrats, as quoted in *Appleton's Annual Cyclopedia,* 1868, 697. I have reversed the order of the sentences.

66. *Jackson Daily Clarion,* November 4, 1869, 2; ibid., May 19, 1868, 2.

67. "Memorial of the Citizens of Louisiana," Senate Judiciary Committee Papers, 40th Cong., Record Group 46, National Archives.

68. *Montgomery Daily Advertiser*, January 7, 1868, 2.

69. William C. Hines, "Frustration, Factionalism, and Failure: Black Political Leadership and the Republican Party in Reconstruction Charleston, 1865–1877" (Ph.D. diss., Kent State University, 1979), 185.

70. Lawrence N. Powell, "The Politics of Livelihood: Carpetbaggers in the Deep South," in *Region, Race, and Reconstruction: Essays in Honor of C. Vann Woodward*, ed. J. Morgan Kousser and James M. McPherson (New York, 1982), 315–47; Mark W. Summers, *Railroads, Reconstruction, and the Gospel of Prosperity: Aid under the Radical Republicans, 1865–1877* (Princeton, N.J., 1984), 126–28.

71. *Jackson Weekly Clarion*, June 2, 1870, 2; ibid., November 23, 1871, 2.

72. We badly need a sophisticated study of fiscal policy and management in the Reconstruction South. Traditional accounts rely on what may be doctored Conservative and Democratic accounts, stress increased property taxes without noting that taxes on slave property had been eliminated, do not try to adjust tax rates for low tax assessments or payment in depreciated state scrip and bonds, and fail to take into account a host of other factors. One can find the traditional horror story of debt and high taxation recounted in the Dunningite studies cited in n. 4 above and in C. Mildred Thompson, *Reconstruction in Georgia: Economic, Social, Political, 1865–72* (New York, 1915), 207–34; and Simkins and Woody, *South Carolina during Reconstruction*, 175–79. Revisionist histories have been more sympathetic, but they still chronicle a rather dismal tale. See Harris, *The Day of the Carpetbagger*, 295–300; Taylor, *Louisiana Reconstructed*, 187–208, 265–67; Summers, *Railroads, Reconstruction, and the Gospel of Prosperity*, esp. 158–59, 196–208, 280–85; and J. Mills Thornton, "Fiscal Policy and the Failure of Reconstruction in the Lower South," in Kousser and McPherson, *Region, Race, and Reconstruction*, 349–94.

73. Horace Greeley, *Mr. Greeley's Letters from Texas and the Lower Mississippi . . . ; Address to the Farmers of Texas, and His Speech on His Return to New York, June 12, 1871* (New York, 1871), 51.

74. Thornton, "Fiscal Policy and the Failure of Reconstruction," 351.

75. Harris, *The Day of the Carpetbagger*, 299.

76. *Report of the Auditor of the State of Alabama for . . . 1873* (Montgomery, Ala., 1873), 108–9.

77. William Pitt Kellogg, *Annual Message of His Excellency, Wm. Pitt Kellogg, to the General Assembly of Louisiana, Session of 1874* (New Orleans, 1874). Thornton reports that interest payments equaled 22 percent of South Carolina's disbursements in 1876 and 32 percent of Florida's. Thornton, "Fiscal Policy and the Failure of Reconstruction," 384.

78. Thornton, "Fiscal Policy and the Failure of Reconstruction," 382–85.

79. Edward King, "The Great South: The South Carolina Problem," *Scribner's Monthly* 8 (1874): 139.

80. W. W. Boyce to Schurz, May 8, 1874, Schurz Papers, Manuscripts Division, Library of Congress, Washington, D.C.

81. *Alexandria* (La.) *Caucasian,* August 1, 1874, 2.

82. *Natchez Democrat,* January 15, 1875, as quoted in Harris, *The Day of the Carpetbagger,* 645.

83. *Jackson Weekly Clarion,* March 11, 1875, 2.

84. For example, Gillette, *Retreat from Reconstruction,* 190–96, 197–279; Robert F. Durden, *James Shepard Pike: Republicanism and the American Negro, 1850–1882* (Durham, N.C., 1957); and Patrick W. Riddleburger, "The Break in the Radical Ranks: Liberals vs. Stalwarts in the Election of 1872," *Journal of Negro History* 44 (1959): 136–57.

85. Francis Parkman, "The Failure of Universal Suffrage," *North American Review* 126 (1878): 20; J. Francis Fisher, as quoted in Simon Sterne, *On Representative Government and Personal Reputation* (Philadelphia, 1871), 74; Simon Sterne, *Suffrage in the Cities* (New York, 1878), 26. See Benedict, "Laissez-Faire and Liberty," 306–7; and McGerr, *The Decline of Popular Politics,* 45–50.

86. *New York Times,* May 8, 1876, 4.

87. *Nation,* December 7, 1871, 364; "Socialism in South Carolina," ibid., April 16, 1874, 247.

88. Benjamin F. Butler, *The Negro in Politics: Review of the Recent Legislation for His Protection . . .* (Lowell, Mass., 1871), 11.

89. *Beauregard and Wesson* (Miss.) *Times,* September 3, 1874, as quoted in Harris, *The Day of the Carpetbagger,* 637–38.

90. S. R. Cockrill to Andrew Johnson, January 9, 1868, Johnson Papers, Manuscripts Division, Library of Congress (emphasis added).

91. Benjamin F. Perry, "Gov. Perry's Address to his Constituency," in Perry, *Biographical Sketches of Eminent American Statesmen with Speeches, Addresses and Letters* (Philadelphia, 1887), 214.

92. George W. Blount to Matthew W. Ransom, August 8, 1874, Ransom Papers, Southern Historical Collection, University of North Carolina, Chapel Hill.

93. William Y. Thompson, *Robert Toombs of Georgia* (Baton Rouge, 1966), 242.

94. S. B. French to Samuel J. Tilden, November 21, 1875, Tilden Papers, New York Public Library.

95. For a discussion of the Redeemer constitutions, see Perman, *The Road to Redemption,* 193–220. The constitutions themselves may be found in Swindler, *Sources and Documents.* For northern constitutions in the 1870s and 1880s, see Hyman and Wiecek, *Equal Justice under Law,* 356–57; and Morton Keller, *Affairs of State: Public Life in Late Nineteenth Century America* (Cambridge, Mass., 1977), 319–20.

249

Part Five

Constitutionalism in the Twentieth-Century South

I
t is a truism that the twentieth century has produced sweeping changes in the South's social and political order. Urbanization and industrialization transformed the rural economy of the region and gradually undermined states' rights constitutionalism. Southern politics were increasingly integrated into the national two-party system. Groups previously excluded from meaningful participation in public life, such as blacks and women, pushed for a share of power. Moreover, after World War II new constitutional norms of equal protection prompted the federal government to attack racial segregation in the South.

Although traditional constitutional values have not completely disappeared, twentieth-century southerners have made substantial adjustments in the face of the centralizing tendency of the federal Constitution. The chapters in this section treat aspects of that story and suggest possibilities for future research. Peter Graham Fish investigates Judge John Parker's handling of economic issues during the 1920s. A strong proponent of business growth, Parker tended to uphold state regulations and sought to balance national economic policy with the needs of regional development. David R. Colburn and Steven F. Lawson offer insights into Florida's reaction to the school-desegregation mandate of *Brown v. Board of Education*. Colburn presents a case study of the constitutional politics of implementing the *Brown* decision in the Sunshine State; he demonstrates that state leaders retained considerable latitude to influence events in carrying out constitutional standards. Lawson considers the effort of the Florida Legislative Investigation Committee to

251

hamper the activities of the NAACP. This controversy produced the landmark *Gibson* ruling in which the U.S. Supreme Court curtailed legislative investigation by recognizing an associational right to privacy. Mary K. Bonsteel Tachau breaks new ground in her essay dealing with women and constitutionalism; she traces the slow movement toward equal rights for women in the section and argues that much further work remains to be done.

Torchbearer for Pre–New Deal Southern Economic Development: Judge John J. Parker of the U.S. Court of Appeals for the Fourth Circuit

Peter Graham Fish

The South, Law, and Economic Development

Despite a historic commitment to agriculture, many southerners realized by the beginning of the twentieth century that their region required enhanced commercial and industrial development in order to become competitive within the national economy. For them the 1920s were a time of hope when the prospect of bringing prosperity to the South seemed at hand. World War I had ended; the Great Depression had not yet begun. A legacy of prewar progressivism persisted at the state government level, manifested by what George B. Tindall has termed "business progressivism."[1] Yet amid the economic boosterism of the period, private property rights continued to enjoy powerful intellectual and judicial protections.[2] The war had muted sectionalism and fostered national political integration.[3] So, too, had it given impetus to centralizing impulses already coursing through the national economy.[4] But at the same time, earlier variants of

253

state mercantilism, together with the presence of distinct southern regional economic interests, persisted, constitutionally clothed with immunity from national preemption by the time-worn doctrine of "dual federalism."[5] Where to draw the lines between government and enterprise, and among occasionally competing state, regional, and national interests, perplexed policy makers who sought to promote economic development of the New South. Southerners, like citizens in other sections of the nation, grasped the instrumental role that courts and judges could play in achieving such development.[6] And the federal judiciary in the South would prove to be a particularly important vehicle of economic policy, especially during the years 1925 to 1933. Even though the impetus for the growth of the region's economy typically lay with private, local, or state initiatives, federal district and appeals courts also exercised considerable influence.[7] They used their authority to invoke constitutional limitations, federal statute law, and prior decisions to channel these economic initiatives.[8] To be sure, authoritative disposition of economic questions transformed into legal issues rested with the U.S. Supreme Court. But regional courts of appeals and three-judge district courts processed such economics-laden cases, finally adjudicated many of them, and transmitted some to the high Court.

Although scholars have lavished attention on the role of southern federal judges in the civil rights revolution of the 1950s and 1960s,[9] they have generally ignored the contributions of a previous generation of judges to the economic development of the region. This essay explores these developments through the contributions of John J. Parker and his colleagues on the Fourth Circuit Court of Appeals. Their decisions allocated valuable economic resources among litigants as they helped to forge subnational economic development policies that presumably fostered national goals, a behavioral assumption warmly embraced by critics.[10] Yet the roots of these same judges typically sprang from the vicinage of their courts.[11] Consequently, the outlooks and judicial decisions of these judges of courts-in-between predictably reflected inherent tensions between public and private economic spheres of interest and between the claims of regionalism and those of nationalism, tensions that were part and parcel of the New South credo.[12]

Fourth Circuit Court

Two circuit courts of appeals provided the sole regional judicial forum available in the South: the Fifth, which encompassed the states of the

Deep South, and the Fourth.[13] The latter processed appeals flowing thinly and unevenly from ten district courts in Maryland, West Virginia, Virginia, North Carolina, and South Carolina during the pre-depression years.[14] The appellate litigation raised regionally important economic issues involving state regulatory and taxing powers, the scope of national power respecting private property rights, and conflicts between policies favorable to national economic integration and those perceived as essential to southern economic development. The outcome of these appeals tended to be final and authoritative within the tribunal's jurisdiction; only 2.8 percent of the circuit court's decisions were subsequently even considered by the U.S. Supreme Court.[15] Whether or not reviewed by the high Court, cases adjudicated before the intermediate appellate bench and before three-judge district courts composed of trial and appellate judges[16] produced a policy-oriented constitutional jurisprudence that resonated to the cadences of regional economic development.

The foremost Fourth Circuit exponent for a manifestly regional economic jurisprudence was John J. Parker of North Carolina. He acted as a veritable torchbearer for a juristic version of the New South creed. Like his much-older colleagues on the three-judge circuit bench during the 1920s, Parker could not claim to be a representative luminary of the South. All were Republicans in a circuit including five states, three of which had become integral parts of the solidly Democratic South.[17] And all were in some qualified degree advocates of national economic policies promoted by the Republican party.

Senior Circuit Judge Edmund Waddill, Jr., presided over the court of appeals from 1925 until his death in 1931. Waddill had battled his way through tumultuous Virginia politics, first as a Readjuster and then as a supporter of Republican-sponsored national voting-protection laws, high-tariff policies, and state policies favorable to education and trade.[18] Parker's other colleague, John Carter Rose, died in 1927, to be succeeded by Elliott Northcott of West Virginia.[19] Marylander Rose had emerged from an urban-reform tradition in Baltimore, become a close personal and political ally of Theodore Roosevelt, and supported Bull Moose national social programs protective of labor.[20] Northcott, a self-taught lawyer, climbed the federal political patronage ladder from junior assistant U.S. attorney in the Southern District of West Virginia to the court of appeals.[21] Hailing from a state with pronounced Republican proclivities in presidential elections,[22] Northcott could at least claim a representativeness on his native heath, if not in the circuit as a whole.

255

Parker joined the court in 1925, at age forty,[23] succeeding a Wilson appointee from South Carolina who epitomized the Old South. Charles Albert Woods was eulogized on his death as one who had come to the bar in the midst of Reconstruction and argued "his first cases . . . before alien Judges and negro jurors."[24] Woods's career thereafter flowed in the Palmetto State's political mainstream,[25] a path that would bear precious little resemblance to the prejudicial career of Parker. The court's youngest and most recently appointed member had become a Republican in twentieth-century North Carolina and had run hopeless races as that party's youthful candidate for Congress in 1910, for state attorney general in 1916, and for governor in 1920.[26] By the time he reached the bench, his economic beliefs had been thoroughly formed and publicly articulated. They embraced bedrock tenets of national Republican beliefs prevailing during an era dominated by the fourth American party system.[27] Republicans in the age from McKinley to Hoover promoted individual achievement, the protection of property, and a national industrial policy favorable to business.[28]

Parker the politician echoed the party's themes, albeit with regionally biased qualifications. He lauded the GOP as the foremost political champion of the "right of private property."[29] Property was the key to economic progress. Populist antagonism to corporate organization, a foundation of that progress, threatened "to wreck the industrial prosperity of the State" and early received his condemnation.[30] The entrepreneur, standing poles apart from the populist, held the key to the long-awaited emergence of the New South.

The New South creed advanced at the time of Parker's birth in 1885 by Henry W. Grady emphasized economic conditions necessary for southern progress: industrialism, diversification, and regional development.[31] Parker enthusiastically embraced these Hamiltonian elements. Abundant natural resources and concomitant hydroelectric power potential would "make the state the greatest manufacturing section of the country."[32] Only human initiative was needed. Like President Coolidge, whom he paraphrased, the future jurist suggested "that a man who builds a factory confers a blessing upon the state. He furnishes investment for capital, employment for labor, and a home market for the farmer's product."[33] Establishment of a banking institution likewise served the same function; it thus became "the attendant of prosperity and the harbinger of progress."[34]

"Progress," in Parker's mind, encompassed more than material benefits, as did the word for Henry Horace Williams, Parker's undergraduate mentor at the University of North Carolina. The iconoclastic philosophy professor, who made a profound impression on Parker,[35] compared the commercial North with the agrarian South and noted the different degrees of individual freedom extant in the respective regions, concluding that "wherever there are business people there is a free people."[36] Herbert Hoover's 1928 presidential election landslide seemingly attested to the impending achievement of these linked goals and to the Republican party as the instrument of that result.[37] The GOP standard-bearer's victory seemingly promised enhanced party competition in the eleven states of the Old Confederacy, where Hoover had carried the electoral votes of five states.[38] Hoover's feat meant to Parker nothing less than "the dawning of a new day for the South, . . . the day in which the South will see a greater measure of progress and prosperity as well as a greater measure of liberty."[39]

Governmental nurture, not laissez-faire, would bring forth economic plenty and individual freedom. Public ownership of land or operation of a business was, Parker believed, generally "wrong in principle and mischievous in practice."[40] However, he welcomed state promotion of economic development. Parker, as the GOP's gubernatorial candidate in 1920, promised centralized state-sponsored cooperative marketing,[41] "a liberal system of rural credits,"[42] adequate state-financed public schools,[43] and a vast highway-construction program.[44] These economic infrastructure proposals fit comfortably with the New South creed.

The national government should also be harnessed to the cause of southern economic development. Parker never doubted that the region's sluggish economic performance sprang in part from stubborn resistance to the protective external tariff.[45] The Democratic-supported tariffs intended solely for revenue purposes brought "ruin and disaster to the business of the United States."[46] High tariffs, on the other hand, had once seemingly caused the New England cotton mills to prosper. As textile mills flourished across Dixie, it would be, he protested, nothing short of "colossal stupidity to destroy the protective tariff . . . when it is protecting us instead of New England."[47] Thus selected national economic policies could be fully compatible with southern regionalism.

Traditionalists might seek regional economic autonomy for the South as a means of protecting white supremacy from erosion by broad nationalistic tides responsive to national economic or political integration.[48] But neither as Tar Heel politician nor as judge did Parker ever

257

suggest that national regulation of economic life might serve as a precursor to centralized control of race relations in the South. For him, the economic and social issues remained separate, the former to be treated pragmatically with an eye to state-regional autonomy or national integration as determined by the perceived benefits likely to be derived from either course.

Affirming State Power

Business Regulations

The performance of Parker the jurist matched positions previously articulated by Parker the politician. Notwithstanding the prevailing Lochneristic jurisprudence of the Supreme Court,[49] the Fourth Circuit judge proved no "man against the State."[50] On the contrary, he regarded state and local business regulations as conducive to economic progress, not as threats to it. A directive from one North Carolina city ordering a railroad to replace wooden bridges with more fire-resistant concrete structures met with his approval notwithstanding the railroad's fusillade of constitutional objections. "Progress and development" had visited other municipalities since the turn of the century, he declared, and they had required "many things . . . for the public safety which were not necessary then."[51] Neither the commerce-clause arguments, which he dismissed as "so frivolous as not to merit discussion,"[52] nor substantive due-process attacks prevailed.[53] An obligation-of-contract argument received short shrift on grounds that the railroad enjoyed at most a municipally granted license, not a vested right in its property.[54] Surely, Lincolnton had never "intended to surrender for an indefinite future" its power to protect the public welfare. Had it so intended, "the contract would have been void, because contrary to public policy."[55]

Self-restraint similarly characterized Parker's treatment of other state regulatory efforts.[56] He deferred to Virginia's efforts to combat a deadly threat to a segment of its agricultural economy posed by cedar rust, a fungus disease that infects apple trees. To protect its valuable apple crop, Virginia enacted procedures for destruction of the less valuable cedar tree hosts. Against a Fourteenth Amendment substantive due-process attack[57] Parker refused to enjoin this exercise of the state's police powers because the regulation "does not authorize the taking of one man's property for another man's benefit, but is a reasonable regulation of the

258

use of property in furtherance of the public welfare."[58] Consequently, the due-process clause did not bar Virginia from saying "that in the enjoyment of property the owner shall not use it in such a way as to endanger the rights and property of others."[59]

Property rights of the Suncrest Lumber Company, likewise, were subordinated to state police powers. The Delaware corporation's vast stands of valuable virgin timber in western North Carolina fell within the boundaries of the projected Great Smoky Mountains National Park.[60] In pursuit of the park's several purposes, including recreation, tourism, forest preservation, and water conservation, the North Carolina Park Commission condemned privately owned lands and barred clear-cutting in order to prevent decimation of the projected parkland pending condemnation proceedings.[61] The company reacted to the commission's order by seeking an injunction against state interference with exploitation of its mountain holdings. Before a three-judge district court, the agency fought and won its first serious legal battle[62] when Parker asserted "that, if the State has a right to take property for a public use, it has the right while engaged in the act of taking to prevent it from being so mutilated as to destroy the use which it has for the public."[63]

Tax Power

Taxing powers provided an essential support for state financing of public services essential to economic progress. Real and personal property constituted traditional subjects of this power. But in the 1920s South Carolina faced a severe public finance crisis associated with relatively static real property values and declining personal property values.[64] As tax collections foundered,[65] the state sought to find alternative revenue sources in order to stabilize its per capita tax levy on real and personal property.[66]

Parker looked benignly on South Carolina's imaginative excise and income tax policies.[67] Unfavorably disposed toward use of federal equity courts as refuges for those injured by the exercises of state taxing power,[68] he approved some of the necessitous state's taxation strategies. It was true that "the power to tax is the power to destroy," Parker declared in Marshallian prose, but he added that "while the state legislature ought not exercise the taxing power unjustly, the federal courts have no power to enjoin the tax because they deem it unjust or unfair."[69] The South Carolina Chain Store Tax of 1930 was upheld against Fourteenth Amendment limitations.[70]

He similarly did not believe that the commerce clause prevented states from obtaining vital revenue by taxing goods that moved in interstate commerce. Charleston tobacco dealers thus failed in their attempt to enjoin collection by the South Carolina Tax Commission of an excise tax effected by means of stamps affixed to individual items shipped in inter-state commerce and awaiting further shipment either out of state or within state for local sale. Parker observed in *Doscher v. Query* that

> just as the commerce clause will not protect property from taxation after its interstate journey has ended and it has come to rest and become part of the general mass of property within the state, neither will that clause protect from taxation . . . goods [that] have been transported in interstate com-merce . . . and are intended for shipment to other states, if they have reached the destination of their first journey and are being held by their owner for disposition in the ordinary course of business, and the stoppage be not a mere temporary delay in transportation.[71]

Against commerce-clause–based arguments, Parker also upheld both South Carolina's nondiscriminatory gasoline tax on fuel purchased within the state by then-fledgling interstate air carriers[72] and the state's excise tax on electric power.[73] Even a tax on electric current generated within the state for sale in interstate commerce did not violate the com-merce clause because Taft Court decisions had made clear that local pro-duction was "not in itself such commerce."[74] Electric power generated outside South Carolina and wheeled into that state posed a more diffi-cult question. Again Parker deferred to state power. Invoking Chief Jus-tice Marshall's "original package" doctrine,[75] he held that when "the interstate journey of the current is ended and it becomes mingled with the current which the power company distributes and sells within the state, its sale unquestionably becomes subject to taxation by the state."[76]

Curbing State Power

Not every state economic regulation and revenue policy received Par-ker's approval. Those he invalidated typically reflected clear Supreme Court mandates to be followed by subordinate lower federal courts, or the salient policies pitted localistic interests against larger regional eco-nomic interests. Fourteenth Amendment due-process and equal-protec-tion restraints occasionally shielded private enterprises from state regulatory power,[77] as when the Carolina and Northwestern Railway Company defeated one town's attempt to collect a paving assessment on the line's right-of-way. In the then-prevailing substantive due-process tradition, Parker held that the assessment "was unquestionably unreasonable and confiscatory" because it "did not enhance in any substantial degree the utility or value of [the railroad's] property." Whether or not the $5,415 assessment also burdened interstate commerce remained unanswered.[78]

Restraint imposed by the existence of national commerce power figured importantly in other cases involving state pursuit of anticompetitive economic policies in hard times. An attempt by South Carolina to deny use of its roads to an interstate bus line raised a constitutional question "so repeatedly answered in the negative as not to justify further discussion of the principles involved."[79] Few appeals, however, involved such blatantly protective state regulations. Rather, they arose out of challenges to a state's neo-mercantilist tax policies, which served to transfer financial burdens to citizens of contiguous states within the South Atlantic region. Especially egregious was South Carolina's Radio Tax Act of 1930, which imposed a privilege tax prorated according to the value and thus presumably the capacity of the approximately fifty thousand radio sets then owned by South Carolinians for receiving distant signals.[80] When Station WBT of Charlotte sought to enjoin this burden on what the court termed "a necessary instrument of interstate commerce," Parker joined colleagues in holding the tax invalid.[81] Nor did he look kindly on that same state's corporate income tax, which levied a mileage tax on a railroad's income derived from traffic on its North Carolina as well as on its South Carolina tracks. Cited as authority was his own opinion in *Gramling v. Maxwell,* holding as "clearly and unmistakeably unconstitutional" a fifty-dollar North Carolina license tax discriminatorily imposed on a nonresident peach grower who peddled his South Carolina–grown crop in western North Carolina.[82] Quoting extensively from Associate Justice Stephen J. Field's landmark opinion in *Welton v. Missouri,* Parker asserted that the Tar Heel State had effectively enacted "a protective tariff against the products of other states."[83]

Parker's treatment of state regulatory and revenue powers reflected a sense of judicial modesty in pursuit of southern economic development. Conflicts between private property rights and exercises of state regulatory powers found Parker deferring to the state's interest in promoting the more inclusive economic interests of agriculture and natural resources conservation. In numerous tax cases, he repeatedly acted to mark the outer boundaries of state revenue-raising measures so vital to the development of public services that might undergird industrialism, diversification, and regional economic development. Yet he fully realized that the same taxes intended for beneficent ends could suppress critical economic enterprises and regional free trade and prosperity. Thus did he labor to unleash state power as a means of realizing the tenets of the New South creed while simultaneously restraining populist and neo-mercantilist exercises of that power which threatened to subvert those tenets.

Judicial Nationalism

If Parker generally sought to unleash state power as a means of ordering economic life, he proved no enemy of national power. Others, however, took a different stance. Southern politicians of his and of an earlier post–Civil War generation had railed against federal judges and federal courts as diabolical instruments of northern economic exploitation of the South. They had labored to curb the organization, jurisdiction, and equity powers of the U.S. courts.[84] Parker, however, stood apart from these sometimes deafening and demagogic critics of the national judiciary. He was an outspoken judicial nationalist—but always with a regional bias!

The power and status enjoyed by judges of the lower federal courts made him proud. Evisceration of either attribute elicited his condemnation. When a district court colleague allowed a bankrupt to seek state court appointment of receivers, Parker deplored the action as anomalous. U.S. judges, he stated, "should be slow to decide that a federal court of equity can relinquish its jurisdiction or admit its impotency."[85] Criticized, too, were various judge-weakening congressional measures inspired by Progressives anxious to curb the federal courts.[86] Attempts to deprive federal courts of their jurisdiction under the diversity-of-citizenship clause of the Constitution impressed Parker as especially serious threats to development of a harmonious national common law.[87] "This is the most dangerous attack made on the Judiciary in recent years," he warned Chief Justice Charles Evans Hughes and presiding federal appellate judges at the 1932 Conference of Senior Circuit Judges. The proposal constituted nothing less than an "attempt to destroy the

Judiciary" by removing a significant segment of what Parker considered part of the stately jurisdiction of the federal courts.[88] That jurisdiction had, since 1842, when Supreme Court Justice Joseph Story handed down his opinion in *Swift v. Tyson*,[89] brought monetarily important cases to U.S. courtrooms, clothed its judges with broad discretion in the absence of relevant state statutes, and enabled them to shape a distinct and nationally uniform general common law of contracts, agency, negotiable instruments, insurance, negligence, and torts.[90]

The much-criticized diversity jurisdiction received Parker's warm embrace in *Hewlett v. Schadel*. *Swift*, he decided, meant that state legislative silence unshackled federal judges "to follow their independent judgment in applying the rules of the common law."[91] Nowhere were the imperatives of Story's handiwork more germane than in Goldye Hewlett's suit against her speeding motorcyclist boyfriend for multiple injuries that she received in a collision. Parker the judge and Parker the father of a teenage daughter resisted applying Virginia's judicially created "guest" doctrine. Its application would have required affirmance of the trial court's directed verdict for the defendant, whose actions had fallen short of the doctrine's "gross negligence" liability standard. It perturbed Parker "that a young man who takes my daughter to a party in an automobile is bound to use only a slight degree of care . . . for her safety." Invoked in place of the guest doctrine, which he condemned as "pure nonsense and unjustifiable on any theory of law or public policy," was the "general" law.[92] One purpose of that national jurisprudence was to "unify so far as possible the rules under which the people of the various sections of the country may use the highways which are now so largely devoted to interstate travel and commerce."[93] Armed with Story's nationalistic judicial legacy, Parker expressed confidence that the federal courts would ever continue to weld "these United States into a single nation . . . to foster interstate commerce and communication and the uninterrupted flow of capital for investment into the various parts of the Union, [and to sustain] the public credit and sanctity of private contracts."[94]

The judge's nationalistic proclivities surfaced in deferential treatment of the federal government as an ordinary civil litigant as well as in public-law litigation.[95] When the navy stored high explosives distressingly close to aggrieved nearby property owners, Parker considered "it unthinkable that the courts should enjoin as a nuisance the use of property by a co-ordinate branch of the government, the executive, where such use is authorized by a valid act of the other co-ordinate branch, the legislature."[96] Nor in a case challenging the constitutionality of a federal estate tax did he believe that "the statute ought to be held unconstitutional unless it clearly violates the Constitution and then only by the Supreme Court."[97]

Conflicts between federal and state laws were resolved in favor of the former. Once Congress had invoked its enumerated and plenary power over commerce, regulatory legislation enacted in its pursuance swept aside clashing state laws. Preemptive federalism thus found favor with Parker in *United States v. Lindgren,* a case juxtaposing the Merchant Marine (Jones) Act of 1920 and Virginia's Wrongful Death Statute.[98] Citing *Cooley v. Board of Wardens of the Port of Philadelphia*[99] and the *Second Employer's Liability* case,[100] he held that congressional silence meant that "the states might occupy the field, but . . . as soon as Congress acted, the legislation of the states was superseded, and that of Congress became supreme and exclusive." A "dual federalism" position would squarely conflict with a legislative purpose of fostering national uniformity through preemption "of the death statutes of the several States."[101]

Parker's adherence to judicial nationalism was tightly bound up with enhancement of the power and status of the U.S. courts. Never did he move to join the camp of those ranged in opposition to the federal judiciary. Instead, he vigorously defended what he perceived as the jurisdictional cornerstone of that system's power, independence, and integrity. Neither did he regard private property claims as inherently superior to those of the government. On the contrary, he deferred to the latter in such litigation. And as with judicial policy making under the diversity jurisdiction, federal preemption of state laws impressed him as an often desirable means of achieving harmony in national law. But not every step away from juristic decentralization fostered and protected by federalism met with his approval.

Regionalism Ascendant

Appeals that pitted national interests against southern regional interests tested Parker's fidelity to judicial nationalism. Federal government activism could promote development of an economically viable New South. On the other hand, Hamiltonian initiatives from Washington could have exactly the opposite effect.[102] How to temper national policies injurious to regional growth perplexed Parker in cases involving national banking, conservation, and railroad freight-rate policies.

Federal Reserve Bank of Richmond

Parker as lawyer had represented southern country banks then warring against the Federal Reserve's "par clearance" system. In the U.S. Supreme Court he had defeated the central bank's attempt to establish a national clearinghouse system whereby onerous exchange charges were imposed on checks tendered at Reserve Bank counters by country banks.[103] Notwithstanding the proclaimed intentions and hopes of those who supported the Federal Reserve Act of 1913 that its enactment would dethrone Wall Street financial power and regionally diffuse it,[104] Parker as judge implicitly questioned the Reserve system's centralizing tendencies as a development antithetical to southern interests. Yet he proved unable to curb the Federal Reserve Bank of Richmond. "I have been sweating for a week over the opinion" in *Federal Reserve Bank v. Early,* he wrote. After reading "all of the cases cited and a great many others and . . . looking at the case from every angle . . . ," he found that the national clearinghouse's claim to the deposit balance of one of South Carolina's numerous insolvent banking institutions seemed unassailable.[105] "I started out to write an opinion on the other side of the proposition," he confessed, "but I found that it would not write that way."[106] A disappointed Parker held that "the deposit balance in favor of the insolvent bank should be applied to checks as the Federal Reserve Bank contends."[107] The decision effectively accorded a preferential claim on deposit reserves of failed banks to remote users of the Federal Reserve clearinghouse system over local depositors and other creditors of such insolvent financial institutions.

Southern Utilities

Parker had resoundingly affirmed the exercise of governmental power as against an asserted right of private property in the *Suncrest Lumber* case, wherein national and regional interests had been complementary.[108] Federal condemnation of the Duke-owned Southern Power Company's right-of-way across Nantahala National Forest, however, encouraged close scrutiny of this interference with a cornerstone of the region's economic infrastructure. As the utility's brief stressed, the electric power generated by the company went out "to cities and towns, cotton mills, and other industrial enterprises, and to the public generally," and the transmission lines in question also "constitute[d] the sole connecting link between the . . . system of the defendant and that of the Georgia Railway & Power Company and . . . the system of other power companies lying in the south of the defendant's system."[109]

To sever vital connections between power grids in the region would cause irreparable loss to the public, jeopardize national defense capabilities, and reduce "interchange of electric power between the great industrial centers of the Piedmont section of North and South Carolina."[110] Parker agreed. The land in question had been obtained for laudable conservation purposes that hardly suffered from rights-of-way enjoyed by public utilities. But interference with their lines would certainly "involve inconvenience with loss to the public and needless expense to the government."[111] Furthermore, Congress had never intended to endow the Department of Agriculture with power "to condemn the rights of way of railway and power companies for forestry purposes merely because they happen to be situated on forest lands acquired by the government.[112]

Intrastate Freight Rates

Freight rates established by the Interstate Commerce Commission had far-reaching implications for southern life. The ICC-fixed rates constituted a national internal tariff system perceived as responsible for perpetuating the South's colonial economy and subordinating it to the economic hegemony of the northern metropole.[113] The 1920 North Carolina Republican platform, on which Parker had run for the governorship, attacked the interregional rate differentials established by the national regulatory agency because they levied "upon our people an unjust and enormous burden of taxes in the form of excessive freight rates."[114] Criticism of the commission coincided with substantial augmentation of its powers under the Transportation Act of 1920 and with the agency's domination by the major interstate rail carriers.[115]

Parker affirmed exercises of Congress's power to regulate interstate commerce in order to protect that commerce from harmful consequences flowing from intrastate activities.[116] But like Chief Justice William Howard Taft, he perceived a clear distinction between freight shipped in intrastate commerce and that carried in interstate commerce.[117] The distinction became significant for local consumers, shippers, and producers because classification of commerce as intrastate

266

meant subjecting goods used within the several states to rates set by state agencies at levels often below those authorized by the ICC.[118]

In an opinion that Parker deemed among his "most important,"[119] he rejected a regional rail carrier's contention that petroleum shipped interstate by sea to a tank storage depot at the port of Wilmington and thereafter distributed in railway tank cars to some twenty thousand Tar Heel customers constituted continuous shipments in interstate commerce.[120] Instead, he held in *Atlantic Coast Line Railroad and Seaboard Air Line Railway Co. v. Standard Oil Company of New Jersey*[121] that at Wilmington the oil and gasoline "came to rest and lost their identity in complainant's storage tanks and were mingled with its general stock." Consequently, shipments from the North Carolina port constituted "independent movements" within the meaning of a Brandeis-coined test advanced in *Baltimore & Ohio Southwestern Railroad Co. v. Settle*, and the applicable rates became those approved by the North Carolina Corporation Commission for intrastate shipments, rather than the higher ICC-fixed interstate rates.[122]

ICC rates and orders encountered similar judicial hostility in another case,[123] but several that portended either lower costs or enhanced intraregional competition or both were approved.[124]

At the critical decisional points where federal judges enjoyed discretion, Parker's regional proclivities surfaced. They emerged in cases arraying national power against southern regional interests in economic development. Centralized versus decentralized banking system models, amorphous national conservation interests versus regionally vital electric power transmission, and locally beneficial low freight rates versus nationally desirable higher freight rates all constituted issues on which Parker aligned himself with local and regional as against national interests. His decision-making approach involved the parsing of often complex facts of the cases, reasoned exposition of statutes and constitutional doctrines, and a pragmatic, if usually implicit, policy determination compatible with the tenets of the New South creed. It was an approach that suffused judicial resolution of conflicts involving the southern bituminous coal industry.

Southern Coal Industry

On no other subject did the Fourth Circuit confront greater tension between national and regional economic interests than in cases involving the labor-intensive bituminous coal industry of the southern Appalachians. And in no other area did a policy-based pro-South jurisprudence so strikingly emerge during the decade before the New Deal as in defense of the threatened coal industry. At stake was (1) that industry's transportation costs regulated by the ICC, (2) its labor costs dependent on avoidance of high uniform and nationwide wage scales, and (3) its price-fixing powers. Favorable resolution of these three key issues meant apparent preservation of regionally important mining enterprises. The ultimate beneficiary, however, might well be manufacturers in the northern metropole blessed with a cheap and assured supply of coal.[125] These consumers did not appear before the circuit court. Instead, southern coal operators came before Parker and his colleagues and related doleful tales of their bare survival, tales that became the focus of the court's attention.[126]

The trial and appellate courts in the circuit heard about intersectional economic strife that reached new heights in the 1920s. Coal shortages and soaring prices during World War I had induced a boom in bituminous coal and related development of new mines in the southern Appalachians. With demobilization and enhanced competition from petroleum and natural gas, the coal industry confronted vast surplus capacity, an inelastic demand for its product, and slipping prices and profits.[127] Operator survival in this laissez-faire jungle meant cuts in either or both of the key factors that determined coal costs to the consumer: transportation and labor.

Lake Cargo Coal Case

Anchor Coal Co. v. United States called into question ICC-fixed coal freight rates and the consequences for the region's economy of such nationally established charges.[128] The suit by southern operators to enjoin rates on their coal shipped into the lucrative Great Lakes industrial market reflected acute intraindustry and intersectional rivalry for dominance in "Lake Cargo Coal." Northern operators in the Central Competitive Field stretching from western Pennsylvania into Illinois enjoyed a natural advantage in their geographical proximity to industrial markets, an advantage offset by prevailing union wage scales, which raised production costs to levels exceeding those of the southern operators.[129]

Inroads made by southern bituminous in Great Lakes markets evoked protests from northern operators and action by the ICC. At issue were the Lake Cargo Coal rates charged by railroads. Rates on a per-ton basis from nearby northern fields ranged below those charged to remote producers in southern West Virginia, Kentucky, and Tennessee.[130] Higher total transportation costs, even if much lower per mile, required that southern operators achieve the smallest possible per-ton rate differential from mine to market. From mid-1922 to mid-1927 the differential between the benchmark Pittsburgh and Kanawha rates stood at twenty-five cents.[131] But in August 1927 the northern carriers, with ICC permission, reduced their rates by twenty cents, thereby increasing the differential to forty-five cents. Southern roads retaliated. They lowered their rates by the same amount and restored the former twenty-five-cent differential. Appeals for protection by the northern carriers won an ICC order directing their sectional competitors to suspend the unauthorized twenty-cent rate reduction and to justify its reinstatement.[132]

When their justification failed to satisfy the commission, southern coalmen, led by Wall Street lawyer John W. Davis, went into the U.S. Court for the Southern District of West Virginia to enjoin enforcement of the agency's rate-suspension order and justification requirement.[133] Three days of what Parker termed a "strenuous hearing" were followed in March 1928 by his selection as author of the three-judge district court's opinion.[134] The *Lake Cargo Coal Rate* opinion reflected his conviction that the ICC's rate-suspension order presented "a question fraught . . . with the gravest consequences to the future of the country, if the power asserted . . . can be sustained." Answering this question required an activist approach. It would be necessary, he stated at the outset, "to look behind the ICC's conclusions on the reasonability of rates and ascertain exactly what it is that it has done, and upon what facts and upon the application of what principles it has arrived at its conclusion."[135] What the agency had done seemed self-evident to Parker's colleague on the three-judge panel, resident District Judge George W. McClintic. It had played sectional favorites, affording "a 'special providence' for the Ohio and Pittsburgh coal operators, rather than thinking of the consumers in the northwestern states or the southern carriers or coal operators."[136]

The immediate question before the court involved statutory construction. Had Congress empowered the agency to make national economic policies? Quoting voluminously from commission reports reciting the collapsed state of the beleaguered bituminous industry in the North, Parker indicated that he thought it

> perfectly evident . . . that, in reducing the rates from the northern field, and in directing the cancellation of the reduction from the southern field, the

Commission was primarily concerned, not in fixing rates, but in fixing the differential which was to prevail between the two fields and that the Commission based its action upon the shift of tonnage from the northern to the southern field and the industrial conditions resulting therefrom.

Wielding the rate-fixing power to correct displacement of northern coal in the Lake Cargo market was not, he declared in echoing McClintic, a "regulation of rates, but regulation of industrial conditions under the guise of regulating rates." The commission had taken account of transportation as well as production and employment in "an effort to equalize industrial conditions or offset economic advantages [of the South]."[137]

In reaching its rate decision, the ICC had relied on the 1925 Hoch-Smith Resolution, a farm-relief measure, which authorized the agency to adjust rates in order to correct those found "unjust, unreasonable, unjustly discriminatory, or unduly preferential, thereby imposing undue burdens, or giving undue advantage as between the various localities and parts of the country."[138] Parker held in the *Lake Cargo Coal Rate* case, the federal judiciary's first interpretation of the resolution, that the statutory language constituted "no more than a general declaration that freight rates shall be adjusted in such a way as to provide the country with an adequate system of transportation." Surely, Congress had never intended "by this language to create in the Commission an economic dictatorship over the various sections of the country, with power to kill or make alive." Today, the ICC took aim at southern coal. Tomorrow, he warned, its target could be "cotton manufacturing, . . . fruit growing, . . . furniture manufacturing, in short, . . . every branch of industry."[139]

If the ICC had exceeded its rate-fixing powers, could Congress remedy the deficiency by empowering the regulatory agency to weigh intersectional economic conditions in setting rail tariffs? Probably not. In an *obiter dictum*, Parker invoked the Supreme Court's sectionally beneficial decision in *Hammer v. Dagenhart*,[140] a case that had arisen out of the North Carolina textile industry. The decade-old precedent solidly supported his contention that Congress "could not give the Commission power to fix rates to equalize industrial conditions."[141] Regulation of production lay within the police powers of the states, powers reserved to them by the Tenth Amendment. Furthermore, Parker suggested but did not decide that such a rate-fixing basis likely violated the due-process clause of the Fifth Amendment in that the rates promulgated would necessarily be "unreasonable and constitute an unprecedented interference with the industrial conditions of the country."[142] Dixie's hard-pressed coal industries would probably be especially disadvantaged by the national regulatory agency's rate-making policies.

Red Jacket

New South industries seemingly needed protection not only from unfavorable freight rates set by the ICC but also from imposition of national labor standards. As an isolated and low-wage labor market, the South enjoyed a competitive edge in common markets against products from regions with higher labor costs and/or more capital-intensive industries.[143] Standardized national wages and working conditions threatened this regional advantage, thereby inflicting economic losses on both southern producers and their labor forces.[144] The United Mine Workers of America (UMWA), in its quest for monopoly control over the price of all coal mine labor, posed just such a threat to regional economic development. Without judicial intervention to foil unionization, an advocate for the southern operators predicted, "the Union will succeed in the end in forcing . . . non-union mined coal of West Virginia out of competition in the markets of the country with the coal produced by Union operators and miners under Union rules and regulations and sold at prices determined by the Union."[145]

The violent and emotion-laden labor conflict in the bituminous coalfields of southern West Virginia, dramatized for modern movie audiences by director John Sayles in his 1987 pro-union film *Matewan*,[146] reached the Fourth Circuit Court in *United Mine Workers of America v. Red Jacket Consolidated Coal and Coke Co.* This case would play a prominent role in later defeating Parker's confirmation as associate justice of the U.S. Supreme Court.[147] But in 1927, when it came before the Fourth Circuit bench, its primary importance involved application of the Sherman Anti-Trust Act to John L. Lewis's union, the union seeking to organize the West Virginia miners.[148] The act's application hinged, in turn, on discovery of a relationship between the UMWA's organizational strategies and interstate commerce.

Resolution of the jurisdictional question reflected Parker's fidelity to judicial nationalism. He followed Chief Justice Taft's holding in the *First Coronado* case.[149] In that 1922 labor decision Taft had declared, as Parker explained, "that coal mining is not commerce, and that ordinarily interference with coal mining could not be said to be interference with interstate commerce." But Parker entertained "no doubt that . . . interference with coal mining did interfere with interstate commerce in coal as a natural and logical consequence."[150] The Supreme Court had said as much in its *Second Coronado* decision.[151] The rule of that case, not that of *First Coronado*, applied in *Red Jacket*,[152] because the union, by calling a strike in order to organize the bituminous coalfields of West Virginia, surely "intended to interfere with the shipment of coal in interstate commerce," even in the absence of any evidence of interference with the actual transportation of coal.[153]

The facts spoke for themselves. The 316 coal companies joined as parties in the *Red Jacket* case produced forty million tons a year, over 90 percent of which went into interstate commerce. "Interference with the production of these mines," he reasoned, . . . "would necessarily interfere with interstate commerce in coal to a substantial degree." This result suggested a conspiratorial intent, within the scope of the act, to prevent interstate shipments of southern coal. "It was only as the coal entered into interstate commerce," Parker noted, "that it became a factor in the price and affected defendants in their wage negotiations with the union operators. And in time of strike, it was only as it moved in interstate commerce that it relieved the coal scarcity and interfered with the strike."[154]

Once Parker's broad conception of national commerce power had brought the UMWA's local organizing activities within the court's federal-question jurisdiction, he considered the scope of freedom to be accorded the union in its efforts to penetrate and organize the West Virginia coal miners employed under antiunion "yellow-dog" contracts.[155] Resolution of this issue depended on the nature of the union and on Supreme Court precedents. The UMWA, headquartered in Indianapolis in the midst of the Central Competitive Field,[156] clearly acted as a remote third-party interloper whenever its organizers appeared in West Virginia. Thus Parker correctly regarded the conflict not as one between that state's coal operators "and their [nonunion] employees over wages, hours of labor, or other cause, but [one] . . . between them as nonunion operators and the international union which is seeking to unionize their mines."[157]

Hitchman Coal and Coke Co. v. Mitchell,[158] a case originating in the Fourth Circuit and decided by the high Court in 1917, together with that circuit's 1926 decision in *Bittner v. West Virginia-Pittsburgh Coal Co.*,[159] controlled the extent of permissible strategies available to unions such as the UMWA. Both precedents advanced injunctions as remedies for protecting nonunion or yellow-dog contracts under the constitutionally based "liberty-of-contract" doctrine previously approved in *Adair v. United States*[160] and *Coppage v. Kansas*.[161] Language of the *Hitchman* decree had pervaded Waddill's *Bittner* opinion as well as the trial court's rendition of *Red Jacket*.[162]

Hitchman barred union organizers from peacefully persuading workers under yellow-dog contracts to break their contracts by joining the union while remaining in their employers' work force.[163] It also prevented union agents from merely persuading employees to join up and, honoring their contracts, leave their employment in order to strike. This anti-enticement provision was augmented by another preventing persuasion of "any of plaintiff's employees to refuse or fail to perform their duties as such."[164] *Hitchman* and its progeny, including *Bittner*, thus effectively walled off nonunion workers in the southern bituminous fields from the blandishments of national union organizers.

UMWA efforts to distinguish *Hitchman* by confining its prohibitions to union-organizing strategies involving violence, fraud, and/or deceit, factors present in *Hitchman* but not in *Red Jacket*, foundered on the sweeping language of the decree itself, which restrained even "peaceful persuasion."[165] Nor did section 20 of the 1914 Clayton Act apply.[166] That section prohibited issuance of injunctions against nonviolent persuasion tactics used by unions. *Duplex Printing Press Co. v. Deering* had made clear, however, that this statutory restraint on federal judicial power applied only to conflicts between an employer and his own employees or prospective employees.[167] It did not protect a remote third-party union's peaceful intervention on behalf of the employer's workers and all other similarly situated employees. Chief Justice Taft thereafter modified *Duplex* in *American Steel Foundries v. Tri-City Central Trades Council* to permit peaceful persuasion when the union involved was a geographically local one.[168]

The UMWA fit within neither the *Duplex* nor the *Tri-City* interpretation of the Clayton Act's protective shield. With a membership generously pegged by Parker at 475,000 and with local affiliates spanning the North American continent, the union bore precious little resemblance to the geographically confined Tri-City Central Trades Council, composed of thirty-seven craft unions clustered in three Illinois towns. And the UMWA's goals were different too. It sought not standardization of wages and working conditions in a confined locality but their standardization on a national industry-wide basis.[169]

Impelled by advice received from dying colleague John C. Rose[170] and by his own latent sympathy for working men and women, which had emerged in political appeals made in the 1920 gubernatorial campaign,[171] as well as in judicial opinions,[172] Parker limited the *Hitchman* doctrine. He held that union agents might peacefully persuade non-union employees (1) to leave their employment and join the union in order to go on strike and (2) to refrain from entering the employees' workplace during a strike against it. What the union could not do was "to approach a company's employees, working under a contract not to join the union while remaining in the company's service, and induce them, in violation of their contracts, to join the union and go on strike for the purpose of forcing the company to recognize the union or of impairing its power of production." *Hitchman,* Parker declared, "is conclusive of the point involved here."[173] But the sole "point involved" was actual or attempted contract breaking, an unlawful act that occurred only when an employee joined the union while remaining in the employer's workforce. *Red Jacket*'s decree, as he stated, was "certainly not so broad as that of the decree approved by the Supreme Court in *Hitchman Coal and Coke Co. v. Mitchell . . .* which also enjoined [any] interference with the contract by means of peaceful persuasion."[174]

Red Jacket reflected a cautious balancing of the competing interests of labor and management within the rigid confines of the labor law current at the time.[175] Parker weighed organized labor's interest in communicating its message to nonunion miners, recruiting them into union ranks, organizing the mines, and thereafter developing a collective-bargaining relationship conducive to improved standardized wages and working conditions for individual coal miners. At the same time, he took account of the interests of the southern bituminous operators. Their regionally important production and employment capabilities depended on an ability to offer their soft coal at marginally lower market prices, which, in turn, rested partially on wage scales remaining below uniform industry-wide scales prescribed by the UMWA and on the enforcement of yellow-dog contracts as a defense against injurious strikes intended to promote the union's goals.

Appalachian Coals, Inc.

Notwithstanding protection accorded the faltering soft coal industry by the *Lake Cargo* and *Red Jacket* decisions, conditions in the southern coalfields went from bad to worse as the Great Depression began.

Shrinking markets, sinking prices, and demoralization of an ever-smaller labor force caused desperate operators in Virginia, West Virginia, Kentucky, and Tennessee to establish a sales cartel early in 1932. Appalachian Coals, Inc., consisted of 137 producers who, in 1929, mined 54 percent of all bituminous extracted in the southern fields and 12 percent of total soft coal produced east of the Mississippi River. Their sales predominated in competitive markets from the Carolinas and Georgia westward to Indiana, southern Michigan, and the Great Lakes region. Once the cartel had been created, the Department of Justice acted to enjoin its operations under the Sherman Anti-Trust Act.[176]

Following hearings on *United States v. Appalachian Coals, Inc.,* before a three-judge district court wholly composed of the circuit judges, Parker expressed doubts about the erstwhile cartel's capacity for success in stabilizing coal prices.[177] Yet he "started into the case with the feeling that the combination ought to be upheld and that it could be upheld under the decisions in the *Steel* and *Harvester* cases."[178] The association had "been acting fairly and openly, in an attempt to organize the coal industry and to relieve the deplorable conditions resulting from over-expansion, destructive competition, wasteful trade practices, and the inroads of competing industries."[179]

However justifiable the combination, hopes for eluding the Anti-Trust Act were soon dashed by close examination of Supreme Court precedents and the late Judge Rose's decision in *United States v. American Can Co.*[180] The then district judge used the Supreme Court's "rule-of-reason" standard to distinguish monopolies arising out of natural and legitimate business expansion from those caused by unnatural and illegitimate acquisitions intended to restrain interstate trade or to create monopolies.[181] Appalachian Coals, Inc., clearly fell into the latter category. Agency members, independent coal operators who together controlled "a substantial part of the trade," had agreed to fix uniform selling prices in order to eliminate competition among themselves. Such an agreement suggested a plan to fix monopoly prices in consuming markets "forbidden by the Sherman Act."[182]

Parker regretted the conclusion. "We sympathize with the plight of those engaged in the coal industry, whether as operators or as miners," he wrote, "but we have no option but to declare the law as we find it. We cannot repeal acts of Congress nor can we overrule decisions of the Supreme Court interpreting them." Quite possibly a cooperative coal-marketing agency offered the sole hope for relieving the industry's economic distress. That remedy, however, was one "which addresses itself to the lawmaking branch of the government.[183]

The Supreme Court, not Congress, soon acted to protect a major regional industry. A week prior to Franklin Roosevelt's first inauguration, Chief Justice Hughes held that an unreasonable restraint of trade did not arise from mere establishment of a cooperative enterprise that affected market conditions, especially when that combination had a laudable purpose and, as Parker had shown, no capacity for becoming a monopolistic menace.[184] The Court took cognizance of the reality that "when industry is grievously hurt, when producing concerns fail, when unemployment mounts and communities dependent upon profitable production are prostrated, the wells of commerce go dry."[185] The Sherman Act did not mandate that outcome.

Reversal by the high Court both bemused and pleased Parker. The Court had reached its conclusion, he noted, by overruling "some of its former decisions, which, of course, that Court has a right to do." That its policy-actuated holding overturned his own opinion did not make him "feel at all bad for I think that I would have decided the case exactly as the Supreme Court did if I had not felt bound by its former decisions."[186]

Conclusion

John J. Parker and his colleagues produced on the Fourth Circuit from 1925 to 1933 a constitutional jurisprudence that was at once nationalistic and regionalistic. New South ideological impulses permeated the judicial treatment of economic issues. Although constrained by the abilities of aggrieved parties to litigate and appeal, by the reach of federal jurisdiction, by existing judicial precedents, and by the circumscribed position of a judge who sat on an intermediate appellate court, Parker adjudicated appeals that enabled him to help shape economic relationships from Maryland to South Carolina and from the Appalachians to the Atlantic.

His opinions manifested previously articulated support for the empowerment of state governments. Economic development required affirmative exercises of constitutionally reserved state police powers sufficient to provide necessary public services against private property rights then enjoying broad Supreme Court protection. As a judicial nationalist, he vigorously wielded federal common-law jurisprudence and acted with self-restraint toward exercises of constitutionally enumerated national powers. Conflicts between state and national powers or between regional entrepreneurs and national regulations detrimental to southern economic interests challenged Parker. Aware that the South stood outside the nation's economic mainstream, he labored to clothe such regional interests with judicial protection. Ulterior motives associated with preservation of the racial status quo did not figure in his assessments. In fact, his lone judicial opinion handed down from 1925 into 1930 that spoke directly to the race question actually threatened the racial status quo at its most sensitive points, intermarriage and residential living patterns.[187]

The financially pressed southern bituminous coal industry received his special solicitude. Elements of dual federalism and Marshallian nationalism combined in adjudication of these coal cases to produce a peculiar pragmatic, policy-oriented and regionally biased constitutional jurisprudence, as proffered in the *Lake Cargo* case and as realized in the controversial *Red Jacket* decision. The latter invoked a nationalistic conception of the commerce power combined with a balanced consideration of union-operator relationships then controlled by Supreme Court decisions based on the liberty-of-contract doctrine. Although favorable to the operators, Parker's *Red Jacket* necessarily protected the jobs of southern miners while at the same time according some union access to employees working under yellow-dog contracts.

Harsh economic realities that characterized the South during the late 1920s and that spurred creation of Appalachian Coals, Inc., became a national phenomenon when the Great Depression tightened its grip on the country. As Parker had generally viewed with equanimity state and federal activism in economic matters, so he looked benignly on regionally beneficial economic policies implemented by the early New Deal. In March 1934 he assured the Florida State Bar Association that if Congress, under its commerce powers, "may legislate for the purpose of preserving free competition, it may, when this free competition is on the verge of destroying industry itself, legislate to eliminate its destructive features and in the interest of controlled cooperation." Nor did he see any reason why, under the general-welfare clause, the "national government should not foster the healthy growth and development of [the] nation by encouragement to agriculture, industry, education, road building and other activities essential to the national welfare."[188] His constitutional jurisprudence followed suit.[189]

Themes of judicial nationalism struck by Parker in his 1934 address and in decisions handed down during the New Deal attest to the instrumental nature of his earlier constitutional jurisprudence. It was a defensive jurisprudence endowed with a high, if rarely articulated, policy content. Once national economic programs benefited rather than threatened southern economic interests, distinctively regional interpretations of federal laws and the Constitution became unnecessary. But in the transition era before the New Deal, such judicial strategies seemed of critical importance to the promotion, even the survival, of southern economic interests. Thus in the realm of law and economics there developed and flourished, during the twilight of an expiring economic order, a judge-made southern constitutional tradition. It was marked by a combination of realism and optimism, by a sober reflection on the painful economic plight of the region, and by an eternal optimism about the future of its human and natural resources. That this New South jurisprudence, largely separated from the region's then-peculiar race issue, emerged from the efforts of a single U.S. judge suggests a behavior possibly replicated by other federal judges in other circuits geographically remote from America's industrial heartland.

Notes

I am grateful for financial support provided by grants from the Duke University Research Council and "Project '87," sponsored by the American Political Science and American Historical associations. I am indebted to Duke law students Mario A. Ponce and David Leff for copyediting assistance and to Sandra L. Perkins for manuscript preparation.

1. George B. Tindall, *The Emergence of the New South, 1913–1945*, vol. 10 of *A History of the South*, ed. Wendell Holmes Stephenson and E. Merton Coulter (Baton Rouge, 1967), 223–33.

2. Alpheus Thomas Mason, *The Supreme Court from Taft to Warren* (Baton Rouge, 1968), chap. 2.

3. Tindall, *Emergence of the New South*, 69.

4. Harry N. Scheiber, "Federalism, the Southern Regional Economy, and Public Policy since 1865," in *Ambivalent Legacy: A Legal History of the South*, ed. David J. Bodenhamer and James W. Ely, Jr. (Jackson, Miss., 1984), 86–93. See also Harry N. Scheiber, "State Law and 'Industrial Policy' in American Development, 1790–1987," *California Law Review* 75 (1987): 425–26.

5. Scheiber, "Federalism, the Southern Regional Economy, and Public Policy," 80–86; Scheiber, "State Law and 'Industrial Policy,'" 426–27.

6. See Wallace Mendelson, *Capitalism, Democracy and the Supreme Court* (New York, 1960); James Willard Hurst, *Law and the Conditions of Freedom in the Nineteenth-Century United States* (Madison, Wis., 1956); Bruce A. Ackerman,

Private Property and the Constitution (New Haven, Conn., 1977); and Tony Allan Freyer, *Forums of Order: The Federal Courts and Business in American History, Industrial Development and the Social Fabric*, vol. 1 (Greenwich, Conn., 1979).

7. See Carter Goodrich, ed., *The Government and the Economy: 1783–1861* (Indianapolis, 1967); Stephen Skowronek, *Building a New American State: The Expansion of National Administrative Capacities, 1877–1920* (Cambridge, 1982), chaps. 1, 2, 5, 8; and Dewey W. Grantham, *Southern Progressivism: The Reconciliation of Progress and Tradition* (Knoxville, Tenn., 1983), 4–9, 301–18.

8. See act of July 2, 1890, chap. 647, 26 Stat. 209 (see William Letwin, *Law and Economic Policy in America: The Evolution of the Sherman Antitrust Act* [New York, 1965]); and act of February 4, 1887, chap. 104, 24 Stat. 379 (*see* Avi Hoogenboom and Olive Hoogenboom, *A History of the ICC: From Panacea to Palliative* [New York, 1976]).

9. See Jack Bass, *Unlikely Heroes: The Dramatic Story of the Southern Judges of the Fifth Circuit Who Translated the Supreme Court's Brown Decision into a Revolution for Equality* (New York, 1981); Charles S. Bullock III and Charles M. Lamb, eds., *Implementation of Civil Rights Policy* (Monterey, Calif., 1984); Charles V. Hamilton, *The Bench and the Ballot: Southern Federal Judges and Black Voters* (New York, 1973); Jack W. Peltason, *Fifty-Eight Lonely Men: Southern Federal Judges and School Desegregation* (New York, 1961).

10. Scheiber, "Federalism, the Southern Regional Economy, and Public Policy," 77–79.

11. Each of the judges of the Court of Appeals for the Fourth Circuit who sat during 1925–33 resided in the state of his birth at the time of his appointment (Woods: South Carolina; Waddill: Virginia; Rose: Maryland; Parker: North Carolina; Soper: Maryland). Senate Committee on the Judiciary, *Legislative History of the United States Court of Appeals and the Judges Who Served during the Period 1801 through March 1958*, 85th Cong., 2d sess., 1958, Committee Print, facing 78. Of the fifteen district judges who sat during the period 1925–33, only three (20 percent) were born outside the states in which they resided at the time of their appointments: William C. Coleman (D.Md.), born in Kentucky; Henry Clay McDowell (W.D.Va.), born in Kentucky; and Luther B. Way (E.D.Va.), born in North Carolina. *Judges of the United States*, 2d ed. (Washington, D.C., 1983). See J. Woodford Howard, *Courts of Appeals in the Federal Judicial System: A Study of the Second, Fifth, and District of Columbia Circuits* (Princeton, N.J., 1981), chap. 1.

12. Howard, *Courts of Appeals*, chap. 1.

13. From and after the act of July 23, 1866, chap. 10, sec. 2, 14 Stat. 209 (codified in the act of March 3, 1911, chap. 231, sec. 116, 36 Stat. 1131), the states within the Fourth Circuit were Maryland, West Virginia, Virginia, North and South Carolina; the states within the Fifth Circuit were Georgia, Florida, Alabama, Mississippi, Louisiana, and Texas. The same act also included Kentucky and Tennessee within the Sixth Circuit.

279

14. *Rank Order of Mean Case Filings in U.S. Courts of Appeals: Fiscal Year (July 1–June 30) 1926–1933*

Circuit	Mean Filings	Circuit	Mean Filings
2	517.6	3	240.7
8	339.6	10	185.8 (FY 1929–33)*
9	323.6	7	184.8
5	316.8	4	144.9
6	267.0	1	118.0

Source: Department of Justice, *Annual Report of the Attorney General of the United States* (Washington, D.C., 1926–33).
*Created by act of February 28, 1929, chap. 363, 45 Stat. 1346.

The circuit boundaries extant in 1925–33 were established by the act of July 23, 1866, chap. 10, sec. 2, 14 Stat. 209 (codified in the act of March 3, 1911, chap. 231, sec. 116, 36 Stat. 1131); see 28 U.S.C. sec. 41 (1982). The sources of the Fourth Circuit appellate caseload from 1925–1930 were:

Rank	Source	No. Appeals (N = 543)	% Caseload
1.	Dist. of E.Va.	112	20.6
2.	Md.	111	20.4
3.	S.W.Va.	85	15.7
4.	E.S.C.	58	10.7
5.	E.N.C.	58	10.7
6.	W.N.C.	48	8.8
7.	N.W.Va.	45	8.3
8.	W.Va.	28	5.2
9.	W.S.C.	24	4.4
10.	M.N.C.	10	1.9 (1927–30)*

Source: F.2d.
*Established by act of March 2, 1927, chap. 276, 44 Stat. 1339.

15. From 1925 to 1930 the Supreme Court granted 15 writs of certiorari while the Fourth Circuit Court of Appeals terminated 608 cases.

16. The Expediting Act of February 11, 1903, chap. 544, 32 Stat. 823, required three-judge district courts in any case brought by the United States under the Anti-Trust or Interstate Commerce acts. The act of June 20, 1906, chap. 3591, 34 Stat. 584, 592, required the same procedure in cases seeking to restrain, set aside, or annul an order of the Interstate Commerce Commission.

The act of June 18, 1910, 36 Stat. 557, enacted in the wake of Ex Parte Young, 209 U.S. 123 (1908), required three-judge trial courts in cases to enjoin state offices from enforcing allegedly unconstitutional state statutes; the act of March 4, 1913, 37 Stat. 1013, extended the same provision to suits seeking to restrain enforcement of orders of state administrative boards and commissions. The act of August 12, 1976, chap. 160, 90 Stat. 1119, substantially reduced the three-judge district court requirement. See Charles Alan Wright, *The Law of Federal Courts,* 4th ed. (St. Paul, Minn., 1983), 295–99.

17. See V. O. Key, Jr., *Southern Politics in State and Nation* (New York, 1949), 10 (noting that Maryland and West Virginia were not among the eleven states composing the "Solid South").

18. Peter G. Fish, "From Virginia Readjuster to United States Senior Circuit Judge: The Ascent of Edmund Waddill, Jr. (1855–1931)," *American Journal of Legal History* 30 (1986): 200–213, 231–33.

19. Rose, J., died on March 26, 1927, as reported in 18 F.2d iv (1927). Northcott was nominated on April 6, 1927 (recess) (*Register of the Department of Justice and the Judicial Offices of the United States* [Washington, D.C., 1928], 18); he was renominated on December 9, 1927 (*Congressional Record,* 70th Cong., 1st sess., 1927, 69, pt.1:359), and confirmed on December 15, 1927 (ibid., 692).

20. For Rose as an urban reformer, see James B. Crooks, *Politics and Progress: The Rise of Urban Progressivism in Baltimore, 1895–1911* (Baton Rouge, 1968), 211 n. 26; Jack Temple Kirby, *Darkness at the Dawning: Race and Reform in the Progressive South* (Philadelphia, 1972), 46ff.; and John C. Rose, "Politics and the Race Question in Alabama," *Nation,* September 20, 1894, 211. For his friendship with Theodore Roosevelt, see Edmund Morris, *The Rise of Theodore Roosevelt* (New York, 1979), 433–37; and Rose to Roosevelt, December 14, 1908, Theodore Roosevelt Papers, microfilm roll 86, Manuscripts Division, Library of Congress, Washington, D.C. For his support of national social welfare reforms of the Progressive party, see Rose to Roosevelt, October 19, 1906, ibid., microfilm roll 69 (federal employers' liability legislation and child labor legislation).

21. On Northcott's legal education, see "Elliott Northcott of the Cabell County Bar," *Annual Report of West Virginia Bar Association* 62 (1946): 114. On Northcott as assistant U.S. attorney (S.D.W.Va. 1898–1905), see *Register of the Department of Justice* (1898), 108; ibid. (1902), 165; and ibid. (1904), 155. As U.S. attorney (S.D.W.Va. 1905–9, 1922–27), Northcott was nominated on December 6, 1905 (*Congressional Record,* 59th Cong., 1st sess., 1905, 40, pt.1:157); confirmed on December 12, 1905 (ibid., 328); nominated on January 20, 1922 (ibid., 67th Cong., 2d sess., 1922, 62, pt.2:1456); confirmed on January 24, 1922 (ibid., 1643); renominated on February 6, 1926 (ibid., 69th Cong., 1st sess., 1926, 67, pt.3:3448); and confirmed on February 15, 1926 (ibid., pt. 4:4002). As West Virginia public service commissioner (1915–17), he was appointed on March 26, 1915, reappointed June 1, 1915, and appointed chairman June 1, 1915; he resigned March 1, 1917 (West Virginia,

Public Service Commission: Opinions of the Commission, 1913–1921 [Charleston, W.Va., 1921], 1:5). As envoy extraordinary and minister plenipotentiary to Colombia, he was nominated on April 20, 1909 (*Congressional Record*, 61st Cong., 1st sess., 1909, 44, pt.2:1417); and confirmed on April 23, 1909 (ibid., 1522). For appointment to a position in Nicaragua, he was nominated on January 9, 1911 (ibid., 3d sess., 1911, 46, pt.1:675); and confirmed on the same day (ibid., 679). For the same position in Venezuela, he was nominated on December 21, 1911 (ibid., 62nd Cong., 2d sess., 1911, 48, pt.1:597); and confirmed on the same day (ibid., 598). See *Register of the Department of State: 1913* (Washington, D.C., 1913), 125.

22. Svend Peterson, *A Statistical History of the American Presidential Elections* (New York, 1963), 162 (reporting that the Republican presidential candidate carried West Virginia in 1896, 1900, 1904, 1908, 1920, 1924, and 1928).

23. Nominated on October 3, 1925 (recess) (*Register of the Department of Justice* [1927], 18); renominated on December 8, 1925 (*Congressional Record*, 69th Cong., 1st sess., 1925, 61, pt.1:499); confirmed on December 14, 1925 (ibid., 769).

24. *Memorial Proceedings, Charles Albert Woods, Died June 21, 1925* (Richmond, Va., 1925), 73 (eulogy by Tazewell Taylor), 25 (eulogy by Douglas McKay).

25. U. R. Brooks, *South Carolina Bench and Bar* (Columbia, S.C., 1908), 1:84–86 (reporting that Woods served as trustee of Winthrop and Wofford colleges and declined the presidency of the University of South Carolina); 43 S.E. iii, n. 12 (1903) (reporting Woods's election as associate justice of the South Carolina Supreme Court on January 28, 1903); 79 S.E. v, n. 4 (1913) (reporting his resignation on June 7, 1913).

26. *A Pocket Manual of North Carolina for the Use of Members of the General Assembly, Session, 1911* (Raleigh, N.C., 1911), 178 (1910 election data); *North Carolina Manual for the Use of the Members of the General Assembly, Session, 1917* (Raleigh, N.C., 1917), 274–93 (1916 election data); *North Carolina Manual, 1921* (Raleigh, N.C., 1921), 315–16 (1920 election data).

27. Paul Kleppner, "Critical Realignments and Electoral Systems," in *The Evolution of American Electoral Systems*, ed. Paul Kleppner et al., Contributions in American History, no. 95 (Westport, Conn., 1981), 3–32; Walter Dean Burnham, "The System of 1896: An Analysis," in ibid., 147–202.

28. See William H. Harbaugh, "The Republican Party, 1893–1932," in *History of U.S. Political Parties, 1910–1945: From Square Deal to New Deal*, ed. Arthur M. Schlesinger, Jr. (New York, 1973) 3:2069–125; and "Herbert Hoover, Rugged Individualism Speech, New York, October 11, 1928," reprinted in ibid., 2229–39.

29. *Durham* (N.C.) *Morning Herald*, October 2, 1924, 2.

30. *University of North Carolina Record: The One Hundred and Twelfth Annual Commencement* 54 (1907): 5.

31. Grantham, *Southern Progressivism*, xvi.

32. Address by John J. Parker (fragment in Parker's longhand, n.d.), William S. Ward Files, re *United States v. J. L. Philips et al.*, vol. 3, box 34, Records of the Claims Division, Department of Justice Records, Record Group 60, National Archives, Washington, D.C.

33. *Greensboro* (N.C.) *Daily News*, June 27, 1920, 2. See Arthur M. Schlesinger, Jr., *The Crisis of the Old Order, 1919–1933* (Boston, 1957), 57 (quoting Coolidge as saying that "the man who builds a factory builds a temple").

34. John J. Parker, "North Carolina Banking" unpublished manuscript, ca. 1910), 69, Banks in North Carolina Papers, box 550, Southern Historical Collection, University of North Carolina, Chapel Hill.

35. Robert Watson Winston, *Horace Williams: Gadfly of Chapel Hill* (Chapel Hill, N.C., 1942), 113.

36. *Logic for Living: Lectures of 1921–1922 by Henry Horace Williams*, ed. Jane Ross Hammer (New York, 1951), 255–56.

37. Hoover won 58.22 percent of the popular vote and 444 electoral votes to Alfred E. Smith's 87 votes. Peterson, *Statistical History*, 89–90.

38. Hoover won Florida (58.83 percent), North Carolina (54.87 percent), Tennessee (53.76 percent), Texas (51.77 percent), and Virginia (53.91 percent). Ibid., 90.

39. Parker to George Edward Flow, November 20, 1928, John J. Parker Papers, box 18, Southern Historical Collection.

40. *Greensboro Daily News*, March 4, 1920, 10.

41. *Winston-Salem* (N.C.) *Union Republican*, July 8, 1920, 1. See also ibid., September 30, 1920, 6.

42. Ibid., September 30, 1920, 6.

43. *Greensboro Daily News*, July 21, 1920, 10.

44. *Winston-Salem Union Republican*, March 11, 1920, 5; *Charlotte* (N.C.) *Observer*, April 18, 1920, 8.

45. *Charlotte Observer*, October 30, 1920, 2.

46. *Greensboro Daily News*, November 2, 1924, 4. See also Parker's attacks on the tariff-for-revenue Underwood Act (act of October 3, 1913, 38 Stat. 114), in *Greensboro Daily News*, November 2, 1916, 1.

47. *Greensboro Daily News*, November 2, 1924, 4.

48. Scheiber, "Federalism, the Southern Regional Economy, and Public Policy," 91–93.

49. Lochner v. New York, 198 U.S. 45 (1905). See Charles W. McCurdy, "The Roots of 'Liberty of Contract' Reconsidered: Major Premises in the Law of Employment, 1867–1937," *Yearbook 1984: Supreme Court Historical Society*, 20–33.

50. See J. Francis Paschal, *Mr. Justice Sutherland: A Man against the State* (Princeton, N.J., 1951).

51. Carolina & Northwestern Railway Co. v. Town of Lincolnton, 33 F.2d 719, 721 (4th Cir. 1929). See also memorandum on case no. 2844, ibid.,

Parker Papers, box 48; and U.S. Constitution, art. I, sec. 10, cl. 1; art. I, sec. 8, cl. 3; amendment 16, sec. 1.

52. Memorandum on case no. 2844.

53. See Carolina & Northwestern Railway Co., 33 F.2d at 721.

54. Memorandum on case no. 2844.

55. Carolina & Northwestern Railway Co., 33 F.2d at 721. See also Lynchburg Traction and Light Co. v. City of Lynchburg, 16 F.2d 763 (4th Cir. 1927) (upholding city-ordered trolley fare reduction on service in annexed areas as against obligation of contract claim based on higher-fare franchise for service in formerly unincorporated areas).

56. See Gloucester Seafood Workers' Association v. Houston, 35 F.2d 193 (4th Cir. 1929) (upholding state's power to exclude oyster harvesters from navigable waters).

57. Kelleher v. Schoene, 14 F.2d 341 (W.D.Va. 1926) (denying interlocutory injunction); Kelleher v. French, 22 F.2d 341 (W.D.Va. 1927) (denying permanent injunction).

58. Schoene, 14 F.2d at 343.

59. Ibid., *affirmed per curiam*, 278 U.S. 563 (1928) (citing "the authority of Miller v. Schoene," 276 U.S. 272 [1928] [per Stone, J.], wherein the Supreme Court, in a companion case appealed from the Supreme Court of Appeals of Virginia, had used reasoning similar to Parker's).

60. Suncrest Lumber Co. v. North Carolina Parks Commission, 30 F.2d 121, 123 (W.D.N.C. 1929).

61. The state acted pursuant to the act of May 22, 1926, chap. 363, 44 Stat. 616. See Willard B. Gatewood, Jr., "North Carolina's Role in the Establishment of the Great Smoky Mountains National Park," *North Carolina Historical Review* 37 (1960): 167, 171–72.

62. Gatewood, "North Carolina's Role," 177.

63. Suncrest Lumber Co., 30 F.2d at 127.

64. *Assessed Value of Property in South Carolina (in millions of dollars at 25 percent rate)*

	1921	1922	1923	1924	1925	1926	1927	1928	1929	1930
Real	212.5	218.0	218.9	219.9	221.1	223.4	223.1	221.6	225.7	213.4
Personal	189.5	218.0	205.1	208.7	209.0	201.5	199.1	203.9	200.7	202.0
Other	91.8	—	—	—	—	—	—	—	—	—
Total Taxable	493.8	436.0	424.0	428.6	430.1	424.9	422.2	425.5	426.4	415.4
Per Capita (in hundreds of dollars)	291.8	252.5	243.1	243.3	243.3	232.7	228.8	246.0	245.8	238.7

Source: Department of Commerce, Bureau of the Census, *Financial Statistics of States, 1921–1930* (Washington, D.C., 1922–32)

65. *Seventeenth Annual Report of the South Carolina Tax Commission* (1932), 5–6.

66. *Eighteenth Annual Report of the South Carolina Tax Commission* (1933), 7 (reporting that "South Carolina has, since 1922, by the enactment of special tax statutes, done more than any other state in relieving general property of the cost of state and school government").

67. Parker to Henry H. Watkins, June 24, 1927, re Southern Railway Co. v. Query, 21 F.2d 333 (E.D.S.C. 1927), 5, Parker Papers, box 17.

68. See Henrietta Mills Co. v. Rutherford County, 26 F.2d 799 (W.D.N.C. 1928).

69. Memorandum on South Carolina Power Co. v. South Carolina Tax Commission, 52 F.2d 515 (E.D.S.C. 1931), 2, Parker Papers, box 56 (paraphrasing Marshall, C. J., in McCulloch v. Maryland, 4 Wheat. 316, 431 [1819], "that the power to tax involves the power to destroy; that the power to destroy may defeat and render useless the power to create"); South Carolina Power Co., 52 F.2d at 519 (stating that the power tax was fair because it fell on electric current generated by "hydroelectric companies which utilize the water power in the rivers of South Carolina, one of the great natural resources of that state").

70. Southern Grocery Stores v. South Carolina Tax Commission, 55 F.2d 931 (E.D.S.C. 1932). See ibid., 933 (citing State Board of Tax Commissioners of Indiana v. Jackson, 283 U.S. 527 [1931]; Great Atlantic and Pacific Tea Co. v. Maxwell, 284 U.S. 575 [1931]; and Great Atlantic and Pacific Tea Co. v. Morrissett, 48 F.2d 911 [E.D.Va. 1931] [upholding state license tax on distributing houses], *affirmed,* 284 U.S. 584 [1931]).

71. 21 F.2d 521, 526 (E.D.S.C. 1927) (citing as authority Texas Co. v. Brown, 258 U.S. 466 [1922]; and Sonnenborn Brothers v. Cureton, 262 U.S. 506 [1923]).

72. Eastern Air Transport Inc. v. South Carolina Tax Commission, 52 F.2d 456 (E.D.S.C. 1931).

73. South Carolina Power Co., 52 F.2d 515; ibid., 60 F.2d 528 (E.D.S.C. 1932).

74. South Carolina Power Co., 52 F.2d at 524 (citing United Leather Workers International Union v. Herkert and Meisel Trunk Co., 265 U.S. 457 [1924]; and United Mine Workers of America v. Coronado Coal Co. [First Coronado Case], 259 U.S. 344 [1922]).

75. Brown v. Maryland, 12 Wheat. 419, 441–42 (1827) (holding that "when the importer has so acted upon the thing imported that it has become incorporated and mixed up with the mass of property in the country, it has, perhaps, lost its distinctive character as an import, and has become subject to the taxing power of the state; but while remaining the property of the importer, in his warehouse, in the original form or package in which it was imported, a tax upon it is too plainly a duty on imports to escape the prohibition in the Constitution").

285

76. South Carolina Power Co., 60 F.2d 528, *affirmed sub nom.* Broad River Power Co. v. Query, 288 U.S. 178 (1933) (per Hughes, C. J., rejecting asserted equal-protection and federal preemption grounds and not mentioning the unasserted commerce-clause ground).

77. See Bluefield Water Works and Improvement Co. v. Public Service Commission of West Virginia (S.D.W.Va. May 2, 1927) (stenographic transcript), U.S. Supreme Court nomination file of John J. Parker, SEN 71B–A3, tray 15, Committee on the Judiciary, Records of the U.S. Senate, Record Group 46 National Archives; *Fourteenth Annual Report of the Public Service Commission of W.Va., 1926–1927* (Charleston, W.Va., 1927), 157–58; and *Fifteenth Annual Report of the Public Service Commission of W.Va. 1927–1928* (Charleston, W.Va., 1928), 225–26 (setting utility's electric power rates in conformity with Bluefield Water Works and Improvement Co. v. Public Service Comm'n of W. Va., 256 U.S. 679 [1923] [per Butler, J.]). See also Southern Ry. Co. v. Shealy, 18 F.2d 784 (E.D.S.C. 1927) (disapproving a state regulatory commission's order requiring a regional rail carrier to grant a tiny competitor access to its interstate track network); and Standard Oil Co. of New Jersey v. City of Charlottesville, Va., 42 F.2d 88 (4th Cir. 1930) (overruling a local government's refusal to permit the oil company's erection of a filling station in a residential neighborhood).

78. Carolina & Northwestern Railway Co. v. Clover, S.C., 46 F.2d 395, 399, 397 (4th Cir. 1931).

79. Blease v. Safety Transit Co., 50 F.2d 852, 855 (4th Cir. 1931).

80. Act of March 31, 1930, no. 768, *S.C. Acts and Joint Resolutions of the General Assembly* (Columbia, S.C., 1930), 1292 ("to provide for the levy and collection of a tax upon all radio sets in the state of South Carolina and to provide for penalty for the failure to pay said tax," the act established in section 1 a graduated tax of $0.50 for sets costing $50.00 or less, $1.00 on those costing $50.01–200.00, $2.00 on those costing $200.01–500.00, and $2.50 on those costing $500.01 or more); Station WBT v. Poulnot, 46 F.2d 671, 672 (E.D.S.C. 1931).

81. Station WBT, 46 F.2d at 676.

82. Piedmont & Northern Railway Co. v. Query, 56 F.2d 172, 175 (E.D.S.C. 1932) (citing Gramling v. Maxwell, 52 F.2d 256, 261 [W.D.N.C. 1931]). The relevant statutory text is cited in *Gramling* at 257: "Sec. 121½ (a) Any person, firm, or corporation who or which shall carry on the business of selling or offering for sale fresh fish, fresh fruits and/or vegetables, and who or which does not maintain a permanent place of business in this State, shall apply for in advance and procure from the Commissioner of Revenue a State license for each truck operated, and shall pay for such license a tax of fifty dollars ($50.00). (b) This section shall not apply to those persons, firms, or corpora-

tions selling or offering for sale fruits and/or vegetables, if such fruits and/or vegetables are grown in this State, or the fresh fish are taken in the waters of the State."

83. Gramling, 52 F.2d at 258 (quoting Welton v. Missouri, 91 U.S. 275, 279 [1876]); see Nutt v. Ellerbee, 56 F.2d 1058 [E.D.S.C. 1932] [Parker, J., concurring in holding that a state license tax based on the gross revenues of an interstate contract motor freight hauler rather than on revenue earned within the taxing state was an unconstitutional burden on interstate commerce).

84. Scheiber, "Federalism, the Southern Regional Economy, and Public Policy," 73–80.

85. Memorandum on case no. 2522, Fisheries Products Co. v. Timmons, 16 F.2d 266 (4th Cir. 1926), Parker Papers, box 48.

86. See "Report of the Standing Committee on Jurisprudence and Law Reform," *American Bar Association Report* 50 (1925): 410–14. Measures disapproved included proposals to (1) conform federal civil procedures to state practices, S.624 (68th Cong., 1st sess.), and (2) eliminate federal diversity jurisdiction, S.315 (70th Cong., 1st sess.), H.R. 8892 (72d Cong., 1st sess.), S.939 and S.3243 (72d Cong., 1st sess.). See also John J. Parker, "The Federal Jurisdiction and Recent Attacks upon It," *American Bar Association Journal* 18 (1932): 435; and memorandum by John J. Parker "In re H.R. 8892" (July 21, 1937), 2–3, Parker Papers, box 66.

87. U.S. Constitution, art. III, sec. 2.

88. "Conference of the Chief Justice of the United States with the Senior Circuit Judges of the Ten Judicial Circuits," September 30–October 1, 1932 (stenographic transcript), 239–40, U.S. Judicial Conference Files, Administrative Office of the United States Courts, Washington, D.C.

89. 16 Pet. 1, 18 (1842), *reversed,* Erie Railroad Co. v. Tompkins, 304 U.S. 64 (1938).

90. See Wright, *The Law of Federal Courts,* chap. 9; and Senate Committee on the Judiciary, *Limiting Jurisdiction of District Courts of the United States: Report to Accompany S.939,* 72d Cong., 2d sess., 1932, S. Rept. 530.

91. 68 F.2d 502 (4th Cir. 1934).

92. Memorandum on case no. 3518, Hewlett, 68 F.2d 502, Parker Papers, box 49.

93. Hewlett, 68 F.2d at 503–4.

94. Parker, "The Federal Jurisdiction," 437.

95. See Virginia Shipbuilding Corp. v. United States, 22 F.2d 38 (4th Cir. 1927), *cert. denied,* 276 U.S. 625 (1928) (holding at 51–52 that financial loss "should be borne by the shipbuilding corporation, who when times were prosperous and the contract seemed advantageous, took over the government's interest in the vessels upon an agreement to repay merely the amount which

had been advanced for their construction"); United States v. Neptune Line, Inc., 12 F.2d 568 (4th Cir. 1926) (construing the suits in the Admiralty Act of March 9, 1920, 41 Stat. 525, to hold that the government's maximum liability in a collision between appellee's barge and the *Fort Logan* was only the value of the latter at the time of filing [nil] and not at the time of collision [$100,000]); Newport News Shipbuilding and Dry Dock Co. v. United States, 34 F.2d 100, 109–10 (4th Cir. 1929) (Parker, J., concurring with the holding that the company was liable for the destruction of a government-owned ship but dissenting from the amount of the award because no evidence existed to prove that the government intended to insure the ship other than to act as a self-insurer), *cert. denied*, 280 U.S. 599 (1929); and Virginian Railway Co. v. United States, 13 F.2d 772 (4th Cir. 1926) (placing on the railroad the loss in admiralty incurred in raising the government-owned tug *Barrenfork*), *cert. denied*, 273 U.S. 718 (1926).

96. Ferris v. Wilbur, 27 F.2d 262, 265 (4th Cir. 1928).

97. Memorandum on case no. 2840, United States v. Tyler, 33 F.2d 724 (4th Cir. 1929), Parker Papers, box 48, *affirmed*, 281 U.S. 497 (1929) (per Sutherland, J., holding that a federal estate tax on property owned by a subsequently deceased husband and a living wife as tenants by the entireties did not constitute an unapportioned direct tax prohibited by the U.S. Constitution, art. I, sec. 9, cl. 4).

98. 28 F.2d 725 (4th Cir. 1928) (construing act of June 5, 1920, sec. 33, 41 Stat. 1007).

99. 12 How. 229 (1851).

100. 223 U.S. 1 (1912).

101. United States v. Lindgren, 28 F.2d at 726, 728, *affirmed*, Lindgren v. United States, 281 U.S. 38 (1929).

102. Scheiber, "Federalism, the Southern Regional Economy, and Public Policy," 85, 86, 92.

103. Farmers' and Merchants' Bank of Monroe, N.C. v. Federal Reserve Bank of Richmond, Va., 262 U.S. 651 (1923).

104. See Scheiber, "Federalism, the Southern Regional Economy, and Public Policy," 88–90.

105. Parker to Elliott Northcott, December 21, 1928, re Federal Reserve Bank of Richmond, Va. v. Early, 30 F.2d 198 (4th Cir. 1929), Parker Papers, box 18. See Board of Governors of the Federal Reserve System, *Banking and Monetary Statistics* (Washington, D.C., 1943), 284.

106. Parker to Northcott, December 21, 1928.

107. Federal Reserve Bank of Richmond, Va. v. Early, 30 F.2d at 199, *affirmed*, Early v. Federal Reserve Bank of Richmond, Va., 281 U.S. 84 (1929) (per Holmes, J.). See also Craven Chemical Co. v. Federal Reserve Bank of

Richmond, Va., 18 F.2d 711 (4th Cir. 1927) (holding the Federal Reserve Bank not negligent in handling a check drawn on a bank that failed during transit of the check).

108. Suncrest Lumber Co., 30 F.2d 121.

109. Transcript of record, answer of appellee, case no. 2764, United States v. Southern Power Co., 31 F.2d 852 (4th Cir., 1929), filed August 17, 1928, 9, 17.

110. Ibid., 17.

111. Southern Power Co., 31 F.2d at 856.

112. Parker to William C. Coleman, March 12, 1929, Parker Papers, box 18. See Southern Power Co., 31 F.2d at 856.

113. See C. Vann Woodward, *Origins of the New South, 1877–1913,* vol. 9 of *A History of the South,* ed. Wendell Holmes Stephenson and E. Merton Coulter (Baton Rouge, 1971), 312–17, chap. 11 generally.

114. *North Carolina Manual, 1921,* 300.

115. Act of February 28, 1920 (Esch-Cummins), chap. 91, 41 Stat. 456. See Marver H. Bernstein, *Regulating Business by Independent Commission* (Princeton, N.J., 1955), 49, 90–91.

116. United Mine Workers of America v. Red Jacket Consolidated Coal and Coke Co., 18 F.2d 839 (4th Cir. 1927) (applying Sherman Anti-Trust Act to union interference with local coal mining, the output of which was intended for interstate shipment).

117. Atlantic Coast Line Railroad Co. v. Standard Oil Co., 275 U.S. 257, 272 (1927) (wherein Taft, C. J., approvingly noted Parker's distinction between intra- and interstate commerce drawn in the related case of Atlantic Coast Line Railroad Co. and Seaboard Air Line Railway Co. v. Standard Oil Co., 12 F.2d 541 [4th Cir. 1926]).

118. See Houston, East and West Texas Railway Co. v. United States (The Shreveport Case), 234 U.S. 342 (1914) (per Hughes, J.).

119. Untitled memorandum, ca. March 1930, Parker Papers, box 6 (referring to Atlantic Coast Line Railroad Co. and Seaboard Air Line Railway Co., 12 F.2d 541 [4th Cir. 1926]).

120. Memorandum on cases nos. 2441–42, Atlantic Coast Line Railroad Co. and Seaboard Air Line Railway Co., 12 F.2d 541, Parker Papers, box 48.

121. 12 F.2d 541, *cert. denied,* 273 U.S. 712 (1926).

122. Atlantic Coast Line Railroad Co. and Seaboard Air Line Railway Co., 12 F.2d at 544, 545–46 (quoting Brandeis, J., in Baltimore & Ohio Southwestern Railroad Co. v. Settle, 260 U.S. 166, 173–74 [1922] "the reshipment, although immediate, may be an independent intrastate movement. The instances are many where a local shipment follows quickly upon an interstate shipment and yet is not to be deemed part of it, even though some further

shipment was contemplated when the original movement began. Shipments to and from distributing points often present this situation, if the applicable tariffs do not confer reconsignment or transit privileges"), 541–43. See also Seaboard Air Line Railway Co. v. Lee, 14 F.2d 439 (E.D.N.C. 1926) (wherein Meekins, J., with Parker, J., concurring, held that nitrate fertilizers shipped in foreign commerce from Chile to Wilmington, N.C., had thereafter traveled within the state as "independent movements" and were consequently subject to lower intrastate rates), *affirmed per curiam*, 276 U.S. 591 [1928]). See John J. Parker to Isaac M. Meekins, July 23, 1926, Parker Papers, box 56.

123. United States v. Munson Steamship Line, 37 F.2d 681 (4th Cir. 1930) (holding that the steamship line need not file its rate schedule with the ICC because the line's relationships with connecting rail carriers excluded "a common management for a continuous carriage or shipment within the meaning of the Act of 4 February 1887, §1, 24 Stat. 379" [Interstate Commerce Act], thereby obviating any possibility of monopolistic price-fixing by a railroad endowed with power over water carriers and their rates), *affirmed*, 283 U.S. 43 (1930) (per Hughes, C. J.).

124. Chandler v. Pennsylvania Railroad Co., 11 F.2d 39 (4th Cir. 1926) (upholding ICC interstate freight rates on potatoes shipped intrastate from points in Virginia to ports in that state and clearly destined for foreign export); Atlantic Coast Line Railroad Co. v. United States, 48 F.2d 239 (W.D.S.C. 1931) (affirming ICC orders requiring regional carriers to grant lower through routes and rates to shipments carried by a line in competition with another under the common control of the regional carriers).

125. Woodward, *Origins of the New South*, 314.

126. See Donald L. Horowitz, *The Courts and Social Policy* (Washington, D.C., 1977), 22–23, 31–32, 35–38.

127. Morton S. Baratz, *The Union and the Coal Industry* (New Haven, Conn., 1955), 33; Harvey Mansfield, *The Lake Cargo Coal Rate Controversy: A Study in Governmental Adjustment of a Sectional Dispute* (New York, 1932), 21–27.

128. 25 F.2d 462 (S.D.W.Va. 1928).

129. See Baratz, *The Union and the Coal Industry*, 43; Joseph T. Lambie, *From Mines to Market: A History of Coal Transportation on the Norfolk and Western Railway* (New York, 1954), chap. 14; and David Alan Corbin, *Life, Work and Rebellion in the Coalfields: The Southern West Virginia Miners, 1880–1922* (Urbana, Ill., 1981), 4.

130. Mansfield, *Lake Cargo Coal*, mileage map facing title page and rate chart on 264 (reporting that from 1922 to mid-1927 the Pennsylvania and the Baltimore and Ohio Railroads hauled soft coal mined in Ohio, closest to the Lake ports, a distance of 155 miles at a per ton rate of $1.63 or .011 cents per mile. At the same time, the Norfolk and Western carried Lake Cargo Coal from

the remote Tug River and Pocahontas Fields in southwestern West Virginia northward for 440 miles at $2.06 per ton or .005 cents per mile).

131. *Lake Cargo Coal Freight Rates, 1922–28*

Effective Date	Pittsburgh	North Cents per Mile	Differential			Kanawha	South Cents per Mile
			Cents	Cents per Mi.			
July 1, 1922	1.66	.010	.25	.005		1.91	.005
August 10, 1927	1.46	.008	.45	.003		1.91	.005
April 20, 1928	1.46	.008	.25	.004		1.71	.004

Source: Mansfield, *Lake Cargo Coal*, mileage map facing title page and rate chart on 264.

132. Mansfield, *Lake Cargo Coal*, 104–24.

133. Anchor Coal, 25 F.2d at 463, 469–70.

134. Parker to Edmund Waddill, Jr., March 23 and 26, 1928, Parker Papers, box 18.

135. Anchor Coal, 25 F.2d at 464; United States v. Anchor Coal Co., 279 U.S. 812 (1929) (reversed and remanded *per curiam* with directions to dismiss the bill of complaint and therefore dissolve the injunction because of mootness).

136. McClintic to Parker, March 27, 1928, Parker Papers, box 56.

137. Anchor Coal, 25 F.2d at 466–71 (quotations from 470–71).

138. Anchor Coal, 25 F.2d at 473–74 (quoting act of January 30, 1925, chap. 120, 43 Stat. 802, amending act of February 28, 1920 [Esch-Cummins], chap. 91, 41 Stat. 456).

139. Anchor Coal, 25 F.2d at 474.

140. 247 U.S. 251 (1918).

141. Anchor Coal, 25 F.2d at 472.

142. Ibid., *accord* Ann Arbor Railroad Co. v. United States, 281 U.S. 658 (1930) (per VanDevanter, J.).

143. Gavin Wright, *Old South, New South: Revolutions in the Southern Economy since the Civil War* (New York, 1986), 163.

144. See Stephen B. Wood, *Constitutional Politics in the Progressive Era: Child Labor and the Law* (Chicago, 1968).

145. Brief for Appellees, cases nos. 2492–2503, United Mine Workers of America v. Red Jacket Consolidated Coal and Coke Co., 18 F.2d 839 (4th Cir. 1927), filed October 13, 1926, 234.

146. Reviewed by Vincent Canby, *New York Times,* August 28, 1987, sec. 3, p. 3; and by Michael Buckley, *Films in Review* 38 (1987): 614. See also John Sayles, *Thinking in Pictures: The Making of the Movie "Matewan"* (Boston, Mass., 1987).

147. See Peter Graham Fish, *"Red Jacket* Revisited: The Case That Unraveled John J. Parker's Supreme Court Appointment," *Law and History Review* 5 (1987): 51–104.

148. Red Jacket, 18 F.2d at 843–46.

149. United Mine Workers of America v. Coronado Coal Co. (First Coronado Case), 259 U.S. 344, 407–8 (1922) (citing Hammer v. Dagenhart, 247 U.S. at 272, and stating that "coal mining is not interstate commerce, and the power of Congress does not extend to its regulation as such. . . . Obstruction to coal mining is not a direct obstruction to interstate commerce in coal, although it, of course, may affect it by reducing the amount of coal to be carried in that commerce." But, at 411, Taft, C. J., asserted that "a direct, material and substantial effect" on price or supply of coal or a subjective intent to control those variables would transform a local obstruction into a direct one).

150. Memorandum on cases nos. 2492–2503, Red Jacket, 18 F.2d 839, p. 5, Parker Papers, box 48. See Norfolk and Western Railway Co. v. United States, 52 F.2d 967, 971 (W.D. Va. 1931) (Parker, J., stating that "coal mining is a business entirely separate and distinct from the business of transportation. . . . It has been expressly held that the mining of coal is not commerce even though the coal when mined is to be used or transported in commerce"), *affirmed,* 287 U.S. 134 (1932) (per Roberts, J.).

151. Coronado Coal Co. v. United Mine Workers of America (Second Coronado Case), 268 U.S. 295, 309–10 (1925).

152. 18 F.2d at 845.

153. Memorandum on cases nos. 2492–2503.

154. 18 F.2d at 845–46.

155. Ibid., 845, 848–49.

156. Department of Labor, Bureau of Labor Statistics, *Handbook of American Trade Unions,* bulletin no. 420 (Washington, D.C., 1926), 101 (reporting location of headquarters in Merchants' Bank Building, Indianapolis); *United Mine Workers' Journal* 45 (1934): 6 (reporting location of headquarters, effective June 30, 1934, in the Tower Building, Washington, D.C.).

157. Red Jacket, 18 F.2d at 841.

158. 245 U.S. 229 (1917).

159. 15 F.2d 652 (4th Cir. 1926).

160. 208 U.S. 161 (1908).

161. 236 U.S. 1 (1915).

162. Bittner, 15 F.2d at 657; Red Jacket, 18 F.2d at 842.

163. Hitchman, 245 U.S. at 261–62 (enjoining the union "from interfering

or attempting to interfere with plaintiff's employees so as knowingly and willfully to bring about the breaking by plaintiff's employees, present and future, of their [nonunion] contracts of service known to the defendants to exist").

164. Ibid., 262.

165. See Brief for Appellants, cases nos. 2492–2503, Red Jacket, 18 F.2d 839, filed October 4, 1926, 190.

166. Act of October 25, 1914, chap. 323, sec. 20, 38 Stat. 730, *construed* in Red Jacket, 18 F.2d at 849.

167. 254 U.S. 443, 471 (1921).

168. 257 U.S. 184, 209–10 (1921).

169. Red Jacket, 18 F.2d at 840, 844, 849; American Steel Foundries v. Tri-City Central Trades Council, 257 U.S. at 195.

170. Rose to Parker, March 12, 1927, Parker Papers, box 17.

171. *Greensboro Daily News,* June 27, 1920, 2 (assailing the failure of North Carolina to enact a workmen's compensation law); *Charlotte Observer,* October 30, 1920, 3 (attacking the absence of state labor-protection laws for women and children in mills and factories); ibid., April 18, 1920, 8 (stating that "laboring men have a right to organize . . . , collectively, to enter into agreements with employers").

172. See Manly v. Hood, 37 F.2d 212 (4th Cir. 1930); and George A. Fuller Co. v. Brown, 15 F.2d 672 (4th Cir. 1926).

173. Red Jacket, 18 F.2d at 849.

174. Ibid., *cert. denied,* 275 U.S. 536 (1927).

175. See Bedford Stone Co. v. Journeymen Stone-Cutters, 274 U.S. 37 (1927). See also Norris-LaGuardia Act of March 23, 1932, chap. 90, sec. 4, 47 Stat. 70 (removing jurisdiction of federal courts to restrain "advising, urging, or otherwise causing or inducing without fraud or violence the acts heretofore specified regardless of any such undertaking or promise as is described in Section 3 of this Act"), *held constitutional* in Lauf v. E. G. Shinner and Co., 303 U.S. 323 (1938); but see Bituminous Coal Conservation (Guffey-Synder) Act of August 30, 1935, chap. 824, sec. 4, pt. 3, 49 Stat. 1001 (guaranteeing the right of collective bargaining and other collateral rights enforceable by the Bituminous Coal Labor Board), *held unconstitutional* in Carter v. Carter Coal Co., 298 U.S. 238 (1936). See also National Labor Relations (Wagner) Act of July 5, 1935, chap. 372, sec. 1, 49 Stat. 449, *held constitutional* in N.L.R.B. v. Jones and Laughlin Steel Corp., 301 U.S. 1 (1937); and Bituminous Coal (Guffey-Vinson) Act of April 26, 1937, chap. 127, 50 Stat. 72, *held constitutional* in Sunshine Anthracite Coal Co. v. Adkins, 310 U.S. 381 (1940).

176. United States v. Appalachian Coals, Inc., 1 F.Supp. 339, 339–41 (W.D.Va. 1932) (citing [at 339] act of July 2, 1890, chap. 647, sec. 4, 26 Stat. 209).

293

177. Appalachian Coals, Inc., 1 F.Supp. at 339, 348.

178. Parker to Morris A. Soper and Elliott Northcott, September 13, 1932, Parker Papers, box 22 (referring to United States v. United States Steel Co., 251 U.S. 417 [1920]; and United States v. International Harvester, 274 U.S. 693 [1927], both holding that mere size does not constitute a violation of the Sherman Act).

179. Appalachian Coals, Inc., 1 F.Supp. at 341.

180. Ibid., 343–48 (referring [at 343] to United States v. American Can Co., 230 F. 859 [D.Md. 1916]).

181. American Can Co., 230 F. at 902.

182. Appalachian Coals, Inc., 1 F.Supp. at 348.

183. Ibid., 349.

184. Appalachian Coals, Inc. v. United States, 288 U.S. 344, 372–74 (1933).

185. Ibid., 372.

186. Parker to Edwin Yates Webb, March 20, 1933, Parker Papers, box 23. See Bituminous Coal Conservation (Guffey-Synder) Act of August 30, 1935, chap. 824, sec. 4, pt. 2, 49 Stat. 995 (permitting price fixing), *held unconstitutional* in Carter Coal Co., 298 U.S. 238; and Bituminous Coal (Guffey-Vinson) Act of April 26, 1937, chap. 127, 50 Stat. 72, *held constitutional* in Sunshine Anthracite Coal Co. v. Adkins, 310 U.S. 381 (1940).

187. In City of Richmond v. Deans, 37 F.2d 712 (1930), Parker wrote the court's *per curiam* opinion holding unconstitutional under the equal-protection clause of the Fourteenth Amendment a municipal ordinance barring occupancy of residential dwellings "where the majority of residences on such street are occupied by those with whom such person is forbidden to intermarry" as stipulated in Virginia's Racial Integrity Act of 1924. The Supreme Court denied the city's petition for a writ of certiorari, 281 U.S. 704 (1930). See Parker's memorandum on case no. 2900, City of Richmond v. Deans, 37 F.2d 712 (1930), Parker Papers, box 48; see also Loving v. Virginia, 388 U.S. 1 (1967) (holding unconstitutional the state's anti-miscegenation statute, a revised version of the Act to Preserve Racial Integrity of March 20, 1923, 1924 Va. Acts 534, at issue in the *Deans* case).

188. John J. Parker, "The Crisis in Constitutional Government," *Commercial Law Journal* 39 (1934): 382.

189. Parker upheld (1) the Tobacco Inspection Act of August 23, 1935, chap. 623, 49 Stat. 731, as a valid exercise of national commerce power, Wallace v. Currin, 95 F.2d 856 (4th Cir. 1938), *affirmed,* 306 U.S. 1 (1939); (2) the National Industrial Recovery Act of June 16, 1933, title II, sec. 203, 48 Stat. 202 (authorizing the Public Works Administration to loan federal funds to a county for construction of an electric power plant), Greenwood County, S.C. v. Duke Power Co. (Buzzard's Roost Case), 81 F.2d 986 (4th Cir. 1936), *re-*

versed, 299 U.S. 259 (1936); Duke Power Co. v. Greenwood County, S.C., 91 F.2d 665 (4th Cir. 1937), *affirmed,* 302 U.S. 485 (1938); and (3) the Frazier-Lemke Farm Mortgage Moratorium Act of June 28, 1934, chap. 869, 48 Stat. 1289, Bradford v. Fahey, 76 F.2d 628 (4th Cir. 1935), *questioned,* Louisville Joint Stock Land Bank v. Radford, 295 U.S. 555, 573 (1935).

The Florida Legislative Investigation Committee and the Constitutional Readjustment of Race Relations, 1956–1963

Steven F. Lawson

L aw has played a central role in structuring race relations in the United States. Though violent confron-
tation accompanied the civil rights struggle, the most significant battles
were fought in courthouses and legislatures as well as in the streets.
Segregationists resorted to violence and intimidation, but they were as
likely to respond to civil rights demands by shaping the law to their own
ends. In firm control of political and judicial power, white leaders in the
South fashioned new statutes to forestall integration. Passage of such
legislation and its interpretation in the courts was challenged by civil
rights organizations and sometimes defeated; yet white southern politicians did succeed in managing the legal system to reduce the pace of
racial change.

Southern politicos defended their efforts to maintain white supremacy
on democratic grounds, in the name of majority rule. Following the
pathbreaking *Brown v. Board of Education* ruling in 1954, Governor
LeRoy Collins of Florida championed continued racial separation by in-

voking the principles of the Declaration of Independence. "The feeling for segregation is so deep rooted," Collins remarked, "that proposals to abandon such violate the 'consent of the governed' . . . which is essential in our democratic society to give substance and strength to law."[1] This majoritarian emphasis virtually ignored the concept of minority rights, except when applied to state prerogatives. According to white leaders, the Tenth Amendment to the federal Constitution, reserving undelegated powers to the states, took precedence over the nine articles of the Bill of Rights relating to individual freedoms. Southern leaders viewed their society in organic terms in which the interests and values of communities and the state merged together in a common bond and paternalistic whites took care of blacks. The emphasis was on conformity rather than dissent. As the historian Numan Bartley pointed out, southerners designed their political theory for the "promotion of social and ideological orthodoxy."[2]

Southern segregationists used law as a preservative instrument; nonetheless, many civil rights proponents considered the legal system a powerful tool for social change. Since 1909 the National Association for the Advancement of Colored People (NAACP) had employed a case-by-case approach to obtain equality for blacks. Seeking the rights guaranteed to all Americans within the framework of the Constitution, the NAACP specifically sought redress under the Fourteenth and Fifteenth amendments. In pursuing this goal, the NAACP operated according to the traditional ground rules of the American legal system, fighting for reformist ends by conventional means. "By no manner of speaking," one of its officials asserted, "can remedy so sought be called acting in irresponsible haste or proceeding in an extreme manner."[3]

White southerners did not agree. During the post–World War II era of McCarthyism, enemies of the NAACP equated it with the Communist party. Nationwide the cold war's anti-Communist enthusiasts questioned the patriotism of labor, liberal, and civil liberties groups that advocated progressive social change of any type. Distinctions between subversion and radicalism, Stalinism and New Deal liberalism, security and loyalty, were blurred in an atmosphere of political hysteria. In the South, where labor and liberal groups were scarce, the NAACP with its tightly organized network of branches provided a convenient target for conservatives. The organization's opponents defended segregation as 100 percent American and denounced the NAACP as an alien conspiracy. They claimed that the association was directed by outsiders from its

New York City "Kremlin" with the intent of undermining the southern way of life by brainwashing contented Negroes to persuade them to revolt.

In the sense that civil rights organizations were working to overthrow the system of white supremacy, segregationists were correct in perceiving the NAACP as a threat.[4] However, they were wrong in considering the national association a front for Communism. Like other liberal groups opposed to Stalin's brand of left-wing authoritarianism, the NAACP purged Communists from its ranks in the postwar years. In 1950 the national convention of the NAACP adopted a resolution condemning Communism and provided machinery to expel suspected Communists from membership. In cooperation with other anti-Communist liberal and labor groups, NAACP officials composed a blacklist of Communist-tainted organizations for their branches to avoid and distributed dossiers on party activists to lessen the danger of infiltration. Not surprisingly, this internal housecleaning won the official endorsement of the FBI's J. Edgar Hoover and the House Committee on Un-American Activities (HUAC).[5] Despite these commendations, the NAACP could never secure a clean bill of health in the South so long as it continued challenging Jim Crow.

Following the *Brown* decision, southern states combated the NAACP, which they considered a subversive organization. Starting from the premise that the national association conspired to violate the duly established laws of segregation, they attempted to restrict its ability to function. Alabama prosecuted the NAACP for failing to register as an out-of-state corporation and waged a relentless battle to require the group to turn over its membership list. Given the hostile, anti–civil rights climate, such public exposure would endanger current members and make it difficult to recruit new ones. Registration laws to obtain the records of the NAACP were popular in many states, as were those aimed at preventing the organization from sponsoring litigation, the lifeblood of its program. South Carolina went so far as to bar NAACP members from public employment, and Louisiana prohibited teachers from advocating integration of the schools. A number of states also created investigation committees aimed officially at uncovering some kind of wrongdoing by the NAACP but actually intended to intimidate the association through the glare of unfavorable publicity. Indeed, the purpose of these varied measures was to criminalize the activities of the NAACP, stigmatize its followers, and minimize political dissent.[6]

Florida joined the counterattack against integration and its proponents. A gerrymandered state legislature, in which a majority of lawmakers were elected by less than 15 percent of the population, passed an interposition resolution nullifying the controversial *Brown* opinion. Extreme segregationist proposals were tempered by the gubernatorial leadership of LeRoy Collins, a moderate who preferred to "meet the segregation problem in a peaceful and lawful manner . . . [and] not engage in defiance of constituted authority nor in agitation of furor and disorder."[7] His opposition to interposition and his successful support of the Pupil Placement Act, which permitted school segregation for reasons other than race, reflected his cautiously measured approach to the matter. Yet on one issue the governor and the legislature agreed: the NAACP was providing "irresponsible leadership" in stirring up racial turmoil.[8]

In 1956 the lawmakers acted directly to hamper the premier civil rights organization in the state. Prodded by Charley Johns, an outspoken proponent of segregation, a special session of the assembly formed an interim committee to investigate groups that endangered "the well being and orderly pursuit of . . . personal and business activities by the majority of the citizens of the state."[9] Though the measure did not single out the NAACP by name, its sponsors aimed their sights on the association, which they charged with disturbing the racial peace and violating segregation laws. At the same time, the Florida Legislative Investigation Committee (FLIC), with a one-year authorization, gave moderates an opportunity to explore less radical ways of fighting the integrationist forces.[10] Seeking to undermine the NAACP, they made common cause with conservatives in their belief that the group was an enemy of the state and that its "true purpose . . . is Communist inspired," as well as incorporating a "definite desire for financial gain."[11] Collins may have entertained doubts about the necessity of such a committee to supplement his preferred Pupil Placement Act, but he did not veto the FLIC bill, allowing it to become law without his signature.[12]

As the chief target of this legislation, the NAACP prepared to protect itself. Having learned from its experiences in Alabama, the association requested its Florida affiliates to place their crucial membership lists out of reach of state investigators. As soon as the committee was established in August 1956, the Florida State Conference of NAACP Branches dispatched several of its lawyers to visit every chapter around the state "for the purpose of inspecting records and gathering membership" files. Association officials believed that this material would be protected by the attorney-client privilege of confidentiality, but to be on the safe side they packed up the records and shipped them to NAACP headquarters in New York City. Then they steeled themselves "for the onslaught."[13]

The attack came early the following year when the committee decided to hold public hearings. The seven-member committee contained four representatives from the house and three from the senate, including Charley Johns. Balanced with lawmakers from northern and southern sections, rural and urban areas, the group was chaired by Representative Henry Land of Orlando, who had a reputation as a racial moderate. To direct its probe, the committee employed Mark Hawes, a criminal attorney from Tampa, who had most recently prosecuted participants in the Tallahassee bus boycott. Meeting in February and March 1957, the FLIC conducted inquiries in Tallahassee and Miami, where it subpoenaed NAACP officials to answer questions about the workings of their association. The committee denied that it intended to engage in a witch-hunt and insisted that it was merely trying to uncover those organizations breaking the laws of the state.[14]

The committee searched for ways in which the NAACP might have behaved improperly and focused its spotlight on the organization's role in handling lawsuits. Hawes questioned a series of witnesses to find out the connection between the NAACP and the attempted desegregation of buses in Tallahassee, the University of Florida Law School, and public schools throughout the state. The committee counsel sought to prove that, contrary to the code of ethics of the state bar association, the NAACP solicited litigants to file integration cases, financed their way through the courts, and directed them by its own attorneys without the specific authorization of all the plaintiffs.[15] NAACP lawyers adamantly denied these allegations and swore that "contrary to popular belief, we don't go out looking for plaintiffs. In fact, we have more volunteers than we can think of using."[16]

The NAACP aroused suspicion about its practices by refusing to release its records. As had his counterparts in other southern states, Hawes tried to obtain the files in hope of casting doubt on the organization's activities and exposing the names of local members to unfavorable community sentiment. His quest for the documents led him and the committee to Miami and one of the most active NAACP chapters in the state. He and the committee learned from Ruth Perry, the secretary of the local branch and of the state conference of branches, that she had turned over her files to Grattan E. Graves, Jr., an NAACP attorney from Miami and part of the team of lawyers that gathered branch records throughout Florida. Called to testify on February 25, Graves revealed that under instruction from the national office, he had sent the records to the NAACP's headquarters in New York. Both Graves and Perry agreed to the committee's request to try to have the desired material returned. This effort proved fruitless, as the executive secretary of the NAACP, Roy Wilkins, declined to disclose membership lists and other confidential information "because of reprisals visited upon those whose names have become known."[17]

This dispute underscored the negative publicity the hearings brought the NAACP. The civil rights group could take scant pleasure in the fact that the FLIC had also spent several days probing into white extremist groups such as the Citizens' Council. Investigating the NAACP alongside the Citizens' Council had the effect of reinforcing the image of the association as a lawbreaking, radical organization. Its shipment of records outside the state only heightened this impression. The *Tampa Tribune* concluded that the inquiry "has brought substantial discredit to the [NAACP]" and condemned the association's "defiance of a duly constituted arm of the Commonwealth."[18]

Shortly after the hearings adjourned, the NAACP faced a fresh challenge from the legislature. In April members of the investigation committee introduced into each chamber a package of five bills aimed at undermining the NAACP. The measures resembled those adopted by other southern states: three of them made it illegal to solicit lawsuits, prohibited attorneys employed by an association from representing individual members of the group, and barred individuals or organizations not party to litigation from financing or participating in a lawsuit. Another proposal required all groups that tended "to destroy the peace, tranquility and good order" of a community to register with and submit annual membership and financial records to the secretary of state. If laws such as these had been on the books, one of their sponsors declared, "most of our schools suits would have been dismissed."[19] The remaining measure extended the life of the FLIC for two years.

Despite considerable interest in these bills, only the one to renew the investigation committee passed. The antibarratry and registration measures, approved unanimously by the senate, went down to defeat in the house, where lawmakers feared that their broad wording might adversely affect other business, social, and fraternal organizations. Apparently the FLIC provision posed no similar problem to the representa-

301

tives, for it passed overwhelmingly, with only one dissenting vote. The committee offered a familiar vehicle for proceeding against desegregation, and at the same time the legislators significantly expanded the committee's scope. They instructed its members to examine the influence of Communism in provoking racial agitation, a subject that had been virtually ignored during the previous hearings.[20] Even Collins, whose support for the committee had been cool, declared that extending its term "may have some merit because its conduct has been praiseworthy."[21]

Lawmakers thought the committee a more acceptable way of restricting the NAACP than adopting complicated legislation whose side effects might be harmful. They justified the extension measure as an appropriate response to the "great abuse of the judicial processes of the courts in Florida,"[22] presumably with the NAACP's civil rights litigation in mind.

Defeat of the antibarratry package did not free the NAACP from continuing challenges to its legal practices. In the wake of the hearings, the FLIC's counsel, Mark Hawes, concluded that the NAACP's activities were "contrary to the spirit and letter of the canons of ethics and general laws governing the practice of law in Florida."[23] Consequently, in September 1957, he sent the transcript of the testimony to the Florida Bar Association to determine whether the NAACP had violated rules governing the conduct of attorneys. Early the next year a preliminary investigation concluded that five leading NAACP lawyers in Florida had acted unprofessionally in handling school-desegregation litigation.[24] Despite this finding, the bar association eventually cleared the civil rights counselors. In "unalterable" disagreement with the "precepts of the NAACP," its leaders nonetheless tried to approach the issue dispassionately and decided that no unethical conduct by the individual lawyers had taken place.[25] Most likely they preferred that the legislature and its investigative committee deal directly with the NAACP, rather than dragging themselves publicly into the controversy.

The FLIC was more than willing to oblige, especially with Senator Charley Johns installed as its new chair. An arch-segregationist and a foe of Collins's brand of racial moderation, Johns wielded the weapon of anti-Communism against the NAACP. Before launching a new round of hearings in February 1958, he announced that the committee had in its possession "information regarding Communistic activities in several phases of life in Florida."[26] Borrowing a page out of Joseph McCarthy's book, he brought Dr. J. B. Matthews, a former aide to the Wisconsin senator, to testify at Tallahassee. Matthews, who several years earlier had been forced to resign from McCarthy's subcommittee for accusing Protestant clergy of being an integral part of the Communist apparatus, informed Johns and his colleagues that the Communists had been "directly involved in every major race incident of the past few years." He also encouraged the committee to pick up the trail of the NAACP, which, he said, "for the past 30 years . . . has been a prime target of Communist penetration."[27]

Johns did not need much encouragement, and at the end of February he took the committee to Miami to demonstrate that the "Communist Party and the NAACP are tied up together in Florida."[28] The committee's investigators had done their homework and produced two witnesses who admitted having once belonged to both the Communist party and the NAACP. Their testimony, however, proved less than conclusive. Neither informant currently was an NAACP member, and though one could recall seeing some of his Communist comrades at association meetings, his memory was vague concerning the details of these encounters. Nor did the committee find out more from questioning a left-wing lawyer who had defended NAACP clients in the past but had severed his connection with the organization around 1954 to avoid embarrassing it with his progressive affiliations.[29]

Having learned nothing about any present link between the NAACP and Communism, the FLIC subpoenaed officials of the civil rights group to testify, along with alleged functionaries of the Communist party in Florida. The association came prepared. It had checked out the informants and the accused Communists and concluded that "either they were not members [of the NAACP] in the past or if so are not currently active." To safeguard its membership roster and other records from inspection by the committee, the Miami chapter of the NAACP placed all its files in the hands of its president, Father Theodore R. Gibson, the rector of Christ Episcopal Church.[30] In addition, the branch officers decided not to respond to questions related to individual membership in their organization. Ruth Perry explained that to answer such questions would be "an invasion of my rights to due process of law and freedom of speech and association" guaranteed by the First and Fourteenth amendments. She further denied that the NAACP was infested with Communists.[31]

Perry's testimony sparked fireworks. Perhaps because she was a white woman fighting for black equality, she triggered an angry reaction from committee members. Representative W. C. "Cliff" Herrell of Dade

County, Perry's home county, called her performance a "disgrace" and declared her "not fit to be a citizen of Florida." Mrs. Perry, the granddaughter of South Carolina slaveholders, also received a tongue-lashing from Representative J. B. Hopkins of Pensacola for attempting "to hoodwink and deceive the people of Florida."[32] Denying they were engaged in a witch-hunt, the interrogators wondered why the NAACP refused to cooperate if it had nothing to hide. These sharp words did not shake Perry's resolve. Although she found the experience "harrowing," she refused to comply, in the belief that her constitutional rights were at stake.[33]

Gibson and the rest of his NAACP colleagues also refused to answer questions about suspected Communist members in their organization. Gibson conveyed his disdain most emphatically when, following the attack on Perry, he declined to testify, called the committee a "star chamber . . . disqualified . . . to sit as an objective fact-finding body," and dramatically walked out of the hearing room.[34] Joining Gibson in his beliefs was Reverend Edward T. Graham, a former officer of the Miami chapter, who maintained membership in the association as well as in the American Civil Liberties Union (ACLU). He and Gibson were the city's most prominent black ministers actively fighting for civil rights. Graham had tried unsuccessfully to obtain a court order blocking the hearings, and when forced to appear, he would not tell the committee whether he currently belonged to the NAACP. "I have the right to peaceably assemble and to lawfully work for my ideals," he declared to his inquisitors.[35]

Whereas Gibson, Graham, and their colleagues cited the First and Fourteenth amendments to justify their silence, the alleged Communists who were called to testify took the Fifth Amendment in addition to the other two constitutional provisions.[36] The difference was crucial, because the NAACP based its position on freedom of speech and association and not on the right to invoke the privilege against self-incrimination. However, this distinction was often lost on a public that during the 1950s had come to equate failure to testify before investigation committees with an implied admission of guilt. Mark Hawes reinforced this impression by asserting: "It is significant that the NAACP choose to resort to identical tactics used by the Communist Party to fight these hearings."[37] Collins did little to dispel this view. He refused to comment on how the committee was conducting its investigation under Johns, answering instead that the "public will hold them [sic] accountable and responsible for their actions."[38]

Actually it would be up to the courts rather than public opinion to determine the future of the so-called Johns Committee and the NAACP. After the panel obtained a decree from a state circuit judge ordering the defiant witnesses to testify under threat of a contempt citation, the case was appealed to the Florida Supreme Court. The legal questions involved the clash between a state legislative committee that sought to compel testimony as part of an official investigation and individuals who claimed the right to associate freely without fear of reprisal. When did the right to privacy of members of a group give way to the state's right to safeguard its internal security from the widely recognized menace of Communism? Though the NAACP engaged in political dissent in an open and lawful manner, could a southern state government that considered the civil rights cause obnoxious restrain the organization in a fashion that might be deemed permissible? In short, could state authorities wield the hammer of anti-Communism to club the NAACP into submission?

In answering these questions, the Florida judiciary had some recent precedents for guidance. Under the leadership of Chief Justice Earl Warren, the U.S. Supreme Court had ruled on the separate issues of legislative probes of Communism and the associational privacy of the NAACP. In a series of cases in 1956 and 1957, the high tribunal reined in HUAC to check it from misusing congressional investigatory power "to expose for the sake of exposure"; restricted a similar agency in New Hampshire from forcing a witness to testify because its statutory authorization was too vague and imprecise; and struck down a Pennsylvania antisedition law on the ground that it had been superseded by federal legislation.[39]

While limiting the scope of governmental activities in the area of loyalty and security, the Supreme Court also impeded Alabama from forcing the NAACP to disclose its membership rosters. The state had attempted to obtain NAACP records through its law requiring foreign corporations to register. Weighing the ability of the civil rights group to operate in a hostile climate if the names of its members were revealed against the state's concern for regulating outside enterprises, the unanimous Court declared that the state "has fallen short of showing a controlling justification for the deterrent effect on the free enjoyment of the right to associate which disclosure of the membership lists is likely to have."[40]

These pronouncements seemed to buttress the NAACP's position in Florida. Led by Robert Carter, the NAACP's general counsel, and Grattan Graves, Jr., the Miami attorney who was also a party to the suit, the civil rights plaintiffs petitioned the state supreme court to set aside the order against them. To coerce them to testify and produce membership records, their attorneys argued, violated their freedom of association protected by the First Amendment and incorporated into the due-process clause of the Fourteenth Amendment. They insisted that the FLIC had not satisfied the standard, established in the Alabama case, that permitted the state to interfere with their constitutionally protected rights only by proving its interest to be dominant and compelling. The committee had not met this standard, the NAACP claimed, because the statute creating it was loosely worded and its announced purpose of examining Communist penetration bore no reasonable relationship to the NAACP, which neither allowed Communist members nor sanctioned violence. The attorneys emphasized that the exposure of the names of the rank and file to public scrutiny would have a chilling effect on freedom of association in a state where NAACP members constituted "a weak and unpopular minority."[41]

The appellant witnesses reinforced their position with the Supreme Court's rulings on the scope of legislative inquiries and state antisubversion laws. Based on the HUAC case, *Watkins v. United States,* they contended that the FLIC had not shown "with unmistakable clarity the precise relationship between the questions propounded and the inquiry authorized." Without such specificity, the committee had embarked on a "fishing expedition," conducted a "mock trial," and treated such witnesses as Ruth Perry in a "highly prejudicial" way. Had Communist infiltration, rather than public humiliation, been the real purpose of the hearing, the lawmakers would have focused on the association's demonstrated activities and not on the names of its members.[42] In addition, relying on *Pennsylvania v. Nelson,* the petitioners claimed that federal laws against subversion had preempted the field and blocked state lawmakers from investigating a subject on which they had no constitutional authority to legislate.[43]

The committee's counsel, Mark Hawes, denied that these decisions supported the NAACP's position in this instance. He contended that *Alabama* did not prohibit a state from compelling testimony and obtaining membership files so long as it proved a substantial need. Hawes claimed that Florida had shown ample reason for its attempt to discover "the degree to which . . . known Communists . . . have penetrated, infiltrated, and influenced the actions of the Miami Branch of the NAACP."[44]

The FLIC attorney flatly disputed that the issue involved race or attempts to avert desegregation. He asked the court whether or not a sovereign state could take measures to protect itself from the Communist menace. *Pennsylvania v. Nelson* did not keep Florida from conducting investigations on the subject because article V of the U.S. Constitution empowered states to initiate proceedings to amend the governing document. Hawes suggested that Florida's legislature might use the information obtained from the hearings to overcome the effects of the *Nelson* decision through the prescribed constitutional revision. Furthermore, he dismissed the charge that the committee had conducted its inquiry irresponsibly or with prejudice by pointing out that it had also investigated white-supremacist groups. Having discounted any hint of bias, Hawes could not resist insinuating that the NAACP's "false accusations . . . [were] a typically Communist tactic of resistance to investigation."[45]

The Florida Supreme Court fundamentally agreed with Hawes's arguments. Speaking for a unanimous bench, on December 19, 1958, Justice Campbell Thornal reaffirmed that legislatures had the power to conduct investigations toward a valid objective but warned against "exercising it . . . sadistically . . . as a media to hunt witches." He concluded that the FLIC had acted properly and praised Johns for clearly informing witnesses about the subject of the inquiry, thus enabling them to determine the pertinency of the questions posed. With respect to the manner in which the committee allegedly mistreated the appellants, particularly Perry, Thornal asserted that confronted by "defiant and recalcitrant witnesses," the panel exhibited "a degree of patience and composure customarily demanded only of judicial officers."[46]

In reaching its opinion, the tribunal distinguished this case from recent Supreme Court opinions. Thornal denied that *Pennsylvania v. Nelson* prevented a state from coping "with purely internal problems," protecting the "welfare of its people," and acquiring information that might "set in motion the amending procedure" of the U.S. Constitution. In contrast to the situation in *Alabama*, Thornal found that Florida had sufficiently demonstrated a compelling reason to obtain the names of NAACP members, whereas the civil rights groups had failed to prove that the "identification of members would have a deterrent effect on freedom of association."[47]

Convinced that the committee had acted correctly and that the NAACP would suffer no stigma by cooperating with the agency, the state high court issued a decree tailored to fashion a delicate balance between the competing interests of the litigants. In a masterful stroke of judicial deci-

307

sion making, Thornal held that the FLIC was entitled to secure the information it demanded, though he granted the NAACP nominal protection of its privacy. He ordered the witnesses to answer the disputed questions about Communists in the organization, "based upon . . . reference to available membership lists." This procedure allowed the civil rights officials to keep the records in their possession but forced them to reveal whether persons named by the committee as Communists were on the lists. The court found no evidence that merely by answering such questions would NAACP adherents suffer from guilt by association, "contrary to their own protestations of absolute innocence."[48]

The NAACP appealed this decision to the U.S. Supreme Court, which on June 22, 1959, refused to grant a review. Though the justices did not publish their reasons, most likely they refrained from considering the case because it had not yet reached a final judgment. They expected the petitioners to go back before the committee, refuse to cooperate once again, and be held in contempt. At that stage of punishment, the high bench would probably hear the case.[49] Whatever might happen in the future, the NAACP felt "very discouraged and frustrated." Ruth Perry lamented that the Johns Committee was "convinced now that the Supreme Court thinks we are all Red down here."[50]

Her concern proved well founded. Revived by the legislature in 1959, the FLIC convened hearings in Tallahassee on November 4 and 5. Charley Johns remained a member of the panel, and his successor as chair, Representative Cliff Herrell, proved no less willing to pursue Communists. Herrell had clashed with Perry at the hearing the previous year, and he took precautionary measures to assure that the committee met its constitutional obligations of fairness. He opened the inquiry by carefully reading a statement explaining the committee's desire to examine Communist penetration of organizations dealing with race relations and admonished against drawing an inference that a subpoenaed witness was a likely Communist.[51]

Having established the basis for the pertinency of their forthcoming questions and disavowed any feelings of bias, the legislators first summoned several white Floridians they suspected of belonging to the Communist party in the state. After listening to their refusal to answer any questions, the panel called its chief investigator to the stand. R. J. Strickland informed the group about what it presumably already knew: fourteen people, including the recalcitrant witnesses, were Communists who had attended NAACP meetings in Miami. However, a subsequent witness, Arlington Sands, a self-confessed former Communist who had once belonged to the NAACP but had not been active since the late 1940s, cast some doubt on Strickland's evidence. Although Sands had been a source for much of that information, he publicly disputed the investigator's claim that he had personally encountered most of the accused Communists at NAACP meetings.[52]

Only the NAACP officers could confirm whether the persons named by the committee belonged to the Miami branch. This they refused to do. The association's representatives had no objection to testifying whether they recalled seeing an individual, designated as a Communist, at NAACP meetings or whether they recognized such persons as members of the group. However, they declined to check their memories against the membership lists, which Gibson held exclusively in his possession. "If people who join our organization discover that we are going to disclose their identity in the organization," the Miami chapter president told the committee, "that is a sure way that our organization would be wrecked." Instead, Gibson willingly answered questions about individuals the committee identified as Communists, though he denied knowing any of them as NAACP members. Nor did any of the remaining branch officials recognize the suspected subversives. In addition, Reverend Edward Graham, who was not an NAACP official, refused to reply whether he was a member of the civil rights group for fear that it would jeopardize "his right to privacy."[53]

The NAACP witnesses had walked a thin line in their appearance before the FLIC. Their commitment to free speech and association did not prevent them from answering questions about individuals named as Communists. After all, their organization had taken a strong stand in purging Communists from its ranks. They complied with the judicial order to respond to the committee's questioning, but they refused to follow the court's decree to have membership rolls available for consultation. It was one thing to discuss possible members of the Communist party, an organization that they agreed was illegitimate, and another to expose their own lawful association to public inspection.[54]

The FLIC refused to accept the NAACP's reasoning and initiated contempt proceedings against Gibson, as official custodian of the files, and Graham, for declining to answer questions about his membership in the association. Despite a court order instructing them to testify on April 5, 1960, the two civil rights activists once again defied the committee. The following month, Circuit Judge W. May Walker of Leon County (Talla-

309

hassee) held a hearing on the violation of his decree. Though a parade of witnesses testified that membership in the NAACP had declined and its officials had been threatened since the beginning of the investigation committee hearings in 1957, the judge did not find the evidence believable and ruled against the defendants. Even if he had discovered the necessary "substantial risk of deterrent effect," Walker held that the interest of Florida in investigating Communist subversion was "so grave, pressing and compelling" as to override the rights of Gibson and Graham.[55] Ordered to appear before the committee on July 27, they refused to acquiesce in its demand for information. As a result, Walker found them in contempt and levied twelve-hundred-dollar fines and six-month prison sentences.[56]

Both appealed to the state supreme court. Gibson's counsel, Robert Carter, argued that his client saw no distinction between taking the membership list to the committee for reference and turning it over to the panel. As far as he was concerned the results would be the same: fear and intimidation of present and prospective NAACP members and supporters. Together with Graham's ACLU attorneys, Howard Dixon and Tobias Simon, Carter claimed that Florida had to do more than suggest that alleged Communists were associated with the NAACP; rather, the state had to prove "that the activities of the organization are subversive or tend to be subversive."[57] This it had not done, except to charge that some Communists might have belonged to the Miami branch before 1950. The civil rights counselors also pointed out that the U.S. Supreme Court had recently overthrown an attempt by Little Rock, Arkansas, to force disclosure of NAACP membership rolls as an otherwise legitimate function of its municipal licensing and taxing authority. As in that case, they contended, governmental officials in Florida had failed to prove that their need for information outweighed the "demonstrated deterrent effects upon the witnesses."[58]

The opposing counsel applied a different standard to address the constitutional question. Mark Hawes asserted that to subordinate the rights of witnesses all the state had to do was "exhibit a legitimate . . . interest in the subject matter of the investigation" and ask questions that were pertinent to obtaining the desired information. In contrast to the circumstances in the Little Rock case, Hawes found a sufficient connection between the FLIC's inquiry into Communism and the agency's effort to identify specific NAACP members. Besides, he claimed that the witnesses had produced insufficient evidence to show the harm in testifying.[59]

On December 30 the state supreme court upheld the verdict for Gibson but not Graham. On behalf of a unanimous bench, Justice Thornal asserted that the custodian of the NAACP records had to consult them to authenticate his testimony. He declared that this procedure did not have a deterrent effect on "legitimate and good faith members of the NAACP" because their names would not be exposed to public disclosure. As for the alleged Communists, they were "not entitled to the same associational privacy." However, in a surprising opinion with respect to the question of Graham's membership in the NAACP, the justice could not discern the committee's dominant interest in obtaining a response. Thornal argued that the FLIC had not specifically linked Graham to any Communist affiliation, it could obtain the relevant information about subversive infiltration of the NAACP from Gibson, and its efforts could lead to reprisals against the witness for admitting that he belonged to an "organization perfectly legitimate but allegedly unpopular in the community."[60]

The tribunal's companion decisions complicated the situation for the NAACP. In reaching different outcomes, the state judges appeared to follow the kind of balancing process that the U.S. Supreme Court had sanctioned in weighing governmental power against the rights of individuals. In the face of adverse consequences, a person did not have to testify about membership in the NAACP, whereas an authorized NAACP official could not refuse if the state demonstrated an appropriate interest in the answer. To win a reversal for Gibson, his lawyers would have to show convincingly that the lower court's ruling did not adequately safeguard the constitutional rights of innocent NAACP members or the group as a whole. If they failed, other southern states, so far blocked in their attempts at exposure, would most likely succeed in eliciting the names of NAACP members under the guise of uncovering Communists. "The Gibson case," Roy Wilkins declared, "is of strategic importance to the survival of the civil rights movement in Florida and the entire southeast."[61]

The prospects of victory appeared mixed. From 1959 to 1961 the Supreme Court moved in opposite directions in cases involving southern efforts to hamstring the NAACP and governmental attempts to extend the scope of investigations into Communism. In the former area, the

Court struck down an Arkansas statute that required public school teachers to file an annual list of all organizations they had belonged to during the past five years. The high bench ruled that although a state could inquire into the competence of its teachers, on this occasion its methods were too sweeping and infringed upon personal liberties. The Court reached a similar conclusion in voiding a Louisiana law calling for out-of-state associations to submit their membership rosters along with affidavits swearing that their officers were not Communists.[62] In contrast, the tribunal enlarged the range of legislative discretion in probing Communist affiliations and narrowed the options of witnesses who stood behind the shield of the First Amendment to keep from testifying. In three cases involving HUAC and one concerning an investigative panel in New Hampshire, the justices ruled that the government's interest in self preservation outweighed the individual's rights in associational privacy.[63]

After the Court agreed to hear the Gibson case in the fall of 1961, NAACP attorneys had to convince the justices to reconcile the competing lines of precedent in favor of their civil rights cause. In light of recent decisions upholding HUAC's broad sway in questioning alleged Communists, Robert Carter and his associates dropped their previous argument that the Florida statute creating the FLIC was "unconstitutionally vague and inexplicit."[64] Instead they attempted to prove that the committee had failed to show a "nexus" between Communist activities and the NAACP. Without such a concrete demonstration, they argued, the interest of the state in obtaining information about subversion failed to justify the deterrence to Gibson's freedom of association resulting from compulsory disclosure.

On this basis, they distinguished Gibson's case from the HUAC rulings. Because Gibson himself was not accused of being a Communist and his organization did not have any relationship with Communist activities, the FLIC did not have sufficient reason to invade his right of privacy. Carter reviewed the NAACP's history of anti-Communism and pointed out that the committee's main informer, Arlington Sands, had failed to identify suspected Communists as NAACP members. Thus the committee lacked the requisite probable cause for believing that Gibson had any valid testimony to offer and could not compel him to respond. "Undoubtedly, a mere assertion that a subordinating interest exists or a mere statement that the committee has 'knowledge' that subversives are infiltrating the organization," Carter maintained, "does not constitute justification for intrusion" on personal liberties.[65]

Because there was no tangible evidence to connect Communism with the civil rights group, NAACP lawyers insisted that Gibson should not be forced to divulge the names of the organization's members even under the carefully drawn guidelines adopted by the Florida Supreme Court. Carter argued that it made no difference whether the NAACP branch president handed over the entire membership list or merely checked it to confirm the identity of particular members. Under either circumstance subversion would be linked with the NAACP and aspersions would be cast on an innocent organization. By bringing into doubt the loyalty of the group, public disclosure would generate reprisals against current members and scare off prospects from joining.[66]

Naturally, Mark Hawes reached the opposite conclusion. He failed to comprehend how the "disclosure of membership of a person shown to be a member of the Communist Party would work . . . [a] deterrent effect upon loyal and patriotic members of the organization." Only acknowledged subversives would suffer, and they had no constitutional guarantee to remain anonymous. Besides, the FLIC counsel denied the claim that the committee had not sufficiently linked the NAACP with Communist activities. His brief pointed out that the committee's chief investigator had introduced evidence of Communist infiltration, and the civil rights group admitted in its 1950 resolution that Communist penetration was a serious problem. He assured the Court that the FLIC harbored no desire to expose the NAACP to reprisals and noted that the panel had been evenhanded in investigating white segregationists as well as civil rights groups.[67]

These contending arguments underscored the dilemma faced by the Court. This case fell between the pro-NAACP rulings on one hand and the anti-Communist decisions on the other. Because a majority of five justices had come to favor a broad interpretation of investigative power, the civil libertarians on the bench worried about the outcome here. One of Chief Justice Warren's law clerks admitted that the current case was weaker than those in Alabama and Arkansas because the Miami chapter president had not been coerced to turn over the entire membership rolls to the committee. Moreover, the NAACP's assertion of a right to protect its members was "somewhat feeble in view of the fact that . . . [Gibson] indicated he would willingly testify from his own memory as to" the identity of possible Communists. Most likely mirroring the chief justice's thinking, the aide believed nonetheless that the lower court's ruling should be reversed or every southern state would seize the opportunity to harass the NAACP under the banner of anti-Communism.[68]

However, the liberals initially did not have the votes. With Felix Frankfurter and John Marshall Harlan in the lead, the Court split five to four in support of the FLIC's position. On March 13, 1962, Harlan circulated to his brethren the draft of a majority opinion affirming the lower court decision. He argued that to pass constitutional muster a legislative committee, "in pursuit of an otherwise legitimate state or federal inquiry, must act responsibly and not irrationally." To obtain information from a witness, a committee did not have to prove "probable cause" in meeting the same high standards as it would in securing a search warrant under the Fourth Amendment. Accordingly, after examining the record, Harlan concluded that the FLIC acted reasonably. To hold differently, he declared, would mean granting preferential treatment to the NAACP and freeing Gibson from responding "to a legitimate official inquiry with the same degree of responsibility that is demanded of officials of other organizations."[69]

A stroke of fate saved Gibson. Frankfurter became seriously ill in April 1962, and his absence from participation in the deliberations held up final disposition. Without Frankfurter, the justices deadlocked at four apiece. The delay caused by his illness forced the Court to schedule the suit for reargument the following term. In the meantime, Frankfurter retired in August, and Arthur Goldberg took his seat.[70]

This personnel change produced a majority of five behind the NAACP. Speaking for his brethren on March 25, 1963, Goldberg asserted that before the legislative committee could infringe upon First Amendment rights it had to demonstrate a direct connection between the NAACP and subversive activities. He demanded a higher standard of proof than in previous cases involving accused Communists, because in this instance the NAACP was "a concededly legitimate and nonsubversive organization." Goldberg's review of the record found the evidence linking the NAACP and Communism "indirect, less than unequivocal, and mostly hearsay." Thus the committee's demand for disclosure threatened the "constitutionally enshrined rights of free speech, expression, and association" of an unpopular but innocent group.[71]

Goldberg occupied the middle ground between the absolutist and minimalist approaches toward civil liberties. Representing the former, Hugo Black and William O. Douglas agreed with the result but issued separate concurring opinions. They insisted that the Bill of Rights protected individuals and groups in associating with non-Communists as well as Communists, and they denied that the principle of innocence by association, as enunciated by Goldberg, was any more constitutionally valid than was guilt by association. "One man's privacy," Douglas asserted, "may not be voided because of another's perversity."[72] In sharp contrast, Harlan delivered a dissenting opinion that criticized the majority for distinguishing between a government's power to investigate "Communist infiltration of organizations and Communist activity by organizations." Neither could he fathom the difference between Gibson's willingness to testify from memory and his refusal to verify his recollection by consulting the membership records. Nor could the justice understand how the Court, in searching for a nexus, could require "an investigating agency to prove in advance the very things it is trying to find out."[73]

The majority ruling conferred on so-called innocent organizations an associational right to privacy guaranteed by the Constitution. The NAACP may have been viewed by white southerners as on a par with Communism, but the Supreme Court disagreed. The majority of the justices apparently recognized, without explicitly stating so, that the FLIC probe was part of a larger program to discredit a respected civil rights group.[74] Though members of illegitimate Communist or Communist-infiltrated groups presumably did not share the constitutional protection afforded to those in lawful ones, the high tribunal's decision also made it more difficult for legislative committees to investigate them. The judiciary would continue to balance governmental and individual interests in each case; however, as a consequence of *Gibson,* associational privacy would be assigned a higher priority than investigative rights, "especially where prospects for legislation are slight and the political overtones are obvious."[75]

The *Gibson* decision effectively stifled Florida's legislative probe of the NAACP. A verdict unfavorable to Gibson would have signaled the go-ahead for the FLIC to resume its anti–civil rights efforts. As late as 1961, while the case was still pending, Charley Johns chaired hearings to search for Communist influence in the burgeoning racial protest across the state. The inquiry focused on the activities of the Southern Conference Education Fund, a group cited as a Communist front by HUAC, and the Johns Committee managed to link it to the NAACP in absentia.[76] The *Gibson* opinion brought an end to further committee efforts to investigate the NAACP, and public support for such attempts waned.

315

The *Miami Herald* called Gibson's victory "just," and the *Miami News* agreed that it was "strongly in the American tradition."[77] Within two years, the legislature allowed its investigative agency to expire.

The impact of the FLIC on the NAACP cannot be measured precisely. Undoubtedly, the FLIC struggle and the uncertainty of its outcome took a toll on NAACP energies and finances; time and money spent challenging the committee could have been used elsewhere for the frontal assault on racial discrimination. Civil rights activists suffered reprisals and had to live constantly with the possibility of intimidation. As a result, membership in the organization temporarily declined, and the group found it difficult to sign up new recruits.[78] However, the NAACP outlasted its nemesis, and unlike its counterparts in Alabama and Louisiana, the association did not cease functioning in Florida while the judicial conflict dragged on. It continued to file lawsuits attacking segregated education and public facilities, and in 1960 its youth councils led successful sit-in demonstrations against Jim Crow lunch counters throughout the state. By that time the drop in membership had been reversed, and the association promoted the *Gibson* case to stimulate interest in its cause. Rather than breaking the NAACP, the FLIC battles bolstered the esprit de corps of civil rights advocates and, as Ruth Perry put it, generated a "new faith in the rightness of our cause."[79]

The NAACP survived for several reasons. The segregationists were not as solidly united in Florida as they were in other states of the region. Traditional southern racial values were voiced by rural and small-town lawmakers from north Florida, whose influence was inflated in a malapportioned legislature. Yet growing urbanization in the southern half of the state and the declining percentage of blacks in the population tended to lessen the intensity of racial obstructionism, without eliminating it.[80] As in neighboring states, Florida legislators enacted an interposition resolution and a pupil-assignment law to deter integration, but they failed to pass massive resistance bills that closed public schools and shut down the operation of the NAACP. Though racial moderates accepted the validity of the FLIC, they did so without enthusiasm and worried about Charley Johns's direction of the panel. They preferred to follow the lead of Governor LeRoy Collins and avoid extremist positions that might impede efforts to promote economic development of the Sunshine State. Still, the committee might have accomplished its mission against the NAACP if not for the outside intervention of the federal judiciary. Despite their differences, Florida's political leaders joined together in shaping the legal system to maintain segregation as long as possible and to diminish the NAACP's opposition. The state's highest tribunal sanctioned that effort, leaving only the U.S. Supreme Court to block it. The *Gibson* opinion assured that the investigative agency had no legitimate way of getting at the civil rights group.

Moreover, the NAACP withstood the constitutional barrage because it commanded the overwhelming allegiance of blacks in the state. While awaiting the final stamp of judicial approval, the association preserved its leadership of the civil rights movement in Florida. The NAACP had a tightly knit network of chapters, and officials such as Father Gibson won the admiration of black Floridians by keeping up the pressure for first-class citizenship on a variety of fronts and by refusing to be intimidated by state officials. Not only did they petition the courts to gain their rights, but they adapted their techniques to provide just enough militancy to satisfy the masses of blacks. Notwithstanding the presence in the state of more activist groups, such as the Congress of Racial Equality and the Southern Christian Leadership Conference, the NAACP retained its preeminence in the field.[81]

The triumph of the NAACP in *Gibson* guaranteed its freedom of association; however, it did not immediately dismantle the structure of discrimination that kept blacks separate and unequal. For all of its dangers, the FLIC was not the greatest obstacle to racial change in the Sunshine State. Its limitations stemmed in part from the ability of the NAACP to tie up the panel in court. The main hurdle to school desegregation, which had spawned the legislative counterattack in the first place, remained the "lawful" statutes on the books permitting the state to circumvent the Supreme Court's 1954 ruling. Until the high tribunal, backed by the legislative and executive power of the federal government, took appropriate action in the late 1960s, the legal roadblocks constructed by Florida to enforce segregation remained intact.

Still, the defeat of the FLIC meant that, as Justice Goldberg noted, constitutional freedoms "are protected not only against heavy-handed frontal attack, but also from being stifled by more subtle governmental interference."[82] Gibson's victory helped ensure that the NAACP would be around to press its unfinished business to a successful conclusion. In the end, its attorneys demonstrated that conservative rules of law could be shaped for progressive ends.

317

Notes

I wish to express my gratitude to Bonnie Stark for her generosity in sharing research materials, to Nancy A. Hewitt for her gentle advice and congenial encouragement, and to Paul L. Murphy for his incisive comments.

1. Statement by Gov. LeRoy Collins, November 19, 1956, PUT-RAC, box 33, RG 102, ser. 776A, T. LeRoy Collins Papers, Florida State Archives, Tallahassee.

2. Numan V. Bartley, *The Rise of Massive Resistance: Race and Politics in the South during the 1950s* (Baton Rouge, 1969), 241.

3. Theodore R. Gibson to the editor of *Look*, May 21, 1958, Branch III, Florida, NAACP Papers, Library of Congress, Washington, D.C.

4. Bartley, *The Rise of Massive Resistance*, 119, 170–71, 245.

5. Wilson Record, *Race and Radicalism: The NAACP and the Communist Party in Conflict* (Ithaca, N.Y., 1964), 164, 212; Walter F. Murphy, "The South Counterattacks: The Anti-NAACP Laws," *Western Political Quarterly* 12 (1959): 389.

6. American Jewish Congress, Commission on Law and Social Action, *Assault upon Freedom of Association: A Study of the Southern Attack on the National Association for the Advancement of Colored People* (New York, 1957), 19, 21; Harry Kalven, Jr., *The Negro and the First Amendment* (Columbus, Ohio, 1965), 70–71.

7. Collins to Edward O. Davis, July 2, 1956, PUT-RAC, box 33, Collins Papers. See also William C. Havard and Loren P. Beth, *The Politics of Mis-Representation: Rural-Urban Conflict in the Florida Legislature* (Baton Rouge, 1962), 6, 43, 80.

8. Thomas R. Wagy, *Governor LeRoy Collins of Florida: Spokesman of the New South* (University, Ala., 1985), 77, 80, 88 (quotation from 77). See Ben C. Willis to Collins, February 9, 1956, PUT-RAC, box 33, Collins Papers, for views similar to the governor's.

9. *Laws of Florida*, chap. 31498 (1956), 396–97.

10. Bonnie Stark, "McCarthyism in Florida: Charley Johns and the Florida Legislative Investigation Committee, July, 1956 to July, 1965" (master's thesis, University of South Florida, 1985) 13–16. The bill passed thirty-four to one in the Senate and seventy-two to fifteen in the House. *Tampa Tribune*, August 22, 1956, 1; *Florida Times Union*, February 3, 1957, 22.

11. A. J. Musselman, Jr., to LeRoy Collins, July 14, 1956, PUT-RAC, box 33, Collins Papers.

12. Stark, "McCarthyism in Florida," 16; *Tampa Tribune*, August 23, 1956, 24. He did so on the ground that the establishment of the committee was a legislative matter.

13. Robert Saunders to Roy Wilkins, February 27, 1957, and Francisco A. Rodriguez to Jack Greenberg, August 22, 1956, *Gibson v. Florida Legislative Investigation Committee*, Legal Files, NAACP Papers. See also Robert L. Carter to William A. Fordham, June 4, 1956, and Fordham to R. A. Gray, July 19, 1956

(registered), ibid.; Saunders to Wilkins, August 23, 1956, "Reprisals in Florida," Administration II, NAACP Papers; and typewritten report, n.d., n.p., Robert Saunders Papers, University of South Florida, Tampa.

14. *Miami Herald*, September 12, 1956, 20A; *Tampa Tribune*, February 5, 1957, 14B; ibid., February 25, 1957, 12; Havard and Beth, *The Politics of Mis-Representation*, 158; Stark, "McCarthyism in Florida," 18.

15. Press release, February 7, [1957], Ruth Perry Files, in possession of the author; Stark, "McCarthyism in Florida," 22.

16. Florida Legislative Investigation Committee (FLIC), *Transcript of Testimony*, 1957, NAACP Investigation Files, 1957–60, Florida Bar Association Papers, Department of Archives, Tallahassee, Fla., 949.

17. Wilkins to Henry Land, reprinted in ibid., 1612. William Fordham had told the committee in Tallahassee on February 4 that the branch files had been rounded up for safekeeping. Ibid., 71, 121–22. For Perry's and Graves's testimony, see ibid., 1143–77, 1180–86, 1360; and Grattan E. Graves, Jr., to Thurgood Marshall, February 25, 1957, Branch III, Florida, NAACP Papers. One last unsuccessful attempt was made before the close of the hearings to secure the pertinent records from the NAACP's Florida field secretary, Robert W. Saunders. See FLIC, *Transcript*, 1957, 1944–2075.

18. *Tampa Tribune*, February 9, 1957, 6.

19. Ibid., quoting Sen. Dewey Johnson, April 17, 1957, 11. See also Stark, "McCarthyism in Florida," 27–28.

20. A Louisiana legislative committee had reportedly supplied the FLIC with evidence of Communist activities in Florida. *Tampa Tribune*, April 16, 1957, 11. During the Tallahassee and Miami hearings, Charley Johns routinely had asked NAACP officials if they were members of the Communist party. FLIC, *Transcript*, 1957, 668, 1068, 1139, 1161.

21. The governor added that the committee "would bring serious harm if its procedure is changed radically." As he had done a year earlier, Collins allowed the bill to become law without his signature. *Miami Herald*, April 21, 1957, 2; *Tampa Tribune*, May 16, 1957, 14A; Stark, "McCarthyism in Florida," 28.

22. *Laws of Florida*, chap. 57–125 (1957), 204.

23. *Tampa Tribune*, June 1, 1957, 6.

24. Mark R. Hawes to Baya M. Harrison, September 26, 1957, and George W. Atkinson to Harrison, February 13, 1958, box 2, NAACP Investigation Files, Florida Bar Association Papers. Though the lawyers represented individual plaintiffs in these cases, the report found that they actually were paid and supervised by the NAACP, contrary to the code against associational lawyers representing clients in personal matters.

25. Paul B. Comstock to Ralph C. Dell, July 22, 1958, box 2, NAACP Investigation Files, Florida Bar Association Papers. See also Dell to O. B. McEwan, July 31, 1958; Jack A. Abbott, "Report of Unauthorized Practice of Law Committee of the Florida Bar," received May 15, 1959; "Findings and Report

before the Grievance Committee from the Seventh Judicial Circuit Division 'A,' " June 24, 1960; "Alleged Unethical Conduct by Members of the Florida Bar Reported by Legislative Investigation Committee, Report of Seventh Judicial Circuit Grievance Committee 'A,' " November 4, 1960; all in ibid. The bar association did believe that the NAACP as an organization was guilty of the unauthorized practice of law, but the record does not show that formal charges were ever brought.

26. *Miami News,* February 7, 1958, 1C.

27. *Miami Herald,* February 11, 1958, 1A, 2C. For a skeptical assessment of Matthews, see *Tampa Tribune,* February 13, 1958, 14A.

28. *Miami News,* June 18, 1958, clipping, Perry Files.

29. *Miami Herald,* February 27, 1958, 1A; ibid., February 28, 1958, 1A; *Tampa Tribune,* February 27, 1958, 1; ibid., February 28, 1958, 15A. The lawyer was Howard Dixon, who worked with the American Civil Liberties Union (ACLU).

30. Robert W. Saunders to Robert L. Carter, February 13, 1958, *Gibson,* Legal Files, NAACP Papers. See also Saunders to Roy Wilkins, November 19, 1957, "Reprisals in Florida," Administration II; ibid.

31. "Preliminary Statement by Mrs. Ruth Perry to the Florida Legislative Investigation Committee at Miami, Florida, February 26, 1958," Perry Files.

32. Petition for Writ of Certiorari to the Supreme Court of Florida, Brief of Petitioners, Theodore R. Gibson, Ruth Perry, Vernell Albury and Grattan E. Graves, Jr., v. Florida Legislative Investigation Committee, U.S. Supreme Court, October Term, 1958, no. 873, pp. 11–13.

33. Ruth W. Perry, "Along Freedom's Road," *Miami Times,* March 8, 1958, clipping, Perry Files. See also *Miami Herald,* March 1, 1958, 2A; and Ruth W. Perry, interview with author, May 24, 1986, Miami. Perry feared that her defiance of the committee might cost her her job as a Miami Beach librarian. Robert Carter to Perry, March 7, 1958, Perry Files; Perry to Carter, March 2 and April 7, 1958, *Gibson,* Legal Files, NAACP Papers.

34. *Miami Times,* March 1, 1958, 1, clipping, Perry Files.

35. In the Supreme Court of Florida, Edward T. Graham v. Florida Legislative Investigation Committee, Brief of Appellant, May 16, 1958, no. 29,493, p. A-10. See also In Re Petition of Graham, 104 So. 2d 16 (1958); and *Tampa Tribune,* February 22, 1958, 16 (for the position of the ACLU, whose attorneys, Tobias Simon and Howard Dixon, represented Graham).

36. The *Miami Herald,* February 27, 1958, 1A, speculated that the names of suspected Communists came from a Dade County grand jury probe in 1954. See also Stark, "McCarthyism in Florida," 42–43.

37. *Tampa Tribune,* August 2, 1958, 16. The use of the Fifth Amendment during the 1950s was a tactic employed not only by alleged Communists but also by suspected mob figures brought before congressional committees. In

1956 the Florida Bar Association had adopted a resolution condemning law-yers who invoked the Fifth Amendment in refusing to answer questions about Communist activities. "The Proposal Re 'Fifth Amendment Lawyers,' " *Florida Bar Journal* 30 (1956): 318. Though the *Tampa Tribune* distinguished the NAACP from "Fifth Amendment Communists," it condemned the group's "un-warranted display of arrogance against the authority of the State of Florida" and argued that its "hostile tactics generate suspicion." March 1, 1958, 6. One notable dissent came from Jack Bell, a popular *Miami Herald* columnist, who recognized the right of the FLIC to investigate NAACP activities but lambasted it for "drag[ging] out that old 'were you ever a Communist' bromide." "The Town Crier," *Miami Herald,* March 9, 1958, clipping, Perry Files.

38. *St. Petersburg Times,* February 19, 1958, 9A. Perhaps in recognition that the committee was singling out the NAACP for attack, its members voted to launch a probe of the Ku Klux Klan. In doing so, they placed the NAACP in the same camp with "all racial troublemakers," according to the *Florida Times-Union,* March 1, 1958, 20.

39. Watkins v. United States, 354 U.S. 178 (1957); Sweezy v. New Hampshire, 354 U.S. 234 (1957); Pennsylvania v. Nelson, 350 U.S. 497 (1956).

40. NAACP v. Alabama, 357 U.S. 449, 466 (1958). In this instance the court could not find that disclosure of the names of NAACP members was necessary to implement the foreign registration act.

41. In the Supreme Court of Florida, Brief of Appellants, Theodore R. Gib-son, Ruth Perry, Vernell Albury and Grattan E. Graves, Jr. v. Florida Legislative Investigation Committee, September Term, 1958, no. 29, 491, pp. 20, 24 (quotation from 20). See also *Tampa Tribune,* July 3, 1958, 3.

42. Supreme Court of Florida, Brief of Appellants, Gibson et al., 1958, 24, 27, 29. Graves also claimed the attorney-client privilege as a basis for not divulging communications between himself and association members.

43. Supreme Court of Florida, Brief of Appellant, Graham, 1958, 4–5.

44. In the Supreme Court of Florida, Brief of Appellee, Theodore R. Gibson, Ruth Perry, Vernell Albury and Grattan E. Graves, Jr. v. Florida Legislative Investigation Committee, no 29,491, August 25, 1958, 27.

45. Ibid., 34. In June 1958 the committee had conducted hearings of the Ku Klux Klan, but in contrast to its efforts against the NAACP, the panel did not recommend any new measures to restrict the white-supremacist group. Stark, "McCarthyism in Florida," pp. 47–48; "Report of Florida Legislative Investiga-tion Committee to 1959 Session of the Legislature," 19–21, photocopy cour-tesy of Bonnie Stark. At these hearings Sheriff Hugh Lewis of Suwanee County, an admitted member of the Ku Klux Klan, took the Fifth Amendment and refused to testify about his possible involvement in a flogging of a black in 1955. For Collins's cautious reaction to this case, see Collins to Charley Johns,

September 15, 1958; *Tampa Tribune,* September 22, 1958, clipping; and Bill Durden to Bill Killian, February 11, 1959, "Race Relations, 1959–1960"; all in LeRoy Collins Papers, University of South Florida Library, Tampa.

46. Gibson v. Florida Legislative Investigation Committee, 108 So. 2d 737,741 (1958).

47. Ibid., 739–40, 743.

48. Ibid., 744, 745. The suspected Communists, Anna Rosenberg and Bertha Teplow, were represented by Robert Ramer. The court also ruled that the attorney-client privilege invoked by Grattan Graves, Jr., did not enable him to avoid answering questions required of his clients. However, the justices asserted that vaguely drawn questions could not satisfy the pertinency requirement. It was not permissible to ask: "Do you know Bertha Teplow?" Rather, the committee had to state the connection between the person and the subject of the inquiry, in this instance that Teplow was a suspected member of the Communist party. See *Tampa Tribune,* December 23, 1958, 12, for praise of Thornal's decision safeguarding both "the order and security of the state . . . [and] the rank and file of the NAACP membership from a random and potentially capricious committee search."

49. SNS to J. M. Harlan, Bench Memo, "Gibson v. Florida Legislative Investigation Committee," no. 873, May 29, 1959, John Marshall Harlan Papers, Princeton University Library, Princeton, N.J. Robert Carter, the NAACP's attorney, correctly guessed the Court's reasoning. Carter to Vernell Albury, Theodore Gibson, Grattan E. Graves, Jr., and Ruth Perry, June 25, 1959, *Gibson,* Legal Files, NAACP Papers. Three justices, Earl Warren, Hugo Black, and William O. Douglas, one short of those required to grant review, voted to hear the case.

50. Perry to Robert L. Carter, June 23, 1959, *Gibson,* Legal Files, NAACP Papers.

51. FLIC, *Transcript of Testimony,* November 4, 1959, 17–19, photocopy courtesy of Bonnie Stark; "Report of Florida Legislative Investigation Committee to 1959 Session," 12, 16–17.

52. FLIC, *Transcript,* 1959, 40, 46, 50, 117–40.

53. Ibid., 63, 86. See also ibid., 89ff.

54. This distinction drew mixed reviews. The *Pittsburgh Courier,* a black newspaper, suggested that the issue was not really Communism but the destruction of the NAACP, and "once in possession of the membership lists, the Cracker dictatorship would immediately proceed to launch a 'cold war' against every NAACP member." November 14, 1959, 13. In contrast, the *Tampa Tribune* pointed out that had the civil rights leaders cooperated, they could have permitted examination of their records "without revealing the entire membership." November 7, 1959, 10.

55. Florida Legislative Investigation Committee v. Gibson, no. 16821, Cir-

cuit Court, 2d Circuit, Leon County, July 19, 1960, 1. See also Circuit Court, *Transcript of Hearing*, May 1960, 41, 70, 77–78, 81, 90–91, 158; and Mark Hawes, Memo, June 11, 1960, and Howard W. Dixon and Tobias Simon, Memo of Respondent, June 23, 1960, Florida Legislative Investigation Committee v. Graham, no. 16820, Circuit Court, Leon County.

56. FLIC, *Transcript of Hearing*, July 27, 1960, in Florida Legislative Investigation Committee v. Gibson, no. 16821, Circuit Court, 2d Circuit, Leon County; *Tampa Tribune*, August 31, 1960, 16.

57. In the Supreme Court of Florida, Brief for Appellant, Theodore R. Gibson v. Florida Legislative Investigation Committee, September Term, 1960, no. 30,661, p. 29.

58. In the Supreme Court of Florida, Reply Brief of Appellant, Edward T. Graham v. Florida Legislative Investigation Committee, September Term, 1960, no. 30,660, p. 1. See also Supreme Court of Florida, Brief of Appellant, Gibson, 1960, 32; Bates v. Little Rock, 61 U.S. 461 (1960); and Kalven, *The Negro and the First Amendment*, 97.

59. In the Supreme Court of Florida, Brief of Appellee, Theodore R. Gibson v. Florida Legislative Investigation Committee; Edward T. Graham v. Florida Legislative Investigation Committee, September Term, 1960, nos. 30,660, 30,661, pp. 3, 8 (quotation from 3).

60. Gibson v. Florida Legislative Investigation Committee, 26 So. 2d 129, 132, 136 (1960).

61. Wilkins to Harry Belafonte, March 2, 1961, "Reprisals in Florida," Administration II, NAACP Papers.

62. Shelton v. Tucker, 364 U.S. 497 (1960); NAACP v. Louisiana, 366 U.S. 293 (1961); Kalven, *The Negro and the First Amendment*, 74–75, 97–100.

63. Barenblatt v. United States, 360 U.S. 109 (1959); Wilkinson v. United States, 356 U.S. 399 (1961); Braden v. United States, 365 U.S. 431 (1961); Uphaus v. Wyman, 360 U.S. 72 (1959); Robert E. Cushman and Robert F. Cushman, *Cases in Constitutional Law*, 3d ed. (New York, 1968), 121; Paul L. Murphy, *The Constitution in Crisis Times* (New York, 1972), 331–34, 345–46; Anthony Lewis, *New York Times*, December 6, 1961, 28.

64. Petition for Writ of Certiorari to the Supreme Court of Florida, Theodore R. Gibson v. Florida Legislative Investigation Committee, Supreme Court of the United States, October Term, 1960, 21.

65. Brief for Petitioner, Theodore R. Gibson v. Florida Legislative Investigation Committee, Supreme Court of the United States, October Term, 1961, no. 70 (6), p. 20. See also Brief for Petitioner, Gibson, Certiorari, U.S. Supreme Court, 1960, 18–19.

66. Brief for Petitioner, Gibson, U.S. Supreme Court, 1961, 25; Brief for Petitioner, Gibson, Certiorari, U.S. Supreme Court, 1960, 17.

67. Brief of Respondent, Theodore R. Gibson v. Florida, Supreme Court of

the United States, October Term, 1961, no. 70 (6), pp. 4 (quoting Hawes), 18, 20.

68. MHB, Bench Memo, "Gibson v. Florida Legislative Investigation Committee," n.d., 10–11, box 232, Earl Warren Papers, Library of Congress. See also TBD, Bench Memo, "Gibson v. Florida Legislative Investigation Committee," n.d., ibid.; and CF, Bench Memo, "Gibson v. Florida Legislative Investigation Committee," March 5, 1961, Harlan Papers.

69. Draft opinion, *Gibson v. Florida Legislative Investigation Committee*, March 13, 1962, 11, Harlan Papers. Potter Stewart to John Marshall Harlan, March 15, 1962, and notations of Tom Clark, March 14, 1962, and Felix Frankfurter, n.d., can be found in the margins of ibid. Shortly before Frankfurter resigned, the conservatives also had lost Charles Whittaker to retirement. His place was taken, however, by Byron White, who supported their position.

70. Earl Warren, memorandum to Justices Black, Douglas, Clark, Harlan, Brennan, Stewart, and White, April 25, 1962, box 352, Hugo Black Papers, Library of Congress; Anthony Lewis, *New York Times*, March 26, 1963, 1.

71. Gibson v. Florida Legislative Investigation Committee, 372 U.S. 539 (1963) at 548, 555, 557.

72. Ibid., 572. See also William O. Douglas, "The Right of Association," *Columbia Law Review* 63 (1963): 1378–79.

73. Gibson v. Florida Legislative Investigation Committee, 372 U.S. at 579, 580. White also dissented because the "net effect of the Court's decision is . . . to insulate from effective legislative inquiry and preventive legislation the time-proven skills of the Communist Party in subverting and eventually controlling legitimate organization." Ibid., 585. See also Kalven, *The Negro and the First Amendment*, 113.

74. Kalven, *The Negro and the First Amendment*, 116; "The Supreme Court 1962 Term," *Harvard Law Review* 77 (1963): 120; Gerald F. Richman, "Constitutional Law: Associational Privacy Afforded to Legitimate Organizations notwithstanding Subversive Infiltration," *University of Florida Law Review* 16 (1963): 496–97; Cushman and Cushman, *Cases*, 122.

75. "The Supreme Court 1962," 122. See also Kalven, The *Negro and the First Amendment*, 119; and Anthony Lewis, *New York Times*, March 26, 1963, 1, and June 23, 1963, 64.

76. FLIC, *Report*, 1961, photocopy courtesy of Bonnie Stark; Stark, "McCarthyism in Florida," 77–78. The focus of the hearings was on Carl Braden, a leader of the Southern Conference, who had been cited for contempt by HUAC and whose conviction was upheld by the U.S. Supreme Court. Despite the FLIC's assumption, the NAACP had tried to steer clear of Braden and his group. Robert W. Saunders to Ruby Hurley, November 30, 1959, Saunders Papers.

77. *Miami Herald*, March 27, 1963, 6A; *Miami News*, March 27, 1963, 16A.

See the *Tampa Tribune*, March 27, 1963, 6B, for a slightly different view. Several years earlier, the FLIC had shifted its attention toward hunting for subversives and homosexuals on the campuses of the University of Florida and the University of South Florida. These probes generated a good deal of political animosity and negative publicity. See Stark, "McCarthyism in Florida," chaps. 3 and 4.

78. Ruth W. Perry to Roy Wilkins, October 31, 1958, Branch III, Florida; Perry to Robert Carter, June 23, 1959, *Gibson*, Legal Files; Lucille Black to Theodore R. Gibson, June 7, 1960, Branch III, Florida; all in NAACP Papers.

79. Ruth Perry, "Along Freedom's Road," *Miami Times*, April, 11, 1959, clipping, Perry Files. See also Perry interview; and Robert W. Saunders, interview with author, September 9, 1986, Tampa, Fla. The figures on membership in Florida were not published separately but were included along with the totals for Georgia, Mississippi, North Carolina, South Carolina, Tennessee, and, until 1957, Alabama. The aggregate figures for this region were 52,365 in 1955; 44,447 in 1956; 26,775 in 1957; 30,245 in 1958; 37,273 in 1959; 44,842 in 1960; 45,077 in 1961; 49,597 in 1962; and 57,450 in 1963. See NAACP, *Annual Report*, 1955–63. The impressionistic evidence suggests that Florida enrollments did not improve until the early 1960s. Robert W. Saunders to Robert Carter, December 7, 1959, Saunders Papers. For promotion of the *Gibson* suit, see Roy Wilkins to Harry Belafonte, March 2, 1961, "Reprisals in Florida," Administration II; Robert L. Carter to Wilkins and Henry Lee Moon, August 31, 1960, "Reprisals in Florida," Administration II; Jesse DeVore to editors, columnists, and writers, January 4, 1961, "Reprisals in Florida," Administration II; Otis D. James and George A. Simpson to Gloster B. Current, March 9, 1961, Branch III, Florida; and Current to Theodore R. Gibson, June 15, 1961, Branch III, Florida; all in NAACP Papers.

80. On the ranking of Florida in qualities of southernness, see Hugh D. Price, *The Negro and Southern Politics: A Chapter in Florida History* (New York, 1957), 8–9.

81. Saunders interview. By targeting the NAACP for harassment, southern white segregationists inadvertently may have strengthened its image among many blacks as the leading organization fighting for racial equality. See Adam Fairclough, *"To Redeem the Soul of America": The Southern Christian Leadership Conference and Martin Luther King, Jr.* (Athens, Ga., 1987), 22–23. On the negative side, some NAACP leaders undermined their more radical civil rights competitors by cooperating with the FBI to provide a source of inside information that could be used against them. David Colburn, *Racial Change and Community Crisis: St. Augustine, Florida, 1877–1980* (New York, 1985), 85.

82. Gibson v. Florida Legislative Investigation Committee, 372 U.S. at 544, quoting Bates v. Little Rock.

325

Florida's Governors Confront the Brown Decision: A Case Study of the Constitutional Politics of School Desegregation, 1954–1970

David R. Colburn

O n May 17, 1954, Florida faced a challenge to its social and legal traditions unlike any encountered since the Civil War. In *Brown v. Board of Education*, the Supreme Court overturned the southern school practice of racial segregation. In their shock and confusion over the decision, state leaders responded cautiously, but they also made clear the South's position. Although Senator Spessard Holland said that he hoped the decision would be met with "patience and moderation" and that there would not be any "violent repercussions," Governor James Byrnes of South Carolina and others announced that they intended to block white and black students from mixing in southern schools. As if to make this position unambiguous, several school districts that had begun construction on additional segregated schools continued with these projects after consulting with political leaders.[1]

President Dwight D. Eisenhower encouraged southern intransigence by privately criticizing the decision. Although he ordered the desegregation of public schools in the nation's capital, he refrained from taking further steps. As he told his aides, "I personally think that the decision was wrong." He later added, "It is all very well to talk about school desegregation—if you remember that you may also be talking about social disintegration."[2]

Black Americans cheered the *Brown* decision and saw it as a bench mark in their historic march toward equality. During the heady days that followed the Court's pronouncement, Thurgood Marshall remarked that "the most gratifying thing, in addition to the fact that we won, is the unanimous decision and the language used. Once for all, it's decided, and completely decided." Black journalist Louis Lomax wrote more personally, "It would be impossible for a white person to understand what happened within black breasts on that Monday . . . we took the white man's laws and won our case before an all-white Supreme Court with a negro lawyer, . . . and we were proud."[3]

The path toward desegregated schools had been a particularly difficult one for blacks in Florida, and despite Marshall's hopes, it would take more than the *Brown* decision to achieve integration. Certainly part of the difficulty was the historic legal commitment to segregation. Like most southern states, Florida had constitutional provisions requiring school segregation. Not only were white and black students forbidden from being "taught in the same school," but the Florida Constitution of 1885 also made it a penal offense "for any individual, corporation or association" to permit such educational practices. Thirty years after the adoption of the constitution, the Florida legislature took steps to prevent any cracks from developing in the segregated system by banning whites from teaching in black schools and black teachers from white schools.[4]

Despite the persistence of racial inequities throughout the first half of the twentieth century, conditions did improve for black schoolchildren in the post–World War II period and for blacks generally. These changes resulted in large measure from a series of Supreme Court decisions that sought to restore meaning to the principle of separate but equal. Florida responded to this mandate in 1947 with the Minimum Foundations Program, which gradually increased expenditures for black schools so that they virtually equaled those for white schools by 1954. Salaries for black and white teachers were also equalized, and the school year was made standard at 180 days.[5]

In addition to the racial advances being forced upon Florida by the federal courts, changes occurred under the guise of economic development and population growth. Florida had suffered tremendously during the depression, and the prospect of new industry and a large consumer base had widespread appeal. Under the direction of the governor's office, the state conducted a vigorous advertising campaign that saw two million people, principally from the Northeast and Midwest, move into Florida between 1940 and 1960.[6]

Floridians did not believe that such changes portended ill for the state. As Ralph McGill, editor of the *Atlanta Constitution*, described the process in regional terms, southern leaders "never saw themselves as carriers of the virus which was to destroy the *status quo*—all the while laboring to bring new industries and payrolls which could only accelerate the changes." Reflecting on the broad-based consequences of these developments, two economists asserted that "production patterns are thoroughly entwined with habits of consumption, attitudes toward work, family patterns, religious values, and the distribution of power. To change one of these requires attention to the ways in which it is tied to all the others."[7] Whether such changes were inextricably linked remains doubtful, but these developments, in concert with others, would influence Florida in profound ways after 1950, helping to alter in the process the status quo and the state's racial traditions.

The state's mild response to the *Brown* decision was closely tied to the social and economic changes that had been under way since the 1940s. The substantial increase in the size of the white population through immigration had reduced the black population to less than 22 percent, the smallest in the state's history and down from 43.7 percent at the turn of the century. As V. O. Key, Jr., pointed out in 1949, there was a close correlation between the size of the black population and a state's penchant for racial extremism.[8] Moreover, the new residents of Florida had little commitment to the state's racial heritage, and they settled in communities (with the exception of Miami) where there were relatively few blacks. The state's heavy dependence on tourism (nearly five million visitors spent one billion dollars in 1954) also discouraged extremism.[9] Tourists were not likely to spend their vacation dollars in communities racked by social unrest.

But this is not to say that the *Brown* decision had little impact on the state. Because Florida was one of only four southern states with no public school integration in the spring of 1954, the decision had grave implications for the state's traditional pattern of public education.[10]

It was the significance of *Brown*, in fact, and the conflict it posed for Florida's racial traditions and constitutional norms, that would thrust the issue into the political arena. In the view of Floridians and southerners generally, the Supreme Court had entered into an area that was fundamental to their society, and it had done so through questionable legal reasoning. Despite the constitutional mandate, they would not readily accept such a change without resorting to political protest. The Court and the Constitution would thus be pushed into the political arena in ways unseen since the antebellum period, and numerous political obstacles would block state compliance with the *Brown* decision.[11]

The first *Brown* decision was issued in the midst of a special Democratic primary to replace the recently deceased governor, Dan McCarty. The two leading opponents, Charley Johns, acting governor for a year and a half, and LeRoy Collins, state senator from Leon County, announced their support for school segregation and then let the matter drop. Both men seemed unsure of the impact of the decision on the campaign and opted instead to concentrate on issues raised in their respective platform.[12]

During Collins's campaign against Johns, he emphasized his business progressivism and his commitment to economic development and educational improvement. Collins actively campaigned downstate, where political scientist H. D. Price identified several hundred thousand new voters who were "relatively unconcerned about the Negro, but very much concerned about continued economic development, further population growth, and more rapid development of industry." Collins's appeal to business progressivism had deep roots in "the 'New South' creed of economic development." Defeating Johns rather easily in the spring primary, Collins captured the general election against a weak Republican opponent in the fall.[13]

Upon assuming office, Collins sought to pursue the political agenda outlined in his platform but quickly found his administration engulfed in the desegregation issue. In the wake of the *Brown* decision, the Supreme Court had invited those southern states that were not part of the original decision to respond to its implications for public education in their communities. Florida joined five other states in accepting the invitation, with Acting Governor Johns endorsing an expenditure of ten thousand dollars for a poll to determine the attitudes of Floridians toward desegregation.[14]

In *Simple Justice,* Richard Kluger wrote that Florida "submitted the most extensive and spirited brief," which pursued a "community attitudes" argument. Prepared by Attorney General Richard Ervin, the brief contended that the only hope to end segregated schooling in Florida without destroying public education was for "the Court to restrain the use of coercive measures where necessary until the hard core of public opinion had softened." Referring to the state's sixty-nine years of segregation and the results of the poll, which showed that 75 percent of all Floridians opposed *Brown*, Ervin warned that a dramatic rush toward integration "would devastate the entire school system." Despite a plea from the National Association for the Advancement of Colored People (NAACP) that there was no evidence to suggest that delay would minimize the unpleasant consequences, the Court seemed to accept the arguments of Florida and the other southern states, deciding against immediate implementation of desegregation and referring the matter to the district courts.[15]

Although Collins had promised voters that he would use all of his lawful powers to maintain a segregated school system, he was reluctant to pursue an extremist position. His platform had emphasized economic growth and educational enhancement, and he knew these developments would not occur in the midst of a racial crisis. How to respond to the public concerns about the implications of *Brown* and yet preserve order and civility so that industrial recruitment efforts and tourism would not be jeopardized was the dilemma that faced Collins. He was additionally confronted with a legislature that was badly apportioned and dominated by rural and black-belt representatives who called for a full-scale resistance to the Court's decision.[16] Finally, he faced reelection in 1956 because he was merely filling the last two years of McCarty's term.

Collins felt additional political pressure from southern congressmen who on March 12, 1956, signed the "Southern Manifesto," which denounced the 1954 *Brown* decision as a "clear abuse" of judicial authority with "no legal basis." This unprecedented criticism of the Supreme Court by southern political leaders strengthened the hand of the massive resisters and made it exceedingly difficult for southern governors to pursue a policy of moderation.[17]

To say that Collins proceeded cautiously would be an understatement, but in the process he laid the foundation for what would be Florida's approach to school desegregation for the next fifteen years. His response to the issue unfolded initially in two distinct but not unrelated ways in March 1956. The first step evolved in reaction to the U.S. Supreme Court's order that Virgil D. Hawkins, a black man, be admitted to the University of Florida's College of Law after a seven-year legal battle in which Hawkins had been repeatedly rebuffed by the state courts. In a statewide radio broadcast that same day, Collins attempted to reassure Floridians that the state was "just as determined as any Southern state to maintain segregation" and that he would personally appear before the Supreme Court to defend the state's position.[18] By offering this personal commitment, Collins sought to maintain control of the desegregation issue rather than allow it to fall into the hands of his rivals for the Democratic gubernatorial nomination. With the primary already under way, Collins faced three rivals who denounced the Supreme Court's decision and offered a variety of proposals to preserve segregation.[19]

The second step reflected Collins's desire to develop strategies to curb desegregation. At an emergency cabinet meeting, he persuaded state officials to call a conference of political and educational leaders to assess the implications of the *Brown* and *Hawkins* decisions. The meeting took place in Tallahassee on March 21 and led to the adoption of four proposals, of which the second—the creation of a committee of lawyers and judges appointed by Collins and Attorney General Ervin to identify ways to preserve segregation—became the centerpiece of Collins's response to school desegregation.[20]

In seeking an approach that would ease the concerns of Floridians and that would avoid extremism, Collins examined the policies of other southern governors, especially those of Luther Hodges, whose ambitious economic-development program in North Carolina paralleled his own. Hodges had appointed a special Advisory Committee on Education (also known as the Piersall Commission after its chairman, Thomas Piersall) in 1955 to address the problems posed by the *Brown* decision. Although the recommendations of the Piersall Commission calmed fears of white North Carolinians and gave the appearance of pursuing a responsible approach to the Court's verdict, the historian William Chafe has described the proposals as "a clear effort to circumvent" *Brown*.[21]

Following Hodges' approach, Collins appointed a seven-member committee, chaired by former circuit court judge L. L. Fabisinski, and charged it with devising a plan the state could use to obtain a Supreme Court review in the *Hawkins* case, developing an effective legal strategy that would preserve "the continuation of segregation in our schools," and establishing guidelines to prevent further deterioration in race relations. In summary, the governor wanted plans that would preserve segregation as well as peace and stability for his economic program. The similarity of the Fabisinski Committee to the Piersall Commission in North Carolina was unmistakable.[22]

Collins's response to the *Hawkins* decision and the convening of a statewide conference on education launched his campaign to retain the Democratic gubernatorial nomination. With racial concerns increasingly dominating southern and Florida politics in the wake of the second *Brown* decision, Collins used the *Hawkins* case to strengthen his reputation as a segregationist in order to deflect criticism from his more extreme opponents, especially Sumter Lowry. Running on a platform that labeled the *Brown* verdict part of an "international Communist conspiracy," Lowry set the tone for the entire gubernatorial campaign, which one reporter characterized as "rolling along like a segregation surrey with a lunatic fringe on top." Collins attempted to link racial stability to increases in investment and tourism, but pressed by his opponents, he found it necessary to promise that "if there is any lawful way, . . . I will maintain segregation."[23]

With very strong support from south Florida, Collins defeated his three opponents without the need for a runoff, and many hailed his victory as a triumph for moderation. But Collins's campaign was moderate only when compared to the racial extremism of his three opponents, and the election results disclosed that the governor's views enjoyed support only in the eighteen south Florida counties and in Leon County, his home. In thirty-four northern, mostly rural, counties, Collins received less than 35 percent of the vote. He was, however, the preferred candidate among black voters, who gave him a ten to one majority because of his relative moderation and his commutation of Walter Irvin's death sentence in Florida's little Scottsboro case.[24]

The election results persuaded Collins that he was pursuing the right course and that he had constructed an effective coalition of urban, mostly southern, white and black voters who supported racial moderation and economic development. He had to move cautiously, however, because the legislature was heavily dominated by rural, black-belt representatives. Despite their predominance in legislative matters, Collins was determined to set the agenda and the parameters of the school-desegregation debate. To achieve this goal, he was dependent on the Fabisinski Committee.

The committee submitted its report to Collins in early July, and its recommendations formed the basis for a special session Collins called on July 20. Proposing a four-point program, the committee report placed special emphasis on the enactment of a pupil-placement law that the members modeled after an Alabama statute. This measure was designed to replace the Student Assignment law adopted in 1955 with a far more complex set of procedures. As Richard Bardolph has written, these laws seemed "eminently reasonable on their face," if somewhat detailed, and yet they "were devastatingly effective as deterrents to integration." In reflecting on this classification system, J. Lewis Hall, a member of the Fabisinski Committee, observed that when educational criteria were combined with residence and moral, cultural, and ethical background, "we may find that the overlapping of white and negro children of equal qualifications will be reduced to a comparatively small percent."[25]

In forwarding the committee's recommendations to Collins, John T. Wigginton, a member of the committee, wrote that "we could not have written such a report, however, without stating very frankly that our sole effort and intention was to devise ways and means of preventing or slowing down the integration of our public schools in order to circumvent the Supreme Court's decision in *Brown v. Topeka.*" Wigginton added that the committee did not think that this purpose should be stated, because the federal court would strike down the legislation proposed by the committee as "a subterfuge to circumvent the Supreme Court's mandate."[26]

In presenting these measures to a special session of the legislature, Collins informed leaders of the house and senate that he would not consider any other proposals on school desegregation. Once the session convened, however, he quickly lost control of the agenda. Legislators from Florida's black belt introduced motions to close state schools if the courts ordered them desegregated and to nullify the *Brown* decision through an interposition resolution. The Fabisinski proposals were passed by both houses, but debate continued over the new proposals. Confronted by a rejection of his more limited approach, Collins resorted to a little-known state constitutional provision that empowered the governor to adjourn a special session when both houses disagreed about the adjournment hour.[27]

In the aftermath of the special session, Collins's policy of moderation faced pressures from two directions. Rural legislators called his action "a low blow" and promised a different outcome in the 1957 legislative session.[28] Also expressing dissatisfaction with Collins's leadership was the NAACP, which denounced the new Pupil Placement Law as the state's way of preserving segregation. Working with black parents, the NAACP persuaded several families to petition the local board of public instruction for admission to white schools. Two school-desegregation suits were filed in Dade County and Palm Beach County when the school boards rejected the reassignment requests.[29]

Collins and his advisers realized that the suits posed a serious threat to the state. He and Attorney General Ervin agreed that the federal courts might well overturn the Pupil Placement Law if it did not provide for some desegregation. But racial concerns among white Floridians ran so strong in 1956 that neither thought raising the issue at the moment would benefit the governor's policies or his legislative program. Collins opted to have his aides follow the progress of the *Shuttlesworth* case in Alabama, which challenged that state's Pupil Placement Law.[30] If the courts overturned Alabama's law, then Florida would review its legislation. But for the time being it would wait.

The governor's efforts to keep Florida from drifting toward extremism faced a particularly difficult time in 1957. In the autumn of that year, Governor Orval Faubus of Arkansas mobilized the state guard to block the desegregation of Central High School. In the ensuing confrontation among Faubus, the federal courts, and the Eisenhower administration, many southerners and Floridians expressed support for Faubus, especially after Eisenhower mobilized federal troops to protect the black students.[31]

In the midst of the crisis, the southern governors met at Sea Island, Georgia, where Collins was scheduled to give a luncheon address entitled "Can a Southerner Be Elected President?" Restating views he had expressed earlier, in his second inaugural address, Collins argued that any serious southern presidential candidate would have to seek "racial harmony and progress" within the context of regional economic prosperity. To wrap itself in a "confederate blanket" would be disastrous for the South, Collins warned, and would stymie the substantial economic development the region had enjoyed since World War II.[32]

Collins's moderate views gained widespread national publicity, and the positive response to his address helped strengthen his position in Florida. Although he received criticism from several advocates of segregation, legislative leaders from south Florida and newspaper editors generally praised his judicious comments. Most Floridians seemed impressed and pleased with the favorable reaction nationally, and this perception would make it difficult for political opponents to overturn Collins's leadership.[33]

The national attention that Collins received quickly faded, however, when he returned to Tallahassee, and developments there pointed out the difficulties faced by a southern moderate who sought to construct a moderate course between the requirements of federal law and the practical realities of state politics. Before the Southern Governors' Conference, Collins had called a special legislative session to consider reapportionment, but the meeting lapsed into a debate over segregation. Angered by events in Little Rock, representatives of the black belt and their allies proposed a bill to close the public schools in Florida if federal troops were ever deployed to enforce desegregation in the state and also a bill to use state funds to establish private schools. Much of the discussion centered on Collins's speech to the conference. In an often-heated series of debates, rural leaders denounced Collins for doing "considerable harm" to Florida's effort to preserve segregation. Urban leaders and south Florida representatives, however, praised him for having "done more than any other man in public office to preserve peace." In a vote that at times seemed to be a referendum on Collins's leadership, both measures were defeated.[34]

Aiding Collins in his effort to carve out a middle ground between the extremes of Little Rock and integration was the U.S. Supreme Court, which, in a startling development during the special session, decided not to order the admission of Virgil Hawkins. Although the Court's decision seemed inconsistent with the *Brown* verdict and incongruous in light of the state's refusal to carry out the previous decisions in the *Hawkins* case, the Supreme Court justices apparently decided to engage in a bit of constitutional politics to ease racial tensions in the wake of the Little Rock crisis. It is also conceivable that the Court saw a chance to encourage Collins's moderate leadership in the South. Whatever the reasoning of the justices, Collins praised the Court for its "conciliatory and understanding position," and he also emphasized to Floridians that the state's desire to work within a legal framework had facilitated this victory.[35]

The year 1957 proved to be a critical one for Florida and the moderate leadership of LeRoy Collins. Despite the social and demographic changes of the 1940s and 1950s, Florida had not pursued a policy that distanced itself on racial matters from its Deep South neighbors. Moreover, although the tremendous population growth suggested that the state was in the process of changing, the new residents had yet to assume a position on race that differed markedly from the prevailing attitudes of native Floridians. Certainly they did not support extremism, but neither

335

were they advocates of school desegregation. Collins's leadership proved critical in providing southern and urban Floridians with an opportunity to give expression to a more reasonable course of action.

Without the support of this large and growing constituency and without the Court's decision in the *Hawkins* case, it is unlikely that Collins could have stayed this course in 1957. During the regular legislative session and the special session in that year, members bombarded their colleagues with a maze of racially inspired proposals, including an interposition resolution, an anti-NAACP package, a last-resort bill that would permit schools to close under a local option to avoid court-ordered desegregation, and a measure to provide state support for private schools. The struggle between Collins and the extremists in the legislature was an extremely difficult one, and although Collins and his allies defeated the last-resort proposal, the NAACP package, and the private school bill, his legislative leaders accepted a compromise proposal that would close public schools when federal troops were deployed (this same measure had been defeated in the 1957 special session) and the interposition resolution. It was a delicate balancing act for Collins throughout the session, and though he allowed certain compromises to occur, he did not commit himself to them. Thus when the legislature adjourned, the governor vetoed the measure that would close schools, stating that "the permissive authority we now have is adequate," and he denounced the interposition resolution as "a fraud" and a measure that "stultifies our state."[36]

Historian Jerrell Shofner has called the interposition resolution "a last-ditch effort to justify the system [of segregation] in terms of state sovereignty along lines enunciated by John C. Calhoun more than a century earlier." This measure and the last-resort school bill marked the high point of Florida's resistance, and the failure of each also represented the collapse of this approach in Florida.[37]

The Collins approach benefited substantially from the collapse of Arkansas's economy in the wake of the Little Rock crisis and the achievements of North Carolina's economy under the moderate leadership of Luther Hodges. Mounting evidence revealed that in closing schools a state courted disaster. According to the industrial development director of Little Rock, Arkansas, "the city had averaged five major new plants per year from 1950 to 1957." In the aftermath of the school crisis, however, the city had failed to add any new companies in four years.[38]

Throughout his last four years in office, Collins repeatedly linked school stability with economic growth. He made frequent reference to developments in Arkansas and in Virginia following the closing of the public schools in Prince Edward County. Rejecting the extremist actions of these and other southern states, Collins tried to focus Florida's attention on the policies and consequences of Luther Hodges' leadership in North Carolina. In several talks, he noted that North Carolina had attracted over 300 million dollars in new investments and twenty-one thousand additional jobs, as opposed to Arkansas and Virginia, which were virtually stagnant because of racial extremism.[39]

The widespread interest in continued economic investment in Florida and Collins's educational campaign produced some results in the state near the end of 1957. In December the Florida Congress of Parents and Teachers met in Orlando and decided to remove all reference to segregation from its policy statement, despite considerable pressure from the White Citizens' Council.[40]

With the state legislature in session only every other year during this period, Collins used the off year in 1958 to build upon "a climate of tolerance" and to begin laying plans for token school desegregation in 1959 to ensure the constitutionality of the Pupil Placement Law. The state received a temporary reprieve from the threat posed by a legal appeal of its law when the Fifth Circuit Court of Appeals ruled in 1958, in *Shuttlesworth v. Alabama*, that the placement statute upon which Florida's was modeled was legal. The court noted, however, that although the law was not on its face unconstitutional, the state would have to demonstrate that desegregation could be accomplished under the act's guidelines.[41]

Relying on the advice of the Fabisinski Committee, the Collins administration developed plans to desegregate the state university system initially. In early discussions, the committee proposed to desegregate the University of Florida and Florida State University simultaneously so that parents could not transfer their children from one school to the other. The members also commissioned a survey to determine faculty, student, parent, and alumni attitudes. On the basis of the survey, members decided to desegregate at the graduate level so that housing would not be a problem, and only at the University of Florida, since Florida State University had only recently become coeducational and it was feared that desegregating a predominantly women's college would cause undue public alarm.[42] George Starke, a married Air Force veteran from Orlando, was selected by the committee and the university as an ideal candidate, and he entered the College of Law in the fall of 1958. In contrast to school desegregation at the University of Alabama and the University of Mississippi, desegregation at the University of Florida occurred without fanfare and without violence.[43] Careful planning and a well-orchestrated media campaign ensured a peaceful process.

Although Collins frequently asserted that the desegregation of elementary and secondary schools was a local matter, he and the Fabisinski Committee worked quietly with school board officials to ensure compliance with the Pupil Placement Law. As it had done with the desegregation of the University of Florida, the administration planned its approach carefully and moved forward only when it was certain that events could be controlled. In 1958 Collins and Judge Fabisinski began to hint to the public that Florida "must be prepared to accept more desegregation." On October 20, Assistant Attorney General Ralph Odum, the cabinet's expert on racial litigation, warned Floridians that despite the *Shuttlesworth* decision, the state's Pupil Placement Law would be overturned if all the public schools remained segregated.[44]

During 1958, members of the Fabisinski Committee talked with Dade County school board officials to see if they would be receptive to desegregation in light of the *Gibson* case, which had been filed in 1956[45] and came before the Fifth Circuit Court on appeal in 1958. School leaders in Dade seemed generally interested in seeking a limited response, but they were reluctant to have theirs be the only county to act. In December Collins invited school officials from Dade, Broward, Palm Beach, Hillsborough, and Pinellas counties to a private meeting to discuss desegregation. After the meeting, he told reporters that it had been arranged by the Fabisinski Committee but that no agreements had been reached. It does appear, however, that Dade officials decided at this meeting to begin preparations to desegregate an elementary school in the fall of 1959 and that Collins agreed to provide financial and legal assistance from the state to facilitate the process.[46]

In February 1959 Dade County school board members voted unanimously to admit four black children to Orchard Villa Elementary School, although the issue had not appeared on the board's agenda published before the meeting. Orchard Villa had been recognized as a problem for school officials because it was located in a neighborhood that had become increasingly black, so that officials had had to employ arbitrary criteria to exclude black children from the school.[47]

The desegregation of Orchard Villa was something of a sham from the beginning, however. Changing residential patterns made it apparent that the school would have become black in the near future. Most whites in the area seemed to recognize the transition and either had already moved or had their homes for sale. When the school opened in the fall, four black children arrived and found that they had only eight white schoolmates. By October only nine whites had reported to Orchard Villa, when school officials decided to increase the number of black students. At the end of the year, 450 black students attended Orchard Villa with only five white students.[48]

Despite the best efforts of the Collins administration, however, the Fifth Circuit Court of Appeals was not fooled by developments in Miami. In January 1960 the court ruled in *Gibson v. Board of Public Instruction of Dade County, Florida,* that the admission of a few blacks under the Pupil Placement Law as a "token" of compliance was not sufficient. The Court ordered Dade officials to submit a plan for desegregation or face an order ending all racial restrictions in its schools.[49]

Despite this setback, Collins's response to the *Brown* decision proved very effective in easing the state through the tumultuous 1950s while still maintaining a segregated school system. Like Luther Hodges in North Carolina, Collins was widely viewed as a moderate and enlightened governor who had found a peaceful way to handle school desegregation. The irony, of course, was that despite Collins's reputation, Florida experienced very little desegregation during his six years in office. Indeed, the state ranked below every other state in the South except Alabama, Mississippi, and South Carolina in the level of school desegregation.

In the aftermath of the Collins era, questions still remained about the state's intention of meeting the requirements of *Brown*. Although Collins had set the state on a particular course, his successor would be free to influence school-desegregation patterns significantly, because so little had been accomplished during the Collins years.

The 1960 Democratic gubernatorial primary offered Florida voters what appeared to be a clear-cut choice between the policies of Governor Collins and those of his opponents. Of the two leading candidates, Doyle Carlton, Jr., had actively supported Collins's leadership as a state senator, whereas Farris Bryant had opposed Collins in the 1956 race and cosponsored the interposition resolution. In an extraordinary development, Collins broke with state tradition and endorsed Carlton, characterizing Bryant's campaign as one of "reaction, retreat and regret" that would set the state back ten years.[50]

Despite the governor's efforts, Bryant captured the nomination by nearly a hundred thousand votes and entered office as a "staunch segregationist." His rhetoric was misleading, however, and it quickly became apparent that Bryant identified his governorship with the state's economic interests. Although he may have wished to keep the schools segregated, he was not prepared to jeopardize business prospects by challenging the federal courts or the federal government. As a student of Bryant's administration has observed, the governor's "approach to the race issue was highly legalistic; that is, he spoke as a states' rights conservative and a segregationist, but he did not indulge in rabble-rousing or impress people as a man likely to condone violence."[51]

Although Bryant decided not to reappoint Collins's biracial advisory committee, he did retain Assistant Attorney General Ralph Odum as his principal adviser on school desegregation. Odum's office had coordinated the legal efforts of the Collins administration, and it would continue to do so under Bryant and his successor, Haydon Burns.[52] Thus, despite the change in gubernatorial leadership between 1954 and 1965, Florida's approach to school desegregation was remarkably consistent because of the crucial role played by Odum and his staff.

Bryant's unwillingness to halt the desegregation process was, as already indicated, heavily influenced by his program to create a favorable climate for business. He told the state chamber of commerce, "My job and that of your government is to create conditions under which you can prosper and at the same time contribute to the improvement of our citizens." He also viewed education as essential to that development: as his chief aide reported, Bryant recognized "an interdependency of Florida's economy and Florida's educational system."[53]

In several respects, Bryant's response to the school-desegregation process was as important as that of LeRoy Collins. Though Collins governed during the most critical period, Bryant had the opportunity to disrupt desegregation and to challenge the federal court decisions in the fashion of George Wallace in Alabama or Lester Maddox in Georgia. Bryant's segregationist platform also had the backing of rural and black-belt legislators who still dominated the halls of the state legislature. However, Bryant chose to function within the law and to accept Collins's view that the schools were a local, not a state, matter.[54] In doing so, he established a precedent by which even the segregationist governors accepted the gradual desegregation of the state's school system and which effectively removed the governor from the process. This precedent was particularly important in the sixties, for each of the governors during this period espoused views very similar to those of Bryant. Thus, whereas Collins laid the foundation for Florida's moderate approach to desegregation, Bryant established the parameters of acceptable action within which Floridians came to expect their governors to act.

If Bryant and his successors, Haydon Burns and Claude Kirk, were tempted to respond in a more extreme fashion, however, increasingly active federal courts stood prepared to challenge them. Between 1959 and 1962 the courts ruled that school boards in Florida had to devise plans to "eliminate . . . discrimination because of color." In 1962 the federal district court in Jacksonville added in *Braxton v. Duval County School Board* that school officials could not assign teachers to schools by race. Moreover, Judge Bryan Simpson ordered the board not to approve any budgets, accept construction programs, allocate funds, or rectify policies that were designed to maintain racially segregated schools.[55]

The attitude of the federal bench was no doubt influenced by the 1963 report of the Florida Advisory Committee to the U.S. Commission on Civil Rights, which charged that "the education and training provided for the Florida Negro is markedly inferior to that provided for his white counterpart." The authors of the report referred to an inadequate educational system for blacks and a persistent effort by state leaders to circumvent the *Brown* decision in order to perpetuate segregation.[56]

In the aftermath of the report, the courts increased pressure on the governor's office and school officials to expand the desegregation process. In 1963 the federal court ordered Escambia County to submit a grade-a-year plan commencing in the fall of 1963 and continuing in successive years until all schools had white and black students.[57] Although the courts were accelerating the pace and extent of desegregation, it was clear that some school systems would not be fully desegregated until well into the 1970s or perhaps the 1980s unless something more dramatic was done.

In July 1964 President Lyndon Johnson signed the civil rights bill into law, and although the new act contained two major provisions that dealt with the desegregation of public schools (title IV) and financial assistance for federal programs (title VI), it was not immediately clear that the act would dramatically affect public schools. Southerners were concerned, however, because regional schools received 200 million dollars in federal aid and the elementary and secondary education bill, which became law in 1965, promised another half billion dollars, thus making the region increasingly dependent on federal support and subject to federal regulations. Although Lino Graglia has contended that the debate in the U.S. Senate over the act suggested that racial balance would not be necessary to receive federal aid, the wording of the law left room for interpretation, and the Johnson administration seized on title VI especially to accelerate the desegregation process.[58]

In January 1965 the newly inaugurated governor, Haydon Burns, sent representatives of his administration to Washington to meet with members of the Department of Education and discuss the implications of the Civil Rights Act. Vernon Sikes, the governor's administrative assistant, and Ralph Odum, still serving as assistant attorney general for civil rights affairs, led a five-man team and were joined by representatives from the other southern states for the briefings. Sikes reported to Burns that he and the others were certain that "enforcement of the Civil Rights Act by the Government is going to be immediate and all-inclusive." Federal officials in Washington made it clear, he observed, that "from now on any federal program must be in a position where it can publicly state in writing that it is now and will remain in full and complete compliance with the nondiscrimination requirements of Title VI." He and others on the team advised Burns "that the Cabinet might well consider taking steps which will facilitate an orderly process of transition for those state agencies not now in compliance with the Civil Rights Act."[59]

Although Burns had been an outspoken critic of the desegregation process, he and his aides realized that the state could not operate the public school system without a continuation of federal aid. Moreover, Floridians had consistently supported Collins's efforts to keep the schools open in the 1950s, and they stood more firmly against such closings in the 1960s after watching the debacle in Prince Edward County, Virginia. Floridians also opposed a reduction in public school funding because most believed that the school system was already underfunded. With few political options, the Burns administration moved to comply with the new federal guidelines, applying for federal financial assistance to help in the process.[60]

Not only did the federal government exert pressure on Florida to desegregate, but the black community also expressed its own frustration with the delays. Sikes noted in his report to Burns that representatives of the NAACP and other civil rights organizations sat in on all the meetings and made it clear that they would closely check the state for compliance. "This will not be an easy transition," Sikes wrote, "for it appears many complaints will be filed the moment any agency submits assurance of compliance under Title VI."[61]

The most dramatic evidence of black dissatisfaction with the desegregation process occurred in Jacksonville in December of 1964, when blacks boycotted the public schools. Black leaders and parents had repeatedly expressed their anger over inadequate funding for black schools and their inability to get their children into better-financed white schools. In early December the Southern Association of Colleges and Schools removed accreditation from all fifteen high schools in Duval County because they did not receive sufficient support to meet minimum educational standards. With officials and teachers angry and frustrated by the decision, the community's black leaders staged a boycott. Rutledge Pearson, president of the Florida NAACP and a social studies teacher at Cookman Junior High School in Jacksonville, reflected the views of many when he complained about "overcrowded classrooms, outmoded curricula and inadequate equipment in Negro schools." The protest lasted for three days, during which as many as twenty thousand black children stayed away from classes. The demonstrations added to concerns of political and business leaders, who feared that the loss of accreditation would stymie their development plans for the city. Taking advantage of these fears, black leaders agreed to halt the boycott only after school officials promised to upgrade schools serving both races to meet the standards set by the Southern Association.[62]

Despite the efforts of the black community and the actions of the federal government and the federal courts, Florida had managed to circumvent all but a minimum of desegregation by employing a freedom-of-choice plan that allowed parents to keep their children in schools with others of their own race. Although the Office of Education determined that sixty of Florida's sixty-seven school districts had taken steps to comply with the guidelines of the Department of Health, Education, and Welfare (HEW) in 1965, only 9.67 percent of Florida's public school students were in desegregated schools. Moreover, sixteen Florida counties had no school desegregation even though they had compliance reports on file with the Office of Education. The state's report to HEW revealed only 25,000 white students attended schools with black stu-

343

dents, although 256,000 black students were attending desegregated schools. Though Burns's administration did not block federal orders to desegregate, then, neither did it expedite the process.[63]

But as Vernon Sikes's report to Burns indicated, the new federal guidelines promised wholesale changes and in a rapid way. In 1966 the Office of Education published revised guidelines for those states with freedom-of-choice plans. The new guidelines required school systems with 8 to 9 percent of their black students in desegregated schools to double that figure in 1966–67 and those with less than 5 percent to triple that figure in 1966–67.[64]

The federal courts added to the sense of urgency, ordering Florida to abandon the school policies of the past and replace them with "unitary, nonracial systems." In a series of decisions culminating in *United States v. Jefferson County Board of Education* (Alabama) in 1967, the Fifth Circuit Court of Appeals stood squarely behind the guidelines prepared by HEW, finding that they offered "the best system available for uniform application and the best aid to the courts." The justices also ruled that school officials had an "affirmative duty" to bring about integrated schools. In April 1968 the U.S. Supreme Court went even further, sounding the death knell for freedom-of-choice plans when it ruled in *Green v. School Board of New Kent County, Virginia,* that such plans had failed to dismantle a dual school system. It ordered the school board to "fashion steps which promise realistically to convert promptly to a system without a 'white' school and a 'Negro' school, but just schools."[65]

In contrast to developments in the 1950s, local school officials operated with very little gubernatorial or legislative guidance in the mid-1960s, and the absence of such interference helped speed the desegregation process. The willingness of Floridians and school leaders to accept school desegregation rather than the alternatives severely limited the state's range of options.

The shift in the public's response to school desegregation revealed itself most dramatically in the Democratic gubernatorial primary of 1966. Both Governor Burns and his leading challenger, Mayor Robert King High of Miami, emphasized their efforts to improve race relations in the state. Where Burns highlighted his appointment of blacks to state offices, High pointed to Miami's success in desegregating its school system and its public facilities. In a surprising result, High easily defeated Burns. Saddled with the unpopular economic and social policies of a Democratic president, however, High's candidacy was politically vulnerable, and he lost his gubernatorial bid to Claude Kirk, the first Republican governor in the twentieth century. Kirk capitalized on public sentiment by acknowledging the legality of school desegregation while denouncing the social dislocation and economic problems created by the liberal policies of President Lyndon Johnson.[66]

Like his predecessors, Kirk placed great emphasis on maintaining and expanding the economic vitality of Florida and at the same time attempted to distance himself from the racial changes that were occurring throughout the state and region. Initially, Kirk ignored the accelerated desegregation plans being mandated by HEW and the federal courts. Shortly before he assumed office in 1967, the Fifth Circuit Court, in a ruling that directly affected four counties in north Florida, ordered six southern states to develop plans for the complete integration of their schools within four months. The justices concluded that it was "not enough for school authorities to offer negro children the opportunity to attend formerly all-white schools. The necessity of overcoming the effects of the dual system in this circuit requires integration of faculties, facilities and activities as well as students." It was a startling decision in its ramifications and the speed with which it was to be implemented. Federal District Court Judge Harrold Carswell responded almost immediately, requiring school representatives from Leon, Escambia, Alachua, and Bay counties to meet with him in three days to develop plans for compliance.[67]

Angered by the extent of the decision, Governors George Wallace, Paul Johnson, and Lester Maddox invited their counterparts in the other southern states to join them in a conference to "protect our schools from unwarranted and unnecessary encroachment by the Federal authorities." But Kirk refused to participate, contending that the meeting would be "divisive and unwise." He also announced that Florida would not rely on any "regional confederation to intercede in its Federal-State relations" and that school-desegregation matters would be resolved in a "forward-looking spirit and [we] urge you individually to do the same."[68]

Besides indicating an unwillingness to challenge the position of the federal courts, Kirk's comments also reflected a growing perception among Floridians that because of demographic changes, the state should no longer be defined in just regional or southern terms. The changes of the preceding twenty years had pushed Florida onto a different stage, and residents were beginning to reassess the state's place in the nation. This

345

development had important implications for the school-desegregation issue, because most Floridians were no longer convinced that the racial traditions of the past were worth preserving, especially if they threatened the state's continued economic growth. Not insignificantly, the state press praised Kirk for adhering to the law and for keeping the state's focus on the future instead of turning back to the past.[69]

As Kirk's administration unfolded, however, public and legislative opposition to his other programs became widespread, and he shifted his position on school desegregation as he approached his reelection campaign in 1970. In part, Kirk turned to a strategy utilized by many southern politicians, who when faced with a particularly difficult campaign sounded the racial alarm in an effort to stampede voters to their candidacy. In part, too, Kirk sought to take advantage of President Richard Nixon's reservations about the direction of school desegregation, especially the use of busing.[70]

Kirk's opportunity to employ his campaign strategy came in December 1969, when the Fifth Circuit Court ordered Manatee County, Florida, to conform to the desegregation requirements of *Alexander v. Holmes County Board of Education* (1969). The court specifically ruled that county officials had to terminate their dual school system and operate only unitary schools. When District Judge Ben Krentzman ordered Manatee officials to commence a busing program on April 6, 1970, to create a unitary system with a ratio of 80 percent white to 20 percent black in each school, Kirk took exception and asked for a special hearing before Krentzman. But Krentzman refused without comment. On January 31 Kirk asserted what he described as his "authority as Chief Budget Officer" of the state to issue an executive order directing Manatee officials not to implement busing to desegregate its schools. Caught between the governor and the federal courts, the school board opted to develop busing plans for the April 6 deadline, principally because Kirk and his predecessors had absented themselves from this process for nearly a decade.[71]

When Krentzman's order went into effect on April 6, Kirk seized control of the schools and suspended the school board and the superintendent of schools. Krentzman immediately ordered the schools returned to county officials and Kirk to appear before him to explain his actions. But Kirk refused, claiming that Krentzman had "overstepped his bounds," and he defied the court by again suspending the school board. In this clash of wills, Kirk's position rapidly eroded. State newspapers roundly condemned him for interfering in a local matter and for jeopardizing the state's moderate reputation. Others denounced the governor for playing politics with the schools. On April 11 Krentzman found Kirk guilty of contempt and fined him ten thousand dollars a day until he surrendered control of the school system. With virtually no public support, Kirk bowed to the judge's demands and directed the school board to comply with Krentzman's desegregation orders.[72]

The Manatee crisis marked the beginning of the end for the school-desegregation issue in Florida. Although the public did not support busing, it was unwilling to violate the law or allow its representatives to do so in order to maintain traditional educational patterns. This acknowledgment of the supremacy of law as interpreted by the federal courts and the federal government signaled the end of the battle. It also brought an end to the traditional southern way of doing things in Florida. Remnants and actions tied to the past would continue, but Floridians had chosen a new course. And as if to demonstrate this abandonment of the past, voters turned Kirk out of office in 1970 and elected his Democratic opponent, Reubin Askew, an advocate of biracial schools.[73]

Facilitating an end to the school-desegregation struggle in Florida were the political and legal changes effected by reapportionment of the state legislature in 1967 and revision of the state constitution in 1968. The changing attitudes on race intersected with these political and constitutional transformations, encouraging the public and its political representatives to reappraise and gradually to abandon school segregation. The decision to begin a new chapter in Florida's history emerged from the confluence of these social, legal, and political developments.

The success of Florida's moderation had been built upon the state's population growth and economic development. It did not represent a desire for a biracial society or an appreciation of past racial inequities: instead, it simply acknowledged new social and economic realities in the state that required a different approach to racial affairs. Not insignificantly, the moderate approach employed by Collins did not result in an improvement in black education through a desegregated school system. Indeed, Collins's approach accepted token desegregation only in order to preserve a segregated system and a stable political order. The dramatic social and economic changes of the postwar period shaped the campaigns and policies of Collins's successors; and although they were more outspoken in their criticism of racial change than Collins, they generally adhered to his moderate approach.

347

And so the state of Florida, prodded by the federal courts, the federal government, and black citizens, gradually desegregated its public educational system. But it did not do so willingly and it achieved desegregation with little understanding or concern for its black population. Black children and black teachers moved from segregated to integrated schools and the change was symbolic, but it lacked deeper significance because of the state's approach to the issue. The change had occurred primarily because of federal government actions, court rulings, and the desire of Florida's residents to acquire the wealth and prosperity that began flowing to the Sunbelt.

Notes

The author would like to acknowledge the advice and criticism of Steven Lawson, Kermit Hall, Paul Murphy, J. Mills Thornton III, and George Pozzetta in preparing this essay.

1. *Congressional Quarterly,* May 21, 1954, 637. Also see William Bagwell, *School Desegregation in the Carolinas* (Columbia, S.C., 1972), 128. Florida state school superintendent Thomas Bailey recommended that "the Negro schools should be constructed as planned." David Colburn, *Racial Change and Community Crisis: St. Augustine, Florida, 1877–1980* (New York, 1985), 25–26.

2. Charles C. Alexander, *Holding the Line: The Eisenhower Era, 1952–1961* (Bloomington, Ind., 1975), 118–19; Robert F. Burk, *The Eisenhower Administration and Black Civil Rights* (Knoxville, 1984), 192. Also see Steven E. Ambrose, *Eisenhower: The President,* vol. 2 (New York, 1984), 191–92.

3. Benjamin Muse, *Ten Years of Prelude: The Story of Integration since the Supreme Court's 1954 Decision* (New York, 1964), 19; Donald R. Mathews and James W. Prothro, *Negroes and the New South Politics* (New York, 1966), 410.

4. Joseph A. Tomberlin, "The Negro and Florida's System of Education: The Aftermath of the *Brown* Decision" (Ph.D. diss., Florida State University, 1967), 9–10, 14.

5. David R. Colburn and Richard K. Scher, *Florida's Gubernatorial Politics in the Twentieth Century* (Tallahassee, Fla., 1980), 244–47; Lewis Killian and Charles Grigg, *Racial Crisis in America: Leadership in Conflict* (Englewood Cliffs, N.J., 1964), 121. In 1943 black teachers in Tampa, Fla., sued successfully in federal court to overturn unequal salary schedules. See McDaniel v. Board of Public Instruction of Escambia, Florida, 39 F. Supp. 638 (N.D. Fla. 1941). Also see Manning Marable, *Race, Reform and Rebellion: The Second Reconstruction in Black America* (Jackson, Miss., 1984), 16. The federal court cases that per-

suaded Florida and southern officials to improve funding for black schools included Missouri ex rel Gaines v. Canada, 305 U.S. 337 (1938); Sipuel v. Oklahoma Board of Regents, 332 U.S. 631 (1948); and Mills v. Board of Education of Anne Arundel County, 30 F. Supp. 245 (D.Md., 1939).

6. Jack Bass and Walter DeVries, *The Transformation of Southern Politics: Social Change and Political Consequence since 1945* (New York, 1977), 109; Colburn and Scher, *Florida's Gubernatorial Politics*, 17–20.

7. McGill, as quoted in William H. Nicholls, *Southern Tradition and Regional Progress* (Chapel Hill, N.C., 1960), 156–57; J. Milton Yinger and George E. Simpson, "Can Segregation Survive in an Industrial Society?" *Antioch Review* 18 (1958): 15.

8. V. O. Key, Jr., *Southern Politics in State and Nation* (New York, 1949), 9. By contrast with Florida, the black population stood in 1950 at approximately 31 percent in Georgia, 32 percent in Alabama, 45 percent in Mississippi, and 39 percent in South Carolina. Only Texas among the former Confederate states had a smaller black population as a percentage of the total than Florida.

9. *New York Times*, March 13, 1956, S4. Very few people migrating to Florida settled in the black belt because it was an economically depressed area. Nonetheless, this region, which extended from the Apalachicola River along the Georgia border to the Suwannee River and then south to Marion County, continued to dominate state politics throughout the period, despite the growth of south Florida. Hugh D. Price, *The Negro and Southern Politics: A Chapter in Florida History* (New York, 1957), 36.

10. Helen L. Jacobstein, *The Segregation Factor in the Florida Democratic Primary of 1956*, University of Florida Social Sciences Monograph Series, no. 47 (Gainesville, Fla., 1972), 8.

11. For many southerners the Court action represented what Justice Felix Frankfurter would later describe, in a reapportionment case, as a "massive repudiation of the experience of our whole past in asserting destructively novel judicial power." Baker v. Carr, 369 U.S. 226 (1962); also cited in Kermit Hall, *The Supreme Court and Judicial Review in American History* (Washington, D.C., 1985), 45. Southerners generally believed that segregation issues were unsuitable for resolution by judges. This view owed its heritage in part to Justice Roger B. Taney's political-question doctrine. See Harold M. Hyman and William M. Wiecek, *Equal Justice under Law: Constitutional Development, 1835–1875* (New York, 1982), 75.

12. Colburn and Scher, *Florida's Gubernatorial Politics*, 76; Earl Black, *Southern Governors and Civil Rights: Racial Segregation as a Campaign Issue in the Second Reconstruction* (Cambridge, Mass., 1976), 93.

13. Colburn and Scher, *Florida's Gubernatorial Politics*, 75–76; Price, *The Negro and Southern Politics*, 95. George Tindall first described the connection

between the business-progressive philosophy and the New South creed when writing on the 1920s. See George B. Tindall, "Business Progressivism: Southern Politics in the Twenties," *South Atlantic Quarterly* 62 (1963): 106.

14. Tomberlin, "The Negro and Florida's System of Education," 58; Richard Kluger, *Simple Justice: The History of Brown v. Board of Education and Black America's Struggle for Equality* (New York, 1975), 724.

15. Kluger, *Simple Justice*, 724–25, 728, 735; Harry S. Ashmore, *Hearts and Minds: The Anatomy of Racism from Roosevelt to Reagan* (New York, 1982), 209–11. The Supreme Court did not postpone its decision or sanction the maintenance of segregation; it simply provided the South with more time when it inserted the clause "with all deliberate speed." Nevertheless, among Floridians there was a sigh of relief and a clear sense that desegregation might well be a decade or perhaps a generation away.

16. *St. Petersburg Times*, March 23, 1956, 6. In 1955, 8 percent of the population could elect a majority in the state senate and 17.1 percent could elect a majority in the house of representatives. Throughout his governorship, Collins fought diligently but unsuccessfully for reapportionment. Colburn and Scher, *Florida's Gubernatorial Politics*, 174. Numan v. Bartley has argued that the apportionment issue became entangled with the desegregation issue and strengthened the position of rural legislators in the South who opposed reapportionment and desegregation. This certainly appears to have been the case in Florida. See Bartley, *The Rise of Massive Resistance: Race and Politics in the South during the 1950s* (Baton Rouge, 1969), 79.

17. Southern Manifesto, as quoted in Bartley, *The Rise of Massive Resistance*, 52–53. See also Stephen L. Wasby, Anthony A. D'Amato, and Rosemary Metrailer, *Desegregation from Brown to Alexander: An Exploration of Supreme Court Strategies* (Carbondale, Ill., 1977), 167–68.

18. Darryl Paulson and Paula Hawkes, "Desegregating the University of Florida Law School: Virgil Hawkins v. The Florida Board of Control," *Florida State University Law Review* 12 (1984): 63–66 (quotation from 65). The state successfully blocked Hawkins's admission to the University of Florida when it established minimum academic and examination criteria for entrance into law school. After nine years Hawkins conceded defeat and in 1960, at the age of fifty-one, entered a master's degree program in public relations and communications at Boston University. Memorandum to the State Board of Education, N.O., Administrative Correspondence, PUT-RAC, 1955–56, Folder—Race Relations, box 33, RG 102, ser. 776A, T. LeRoy Collins Papers, Florida State Archives, Tallahassee (hereafter cited as LCP:FSA).

19. Price, *The Negro and Southern Politics*, 51; Thomas R. Wagy, *Governor LeRoy Collins of Florida: Spokesman of the New South* (University, Ala., 1985), 62–64; Colburn and Scher, *Florida's Gubernatorial Politics*, 77.

20. Folder—Conference on Segregation, March 21, 1956, Speeches, Con-

ferences, 1956–57, (8D)3, LeRoy Collins Papers, University of South Florida Library, Tampa (hereafter cited as LCP:USF); Wagy, *Governor LeRoy Collins of Florida*, 69–70.

21. William Chafe, *Civilities and Civil Rights: Greensboro, North Carolina, and the Black Struggle for Freedom* (New York, 1980), 67–82 (quotation from 68). See also Hodges to Collins, July 20, 1956, Administrative Correspondence, PUT-RAC, 1955–56, Folder—Race Relations (May–December 1956), box 33, LCP:FSA; Folder—Race Relations, 1955–58, (4)4, LCP:USF; and Bartley, *The Rise of Massive Resistance*, 22.

22. Folder—Conference on Segregation, March 21, 1956, Speeches, Conferences, 1956–57, (8D)3, LCP:USF. See also Colburn and Scher, *Florida's Gubernatorial Politics*, 225.

23. Tomberlin, "The Negro and Florida's System of Education," 103–4, 112; *St. Petersburg Times*, March 22, 1956 (see also *ibid.*, March 25, 1956); Governor's Monthly Radio and Television Report to the People, March 12, 1956, 5, transcript, PUT-RAC, 1955–56, Folder—Race Relations, 1955–58, box 33, LCP:FSA. See also Black, *Southern Governors and Civil Rights*, 15.

24. Price, *The Negro and Southern Politics*, 51, 65, 100; Colburn and Scher, *Florida's Gubernatorial Politics*, 76–77; Wagy, *Governor LeRoy Collins of Florida*, 71–73; Tomberlin, "The Negro and Florida's System of Education," 142–43. Irvin's case became a cause célèbre for the NAACP and black leaders in Florida. See Steven Lawson, David Colburn, and Darryl Paulson, "Groveland: Florida's Little Scottsboro," *Florida Historical Review* 65 (1986): 1–26.

25. Richard Bardolph, *The Civil Rights Record: Black Americans and the Law, 1849–1970* (New York, 1970), 390; "Florida's School Assignment Law," Remarks by J. Lewis Hall, September 13, 1956, 10–11, Administrative Correspondence, PUT-RAC, 1955–56, Folder—Race Relations, box 33, LCP:FSA. See also Report of the Special Committee to Recommend Legislative Action Relating to Public School Education, Administrative Correspondence, RAC, 1957–60, Folder—Race Relations, box 73, LCP:FSA; and Jack Greenberg, *Race Relations and American Law* (New York, 1959), 232–40. The pupil-assignment regulations were quite complex and often included such criteria as available room, transportation, neighborhood, teaching capacity, scholastic aptitude, and native intelligence.

26. Memorandum, Wigginton to Collins, n.d., Administrative Correspondence, PUT-RAC, 1955–56, Folder—Race Relations—Advisory Commission, box 33, LCP:FSA. See also Report of the Special Committee to Recommend Legislative Action; and Colburn and Scher, *Florida's Gubernatorial Politics*, 225.

27. Colburn and Scher, *Florida's Gubernatorial Politics*, 225–26; Wagy, *Governor LeRoy Collins of Florida*, 74–75.

28. Wagy, *Governor LeRoy Collins of Florida*, 75.

29. *Southern School News*, July 1956, 2; Theodore Gibson v. Board of Public

Instruction of Dade County, Florida, 272 F.2d 763 (1959); William Holland v. The Board of Instruction of Palm Beach County, Florida, 258 F.2d 730 (1958).

30. Shuttlesworth v. Birmingham Board of Education of Jefferson County, Alabama, 162 F. Supp. 372 (1958).

31. Burk, *The Eisenhower Administration and Black Civil Rights*, 176–86; Bartley, *The Rise of Massive Resistance*, 261–68; Harvard Sitkoff, *The Struggle for Black Equality* (New York, 1981), 29–32.

32. Address to Southern Governors' Conference, September 23, 1957, Press Conferences, Meetings, (8D)2, LCP:USF. See also Wagy, *Governor LeRoy Collins of Florida*, 91–96.

33. Wagy, *Governor LeRoy Collins of Florida*, 94–95; *Atlanta Constitution*, September 24, 1957; *New York Times*, September 24, 1957.

34. *Southern School News*, June 1957, 22; ibid., November 1957, 14. See also Colburn and Scher, *Florida's Gubernatorial Politics*, 226; and Wagy, *Governor LeRoy Collins of Florida*, 100–101.

35. *Southern School News*, November 1957, 14. See also Hawkins v. Board of Control of Florida, 253 F.2d 573 (1958); and Hawkins v. Board of Control of Florida and R. S. Johnson, Registrar, University of Florida, 162 F. Supp. 851 (1958).

36. Colburn and Scher, *Florida's Gubernatorial Politics*, 226. See also *Southern School News*, June 1957, 22; and Wagy, *Governor LeRoy Collins of Florida*, 87–88.

37. Jerrell H. Shofner, "Custom, Law and History: The Enduring Influence of Florida's 'Black Code,' " *Florida Historical Quarterly* 55 (1977): 297.

38. Richard Cramer, "School Desegregation and New Industry: The Southern Community Leaders' Viewpoint," *Social Forces*, May 1963, 384.

39. Governor's Monthly Radio and Television Report to the People, March 12, 1956, 5, transcript, PUT-RAC, 1955–56, Folder—Race Relations, 1955–58, box 33, LCP:FSA. During the Little Rock crisis Collins and Hodges became good friends, and they frequently exchanged correspondence concerning racial legislation and policy matters. See also Gov. Luther Hodges, speech to Rotary Club, New York, June 21, 1956, ibid.; *Southern School News*, January 1957, 8; and press conference, Gov. LeRoy Collins, February 19, 1959, 3, box 338, LCP:USF.

40. *Southern School News*, December 1957, 12.

41. Wasby, D'Amato, and Metrailer, *Desegregation from Brown to Alexander*, 194; Shuttlesworth v. Birmingham Board of Education of Jefferson County, Alabama, 162 F. Supp. 372 (1958).

42. Meetings of Governor's Advisory Commission on Race Relations, November 19, 1957, and January 15, 1958, Administrative Correspondence, RAC, 1957–60, box 73, LCP:FSA. The revised Fabisinski Committee included Dr. J. R. Lee, Jr., a black faculty member from Florida A. and M. Shortly after

being added to the committee, Lee had been promoted from business manager to vice-president at Florida A. and M. in an obvious attempt to increase his prominence in the black community and perhaps also to ensure that he would support the governor's policies.

43. *Southern School News,* October 1958, 17.

44. Ibid., November 1958, 10. See also Muse, *Ten Years of Prelude,* 199; and Robert Howard Akerman, "The Triumph of Moderation in Florida Thought and Politics" (Ph.D. diss., American University, 1967), 131.

45. See p. 333 and n. 26.

46. *Southern School News,* January 1959, 7; *Tampa Tribune,* December 17, 1958, 12.

47. *Tampa Tribune,* February 19, 1959, 1.

48. Jess Yarborough, member, Board of Public Instruction of Dade County, to members of the Legislature, March 19, 1959, Administrative Correspondence, PUR-RAC, 1957–60, box 72, LCP:FSA; *Southern School News,* September 1959, 3; ibid., October 1959, 5; ibid., November 1959, 11.

49. *Southern School News,* January 1960, 6; Gibson v. Board of Public Instruction of Dade County, Florida, 272 F.2d 763 (1959).

50. Colburn and Scher, *Florida's Gubernatorial Politics,* 78–79. See also Wagy, *Governor LeRoy Collins of Florida,* 140–43.

51. Akerman, "The Triumph of Moderation," 172; Black, *Southern Governors and Civil Rights,* 96.

52. Ralph E. Odum, "Review of Public School Segregation in Florida, May 1954–May 1960," Folder—Race Relations, Fowler Commission, 1961, Box 114, ser. 756, Farris Bryant Papers, Florida State Archives (hereafter cited as FBP:FSA); Odum to Bryant, July 27, 1963, Folder—Education, 1963, box 39, ibid.; Vernon P. Sikes, administrative assistant to Gov. Haydon Burns, February 2, 1965, CN-CW, Folder—Civil Rights, 1965, box 10, ser. 131, Haydon Burns Papers, Florida State Archives (hereafter cited as HBP:FSA).

53. John E. Evans, *Time for Florida: Report on the Administration of Farris Bryant, Governor, 1961–1965* (n.p., 1965), 8.

54. Bryant to E. R. Eiesly, September 4, 1962, Folder—Race Relations, 1962, box 113, FBP:FSA; Tomberlin, "The Negro and Florida's System of Education," 207; *Tallahassee Democrat,* September 8, 1963, 22.

55. *Race Relations Law Reporter* 7 (1962): 675–80. See also *Southern School News,* September 1962, 1, 8.

56. Florida Advisory Committee to the U.S. Commission on Civil Rights, *Report on Florida* (Washington, D.C., 1963), 10–12 (quotation from 10).

57. *Southern School News,* February 1961, 7; Tomberlin, "The Negro and Florida's System of Education," 203.

58. Bardolph, *The Civil Rights Record,* 407–9; *Southern School News,* Sep-

tember 1964, 1; ibid., February 1965, 1; Lino A. Graglia, *Disaster by Decree: The Supreme Court Decisions on Race and the Schools* (Ithaca, N.Y., 1976), 46–51; Gary Orfield, *The Reconstruction of Southern Education: The Schools and the 1964 Civil Rights Act* (New York, 1969), 78–88, 93–95; George R. Metcalf, *From Little Rock to Boston: The History of School Desegregation* (Westport, Conn., 1983), 5–7.

59. Memorandum—Sikes to Burns, February 2, 1965, "Report on National Conference, Title VI—Civil Rights Act of 1964," CN-CW, Folder—Civil Rights, 1965, box 10, HBP:FSA.

60. Muse, *Ten Years of Prelude*, 187; Francis Keppel, U.S. commissioner of education, to Thomas D. Bailey, state superintendent of education, May 20, 1965, Folder—Education, 2 of 3, 1965, box 20, HBP:FSA.

61. Memorandum—Sikes to Burns, February 2, 1965, "Report on National Conference, Title VI."

62. Tomberlin, "The Negro and Florida's System of Education," 229. See also *Florida Times-Union*, December 8, 1964, 1; and ibid., December 9, 1964, 1.

63. *Southern School News*, May 1964, 1; ibid., September 1964, 7; ibid., May 1965, 6; Tomberlin, "The Negro and Florida's System of Education," 239.

64. Memorandum—Sikes to Burns, February 2, 1965, "Report on National Conference, Title VI"; *Southern School News*, March 1965, 8; ibid., May 1965, 6; Tomberlin, "The Negro and Florida's System of Education," 189; Orfield, *The Reconstruction of Southern Education*, 142–43.

65. Bardolph, *The Civil Rights Record*, 452–54, 456–57. See also Harvie Wilkinson, *From Brown to Baake: The Supreme Court and School Integration, 1954–1978* (New York, 1979), 113–17; Wasby, D'Amato, and Metrailer, *Desegregation from Brown to Alexander*, 399, 406; United States v. Jefferson County Board of Education, 372 F.2d 836 (5th Cir. 1966); and Green v. School Board of New Kent County, Virginia, 391 U.S. 430 (1968).

66. Black, *Southern Governors and Civil Rights*, 228; Colburn and Scher, *Florida's Gubernatorial Politics*, 81–83.

67. Metcalf, *From Little Rock to Boston*, 10–11. See also Wilkinson, *From Brown to Baake*, 111–13; and Wasby, D'Amato, and Metrailer, *Desegregation from Brown to Alexander*, 378–80.

68. *Tampa Tribune*, April 18, 1967, 2.

69. Ibid., 2, 4B.

70. David R. Colburn and Richard K. Scher, "Race Relations and Florida Gubernatorial Politics since the *Brown* Decision," *Florida Historical Quarterly* 55 (1976): 168–69.

71. Claude R. Kirk, Jr., "A Desegregation Plan for the Manatee County Public Schools," January 1970, Folder—Manatee County, 1970, box 78, ser. 923, Claude R. Kirk, Jr., Papers, Florida State Archives. See also *Memphis Commercial Appeal*, January 24, 1970, 1; Kirk to the southern governors, May 8, 1970, box 1, ser. 926, Kirk Papers, Florida State Archives; *Tampa Tribune*,

January 25, 1970, 1; and Alexander v. Holmes County Board of Education, 38 U.S. *Law Week,* 24L Ed 2d 41 (1969).

72. Colburn and Scher, *Florida's Gubernatorial Politics,* 234–35. See also Kirk to the southern governors, May 8, 1970.

73. Colburn and Scher, *Florida's Gubernatorial Politics,* 84–86.

Women, the South, and the Constitution

Mary K. Bonsteel Tachau

This is an exploratory essay, surveying some of the recent work on the constitutional traditions of some women in the South and suggesting areas for further research. It is written from the perspective of a constitutional and legal historian who is not a specialist in women's history, black history, or southern history. This is not, therefore, a discussion of women's history or a survey of its literature as it applies to the South but an inquiry into some of the constitutional and legal traditions of southern women that are especially fruitful fields for historians to begin (or continue) working. It is not "a time to reclaim" because, considering the possibilities, little has been written thus far and there is not much to reclaim. It is, instead, a call to arms to end the historic invisibility of most aspects of the legal and constitutional position of women in the South.[1]

The word "Constitution" in the title establishes the beginning of the chronology: 1789, when the Constitution went into effect. It will be useful to bring the topic as nearly up-to-date as recent scholarly publications permit. Scholarship is, by its nature, after the fact, and even the law reviews have not encompassed the most recent changes in the constitutional status of women in the South or elsewhere.

Whether the South brings to mind slaves working in the fields and sleeping on the floor outside their owners' bedrooms or magnolias in the moonlight and the romance of the Lost Cause, or Tobacco Road, or the American tragedy that was the Civil War, there is no doubt that the South is a distinctive region. One of the principal factors that makes it distinctive is that it is the region where segregation was required by law.

356

The South does not have a monopoly on racism; it is a national characteristic not confined to the relations between black people and white people. Still, it is the southern experience with slavery and later with mandatory separation of the races that makes the region unique. For the purposes of this essay, "southern" encompasses not only the fifteen slave states but also West Virginia and Oklahoma, because they, too, required racial segregation.[2]

This definition is an ineluctable reminder of the difference between the constitutional position of black women and that of white women in the South. Until slavery was ended, most southern black women simply had no constitutional status as persons; they were chattels, movable personal property. The Constitution stated that their "importation" could not be prohibited before 1808, they were counted in the decennial census in a specified three-fifths proportion to their whole numbers, and as slaves or indentured servants they were to be returned to their owners when they fled into free territories or states. Neither their marriages nor their parentage was recognized by law. They could not give, devise, bequeath, or inherit. Slave women were thus less hidden from (or protected by) the law than were married white women because of the status accorded the institution of slavery in the Constitution. It is instructive that one of the few women named in a prominent constitutional case in the antebellum era was a black woman, Margaret Morgan, the object of the kidnapping in *Prigg v. Pennsylvania.*

We know little about free black women, except that the strictures that applied to all women were exponentially increased by the law codes that applied to free blacks. Their legal and constitutional status was only microscopically better than that of slave women.[3]

And, of course, postbellum emancipation did not greatly change the status of black women. They gained some basic legal rights: the right to have their marriages recognized in law, to make contracts, to sue and be sued. The Fourteenth Amendment brought the right to testify against white people in federal courts and, eventually, the right to testify against white people in state courts. (Not until then did the right to participate in court proceedings have real meaning, because courts have been notoriously casual about the grievances of black people against other black people.) Although theoretically black women gained the right to vote through the Nineteenth Amendment, realistically that right was not enforceable until passage of the Voting Rights Act in 1965. Like white women, they did not enjoy the equal protection of the laws until even

357

later, except where the Supreme Court's decision in *Brown v. Board of Education* prevailed.[4]

The degree to which southern black women enjoyed any of the privileges and immunities of citizens of the United States and the degree of due process afforded them in state and federal courts are questions that await answers. I have not found any comprehensive analysis of the constitutional position of southern black women during the post–World War II years, when some of them, it is to be hoped, were able to realize the promise of the Fourteenth Amendment.[5]

Most of the literature on southern black women of any era has been written and collected in the last generation. It is a subject that demands more attention than it has yet received. According to the statistics that newspapers provide, black women are the lowest-paid members of our society. To judge from my search, they are also among the least studied. Their only rivals, if rivalry it may be called, are native American women and Hispanic women. Two recent articles indicate that vast opportunities await constitutional and legal historians in the area of native American women; surely the same opportunities await those who study Hispanic women—and women of other ethnic minorities, also. Gerda Lerner made a helpful beginning in *Black Women in White America*, a collection of documents. Many of these touch on constitutional issues and could easily be expanded by scholars who could place the experiences of individuals in the context of constitutional history.[6]

The general public, as well as those already interested in women's history and black history, would welcome more accounts of the lives of black women in the South. *The Color Purple* was a notably successful film. "Eyes on the Prize," the public television series about the civil rights movement, showed thousands of black women whose courage brought about profound changes in American society, including the realization of constitutional rights that had long been denied. As one who lived through those years, I have been deeply impressed by the accuracy of the scholarly papers, articles, and books about various aspects of the civil rights movement written by people too young to have participated in it. Everyone over the age of thirty witnessed that great mass movement that brought about major constitutional changes, but we have not written much about the women—both white and black—who participated in it. Indeed, among the rewarding experiences of participation in the civil rights movement was the mutual respect and trust that developed between black and white activists, both men and women. Accounts of how their common commitment to the civil rights revolution transcended race, gender, age, and every other extraneous qualification have not yet been recorded. That history will be a happy assignment for whoever undertakes it.

Thus far, the television producers have given fuller coverage than have the historians. There have been interviews with Linda Brown, but where is the book about the women in the other cases that led to desegregation in education, in public accommodations, in housing? What happened to Autherine Lucy? Television shows us Rosa Parks, but has anyone written her biography? What happened to Fannie Lou Hamer, who at the 1964 Democratic convention pleaded so eloquently for recognition of the Freedom Democratic party and cited the long-forgotten section 2 of the Fourteenth Amendment? And what about the unseen contributors to change: for example, the women who made eighty thousand cheese sandwiches for those who were part of the March on Washington? How did the women in Birmingham, in Selma, and in Atlanta in 1967 feed the thousands of people who came to march with them? (As a woman, I expect that care and housing were women's work; if I am mistaken, that should go into the record, too.)

The 1960s brought mass participation in three different but often related movements: one to achieve civil rights for black Americans, one to end American participation in the war in Vietnam, and one to gain equal rights for women. Some activist women participated in all three. Yet in addition to the differences among these causes, there are differences in the ways in which many of the male leaders of the first two treated women. (Not surprisingly, women have always been the leaders in the women's movement.) One has the impression that the women who participated in the civil rights movement were treated equally with men—in contrast to the treatment that women experienced when they participated in the almost contemporaneous protests against the war in Vietnam. Is this an accurate perception? If it is, what explains the difference? It would certainly be logical if the men who abjured racial inequality also abjured gender-based inequality, but logic seldom determines human behavior. Were the experiences of women different from those of men? Did they play a special role in the civil rights movement?

I regret that on this subject I can only raise questions. We cannot expect many people to write their memoirs, as Daisy Bates and Myrlie Evers have. Activists continue to be activists and seldom take time to recount their own experiences until something forces them to slow down. But there are great opportunities, now, for oral historians to interview the participants while they are still alive and their memories fresh. It is time to gather the letters and other manuscript materials that get thrown away when people move or die. It is time to list the books that activists collected, while the collections are complete. It is certainly time to talk with the members of the older generation whose experiences had taught them to stay "in their place" and who feared for their activist children. Can it possibly have reconciled the mothers of the four little girls killed in the Birmingham church bombing to know that their children's deaths helped arouse the conscience of the nation to the dangers involved when black people tried to realize their constitutional rights? Has it been different for women than for men to live in a time when they have been realizing dreams instead of enduring humiliation? How have black women harnessed the hopes engendered by gaining protection from the Constitution? How have they dealt with the disappointments they have encountered since those heady days of the 1960s?[7]

We have little more evidence about the constitutional traditions of white women in the South. If we begin our study in 1789, we plunge in the middle of what, until a few years ago, was a major controversy in women's history. In 1930 Richard B. Morris published *Studies in the History of American Law, with Special Reference to the Seventeenth and Eighteenth Centuries.* His book contained a chapter on the legal status of women in colonial America in which he asserted that because of new economic and political conditions, they attained a greater measure of individuality and independence than English women. Sixteen years later Mary R. Beard reinforced Morris's position. She emphasized the property rights that married women gained through prenuptial marriage settlements, arranged under the supervision of chancery courts. The prestige of their authors gave what was, in reality, only a hypothesis the status of proved fact. It became the a priori assumption underlying the work of other historians who came to describe the seventeenth century—and even the eighteenth—as a "golden age" in women's status. Unfortunately, none of these people investigated the kinds of primary sources (for example, the wills found in probate records) that would have tempered their optimistic evaluations.[8]

The golden-age thesis gained even more currency when specialists in women's history noted a decline in the status of women in the late eighteenth century as American society became more Anglicized, a decline that was accelerated in the nineteenth century by industrialization. Unfortunately, none of these people did comparative studies of the status of women in England, and nobody was yet studying court records, which would have shown the fragility—indeed, the improbability—of the golden-age thesis. It is, therefore, not surprising that it was a legal historian who buried the thesis in 1983. Marylynn Salmon's review essay "The Legal Status of Women in Early America: A Reappraisal" is a thoughtful historiographical analysis that all historians will appreciate and that should inspire further research.[9]

It is frustrating to realize that any analysis of women's constitutional and legal traditions must begin with men's constitutional and legal traditions. Realistically, however, the subject requires a comparative approach and an approach that is not limited to the South.

The fundamental constitutional right is the right of citizenship, even though many constitutional rights are determined not by citizenship but by the extent of the jurisdiction of the national government. (For example, the Fifth Amendment in theory applies to "*all* persons who are accused of capital or otherwise infamous crimes," and the Sixth Amendment describes the procedures to be followed "in *all* criminal prosecutions" [emphasis added]).

The Fourteenth Amendment provided the first constitutional definition of citizenship. Five years after it was ratified, the Supreme Court began to interpret it in the *Slaughterhouse Cases* (1873). The Court's opinions provide comprehensive definitions of the rights associated with citizenship. It is instructive to examine the justices' lengthy descriptions of the privileges and immunities of citizenship and apply them to southern women.

The majority opinion began with the privileges and immunities protected in article IV of the Articles of Confederation and proceeded to article IV of the Constitution, quoting Justice Bushrod Washington in *Corfield v. Coryell,* an 1823 federal circuit court case arising in Pennsylvania. Washington had written that "it would be more tedious than difficult to enumerate" the fundamental principles that underlie the privileges and immunities "which belong of right to the citizens of all free governments."[10] Nevertheless, it is necessary to be tedious to understand specifically what the members of the Court thought those terms encompassed. The Court listed:

1. Protection by the government, with the right to acquire and possess property of every kind, and

2. The right to pursue and obtain happiness and safety, subject,

nevertheless, to such restraints as the government may prescribe for the general good of the whole.

To these, the Court added other provisions in the original body of the Constitution:

    3. The prohibition against ex post facto laws

    4. The prohibition against bills of attainder

    5. The prohibition against laws impairing the obligation of contracts.

They added rights described in *Crandall v. Nevada* (1868):[11]

    6. To come to the seat of government to assert any claim he [the citizen] may have upon that government

    7. To transact any business he may have with it

    8. To seek its protection

    9. To share its offices

    10. To engage in administering its functions

    11. To have free access to its seaports [and] to the subtreasuries, land offices, and courts of justice in the several States

The Court continued with further items:

    12. The right to demand the care and protection of the federal government over life, liberty, and property on the high seas or within the jurisdiction of a foreign government

    13. The right to peaceably assemble and petition for redress of grievances

    14. The privilege of the writ of *habeas corpus*

    15. The right to use the navigable waters of the United States

    16. All rights secured . . . by treaties with foreign nations

    17. [The privilege] that a citizen of the United States can, of his own volition, become a citizen of any State of the Union by a *bona fide* residence therein

    18. The rights of person and of property

Justice Field, in dissent, added his own emphasis:

    19. Equality of right[:] all pursuits, all professions, all avocations are open without other restrictions than such as are imposed equally upon all others of the same age, sex, and condition

    20. The right of free labor

362

And Justice Bradley, referring to the Declaration of Independence, made his additions:

21. Rights to life, liberty, and the pursuit of happiness [because they] are equivalent to the rights of life, liberty, and property
22. The right to choose one's calling [or profession, or trade][12]

The Supreme Court may not be, as Justice Brennan said in *Cooper v. Aaron*, "the Supreme Law of the Land"—a designation reserved by most of us for the Constitution—but it certainly is the supreme interpreter of the Constitution. In *Slaughterhouse* and its cited opinions, the Court listed twenty-two privileges and immunities of citizenship with surprisingly little repetition. Many of them are irrelevant to the everyday lives of most men and women. Yet if the Supreme Court had guaranteed those twenty-two privileges and immunities to all the people under the jurisdiction of the United States, we would have been a far freer people a century ago.[13]

The *Slaughterhouse* opinions are important because they illustrate an important paradox. Most of the privileges and immunities that the men on the Supreme Court thought were fundamental to citizenship were privileges and immunities that were denied to their wives and to their married sisters and mothers. Moreover, when women asked the members of that Court to extend some of those rights to females, the Court indignantly refused to do so. One need not examine the applicability (or, more often, the inapplicability) of all of those privileges and immunities to women in order to appreciate the irony of the situation. Still, it is instructive to analyze the right to acquire and possess property, because it was repeated. The emphasis that this Court and its predecessors placed on property rights converted what was essentially a matter of private law into a major constitutional principle, thus reinforcing Chief Justice John Marshall's elevation of the contract clause in article I, section 10. In 1873, as in Locke's *Second Treatise on Civil Government* almost two hundred years earlier, men thought that property rights were truly fundamental rights of all mankind. It was not a right of all womankind until after the passage of married women's property statutes.[14]

That topic, of course, brings us to coverture, a subject becoming as familiar to us in the late twentieth century as was its practice a century and a half ago. Under the principles of coverture inherited from English legal traditions, persons who were considered helpless (like infants, idiots, the insane, captives [in Kentucky, that was sometimes a consider-

363

able number of people], and, most important for this discussion, married women) were under various legal disabilities. The consequence of those disabilities was that minors, mentally ill people, and women were "hidden from the law." To be hidden from the law means that one has no legal existence. One who has no legal existence is unable to enjoy some of the basic rights that others enjoy, like the right to own property, which the men on the Supreme Court considered a fundamental privilege of citizenship.

It should be noted that coverture carried compensatory protections. The husband was held responsible for his wife's "necessaries" and, in some state jurisdictions, also for her torts and even for certain crimes. In fact, a married woman was excused from many of her crimes if they were committed in her husband's presence because she was presumed to have acted "in obedience to his will and under his coercion," a presumption recognized in Alabama, and perhaps other states, as recently as 1943. Similarly, spouses could not be convicted of conspiracy in many southern states.[15]

Abolishing coverture is one issue upon which the South was the pioneer. The territory of Arkansas passed the first married women's property act in 1835. Mississippi followed soon after in 1839, Texas and Florida in 1845, the state of Arkansas in 1846, Alabama in 1848. (The better-known married women's property act in New York was also passed in 1848.) The process by which women gained other legal rights relating to property—like the rights to contract, to sue and be sued, to own their own businesses and manage their own affairs and the money they earned—varies from state to state because statutes of general applicability were necessary to supersede the common-law presumption of coverture. The reason why the South was more progressive than other regions where married women's property was concerned is found, *inter alia*, in the Arkansas statute. Legislators who were otherwise totally opposed to women's rights wanted to protect married women's ownership of the family's slaves.[16]

Except in Virginia, what had not begun before the war began soon after it. Nine of the ten Reconstruction constitutions adopted from late 1867 to early 1869 contained the "wonderful reform": the guarantee of property rights to married women. Yet as Suzanne Lebsock and others have pointed out, most of the men who were responsible were interested not in women's rights but in debtor relief, the protection of women from the consequences of indebtedness for which they were not responsible, and guarding their daughters from unscrupulous sons-in-law. For those reasons, in Georgia, North Carolina, and South Carolina, married women's property acts were accompanied by homestead exemptions. These exemptions protected a portion of shelter, land, and implements, up to a stipulated maximum value, from seizure by creditors.[17]

The passage of married women's property acts in so many other states raises the question of Kentucky's tardiness in the nineteenth century. In 1972 Kentucky extended its civil rights statutes to women and was the nineteenth state to ratify the Equal Rights Amendment (ERA); two years later, one statute (with 631 sections) ended gender-based discrimination in statutory and decisional law, and another guaranteed women equal access to housing and to credit. But its married women's property act was not passed until 1894. (Kentucky was also reluctant to ratify the Fourteenth Amendment and did not do so until 1965.) Dozens of Kentuckians know the dynamics that explain why their General Assembly was so progressive in 1972, but little has been written or published on the subject.[18]

The Kentucky experience suggests a question that reaches far beyond Kentucky or, for that matter, the entire South. Historians learn to see things in patterns. Patterns bring cohesiveness to what otherwise would appear to be isolated and inexplicable events. But what explains the differences between states? We need to know what happened in every state, including who did what. "The South" is a manageable region; by my definition it is comprised of only seventeen states. If we had monographic studies of all of the states that are as scrupulously scholarly as those we have of some, we might be able to ask and to answer a truly cosmic question about the role of individuals in influencing history. We need for every state the kind of careful analyses of the politics of southern states that the late V. O. Key published, this time centering on women's issues.[19]

Another area that awaits exploration is the impact of federal land policy on women in the South, both before and after the Civil War. A recent article has unearthed the names of women who, as occupying settlers, were successful claimants to federal grants, and of others who purchased federal land under the series of statutes that were passed by Congress from 1811 to 1834.[20] It is unlikely that any of these women were single women; most were probably widows whose claims perfected those of their deceased husbands. Yet some may have been married women who inherited their land grants. It would be interesting to know the marital status of those women, however few they were. Federal land policy seems to have been less inclusive about ownership than the statutes of some states, but whether federal laws specifically excluded married women from obtaining federal land in states that had married women's property acts is a question worth exploring. Under section 34 of the Judiciary Act of 1789, federal courts were bound by the laws of the states in which they were situated: did federal land policy follow this provision? In the post–Civil War era, did any women receive grants for abandoned land? States, also, had homestead laws; did they vary in their application to women? If they did, what explains the variance?

The justices in *Slaughterhouse* and their counterparts in federal and state courts may have emphasized property rights because many of their families had only recently reached the security of the middle and upper-middle classes, and the continuing political and economic democratization of the nation worried them. The white, usually Anglo-Saxon and Protestant judges, legislators, and members of executive branches who dominated American institutions for so long had always had access to the ballot box and thus tended to take that privilege for granted. Ownership of real property set them apart from others. But to men and women who have never voted, suffrage is the more important issue. The right to vote was the centerpiece of the women's rights movement in every region of the nation. Yet the institution of slavery and the issue of race had unique and important connections with the women's rights movement and had ineluctable consequences in the South.

From the beginning of the republic, many individual women and men had advocated political participation for American women. We all are familiar with Abigail Adams's admonition to her husband to "remember the ladies"—and John's patronizing reply. However, the unified struggle for women's rights began officially at a convention held at Seneca Falls, New York, in 1848. Because the suffrage movement is the most widely studied aspect of women's constitutional rights, its history need not all be repeated here. But from its inception, the women's rights movement, like the Constitution itself, was profoundly affected by slavery. It was at an international antislavery convention that women saw the parallels between their legal condition and that of slaves. It was because these activist women considered slavery so great an evil that they postponed working for their own emancipation and devoted themselves to the antislavery and abolitionist movements. And it was the Civil War amendments that gave women the first tangible promise that they might have legal and political equality.

Southern women had been leaders in the American antislavery movement in the early republic; after all, they knew more about slavery than did women in other sections. It may well have been true, as one southern woman wrote in her diary, that the relations between white men and slave women made all "Southern women . . . abolitionists" and led them to "shudder for the standards of morality in . . . Southern homes." By the 1830s, such ideas could not be expressed publicly, for the South had become a closed society where the issue of slavery was concerned. Feminism, also, was suspect, as was everything that affected the status quo. Thus southern white women were not prominent in the antebellum women's rights movement. Then and for generations later, it simply was not acceptable behavior for southern ladies to participate in controversial political matters. However greatly some southern women may have supported suffrage and other women's rights issues, as their mothers, grandmothers, and great-grandmothers had privately supported the termination of slavery, they could not, and did not, participate publicly. Part of the reason why the Grimké sisters of South Carolina are famous is because they were almost unique.[21]

Fortuitously for my definition of what constitutes the South, the first case raising the issue of women's suffrage to reach the Supreme Court was brought by a southern woman, a native of Missouri. To be accurate, the case was brought by her husband as her "next friend"; as a married woman, Virginia Minor could not sue in her own name. (A designation as a "next friend" is not a commentary on a blissful marriage but is a legal fiction identifying someone other than a guardian who acts in a legal capacity for a person under disability. The term itself is further evidence of the consequences of coverture and was required in some states as recently as the mid-1930s, and perhaps later.)[22]

When *Minor v. Happersett* reached the Supreme Court in 1875,[23] the Court had almost the same membership as in *Slaughterhouse.* The only change was in the chief justiceship; Morrison R. Waite had succeeded Salmon P. Chase. Waite was not Warren. The justices who had earlier listed dozens of rights that came under the privileges-and-immunities clause were not interested in extending them to women, and the chief justice did not encourage them to do so.

The Minors argued that the right to vote was one of the privileges and immunities of citizenship that the states were forbidden to abridge under the terms of the Fourteenth Amendment. To twentieth-century eyes, their argument seems unassailable. It nevertheless was assailed by the Supreme Court, which said that the Fourteenth Amendment was not intended to enfranchise any class of citizens who had previously been disfranchised, and Missouri had not granted women the right to vote. Yet nine years later, in *Ex Parte Yarbrough* (1884), the Court extended federal power to protect the right of black men to vote for members of Congress, although no southern blacks had been enfranchised earlier.[24] Even that gesture was undercut by the Court's earlier decision in *U.S. v. Reese* (1876), which prohibited voting discrimination "on account of race, color, or previous condition of servitude" and thereby challenged the ingenuity of southerners to find other grounds.[25] They soon invented grandfather clauses, understanding-the-Constitution requirements, poll taxes, and similar stratagems to circumvent the Fifteenth Amendment. In those years the Court was a weak reed to lean upon, unless one was a businessman. Legislators were no better: Henry Cabot Lodge's force bill, intended to protect the right of black men to vote, was buried by Congress in 1890. Suffrage for women did not inspire either fear or creativity, only contempt, as the legislative records of Congress and many states attest. Nor did successful candidates for executive offices risk defeat by advocating so controversial an issue.

Yet the struggle went on, in state after state, region after region, eventually reaching the South. There it was greatly complicated by racial attitudes. In the beginning—which for the South was the 1880s—there were alternative strategies. One was to gain a constitutional amendment that would enfranchise all women throughout the nation. The other was to get a state statute that would grant suffrage to women under article I, section 2, clause 1, of the Constitution ("the electors [of the House of Representatives] shall have the qualifications requisite for electors of the most numerous branch of the State legislature") and extend that electoral power to voting for presidential electors and, after ratification of the Seventeenth Amendment in 1913, for U.S. senators.

For many decades the National American Woman Suffrage Association supported both strategies because its leaders thought that any method that extended the franchise to women was a step toward the ultimate goal. However, some of the most prominent southern suffragists preferred the second alternative and founded the Southern States Woman Suffrage Conference (SSWSC), which competed with state chapters of the national organization. To women in the SSWSC, the (Susan B.) Anthony amendment, which involved nationwide suffrage, raised the specter of federal power during Reconstruction and thus the unacceptable possibility of a viable black electorate that included black women. The political equality that the SSWSC sought was one wherein "each state can prescribe the same qualification for its women as it does for its men citizens."[26] In other words, the SSWSC would extend to black women the grandfather clauses and other obstacles that prevented black men from voting. By 1913 southern white women were deeply divided on the racial implications of their own enfranchisement. As the Anthony amendment moved through Congress, the states' rights women earlier associated with the SSWSC tried to eliminate the enforcement provision in its second paragraph. And when that effort failed, they worked against ratification.

Although the racial issue is the most obvious difference between the suffrage movement in the South and elsewhere in the nation, there are also other ways in which the southern experience was distinctive. Southern women had been less involved in the earlier temperance movement, which in the Middle West and East had been a training ground for political action. The distilling industry was less active in opposing suffrage in the South; instead, the opponents of women's right to vote generally rested their case on what they considered chivalrous grounds. Finally, there were virtually no prominent men in the South during the entire period from 1848 to 1920 who supported women's suffrage. When the Nineteenth Amendment was voted on in the House of Representatives, there were only two votes from the states of the Old South in favor of it, one from Virginia and one from North Carolina. The entire delegations of Alabama, Georgia, Louisiana, Mississippi, and South Carolina were uniformly negative. It is ironic that Tennessee was the thirty-sixth state to ratify. And when American women voted in the election of 1920, the Nineteenth Amendment had not been ratified in Virginia, North Carolina, South Carolina, Georgia, Florida, Alabama, Mississippi, Arkansas, Louisiana, and Oklahoma.[27]

Like other citizens, women accept and—to judge by the empirical evidence of their volunteer activities—invite the responsibilities as well as the privileges of citizenship. Those responsibilities include serving on juries. Women were absolutely excluded from jury duty in Alabama until 1966, in South Carolina until 1967, and in Mississippi until 1968. In other southern states, such as Missouri, Tennessee, Florida, and Loui-

369

siana, they were not called as jurors unless they had filed written declarations stating their desire to serve. In *Hoyt v. Florida* (1961), the U.S. Supreme Court upheld the Florida statute despite a challenge based on the equal-protection clause of the Fourteenth Amendment.[28] Fourteen years later, in *Taylor v. Louisiana,* the court invalidated a similar Louisiana statute on Sixth Amendment grounds but by its failure to address the equal-protection issue left the situation confused.[29] In other states, including Georgia, Texas, and South Carolina, women were given child-care exemptions that were not available to men. Child-care exemptions in Virginia and Oklahoma that were gender-neutral on their face were discriminatory in their application because they were granted almost exclusively to women. Not until a series of state statutory revisions in the mid-1970s did the composition of southern juries change significantly.[30]

This situation means that until little more than a decade ago, many southern women were either denied or discouraged from participating in a civic responsibility that, in our legal tradition, goes back to Anglo-Saxon times. The provisions that exempted women discriminated against men who could not claim similar exemptions, regardless of their family responsibilities. These practices also had a differential impact upon litigants because men tend to favor other men, as women tend to favor other women, when it comes to sentencing and awarding damages. Most important of all, juries from which women were excluded did not offer women who were criminal defendants the Sixth Amendment right to an impartial jury from a cross-section of their communities.[31]

State criminal codes offer other instances of differential treatment of women that violate the principle as well as the practice of the Fourteenth Amendment's equal-protection clause. The best known are those relating to sexual conduct, one of the clearest examples of the continuing double standard in our society. One thinks immediately of female prostitution, sometimes called the crime without a victim. It does have its legal victims: the prostitutes and the madams who are prosecuted, although their patrons are not.

The area of law relating to sexual activity that has undergone the greatest changes recently is that involving rape. Despite the insensitivity still exhibited by some male judges in their dicta, the statutes do protect women and girls from heterosexual attack but often do not similarly protect men and boys. Until 1977, as a matter of law and definition, a married woman could not be seduced in Alabama; lack of chastity was a

370

complete bar to conviction. At the same time, it was a felony for a man to seduce an unmarried woman. However, the evidentiary requirements were rather bizarre: the prosecutrix was required to provide corroborative testimony for conviction of sexual crimes—but not for conviction of robbery, which also potentially carried the death penalty. I suspect that if women had had witnesses on the occasions when seduction was likely to occur, there would have been few crimes to prosecute.

There are other examples of differences in the constitutional position of southern women where criminal law is concerned. One that is still on the books, at least in Alabama and Texas, is the "unwritten law" that is, in fact, written in decisional law. A man who kills his wife or her paramour will probably be charged with manslaughter and not with murder, especially if he is a witness to their relationship. Yet there is no corresponding decisional law if a wife discovers her husband with another lover.[32] I have great confidence that all of Phyllis Schlafly's followers have husbands who were chaste at marriage and have been faithful ever since. Any women in her substantial following whose husbands do not meet those requirements, and who learn about the decisional law in at least two states, should be recruited for the next drive to ratify the ERA.

That point raises, of course, the final issue: the ERA and how it fared in the South. Six states ratified it: Delaware, Texas, Maryland, Tennessee, West Virginia, and Kentucky. Eleven of the fifteen states that did not ratify were southern states. Only Maryland, Texas, and Virginia have passed state equal-rights provisions. (Kentucky and perhaps some other states have statutes that approximate state ERAs.) There has been a great deal of speculation but little empirical evidence beyond voting records and public opinion polls to explain the widespread southern opposition to the ERA. On this matter as on others mentioned herein, it is time for the historians to get busy. Now is the moment to gather the evidence for the historians of the future. Just as there are seventeen southern states, there are seventeen different histories, although I expect there are more patterns of similarity than of dissimilarity. It has been fifteen years since Congress passed the ERA. Probably most of the leaders who advocated and who opposed ratification in their states are still around and available for oral history interviews—and they should be obtained now. The ERA battles also provide an opportunity to learn about the followers as well as the leaders. What were the dynamics of their decisions? Have they ever changed their minds or wished they had been on the other side? Thus far, sociologists and political scientists are

371

ahead of historians; we need to tackle the subject. Eight hundred women came to a Kentucky interim legislative hearing in 1974. About half of those present advocated recision of the ERA and half opposed recision.[33] No one thought of taking down everyone's names and addresses: if we had, we could have kept our students busy for years interviewing them. As Lawrence Friedman once said about the opportunities that lie in court records, there are many kilo-Ph.D.'s (the material for a thousand Ph.D. dissertations) out there, just waiting to be written up.

This call to arms is coupled with a plea for empirical evidence. It is ironic but true that legal and constitutional histories have too often been based upon unproved and unprovable assumptions. Rigorous investigation and evidence are needed. The wide variance in women's rights, from state to state, is a guarantee that the women's movement will continue until gender-based discrimination is ended. As we witness the struggle to realize constitutional rights for both men and women in the South and elsewhere, let us gather the evidence for our posterity.[34]

Notes

1. See Paul L. Murphy, "Time to Reclaim: The Current Challenge of American Constitutional History," *American Historical Review* 69 (1963): 64–79; Anne Firor Scott, "On Seeing and Not Seeing: A Case of Historical Invisibility," *Journal of American History* 71 (1984): 7–21; Eleanor M. Boatwright, "The Political Status of Women in Georgia, 1783–1860," *Georgia History Quarterly* 25 (1941): 301–24; W. O. Hart, "Rights of Women in Louisiana," *Louisiana History Quarterly* 4 (1921): 437–58; and Leo Kanowitz, *Sex Roles in Law and Society* (Albuquerque, N.M., 1973).

2. This definition is suggested also in Paul Finkelman, "Exploring Southern Legal History," *North Carolina Law Review* 64 (1985): 86.

3. Leonard P. Curry, *The Free Black in Urban America, 1800–1850: The Shadow of the Dream* (Chicago, 1981); Deborah Gray White, *Ar'n't I a Woman? Female Slaves in the Plantation South* (New York, 1985).

4. The equal-protection clause of the Fourteenth Amendment was not used to protect women against discrimination until *Reed v. Reed*, 404 U.S. 71 (1971).

5. One example of the possibilities that are largely unexplored is Charles H. Martin, "Race, Gender and Southern Justice: The Rosa Lee Ingram Case," *American Journal of Legal History* 29 (1985): 251–68.

6. Mary E. Young, "Women, Civilization, and the Indian Question," in *Clio Was a Woman: Studies in the History of American Women*, ed. Mabel E. Deutrich

and Virginia C. Purdy (Washington, D.C., 1980), 98–110; Frederick E. Hoxie, "Toward a 'New' North American Indian Legal History," *American Journal of Legal History* 30 (1986): 351–57; Gerda Lerner, ed., *Black Women in White America: A Documentary History* (New York, 1972).

7. Daisy Bates, *The Long Shadow of Little Rock: A Memoir* (New York, 1962); Myrlie Evers, *For Me, the Living* (Garden City, N.Y., 1967); Joanne Grant, "Mississippi Politics: A Day in the Life of Ella J. Baker," in *The Black Woman: An Anthology,* ed. Toni Cade (New York: 1970), 56–62. Basic bibliographies for exploring related topics are in *Blacks in America: Bibliographic Essays,* ed. James M. McPherson et al. (Garden City, N.Y., 1971).

8. Richard B. Morris, *Studies in the History of American Law, with Special Reference to the Seventeenth and Eighteenth Centuries* (New York, 1930); Mary R. Beard, *Woman as Force in History: A Study in Traditions and Realities* (New York, 1946).

9. Marylynn Salmon, "The Legal Status of Women in Early America: A Reappraisal," *Law and History Review* 1 (1983): 129–51. This essay contains a useful bibliography supporting her argument as well as surveying other aspects of women's legal status: dower, conveyancing, and the law of separate estates. For a more comprehensive study, see Salmon, *Women and the Law of Property in Early America* (Chapel Hill, N.C., 1986). For recent scholarship on the position of women in the early republic, see Linda K. Kerber, *Women of the Republic: Intellect and Ideology in Revolutionary America* (Chapel Hill, N.C., 1980); and Mary Beth Norton, *Liberty's Daughters: The Revolutionary Experience of American Women, 1750–1850* (Boston, 1980). On the legal status of women in the Jacksonian era, see Norma Basch, "Equity vs. Equality: Emerging Concepts of Women's Political Status in the Age of Jackson," *Journal of the Early Republic* 3 (1983): 297–318.

10. F. Cas. 3230 (1823).

11. 6 Wall. 35 (1868).

12. Butchers Benevolent Association of New Orleans v. Crescent City Livestock Landing and Slaughter-house Company, 16 Wall. 36 (1873).

13. Cooper v. Aaron, 358 U.S. 1 (1958). For an excellent review essay useful as a beginning point for those interested in these and other issues, see Elaine Tyler May, "Expanding the Past: Recent Scholarship on Women in Politics and Work," *Reviews in American History* 10 (1982): 216–33.

14. For example, in Bradwell v. Illinois, 16 Wall. 130, 141 (1873), a case brought by a woman who was refused admission to the bar, Justice Bradley wrote in a concurring opinion, "The natural and proper timidity and delicacy which belongs to the female sex evidently unfits it for many of the occupations of civil life. . . . The harmony, not to say identity, of interests and views which belong, or should belong, to the family institution is repugnant to the ideas of a woman adopting a distinct and independent career from that of her hus-

band. . . . The paramount destiny and mission of woman are to fulfil the noble and benign offices of wife and mother. This is the law of the Creator." Ironically, Myra Bradwell's husband was also an attorney.

15. Marjorie Fine Knowles, "The Legal Status of Women in Alabama: A Crazy Quilt," *Alabama Law Review* 29 (1978): 499.

16. Michael B. Dougan, "The Arkansas Married Woman's Property Law," *Arkansas Historical Quarterly* 46 (1987): 3–26; Elizabeth G. Brown, "Husband and Wife—Memorandum on the Mississippi Woman's Law of 1839," *Michigan Law Review* 42 (1944): 1110–21; Peggy A. Rabkin, *Fathers to Daughters: The Legal Foundations of Female Emancipation* (Westport, Conn., 1980); Norma Basch, *In the Eyes of the Law: Women, Marriage, and Property in Nineteenth Century New York* (Ithaca, N.Y., 1982); Richard H. Chused, "Married Women's Property Law, 1800–1850," *Georgetown Law Journal* 71 (1983): 1359–1425.

17. Suzanne D. Lebsock, "Radical Reconstruction and the Property Rights of Southern Women," *Journal of Southern History* 43 (1977): 195. This article also contains citations to the married women's property statutes passed by the southern states during Reconstruction.

18. Martha Carson, "The Kentucky Married Women's Property Act: An Early Appeal for Justice," *Border States: Journal of the Kentucky-Tennessee American Studies Association* 5 (1985): 20–28.

19. V. O. Key, Jr., *Southern Politics in State and Nation* (New York, 1949).

20. Richard H. Chused, "The Oregon Donation Act of 1850 and Nineteenth Century Federal Married Women's Property Law," *Law and History Review* 2 (1984): 44–78.

21. Mary Elizabeth Massey, "The Making of a Feminist," *Journal of Southern History* 39 (1973): 9. See also Russel Nye, *Fettered Freedom: Civil Liberties and the Slavery Controversy, 1830–1860,* rev. ed. (East Lansing, Mich., 1963); Anne Firor Scott, *The Southern Lady: From Pedestal to Politics, 1830–1930* (Chicago, 1970); and Gerda Lerner, *The Grimké Sisters of South Carolina: Rebels against Slavery* (New York, 1967).

22. In the 1937 case that marked the Supreme Court's "switch in time that saved nine," West Coast Hotel v. Parrish, 300 U.S. 379 (1937), Elsie Parrish was represented in court by her husband as her next friend.

23. 21 Wall. 162 (1875).

24. 110 U.S. 651 (1884).

25. 91 U.S. 214 (1876).

26. Kenneth R. Johnson, "Kate Gordon and the Woman-Suffrage Movement in the South," *Journal of Southern History* 38 (1972): 374.

27. Elizabeth Cady Stanton, Susan B. Anthony, Matilda Joslyn Gage, and Ida M. Harper, eds., *History of Woman Suffrage,* 6 vols. (New York and Rochester, N.Y., 1881–1922); Carol Ellen DuBois, *Feminism and Suffrage: The Emergence of an Independent Women's Movement in America, 1848–1869* (Ithaca,

N.Y., 1978); Carol Lynn Yellin, "Countdown in Tennessee, 1920," *American Heritage*, 1978, 12–23, 26–35; Janet K. Boles, "Systemic Factors Underlying Legislative Responses to Woman Suffrage and the Equal Rights Amendment," in *The Equal Rights Amendment: The Politics and Process of Ratification of the 27th Amendment to the U.S. Constitution*, ed. Sarah Slavin, Women and Politics, vol. 2 (New York, 1982), 8; A. Elizabeth Taylor, "The Woman Suffrage Movement in Texas," *Journal of Southern History* 17 (1951): 194–215; Kenneth R. Johnson, "Kate Gordon and the Woman-Suffrage Movement in the South," *Journal of Southern History* 38 (1972): 365–92; Paul E. Fuller, *Laura Clay and the Women's Rights Movement* (Lexington, Ky., 1975). The Nineteenth Amendment was rejected by seven southern states. In Alabama the vote was fifty-nine to thirty-one, almost two to one in opposition. Knowles, "Legal Status of Women in Alabama," 482. The husband's right to choose the family domicile also had the effect of limiting women's right to vote. Ibid., 483.

28. 368 U.S. 57 (1961).

29. 419 U.S. 522 (1975).

30. Barbara A. Brown, Ann E. Freedman, Harriet N. Katz, and Alice M. Price, *Women's Rights and the Law: The Impact of the ERA on State Laws* (New York, 1977), 262–68.

31. Stuart S. Nagel and Lenore J. Weitzman, "Women as Litigants," *Hastings Law Journal* 23 (1971): 171–98.

32. Knowles, "Legal Status of Women in Alabama," 488–98.

33. Catherine Arnott, "Feminists and Anti-Feminists as True Believers," *Sociology and Social Research* 57 (1977): 300–306; Kent L. Tendin et al., "Social Background and Political Differences Between Pro- and Anti-ERA Activists," *American Political Quarterly* 5 (1977): 395–408; David W. Brady and Kent L. Tendin, "Ladies in Pink: Religion and Political Ideology in the Anti-ERA Movement," *Social Science Quarterly* 56 (1976): 564–75; Janet K. Boles, *The Politics of the Equal Rights Amendment* (New York, 1979), 1–8.

34. See NOW Legal Defense and Education Fund and Renee Chero-O'Leary, *The State by State Guide to Women's Legal Rights* (New York, 1987).

Select Bibliography

Although constitutional themes have figured prominently in the history of the South, scholars have devoted surprisingly little energy to the study of constitutions and constitutionalism. As the essays in this volume suggest, however, greater attention to constitutional matters may well provide new insights into southern political and legal culture and, in so doing, offer a fuller perspective on the long-standing debate about southern uniqueness. The full range of literature dealing with the South and American constitutionalism is available in *Comprehensive Bibliography of American Constitutional and Legal History, 1896–1979*, ed. Kermit L. Hall, 5 vols. (Millwood, N.Y., 1984). The following bibliography also lists works bearing upon public- rather than private-law matters, although some overlap is inevitable, and upon the concepts of sectionalism and regionalism as they relate to constitutional developments.

Books

Alden, John Richard. *The First South*. Baton Rouge, 1961.

Ayers, Edward L. *Vengeance and Justice: Crime and Punishment in the Nineteenth-Century South*. New York, 1984.

Bagwell, William. *School Desegregation in the Carolinas*. Columbia, S.C., 1972.

Barney, William. *The Secessionist Impulse: Alabama and Mississippi*. Princeton, N.J., 1974.

Bartley, Numan V. *The Rise of Massive Resistance: Race and Politics in the South during the 1950s*. Baton Rouge, 1969.

Bass, Jack, and Walter DeVries. *The Transformation of Southern Politics: Social Change and Political Consequence since 1945*. New York, 1976.

Dauer, Elizabeth Kelly. *Commentaries on the Constitution, 1790–1860*. New York, 1952.

Belknap, Michal R. *Federal Law and Southern Order: Racial Violence and Constitutional Conflict in the Post-Brown South*. Athens, Ga., 1987.

Bennett, Walter Hartwell. *American Theories of Federalism*. University, Ala., 1964.

Bensel, Richard F. *Sectionalism and American Political Development, 1880–1980*. Madison, Wis., 1984.

Berry, Mary Frances. *Black Resistance/White Law: A History of Constitutional Racism in America*. New York, 1971.

377

Beveridge, Albert J. *The Life of John Marshall.* 4 vols. Boston, 1919.

Black, Earl. *Southern Governors and Civil Rights: Racial Segregation as a Campaign Issue in the Second Reconstruction.* Cambridge, Mass., 1976.

Blaustein, Albert P., and Clarence Clyde Ferguson, Jr. *Desegregation and the Law: The Meaning and Effect of the School Segregation Cases.* 2d ed. New York, 1962.

Bodenhamer, David J., and James W. Ely, Jr., eds. *Ambivalent Legacy: A Legal History of the South.* Jackson, Miss., 1984.

Bruce, Dickson D., Jr. *The Rhetoric of Conservatism: The Virginia Convention of 1829–30 and the Conservative Tradition in the South.* San Marino, Calif., 1982.

Burk, Robert F. *The Eisenhower Administration and Black Civil Rights.* Knoxville, Tenn., 1984.

Carpenter, Jesse T. *The South as a Conscious Minority: A Study in Political Thought.* New York, 1930.

Carter, Dan T. *Scottsboro: A Tragedy of the American South.* Baton Rouge, 1969.

———. *When the War Was Over: The Failure of Self-Reconstruction in the South, 1865–1867.* Baton Rouge, 1985.

Cell, John W. *The Highest Stage of White Supremacy: The Origins of Segregation in South Africa and the American South.* Cambridge, Mass., 1982.

Chafe, William. *Civilities and Civil Rights: Greensboro, North Carolina, and the Black Struggle for Freedom.* New York, 1980.

Cole, Arthur C. *The Irrepressible Conflict, 1850–1865.* New York, 1934.

Cooper, William J., Jr. *Liberty and Slavery: Southern Politics to 1860.* New York, 1983.

Coulter, E. Merton, *The South during Reconstruction, 1865–1877.* Baton Rouge, 1947.

Cullen, Charles T. *St. George Tucker and Law in Virginia, 1772–1804.* New York, 1987.

Current, Richard N. *Northernizing the South.* Athens, Ga., 1983.

Daniel, Pete. *The Shadow of Slavery: Peonage in the South, 1901–1969.* Urbana, Ill., 1972.

Durden, Robert F. *The Self-Inflicted Wound: Southern Politics in the Nineteenth Century.* Lexington, Ky., 1985.

Eaton, Clement. *The Freedom-of-Thought Struggle in the Old South.* Rev. ed. New York, 1964.

Elliot, Jonathan, ed. *The Debates in the Several State Conventions, on the Adoption of the Federal Constitution.* 5 vols. Philadelphia, 1836–59.

Ellis, Richard E. *The Jeffersonian Crisis: Courts and Politics in the Young Republic.* New York, 1971.

———*The Union at Risk: Jacksonian Democracy, States' Rights, and the Nullification Crisis.* New York, 1987.

Ely, James W., Jr. *The Crisis of Conservative Virginia: The Byrd Organization and the Politics of Massive Resistance.* Knoxville, Tenn., 1976.

Fairclough, Adam. *"To Redeem the Soul of America"*: *The Southern Christian Leadership Conference and Martin Luther King, Jr.* Athens, Ga., 1987.

Faulkner, Robert K. *The Jurisprudence of John Marshall.* 1968. Westport, Conn., 1980.

Fehrenbacher, Don E. *The Dred Scott Case: Its Significance in American Law and Politics.* New York, 1978.

Finkelman, Paul. *An Imperfect Union: Slavery, Federalism, and Comity.* Chapel Hill, N.C., 1981.

Franklin, John Hope. *The Militant South, 1800–1861.* Cambridge, Mass., 1956.

Freehling, William W. *Prelude to Civil War: The Nullification Controversy in South Carolina, 1816–1836.* New York, 1965.

Freyer, Tony. *The Little Rock Crisis: A Constitutional Interpretation.* Westport, Conn., 1984.

Fuller, Paul E. *Laura Clay and the Women's Rights Movement.* Lexington, Ky., 1975.

Gillette, William. *Retreat from Reconstruction, 1869–1879.* Baton Rouge, La., 1979.

Grantham, Dewey W. *Southern Progressivism: The Reconciliation of Progress and Tradition.* Knoxville, Tenn., 1983.

Green, Fletcher M. *Constitutional Development in the South Atlantic States, 1776–1860.* Chapel Hill, N.C., 1930.

Greenberg, Kenneth S. *Masters and Statesmen: The Political Culture of American Slavery.* Baltimore, 1985.

Greene, Jack P. *The Quest for Power: The Lower House of Assembly in the Southern Royal Colonies, 1689–1776.* Chapel Hill, N.C., 1963.

Harris, William C. *The Day of the Carpetbagger: Republican Reconstruction in Mississippi.* Baton Rouge, La., 1979.

Haskins, George L., and Herbert A. Johnson. *Foundations of Power: John Marshall, 1801–15.* Vol. 2 of *The Oliver Wendell Holmes Devise History of the Supreme Court of the United States.* New York, 1981.

Hill, C. William, Jr. *The Political Theory of John Taylor of Caroline.* Rutherford, N.J., 1977.

Hitchcock, Henry. *American State Constitutions: A Study of Their Growth.* Boston, 1887.

Holt, Michael F. *The Political Crisis of the 1850s.* New York, 1978.

Howard, A. E. Dick. *Commentaries on the Constitution of Virginia.* 2 vols. Charlottesville, Va., 1974.

Hyman, Harold M. *A More Perfect Union: The Impact of the Civil War and Reconstruction upon the Constitution.* New York, 1973.

Hyman, Harold M., and William M. Wiecek. *Equal Justice under Law: Constitutional Development, 1835–1875.* New York, 1982.

Jefferson, Thomas. *Notes on the State of Virginia.* 1781. Reprinted in *The Portable Thomas Jefferson,* ed. Merrill D. Peterson, 11–17. New York, 1975.

Johnson, Michael P. *Toward a Patriarchal Republic: The Secession of Georgia.* Baton Rouge, 1977.

Kaczorowski, Robert J. *The Politics of Judicial Interpretation: The Federal Courts, Department of Justice and Civil Rights, 1866–1876.* New York, 1985.

Keller, Morton. *Affairs of State: Public Life in Late Nineteenth Century America.* Cambridge, Mass., 1977.

Kerber, Linda K. *Women of the Republic: Intellect and Ideology in Revolutionary America.* Chapel Hill, N.C., 1980.

Key, V. O., Jr. *Southern Politics in State and Nation.* New York, 1949.

Kirby, Jack Temple. *Darkness at the Dawning: Race and Reform in the Progressive South.* Philadelphia, 1972.

Kluger, Richard. *Simple Justice: The History of Brown v. Board of Education and Black America's Struggle for Equality.* New York, 1975.

Kousser, J. Morgan. *The Shaping of Southern Politics: Suffrage Restriction and the Establishment of the One-Party South, 1880–1910.* New Haven, Conn., 1974.

Landau, Norma. *The Justices of the Peace, 1679–1760.* Berkeley, Calif., 1984.

Lee, Charles R., Jr. *The Confederate Constitutions.* Chapel Hill, N.C., 1963. Westport, Conn., 1974.

Levy, Leonard. *Jefferson and Civil Liberties: The Darker Side.* Cambridge, Mass., 1963.

Lewinson, Paul. *Race, Class and Party: A History of Negro Suffrage and White Politics in the South.* London, 1932.

Lutz, Donald S. *Popular Consent and Popular Control: Whig Political Theory in the Early State Constitutions.* Baton Rouge, 1980.

McMillen, Neil R. *The Citizens' Council: Organized Resistance to the Second Reconstruction, 1954–64.* Urbana, Ill., 1971.

Magrath, C. Peter. *Yazoo: Law and Politics in the Early Republic: The Case of Fletcher v. Peck.* Providence, R.I., 1966.

Martin, Charles H. *The Angelo Herndon Case and Southern Justice.* New York, 1967.

Mathews, Donald R., and James W. Prothro. *Negroes and the New South Politics.* New York, 1966.

Moore, A. B. *Conscription and Conflict in the Confederacy.* New York, 1924.

Moore, Harry E. *American Regionalism: A Cultural Historical Approach to National Integration.* Roslyn Heights, N.Y., 1938.

Moore, John Henry. *A Study in State Rights.* New York, 1911.

Morgan, Donald G. *Justice William Johnson, the First Dissenter: The Career and Philosophy of a Jeffersonian Judge.* Columbia, S.C., 1954.

Morgan, Edmund S. *American Slavery/American Freedom: The Ordeal of Colonial Virginia.* New York, 1975.

Morris, Richard B. *Studies in the History of American Law, with Special Reference to the Seventeenth and Eighteenth Centuries.* New York, 1930.

Nelson, Margaret V. *A Study of Judicial Review in Virginia, 1789–1928.* New York, 1947.

Novak, Daniel. *The Wheel of Servitude: Black Forced Labor after Slavery.* Lexington, Ky., 1978.

Nye, Russell B. *Fettered Freedom: Civil Liberties and the Slavery Controversy, 1830–1860.* Rev. ed. East Lansing, Mich., 1963.

Orfield, Gary. *The Reconstruction of Southern Education: The Schools and the 1964 Civil Rights Act.* New York, 1969.

Owsley, Frank. *State Rights in the Confederacy.* Chicago, 1925.

Peltason, Jack W. *Fifty-Eight Lonely Men: Southern Federal Judges and School Desegregation.* New York, 1961.

Perman, Michael. *The Road to Redemption: Southern Politics, 1869–1879.* Chapel Hill, N.C., 1984.

Potter, David M. *The South and the Concurrent Majority.* Edited by Don E. Fehrenbacher and Carl N. Degler. Baton Rouge, 1972.

——. *The South and the Sectional Conflict.* Baton Rouge, 1968.

Price, Alice M. *Women's Rights and the Law: The Impact of the ERA on State Law.* New York, 1977.

Price, Hugh D. *The Negro and Southern Politics: A Chapter in Florida History.* New York, 1957.

Pride, Richard A., and J. David Woodard. *The Burden of Busing: The Politics of Desegregation in Nashville, Tennessee.* Knoxville, Tenn., 1985.

Rable, George C. *But There Was No Peace: The Role of Violence in the Politics of Reconstruction.* Athens, Ga., 1984.

Reed, John Shelton. *One South: An Ethnic Approach to Regional Culture.* Baton Rouge, 1982.

Robinson, Donald L. *Slavery in the Structure of American Politics, 1765–1820.* New York, 1971.

Robinson, William M. *Justice in Grey: A History of the Judicial System of the Confederate States of America.* Cambridge, Mass., 1941.

Salmon, Marylynn. *Women and the Law of Property in Early America.* Chapel Hill, N.C., 1986.

Secrist, Horace. *An Economic Analysis of the Constitutional Restrictions upon Public Indebtedness in the United States.* New York, 1914.

Shalhope, Robert E. *John Taylor of Caroline: Pastoral Republican.* Columbia, S.C., 1980.

Stampp, Kenneth M. *The Imperiled Union: Essays on the Background of the Civil War.* New York, 1980.

Stephens, Alexander H. *A Constitutional View of the Late War between the States.* 2 vols. Philadelphia, 1868, 1870.

Tachau, Mary K. B. *Federal Courts in the Early Republic: Kentucky, 1789–1816.* Princeton, N.J., 1978.

Thomas, Emory M. *The Confederate Nation, 1861–1865.* New York, 1979.

Thompson, Edgar T., ed. *Perspectives on the South: Agenda for Research.* Durham, N.C., 1967.

Thornton, J. Mills III. *Politics and Power in a Slave Society: Alabama, 1800–1860.* Baton Rouge, 1978.

Turner, Frederick Jackson. *Sectionalism in American History.* New York, 1932.

Tushnet, Mark V. *The NAACP's Legal Strategy against Segregated Education, 1925–1950.* Chapel Hill, N.C., 1987.

Wiecek, William M. *The Sources of Antislavery Constitutionalism in America, 1760–1848.* Ithaca, N.Y., 1977.

Wilkinson, J. Harvie. *From Brown to Baake: The Supreme Court and School Integration, 1954–1968.* New York, 1976.

Williamson, Joel. *The Origins of Segregation.* Lexington, Mass., 1968.

Wilson, Major L. *Space, Time, and Freedom: The Quest for Nationality and the Irrepressible Conflict, 1815–1861.* Westport, Conn., 1974.

Woodward, C. Vann. *American Counterpoint: Slavery and Racism in the North-South Dialogue.* Boston, 1964.

——. *The Burden of Southern History.* Rev. ed. Baton Rouge, 1968.

——. *The Strange Career of Jim Crow.* 3d rev. ed. New York, 1974.

Wooster, Ralph. *The People in Power: Courthouse and Statehouse in the Lower South, 1850–1860.* Knoxville, Tenn., 1969.

——. *Politicians, Planters, and Plain Folk: Courthouse and Statehouse in the Upper South.* Knoxville, Tenn., 1975.

——. *The Secession Conventions of the South.* Princeton, N.J., 1962.

Articles and Chapters in Books

Barnhart, John D. "The Tennessee Constitution of 1796," *Journal of Southern History* 9 (1943): 534–51.

Basch, Norma. "Equity vs. Equality: Emerging Concepts of Women's Political Status in the Age of Jackson." *Journal of the Early Republic* 3 (1983): 297–318.

Beard, Charles A. "The Constitution and States Rights." *Virginia Quarterly Review* 11 (1935): 481–95.

Bestor, Arthur, Jr. "State Sovereignty and Slavery: A Reinterpretation of Proslavery Constitutional Doctrine, 1846–1860." *Journal of the Illinois State Historical Society* 54 (1961): 117–80.

Boatright, Eleanor M. "The Political Status of Women in Georgia, 1783–1860." *Georgia History Quarterly* 25 (1941): 301–24.

Brown, Elizabeth G. "Husband and Wife—Memorandum on the Mississippi Woman's Law of 1839." *Michigan Law Review* 42 (1944): 1110–21.

Brown, Richard H. "The Missouri Crisis, Slavery, and the Politics of Jacksonianism." *South Atlantic Quarterly* 65 (1966): 55–72.

Caffey, Francis G. "Suffrage Limitation at the South." *Albany Law Review* 4 (1943): 453–64.

Chused, Richard H. "Married Women's Property Law, 1800–1850." *Georgetown Law Journal* 71 (1983): 1359–1425.

Cohen, William. "Negro Involuntary Servitude in the South, 1865–1940: A Preliminary Analysis." *Journal of Southern History* 42 (1976): 31–60.

Cole, Arthur C. "The South and the Right of Secession in the Early Fifties." *Mississippi Valley Historical Review* 1 (1914): 376–99.

Crittenden, Christopher H. "The Surrender of the Charter of Carolina." *North Carolina Historical Review* 1 (1924): 383–402.

Davis, Donald W. "Ratification of the Constitution of 1868—Record of the Votes." *Louisiana History* 6 (1965): 301–5.

Dougan, Michael B. "The Arkansas Married Woman's Property Law." *Arkansas Historical Quarterly* 46 (1987): 3–26.

Elazar, Daniel. "The Principles and Traditions Underlying State Constitutions." *Publius* 12 (1982): 11–25.

Ely, James W., Jr. "American Independence and the Law: A Study of Post-Revolutionary South Carolina Legislation." *Vanderbilt Law Review* 26 (1973): 939–71.

Ely, James W., Jr., and David J. Bodenhamer. "Regionalism and American Legal History: The Southern Experience." *Vanderbilt Law Review* 39 (1986): 539–67.

Finkelman, Paul. "Exploring Southern Legal History." *North Carolina Law Review* 64 (1985): 77–116.

Fish, Peter G. "From Virginia Readjuster to United States Senior Circuit Judge: The Ascent of Edmund Waddill, Jr. (1855–1931)." *American Journal of Legal History* 30 (1986): 199–240.

Fitts, Albert N. "The Confederate Convention: The Constitutional Debate." *Alabama Review* 2 (1949): 189–210.

———. "The Confederate Convention: The Provisional Constitution." *Alabama Review* 2 (1949): 83–101.

Greene, Jack P. "From the Perspective of Law: Context and Legitimacy in the Origins of the American Revolution." *South Atlantic Quarterly* 85 (1986): 56–77.

———. "'Slavery or Independence': Some Reflections on the Relationship among Liberty, Black Bondage, and Equality in Revolutionary South Carolina." *South Carolina Historical Magazine* 80 (1979): 193–214.

Hall, Kermit L. "The Judiciary on Trial: State Constitutional Reform and the Rise of an Elected Judiciary, 1846–1860." *Historian* 46 (1983): 337–54.

————. "Political Power and Constitutional Legitimacy: The South Carolina Ku Klux Klan Trials, 1871–1872." *Emory Law Journal* 33 (1984): 921–51.

Jaffa, Harry V. " 'Partly Federal, Partly National': On the Political Theory of the Civil War." In *A Nation of States,* edited by Robert A. Goldwin, 109–37. 2d ed. Chicago, 1973.

Johnson, Ludwell H. III. "The Confederacy: What Was It? The View from the Federal Courts." *Civil War History* 32 (1986): 5–22.

Kateb, George. "The Majority Principle: Calhoun and His Antecedents." *Political Science Quarterly* 84 (1969): 583–605.

Keller, Morton. "The Politics of State Constitutional Revision, 1820–1930." In *The Constitutional Convention as an Amending Device,* edited by Kermit L. Hall, Harold M. Hyman, and Leon V. Sigal, 87–112. Washington, D.C., 1981.

Knowles, Marjorie Fine. "The Legal Status of Women in Alabama: A Crazy Quilt." *Alabama Law Review* 29 (1978): 427–515.

Lebsock, Suzanne D. "Radical Reconstruction and the Property Rights of Southern Women." *Journal of Southern History* 43 (1977): 195–216.

Lerner, Ralph. "Calhoun's New Science of Politics." *American Political Science Review* 57 (1963): 918–32.

Leslie, William T. "The Confederate Constitution." *Michigan Quarterly Review* 2 (1963): 153–65.

Lutz, Donald S. "The Purposes of American State Constitutions." *Publius* 12 (1982): 11–42.

Malone, Dumas. "Thomas Cooper and the State Rights Movement in South Carolina, 1823–1830." *North Carolina Historical Review* 3 (1926): 184–97.

Martin, Charles H. "Race, Gender and Southern Justice: The Rosa Lee Ingram Case." *American Journal of Legal History* 29 (1985): 251–68.

Nash, A. E. Kier. "Fairness and Formalism in the Trials of Blacks in State Supreme Courts of the Old South." *Virginia Law Review* 56 (1970): 64–100.

Nixon, H. C., and John T. Nixon. "The Confederate Constitution Today." *Georgia Review* 9 (1955): 369–76.

Oakes, James. "From Republicanism to Liberalism: Ideological Change and the Crisis of the Old South." *American Quarterly* 37 (1985): 551–71.

Prescott, Frank W. "The Executive Veto in the Southern States." *Journal of Politics* 10 (1948): 659–75.

Riegel, Stephen J. "The Persistent Career of Jim Crow: Lower Federal Courts and the 'Separate but Equal' Doctrine, 1865–1896." *American Journal of Legal History* 28 (1984): 17–40.

Russ, William A. "Registration and Disfranchisement under Radical Reconstruction." *Mississippi Valley Historical Review* 21 (1934): 163–80.

Scheiber, Harry N. "Federalism, the Southern Regional Economy, and Public Policy since 1865." In *Ambivalent Legacy: A Legal History of the South,* edited by David J. Bodenhamer and James W. Ely, Jr., 69–105. Jackson, Miss., 1984.

———. "Xenophobia and Parochialism in the Early History of American Legal Process: From the Jacksonian Era to the Sagebrush Rebellion." *William and Mary Law Review* 23 (1982): 625–62.

Schlesinger, Arthur M. "The State Rights Fetish." In *New Viewpoints in American History,* edited by Schlesinger, 234–56. New York, 1934.

Shanks, Henry T. "Conservative Constitutional Tendencies of the Virginia Secession Convention." In *Essays in Southern History Presented to Joseph Gregorie de Roulhac Hamilton,* edited by Fletcher M. Green, 203–34. Chapel Hill, N.C., 1949.

Shofner, Jerrell H. "Custom, Law and History: The Enduring Influence of Florida's 'Black Code'." *Florida Historical Quarterly* 55 (1977): 277–98.

Smiley, David L. "Revolutionary Origins of the South's Constitutional Defenses." *North Carolina Historical Review* 44 (1967): 256–69.

Spicer, George W. "The Federal Judiciary and Political Change in the South." *Journal of Politics* 26 (1964): 154–76.

Sturm, Albert L. "The Development of American State Constitutions." *Publius* 12 (1982): 57–98.

Swinney, Everette. "Enforcing the Fifteenth Amendment, 1870–1877." *Journal of Southern History* 28 (1962): 202–18.

Sydnor, Charles. "The Southerner and the Laws." *Journal of Southern History* 6 (1940): 2–23.

Tyler, Lyon G. "The South and Self-determination." *William and Mary Quarterly* 27 (1919): 217–25.

Williams, David McCord. "'Mr. Ash': A Footnote in Constitutional History." *South Carolina Historical Magazine* 63 (1962): 227–31.

Dissertations

Akerman, Robert Howard. "The Triumph of Moderation in Florida Thought and Politics." Ph.D. diss., American University, 1967.

Higginbotham, Sanford Wilson. "Frontier Democracy in the Early Constitutions of Tennessee and Kentucky, 1772–1799." M.A. thesis, Rice University, 1941.

Mauer, John Walker. "Southern State Constitutions in the 1870s: A Case Study of Texas." Ph.D. diss., Rice University, 1983.

Parkinson, George P., Jr. "Antebellum State Constitution Making: Retention, Circumvention, Revision." Ph.D. diss., University of Wisconsin, 1972.

Tomberlin, Joseph A. "The Negro and Florida's System of Education: The Aftermath of the *Brown* Decision." Ph.D. diss., Florida State University, 1967.

Contributors

Herman Belz, Professor of History, University of Maryland, is the author of, among other works, *Emancipation and Equal Rights: Politics and Constitutionalism in the Civil War Era* (New York, 1978) and *Reconstructing the Union: Theory and Policy during the Civil War* (Ithaca, N.Y., 1969).

Michael Les Benedict, Professor of History, Ohio State University, is the author of *The Impeachment and Trial of Andrew Johnson* (New York, 1973) and *A Compromise of Principle: Congressional Republicans and Reconstruction, 1863–1869* (New York, 1975).

David R. Colburn, Professor of History, University of Florida, is the author, with Richard K. Scher, of *Florida Gubernatorial Politics in the Twentieth Century* (Gainesville, Fla., 1980) and *Racial Change and Community Crisis: St. Augustine, Florida, 1877–1980* (New York, 1985), which won the Rembert W. Patrick Award from the Florida Historical Society.

James W. Ely, Jr., Professor of Law and History, Vanderbilt University, is the author of *The Crisis of Conservative Virginia: The Byrd Organization and the Politics of Massive Resistance* (Knoxville, 1976) and coeditor, with David J. Bodenhamer, of *Ambivalent Legacy: A Legal History of the South* (Jackson, Miss., 1984) and, with Theodore Brown, of *The Legal Papers of Andrew Jackson* (Knoxville, Tenn., 1987).

Paul Finkelman, Assistant Professor of History, State University of New York at Binghamton, is the author of *An Imperfect Union: Slavery, Federalism, and Comity* (Chapel Hill, N.C., 1981) and *Slavery in the Courtroom* (Washington, D. C., 1985), which won the Joseph L. Andrews Award from the American Association of Libraries.

Peter Graham Fish, Professor of Political Science, Duke University, is the author of *The Politics of Federal Judicial Administration* (Princeton, N.J., 1973) and numerous articles in history, law, and political science journals; he is completing a biography of Judge John J. Parker.

387

Kermit L. Hall, Professor of History and Law, University of Florida, is the author of *The Magic Mirror: Law in American History* (New York, 1988) and *The Politics of Justice: Federal Judicial Selection and the Second American Party System* (Lincoln, Neb., 1979) and the editor of *A Comprehensive Bibliography of American Constitutional and Legal History,* 5 vols. (Millwood, N.Y., 1985).

Herbert A. Johnson, Professor of Law, University of South Carolina, is the author of *Imported Eighteenth-Century Law Treatises in American Law Libraries, 1700–1799* (New York, 1978) and, with George Haskins, *History of the Supreme Court of the United States, vol. 2, Foundations of Power: John Marshall, 1801–15* (New York, 1981).

David Thomas Konig, Professor of History, Washington University, St. Louis, is the author of *Law and Society in Puritan Massachusetts: Essex County, 1626–1692* (Chapel Hill, N.C., 1979) and of a forthcoming book, *The Constitution of a County Court: Law, Government, and Power in Colonial York County, Virginia* (Charlottesville, Va.).

Steven F. Lawson, Professor of History, University of South Florida, is the author of *Black Ballots: Voting Rights in the South, 1944–1969* (New York, 1976) and *In Pursuit of Power: Southern Blacks and Electoral Politics, 1965–1982* (New York, 1985).

R. Kent Newmyer, Professor of History, University of Connecticut, is the author of *The Supreme Court under Marshall and Taney* (New York, 1968) and *Supreme Court Justice Joseph Story: Statesman of the Old Republic* (Chapel Hill, N.C., 1985), which won the Littleton-Griswold Prize for the best book in legal history.

Donald Nieman, Associate Professor of History, Kansas State University, is the author of *To Set the Law in Motion: The Freedmen's Bureau and the Legal Rights of Blacks, 1865–1868* (Westport, Conn., 1979). He is presently working on an interpretive history of civil rights to be published by Oxford University Press.

Mary K. Bonsteel Tachau, Professor of History, University of Louisville, is the author of *Federal Courts in the Early Republic: Kentucky, 1789–1815* (Princeton, N.J., 1978), which won the Governor's Award of the Kentucky Historical Society.

388

William M. Wiecek, Chester Adgate Congdon Professor of Public Law and Legislation, College of Law, Syracuse University, is the author of, among many other works, *The Sources of Antislavery Constitutionalism in America, 1760–1848* (Ithaca, N.Y., 1977) and, with Harold M. Hyman, *Equal Justice under Law: Constitutional Development, 1835–1875* (New York, 1982).

Index